# Redefining Russian Literary Diaspora, 1920–2020

# FRINGE

*Series Editors*
Alena Ledeneva and Peter Zusi, School of Slavonic and
East European Studies, UCL

The FRINGE series explores the roles that complexity, ambivalence and immeasurability play in social and cultural phenomena. A cross-disciplinary initiative bringing together researchers from the humanities, social sciences and area studies, the series examines how seemingly opposed notions such as centrality and marginality, clarity and ambiguity, can shift and converge when embedded in everyday practices.

Alena Ledeneva is Professor of Politics and Society at the School of Slavonic and East European Studies of UCL.

Peter Zusi is Associate Professor at the School of Slavonic and East European Studies of UCL.

# Redefining Russian Literary Diaspora, 1920–2020

Edited by

Maria Rubins

First published in 2021 by
UCL Press
University College London
Gower Street
London WC1E 6BT

Available to download free: www.uclpress.co.uk

ISBN: 978-1-78735-943-7 (Hbk.)
ISBN: 978-1-78735-942-0 (Pbk.)
ISBN: 978-1-78735-941-3 (PDF)
ISBN: 978-1-78735-944-4 (epub)
ISBN: 978-1-78735-945-1 (mobi)
DOI: https://doi.org/10.14324/111.9781787359413

# Contents

**Part four:** Imagined spaces of unity and difference

# Notes on contributors

**David M. Bethea** is the Vilas Research Professor (emeritus) at the University of Wisconsin-Madison and Professor of Russian Studies (retired) at Oxford University. He has written broadly on Russian poetry, Russian literary culture and Russian thought. At present he is completing a volume of essays on Charles Darwin's ideas in the Russian cultural imagination.

**Pamela Davidson** is Professor of Russian Literature at UCL (University College London). Her research interests embrace comparative literature, modernist poetry, the relationship between religion and culture, Russian literary demonism and prophecy. Her books include *Russian Literature and its Demons, The Poetic Imagination of Vyacheslav Ivanov*, an anthology of poems dedicated to Anna Akhmatova, *Viacheslav Ivanov: A reference guide*, and *Vyacheslav Ivanov and C. M. Bowra: A correspondence from two corners on humanism*. Following the award of a Leverhulme Trust Research Fellowship, she is currently completing a book on prophecy and power in the Russian literary tradition (1650–1930).

**Katharine Hodgson** (Professor in Russian, University of Exeter) works mainly on Russian poetry of the twentieth century. She is the editor, with Joanne Shelton and Alexandra Smith, of a 2017 volume of essays on the changing poetry canon, and in 2020 published, with Alexandra Smith, a book on the twentieth-century poetry canon and Russian national identity. Other publications cover poetry of the Soviet period, particularly Ol'ga Berggol'ts and wartime poetry, as well as the translation into Russian of the work of poets such as Kipling, Heine and Brecht. She is now exploring the way informal associations of poets may have supported cultural transmission and continuity during the Soviet period.

**Mark Lipovetsky** is Professor at the Department of Slavic Languages, Columbia University (New York). He is the author of 10 books and editor or co-editor of 20 volumes on twentieth- and twenty-first-century Russian literature and culture. He is known mostly for his works on Russian postmodernism, New Russian drama, the trickster in Soviet culture, and Dmitry Prigov. He is also one of the four co-authors of the *Oxford History of Russian Literature* (2018). He is a winner of the AATSEEL Award for Outstanding Contribution to Scholarship (2014) and the Andrei Bely Prize for his input to Russian literature (2019).

**Kevin M. F. Platt** is Edmund J. and Louise W. Kahn Term Professor in the Humanities in the Department of Russian and East European Studies and the Program in Comparative Literature and Literary Theory at the University of Pennsylvania. Platt is the author of books and articles on representations of Russian history, Russian historiography, history and memory in Russia, Russian lyric poetry, and global post-Soviet Russian cultures. He is also a translator of contemporary Russian poetry. Most recently, he was the editor of *Global Russian Cultures* (Wisconsin, 2019). He is currently completing a monograph on Russian culture in Latvia.

**Maria Rubins** is Professor of Russian and Comparative Literature at UCL. Her research interests include modernism, exile and diaspora, bilingual writing, Russian-French cultural relations, and Hebrew, Arabic and russophone literatures in Israel. She is the author of several books, including *Crossroad of Arts, Crossroad of Cultures: Ecphrasis in Russian and French poetry* (2000) and *Russian Montparnasse: Transnational writing in interwar Paris* (2015), and over a hundred articles and book chapters. She is a translator into Russian of fiction in English and French, including books by Elizabeth Gaskell, Judith Gautier and Irène Némirovsky.

**Andreas Schönle** is Professor of Russian and Head of the School of Modern Languages at the University of Bristol as well as a Fellow of the British Academy. He is the author of four monographs and three edited volumes. His monographs include *Architecture of Oblivion: Ruins and historical consciousness in modern Russia* (2011) and *On the Periphery of Europe, 1762–1825: The self-invention of the Russian elite* (2018), co-authored with Andrei Zorin.

**Galin Tihanov** is the George Steiner Professor of Comparative Literature at Queen Mary University of London. He has held visiting appointments at universities in Europe, North and South America and Asia. He is the author of five monographs, including *The Birth and Death of Literary Theory: Regimes of relevance in Russia and beyond* (Stanford UP, 2019). Tihanov is an elected member of Academia Europaea, a past president of the ICLA Committee on Literary Theory, and a member of the executive board of the Institute for World Literature at Harvard University.

He is currently writing *Cosmopolitanism: A very short introduction*, commissioned by Oxford University Press.

**Adrian Wanner** is the Liberal Arts Professor of Slavic Languages and Comparative Literature at Pennsylvania State University. Born and raised in Switzerland, he received his PhD in Russian literature from Columbia University in 1992. He is the author of *Baudelaire in Russia* (1996), *Russian Minimalism: From the prose poem to the anti-story* (2003), *Out of Russia: Fictions of a new translingual diaspora* (2011) and *The Bilingual Muse: Self-translation among Russian poets* (2020). In addition he has published six editions of Russian, Romanian and Ukrainian poetry of his own translations into German verse.

# Preface

The UCL Press FRINGE series presents work related to the themes of the UCL FRINGE Centre for the Study of Social and Cultural Complexity.

The FRINGE series is a platform for cross-disciplinary analysis and the development of 'area studies without borders'. 'FRINGE' is an acronym standing for Fluidity, Resistance, Invisibility, Neutrality, Grey zones and Elusiveness – categories fundamental to the themes that the Centre supports. The oxymoron in the notion of a 'FRINGE CENTRE' expresses our interest in (1) the tensions between 'area studies' and more traditional academic disciplines; and (2) social, political and cultural trajectories from 'centres to fringes' and inversely from 'fringes to centres'.

The series pursues an innovative understanding of the significance of fringes: rather than taking 'fringe areas' to designate the world's peripheries or non-mainstream subject matters (as in 'fringe politics' or 'fringe theatre'), we are committed to exploring the patterns of social and cultural complexity characteristic of fringes and emerging from the areas we research. We aim to develop forms of analysis of those elements of complexity that are resistant to articulation, visualization or measurement.

The present volume approaches conceptions of the Russian-language literary diaspora in the twentieth and twenty-first centuries with an emphasis on working 'up' from particular texts and case studies rather than 'down' from preconceived models of diasporic literature. Both older, hierarchical models that posit diasporas as peripheries to a homeland rendered inaccessible, and more recent conceptions, which emphasize the multiplicity of decentred, fluid, hybridized identities, imply particular assumptions about diasporic texts. Notions of nostalgia, preservation or restoration, creative transformation and so on become baked into the analytic model. This volume puts such notions under critical review by examining the ways such models relate to or have been generated by particular texts and authors.

Alena Ledeneva and Peter Zusi,
School of Slavonic and East European Studies, UCL

# Acknowledgements

This project began with a lively gathering in London in May 2018 where, during two exceptionally bright days, we held a workshop to deliberate on the meaning and status of Russian diasporic literature. This workshop was generously sponsored by the UCL Global Engagement Fund and the FRINGE Research Centre. I also wish to extend thanks to the UCL School of Slavonic and East European Studies for granting a research leave that enabled me to focus on the preparation of this book for publication. While in the late stages of its editing I was hosted by the Slavic-Eurasian Research Center of Hokkaido University (Japan), and I express my deep gratitude for this support. Last but not least, I wish to thank all of my fellow contributors for their enthusiasm, stimulating intellectual input and collaborative spirit. The opportunity to work with such a stellar team for two years has been my biggest reward.

Part one
# Conceptual territories of 'diaspora': introduction

# 1

# The unbearable lightness of being a diasporian: modes of writing and reading narratives of displacement

Maria Rubins

An important, if unintended, consequence of the October Revolution and the waves of emigration that followed was the creation of a global polycentric diaspora that has evolved over the last hundred years into a thriving alternative affiliation for Russian culture. The century of Russian dispersion has coincided with a historical period marked by the rise and fall of a variety of competing ideologies, including diverse forms of totalitarianism, nationalism, liberalism, globalism and multiculturalism. Just as the discourse of the 'national character' that can be described in terms of essential features has been viewed with increased scepticism, the romantic myth of the mysterious 'Russian soul' has lost some of its former lustre. Instead, there is a deeper appreciation today of the diverse ways in which cultural identities are constructed, and the context of diaspora provides particularly fertile ground for examining multiple ways of being Russian.

Literary narratives bring into sharper focus complex experiences of displacement, border crossing and adaptation to a foreign environment. For extraterritorial writers, language itself transcends its role as a tool of communication and self-expression and becomes a crucial symbol of identity. Whether they continue to write in their native tongue, switch to another language, alternate between the two, or experiment with creolization, it is never just a creative quest, an artistic act of self-fashioning in a new medium, but also inevitably an existential choice. Each language activates specific cultural discourses and memories.

Each language provides a unique matrix for understanding and interpreting the world. A constant 'double exposure' of cultural, social and linguistic codes prompts authors to reflect on practices of inter-cultural translation or contemplate the limits of translatability. It is through language that they perform their fluid and interstitial identities, and it is in literature that these identities find their most nuanced and sophisticated articulations, not least because literature, in Joseph Brodsky's words, 'is the greatest … teacher of human subtlety'.[1]

Reflecting elsewhere on the hybridity and ambivalence that inform life in diasporic locations, I visualized the archipelago as a trope for the geocultural configuration of the Russian diaspora.[2] Each island within such a cluster possesses its own unique characteristics, exhibits its own internal diversity, and appears to stand alone, while remaining linked to others and to the mainland through the 'memory' of common origins. And just as each island in a chain is located at a different distance from the continent, extraterritorial groups and individuals constantly renegotiate their mental and stylistic proximity to the homeland.

The leaders of the post-revolutionary émigré community in Europe projected their dedication to the national cause and a strong sense of historical calling that consisted for them in preserving the cultural canon. In contrast, later émigrés were more inclined to acknowledge their cultural and national plurality. A journalist once posed the rather trivial question to Brodsky: 'You are an American citizen who is receiving the Prize for Russian-language poetry. Who are you, an American or a Russian?' The poet famously responded: 'I'm Jewish; a Russian poet, an English essayist – and, of course, an American citizen.' More recently, some authors living outside Russia have made dramatic declarations of non-Russianness. The russophone Israeli poet Mikhail Gendelev wrote in the postscriptum to his collected works published in Moscow: 'Я не считаю себя русским поэтом ни по крови, ни по вере, ни по военной, ни по гражданской биографии, ни по опыту, ни по эстетическим переживаниям… Я поэт израильский, русскоязычный' ('I don't consider myself a Russian poet in terms of blood, faith, my military or civil biography, experience, or aesthetic sensibilities … I am a russophone Israeli poet').[3] Or, to quote the writer Zinovy Zinik, who has resided in the United Kingdom since the 1970s, 'Даже когда я пишу по-русски или говорю по-русски, как сейчас, я рассуждаю, глядя на мир с британской точки зрения' ('Even when I write or speak Russian, like now, I am looking at the world from a British point of view').[4]

It would be too simplistic to suggest that, as the century of Russian emigration continued, dislocated literati moved away from an initial nostalgic focus on their homeland and acquired a transnational identity. Or that the dichotomy of centre and periphery (where the homeland is conceived as the centre and diaspora as the periphery) has been progressively displaced by a non-hierarchical, multifocal model, although today this view is endorsed ever more frequently. The Russian-Israeli poet Alexander Barash, for instance, claims that 'the centre of the language empire is located in a place where a good text in this language is being composed at this very moment'.[5] The condition of polycentricity, plurality and unboundedness of the contemporary cultural situation was recently considered in the volume *Global Russian Cultures*. 'Russian cultures' figures here as a master category to project the vision of 'the contingency of all conceptions of Russian culture across space and time' and to counter the claim to any 'proper' belonging of Russian cultural production. The metropolitan space from this perspective carries no more weight than any of the other loci of Russian culture scattered around the globe, just as 'Russian culture' itself cannot be defined through a set of inherent, stable characteristics. As Kevin Platt, the editor of *Global Russian Cultures*, argues in the introduction,

> Both within and without the Russian Federation, Russian culture is fragmented and multiple, and everywhere it is the object of diverse and contradictory institutional, political, and economic forces that seek to define and constrain it. Here, then, is the reality of culture and its emplacement in modern geography: it always exceeds any one location and presents a unity only in perpetually renegotiated multiplicity.[6]

This rethinking of the Russian cultural field resonates with the robust discourse of decentralization promoted by such subdisciplines as diaspora studies, postcolonial studies, World Literature, and translation studies.

And yet, can extraterritorial Russian writing be adequately assessed when viewed uniquely through an ideological lens that privileges centrifugal movement and non-hierarchical structures? Obviously, over an entire century, geographical distance and an increasing gap between Soviet and foreign experiences, mentalities and linguistic idioms produced a significant degree of emancipation and foreignization of russophone literature created abroad. Consequently, the grip of the metropolitan canon as the ultimate measure of artistic worth has been relaxed. At the same time, at various moments over the century, we find the presence of coeval competing patterns of articulating national and postnational identities. The younger Russian-Parisian writers of the first wave exemplify one of the first pockets of 'dissent', resisting the homebound rhetoric and aesthetics predominant in the interwar émigré milieu and instead creating a Russian version of modernist narratives, drawing on Western discourses alongside the national tradition.[7] Another stark example concerns the very different images projected from American exile by Alexander Solzhenitsyn and Joseph Brodsky, both expelled from the USSR in the early 1970s. In contrast to his cosmopolitan fellow Nobel Prize laureate, Solzhenitsyn presented himself as an ultra-nationalist, criticized the West from conventional Russian positions of messianism and spiritual superiority and eventually returned to Russia to assume a role as the chief prophet of Panslavism.

Zinik, quoted earlier, would probably object to being viewed as a Russian émigré. Yet other writers who found themselves abroad for personal reasons during the post-Soviet period later chose to assume an émigré identity (despite the somewhat dated ring of the very word 'émigré' in our globe-trotting era). Thus, Mikhail Shishkin, who has lived in Switzerland since the 1990s, proclaimed at the 2018 Montenegro forum of Russian writers abroad: 'I never considered myself an émigré, but Russia emigrated from me into the Middle Ages. And so I have declared that I am an émigré.'[8]

Considering that the articulations of cultural identities in the Russian diaspora over the last hundred years have been multiple and often mutually exclusive, does diasporic literature generated by this complexity have a common denominator? Can it be juxtaposed against metropolitan literature as a *sui generis* phenomenon? When we compare the extraterritorial corpus with the metropolitan one, in its own way no less complex, we perceive a certain specificity. The nature of this distinctness is quite subtle, however, because it goes far beyond just thematic content, setting, linguistic hybridity, a sense of alienation, nostalgia or emphasis on the workings of memory (although all of these elements constitute what is commonly called the 'poetics of exile' and appear in texts in infinite variations). More significantly, diasporic narratives inscribe experiences that are not easily available within the metropolitan locus, opening up what Salman Rushdie once called 'new angles at which to enter reality'.[9] And while each narrative arises from a unique combination of historical contingencies and the author's individual circumstances, it gives us insight into the human condition from a perspective informed by a 'contrapuntal' awareness of at least two dimensions.[10]

This volume is our collective attempt to examine some of the key 'angles' of entering reality offered by diasporic literature, and to understand how these novel extraterritorial perspectives generate new modalities of writing and reading. Retracing the last century of Russian dispersion through a range of complementary case studies (with an excursus into the nineteenth century to probe an earlier paradigm of the Russian performance of exile), our contributions focus on characteristic ways in which diasporic texts and literary practices reframe Russian master narratives, question the dominant cultural canon, contest standard, authoritative historical interpretations, reshape cultural memory, and reflect experiences of exile, deracination, migration, translingualism and multiple belonging. We assess diaspora writers' responses to foundational rhetorical or ideological fields that have come to define the Russian national canon and cultural politics. These include, in particular, literature's status as a civic religion; the prophetic mission of the writer; the centrality of the proverbial 'accursed questions' (God, the meaning of life and death, etc.); the 'sacred' status of the Russian language; *literaturotsentrizm*; the Orthodox faith (as defined against Catholicism); the ruler as the ultimate arbiter; intellectuals' claim to act as the 'conscience' of the people and their defence of the trampled dignity of the 'little man'; West, East and Russia's position between the two; Eurocentrism; and hegemonic discourses of the Revolution, war and the Siege of Leningrad. Our contributions interrogate not only how diasporic narratives reinterpret metropolitan discourses and rewrite existing tropes but also how they explore unrealized possibilities and engage with topics that have remained marginal or taboo in the homeland.

Such re-examination of the diasporic literary corpus is important, because the mainstream critical reception still resists the idea of its alterity. Since the late 1980s, émigré literature has been published in Russia in millions of copies, generating huge interest among readers and a proliferation of academic studies. A vibrant new field was thus quickly and enthusiastically established, framed by notions of the 'return' of previously banned literature and its 'reunification' with the metropolitan branch. This optic reinforced the perception of diaspora as a discursive space where the pre-revolutionary cultural agenda, suppressed and censored within metropolitan confines, was preserved and fostered, with the conservationist pathos construed as the *raison d'être* of émigré literature. Even when diverse vectors of the Russian literary process within and outside the metropolis were contrasted, diaspora literature was more likely to be set off against Soviet writing, with the latter regarded as a deviation and the former as a continuation of the 'authentic' Russian path (a point of view actively promoted also by those first-wave émigrés who insisted on their mission as cultural 'guardians'). To reframe

Franco Moretti's tropes of trees and waves,[11] the hierarchical nationalist reception tended to portray diasporic literature as a branch of a family tree, underestimating the transformative impact of diverse cultural 'waves' running through its crown. As a result, as they entered the metropolitan field, diasporic narratives were routinely subjected to deformation and manipulation, reminiscent of the processes that frequently accompany texts when they are read by foreign audiences in translation.

In addition to limiting the range of cultural and aesthetic meanings of diasporic texts, the dominant reception perpetuated a traditional scenario that associates exile with trauma and loss, when redemption is offered only by physical, spiritual or textual return home. The repatriation of the literary corpus of Russia Abroad was also used as a vehicle for a transhistorical 'return' of late Soviet culture to the pre-revolutionary 'classical' era, bypassing the Soviet period altogether. Needless to say, in this atmosphere of 'restorative nostalgia' there was very little interest in seeking out aspects of diasporic writing that reflected an intellectual and aesthetic agenda independent of national concerns or indeed critical of the canonical values and discourses deemed crucial for the restoration of the country after seven decades of Communism. Lately, a number of studies have focused on postnational aspects of extraterritorial Russian writing, and there is a growing understanding of diasporic distinctness, but most of these studies examine specific authors, literary groupings or generations.[12] What we aim to do here is to address the phenomenon of diaspora literature more broadly and to articulate a more balanced conceptual framework for further study.

A particularity of the discourse around Russian diasporic legacy has been a considerable disconnect between Russian material and the evolving theoretical reflection on diasporic, exilic and immigrant modes of creativity.[13] Understandably, after the 70-year ban on émigré publications, Russian scholarship saw its primary objective as the collection and systematizing of a massive body of empirical material. The subsequent analysis of the writers' specific situations and the compilation of comprehensive histories of Russian émigré literature took precedence over assessing this legacy within broader conceptual contexts.

Outside Russia, the situation was only marginally different. During the Soviet period, Western researchers showed rather limited interest in Russian émigré literature, notwithstanding the attention paid to a few celebrity cases (such as Nabokov, Solzhenitsyn and Brodsky). The field of 'Russian studies' was mainly oriented towards developments in the

USSR, and focused on Russian classics, Soviet literature and occasionally on some selected exiles, especially if their work lent itself to a politicized reading. Those who arrived from behind the Iron Curtain without any political agenda inspired even less interest than émigrés of longer standing. Assessing the reception of Russian literature in the West in the 1980s, Olga Matich wrote:

> More often than not Russian literature today is read for its political content, both in the Soviet Union and abroad. As a result, the apolitical Russian writer is all but trapped in the stranglehold of politics, even in the West. Following the Russian lead, Western critics tend to apply political criteria to Russian literature and judge it for the most part according to its testimonial and propagandistic value.[14]

Arguably, research on the Russian diaspora as a particular form of cultural expression caught on in Western academe only after it became an established field within the metropolis. This is demonstrated by a dramatic rise in the number of publications, conferences and university courses on Russian emigration from the late 1980s onward. In this respect the evolution of the discipline mirrored the pattern of navigation between national and international spaces of émigré literary texts themselves, complicating the models articulated by World Literature theorists. Although émigré authors were writing beyond national boundaries and often even in 'prestige-bestowing' world literary centres (to use Pascale Casanova's terminology), most remained in relative obscurity until their works began to circulate inside Russia. Only then were they noticed by foreign scholars, critics and publishers and, in translation, ricocheted back to the West, where they were originally created. In this respect, the transformation of Gaïto Gazdanov's status offers a salient example. While in the 1930s he was hailed, along with Nabokov, as one of the two most promising and original young writers in exile, during his lifetime he never managed to transcend a fairly narrow circle of émigré readership and to attain international recognition. Even after the first monograph on Gazdanov appeared in Europe in the 1980s (written by Laszlo Dienes), his books remained the purview of a specialized audience until his canonization in Russia at the turn of the twenty-first century, provoking a true rediscovery of the author abroad.

Irina Odoevtseva's 1987 iconic and widely publicized physical return to Leningrad from Paris, where the disabled octogenarian lived in a cramped flat in solitude and oblivion, literalized the repatriation metaphor. Over the next few years, Odoevtseva's poems and memoirs were published in hundreds of thousands of copies (something most émigré authors could never even imagine), and her government-sponsored apartment near Nevsky Prospect became a pilgrimage destination for journalists, critics and fellow writers. Although Nina Berberova, another prominent figure of first-wave émigré modernism, was pushed into the international limelight not from within Russia but through French translations of her works, it happened as late as 1984. This belated discovery was due to the discerning eye of Hubert Nyssen, the founder of the Actes Sud publishing house. When, once, Nyssen was asked by an interviewer to name contemporary writers who would survive into posterity, he cited Berberova, not least to correct the 'unforgivable oblivion in which she was held by the twentieth century'.[15] There are many more examples that illustrate the low visibility of Russian diasporic writing.

The belated discovery of the extraterritorial corpus and an even greater delay in its theorization explain in part why many conceptual questions have not yet been posed in the Russian context. One of our goals is to bring the study of Russian diasporic literature into conversation with contemporary theories and to test established analytical approaches by using them in a reflective and discriminating manner. Some of our case studies, in fact, show that Russian literary production resists widely adopted models or yields another inflection on interpretative frames often accepted as axiomatic and universal. It is our hope that by questioning some tenets of diaspora theory we can contribute to further theoretical developments in the field.

For the purposes of the present project, we have chosen 'diaspora' as an umbrella category embracing various modalities of Russian extraterritorial existence over the last century, including exile, emigration, cross-border migration, and russophone enclaves in the ex-Soviet republics. In an untheorized sense, diaspora means a community of people who share origins, culture and language distinct from those of the dominant population. During the hundred-year history of Russian dispersion, traditional diasporic communities have proliferated, and many studies have already addressed the rich cultural activities of Russian Berlin, Russian Prague, Russian Paris, Russian Harbin and so on. Some of our case studies reference specific diasporic communities, but in this volume we are mainly concerned with the *concept* of diaspora.

While in critical literature 'diaspora' has been used practically interchangeably with 'exile', its conventional semantics point to a more neutral condition, without foregrounding the ideas of expulsion, loss and suffering which have come to connote exile.[16] An internal plasticity of the Greek word 'diaspora', designating both 'scattering' and 'sowing seeds', enables the balancing of contrasting ideas: banishment, punishment and exile on the one hand, and settling, establishing communities in new locations and ultimate redemption on the other.[17] This ambivalent concept helps to capture diverse forms of Russian global dispersion without over-romanticizing life beyond the nation state, as is often the case when border crossing is viewed through the interpretational prism of exile. Galin Tihanov argues that the twin narratives of exile (that of 'suffering, anguish and distress' and that of 'an enabling factor that unlocks creativity') share common origins in the nation-focused discourse of romanticism. Against the nexus of language, national culture and the poet as its chief enunciator, the exile figures in one of two guises: 'either as a formidable creative genius who manages to safeguard and masterfully employ the national language in the inclement conditions of separation from the nation, or as a detractor, or rather, disbeliever who embraces another culture and language only to wither away ... in sterile suffering'.[18] Tihanov proposes to de-romanticize exile by stripping it of the aura of exceptionality. Incidentally, exile (*izgnanie*) was a preferred definition that circulated in extraterritorial Russian publications practically throughout the entire Soviet period (along with Russia Abroad (*Russkoe Zarubezh'e*), emigration and scattering (*rasseianie*)), while diaspora has been used very infrequently,[19] perhaps because of its lack of romantic pathos.

As an object of theoretical inquiry in the last three decades, the term 'diaspora' has experienced an impressive semantic expansion. Reconfigured as a conceptual rather than geographical or historical category, diaspora has come to connote a 'broad analytical lens'[20] and a 'category of practice, project, claim and stance'.[21] More and more frequently diaspora is discussed 'in terms of ... adaptation to changes, dislocations and transformations, and the construction of new forms of knowledge and ways of seeing the world'.[22] As Igor Maver observes, today's universal 'diasporization' has transformed what used to be specific (trans)cultural practices of displaced people into 'a mode of everyday existence'.[23] Robin Cohen regards 'the sense of uprootedness, of disconnection, of loss and estrangement, which hitherto was morally appropriated by the traditionally recognized diasporas' as signifying 'something more general about the human condition'.[24] Avtar Brah introduced the category of *diaspora space* as the site at which boundaries of belonging and otherness are contested and where 'the native is as much a diasporian as the diasporian is the native'.[25]

Alongside these broadly conceived definitions, diasporic vocabulary is routinely employed in discussions of subaltern histories and minority groups (overlapping to a certain extent with postcolonial discourses). Most studies have focused on three core components of diasporic experience – homeland; migration or border crossing; and otherness in the host society – if only to interrogate them and to redefine their respective significances. In contrast to Said's politically underpinned claim that in the modern world exile is unthinkable without a triumphant ideology of a 'restored people', today's academic discourse is rather sceptical about the ideas of an originary place and the homeland as an object of perpetual nostalgia and desire. Paul Gilroy's trope of a moving ship[26] transferred the focus from the teleology of return to a (real or imagined) national home onto the element of migration and highlighted a spatially disseminated identity, while James Clifford emphasized de-centred, lateral circulations between various parts of a diasporic community.[27] Such categories as diasporic imaginary,[28] rhetorical constructions of the place of origin without actual repatriation[29] and 'diasporic intimacy' between immigrants from different parts of the world, who develop a new type of solidarity with strangers like themselves,[30] have further de-centred the homeland. Furthermore, the relationship with the host society looms large in almost any discussion of diasporians. Viewing diaspora as one of the Others of the (host) nation state has been one of the tenets of diaspora theory since its inception.[31] For Rogers Brubaker, diasporic identity is predicated on difference and boundary maintenance vis-à-vis the adopted country.[32] The same argument can of course be made with regard to the relationship between diasporic consciousness and the metropole.[33] Diasporic subjectivities and diasporic imagined communities are constituted therefore against multiple Others embedded within and across binaries.[34]

Despite the malleability of diaspora as a methodological tool appropriate to the analysis of modern human experiences, some critics who define this concept against and through the nation predict its imminent end.[35] While this may be true for economic or social applications of the term, diasporic cultural and literary practices highlight the limited applicability of binary approaches that juxtapose 'diaspora' against any single point of reference, particularly a nation state conceived either as a homeland or as the host society. In this book, we engage with diasporic literature as a critical perspective, a distinct paradigm of reading extraterritorial narratives, which requires a transnational mode of thinking and problematizes conventional practices of literary criticism underpinned by a nationalist model. Breaking homology between nation, geographical territory and language, diasporic literature transcends the nation as a normative literary space and destabilizes the national language as a habitual code of communication. As our research into the century of Russian extraterritorial writing (including translation and self-translation) demonstrates, diasporic literature is predicated on hybridity; it engages with various localities and responds, often critically or ironically, to diverse master narratives. Spanning the nation and the world at large, it establishes itself as a 'thirdspace',[36] a zone where the national is inscribed within the global and vice versa, generating new forms of knowledge about the human condition. Diasporic creativity is a result of the explosive potential of such fissures and fusions. But living and writing across geographical and imaginary borders often comes at a price. Interstitial subjects, poised between countries, cultures and languages and engaged in self-reflexive negotiation of their position between national and transnational, simultaneously inhabit several worlds and none at all. The unbearable lightness of being a diasporian is underpinned by this ambivalent condition between double commitment and the ultimate inability to commit.

The chapters that follow attempt to illuminate extraterritorial Russian literature through this lexicon, to locate the Russian case on this vast conceptual map, and to offer critical insight into these theories, expanding existing definitions. Various case studies are grouped around several broader themes: performativity, language and space(s).

Part two, '"Quest for significance": performing diasporic identities in transnational contexts', explores, in particular, how diasporic identity is continuously generated and renegotiated by re-enacting various intellectual, emotional and behavioural models drawn from a vast cultural reservoir. The 'quest for significance'[37] which, in Brodsky's view, motivates intellectuals in exile, may push them in different directions. Some formulate their own role by referencing famous prede-cessors, including historical characters (Ovid, Dante, Byron) or mythical ones (Odysseus). Others adapt powerful tropes from the national cultural canon to articulate their position in diaspora. In any event, as Andreas Schönle remarks, exile is never a solitary act, it is rather 'a series of gestures performed with an eye towards a public' (or at least a potential audience), predicated on improvisation. New roles are assumed in response to ever-changing circumstances, producing unexpected shifts in the 'actor's' self-definition.

Part three, 'Evolutionary trajectories: adaptation, "interbreeding" and transcultural polyglossia', brings together two complementary perspectives on various cases of cultural and linguistic hybridity that punctuate writing in diaspora: evolutionary biology and theories of (self-)translation. The notions of adaptation, genetic drift, 'interbreeding' and transcultural polyglossia are used to explain processes that have gradually shaped a new kind of global russophone diaspora.

The final part, 'Imagined spaces of unity and difference', unites three chapters, each engaging in its own way with discursive constructions of space and strategies for inscribing distance from or proximity to the metropolitan versus diasporic networks and discourses. Ranging from the examinations of a poetic anthology and shared electronic media as imagined spaces of unity, to the Siege of Leningrad as the new myth of the homeland, to writers exploiting the benefits of distance from the hubs of russophone cultural activities, these chapters question the category of space itself and the relevance of geographical location to diasporic specificity.

In his chapter, 'Exile as emotional, moral and ideological ambivalence: Nikolai Turgenev and the performance of political exile', Andreas Schönle aims to establish a distinctive paradigm of political exile, which could define the Russian experience for most of the nineteenth and twentieth centuries. His study focuses on Nikolai Turgenev (1789–1871), a Westernized nobleman who espoused liberal views and advocated constitutional reform and the abolition of serfdom. Turgenev sought to implement his ideals through dedicated state service until he was forced to remain in Europe in the wake of the Decembrists' uprising while taking the waters in Germany. In Russia, he was tried in absentia for his prior participation in secret political and literary societies, and despite the fact that these activities were quite remote from the Decembrists' radical programme, he was convicted and given a sentence of capital punishment. He remained in de facto exile until 1857, when he was pardoned by the new tsar, Alexander II. Subsequently, he made three trips to his homeland but continued to reside in France. From abroad, Turgenev repeatedly petitioned the Russian emperor to clear his name and his honour, and wrote treatises on the Russian social and political situation, memoirs, diaries and some verse.

Schönle draws on the study of emotions and on Peter Burke's 'occasionalist turn'[38] as he discusses the emotional, moral and ideological continuities and dislocations brought about by Turgenev's exile. He demonstrates how Turgenev's experience, predicated on a constant oscillation between tragic rupture and emancipatory reinvention, problematizes some of the tenets of exile theory, in particular as articulated by Said, Gilroy and Tihanov. Schönle argues that the Russian exilic paradigm is characterized by profound ambivalence, and outlines its primary aspects:

- absence of a sense of 'true home', as even before emigration exiles experienced alienation from many spheres of life in their homeland; Russia as a home of sorts can only be fantasized from a safe distance; exile then becomes 'the reconfiguration of an alterity vis-à-vis the homeland';
- perception of the adopted Western country as more advanced; a westward move therefore is often regarded as a civilizational leap into a kind of future desired for Russia;
- a tendency to 'look back', even after relocation to a better situation, rather than unconditionally embracing a new life and a Western identity; exiles desire to 'perform an elite political or cultural function in the polity of their homeland' even if their impact is curtailed by censorship of their work in Russia, paucity of émigré outlets, or lack of interest on the part of the former compatriots;
- an ethos of service to their country that prompts exiles to engage in dialogue or negotiation with the ruler.

This model may not capture all variations, but it is a useful benchmark, allowing us to assess the reasons why some of its elements have remained practically unchanged while others have lost their relevance, and so to appreciate better the complex dynamic of Russian diasporization over time.

Émigrés whose departure was triggered by the Revolution of 1917 certainly experienced alienation from their home country, but their attitude may have been different from that of Turgenev, who claimed that one can love the fatherland without respecting fellow countrymen. Post-revolutionary émigrés felt that their familiar homeland had rapidly changed beyond recognition. In emigration they generally cultivated a rather idealized image of pre-revolutionary Russia, remained strongly opposed to the Bolshevik regime, and saw their main mission as working towards its collapse (for some this went as far as supporting Hitler against Stalin during World War II). In contrast, Soviet émigrés of later periods, particularly the 1970s dissidents, were usually quite estranged from the place of their birth from the outset, and if they experienced nostalgia it was directed towards more personal or specific circumstances than the country as a whole. Turgenev criticized the Russian elite, which he considered foreign to the true Russian spirit, while he pictured the serfs as the carriers of wholesome national values. Meanwhile, the revolutionary events that unleashed unprecedented irrational violence destroyed for Russian intellectuals all illusions about the 'devout' and 'morally upright' *narod*.

The point about the attitude to the West as an advanced civilization can also be qualified in the new historical context. True, émigrés in all generations tended to see in Europe a lofty alternative to 'Asiatic barbarism', and for many the only consolation after losing their homeland was the hope that they would be sustained by European culture. Viacheslav Ivanov felt so much at home in his Italian exile (and within the European spiritual and cultural community) that he even referred to those who remained in Russia as living 'abroad'. Joseph Brodsky voiced the resilient belief of the Russian intelligentsia in the advanced and liberal West as late as 1987, in his speech 'The condition we call exile, or acorns away':

> Displacement and misplacement are this century's commonplace. And what our exiled writer has in common with a *Gastarbeiter* or a political refugee is that in either case a man is running from the worse to the better. The truth of the matter is that from a tyranny one can be exiled only to a democracy. ... [A]s a rule what takes place is a transition from a political and economic backwater to an industrially advanced society with the latest word on individual liberty on its lips. And it must be added that perhaps taking this route is for an exiled writer, in many ways, like going home – because he gets closer to the seat of the ideals which inspired him all along.[39]

Yet there was an equally strong counter-current in twentieth-century Russian exilic discourses about the West, distinguished by a profound disillusionment with European values, mentality and mode of life observed at close range. Arguably, the most nihilist narratives ever created in the Russian language, which intensely question European spiritual and ethical foundations, humanist beliefs and human nature itself, were created in emigration against the backdrop of European modernity. Russian philosophers, notably Nikolai Berdyaev, contemplated the advent of what he defined as the 'new Middle Ages'. Having proclaimed the end of the European monopoly on culture in his article 'Konets Evropy' (The end of Europe, 1915), Berdyaev remained an acute critic of the contemporary zeitgeist after emigration. Like many of his contemporaries, he saw World War I as a major turning point of modern history. The war, he wrote, revealed the evil accumulated by humanity, exposed the falsehood of our civilization, and devalued human life: 'Demons of hatred and murder who were set free continue to act in the modern world.'[40] In a 1932 article, 'Dukhovnoe sostoianie sovremennogo mira' (The spiritual condition of the modern world), published in the émigré journal *Put'*, and in his later work *Puti gumanizma* (Paths of humanism, 1946), he developed his theses of human crisis and the dehumanization process brought about by unchecked technical progress (man has not yet become the master of the machine that he invented), acceleration of life and the loss of the individual to the collective.[41]

Along with Berdyaev's writings, Lev Shestov's book *Na vesakh Iova (stranstvovaniia po dusham)* (On Job's scales (pilgrimage across souls), 1929) had a far-reaching impact in the interwar diaspora. Arguably, under the influence of Shestov, Russian émigré writers created their own brand of existentialism, which foreshadowed its subsequent articulations in French and European thought. In some of its manifestations, Russian émigré existentialism is an extreme example of negative anthropology, quite at odds with Sartre's later philosophy of responsibility that urges fellow humans to invest existence with meaning. These explosive texts include Georgy Ivanov's 'Raspad atoma' (The atom explodes, 1938), Gaïto Gazdanov's *Nochnye dorogi* (*Night Roads*, 1939–40, 1951), and narratives by Vasily Yanovsky and other writers of Russian Montparnasse portraying a decaying, ugly and meaningless world beyond redemption. In Vladislav Khodasevich's cycle *Evropeiskaia noch'* (European night, 1927), the soul of the contemporary European is plunged into animalistic slumber, and even art has lost its transfiguring potential.[42]

What accounts for this drastic re-evaluation of the very foundations of European culture, treasured by Russian intellectuals for centuries? The answer lies only partly in the understandable psychological reaction of exiles to the decline of their social and cultural status, their identity crisis and sense of utter irrelevance in the host country. It has perhaps more to do with their culturally construed high expectations, informed by the Russian *idea* about Europe and ignorance of its present condition. Significantly, shortly before his expulsion Berdyaev commented on Russians' dated, idealized perception of Europe, caused by their forced separation from the Western world: 'For many years already, we Russians have been torn away from Western Europe and from its spiritual life. And because we are denied access to it, it appears to us more prosperous, more stable, and happier than it is in reality.'[43] Brought up on European culture, Russian émigrés soon discovered that interwar Europe was no longer the epicentre of the enlightened world – it was profoundly shaken by the experience of the Great War, which had cast doubt on all fundamental ideas, beliefs and feelings, spelling the beginning of the end of European cultural dominance. While the death of traditional forms of culture and humanity became a powerful theme in interwar modernist art and thought more generally, Russian exiles were particularly sensitive to signs of decay, degeneration and fragmentation. After a long history of learning from and competing with Europe, the cognitive dissonance they felt between its lofty image and the uninspiring reality they discovered upon relocation became a source of trauma and pessimism, as Europe could no longer be pictured as a viable alternative to the chaos that had engulfed Russia.

The sense of absurdity and meaninglessness of the world was amplified for exiles because they had left Russia in the midst of bloodshed and looting but came to Western Europe after the war was over. And yet in this peaceful, quite ordinary bourgeois world they encountered similar – if not worse – manifestations of evil, sadism, avarice, perversion, and profound indifference to fellow human beings. In the words of Gazdanov, who fought in the White army for a year before emigrating, 'even the Russian Civil War could not compare with this essentially peaceful existence for its repulsiveness and absence of anything good'. His book *Nochnye dorogi* (*Night Roads*) is an agonizing attempt to comprehend the 'endless and depressing human vileness', intellectual dullness, absence of curiosity, critical thinking, and awareness that he observed in Europeans, who 'lived in a world which was real and actual, which had taken shape long ago and had now acquired a moribund and tragic immobility, the immobility of decline and death'.[44]

This rejection of Europe is a far cry from occasional sceptical remarks expressed by some nineteenth-century Russian intellectuals, including Westernizers like Alexander Herzen, whose example serves as a variation of Turgenev's performance of exile. In his letters from France and Italy, Herzen also refers to Europe as a decaying world. In comparison with Russia with its future, if yet unrealized, potential, Europe's older civilization appears but a repository of obsolete achievements. But his assessment contains no sense of an imminent apocalypse that would invalidate his belief in historical teleology. For Herzen, it is Europe's age and the wealth of its cultural treasures that pull it down: 'Europe is sinking because it cannot get rid of its freight, which contains many gems acquired in the course of a long and dangerous voyage.'[45] Nothing is further from his mind than a denial of European experience or the significance of its accumulated 'wisdom' for Russia's own historical path:

[I]sn't the birthplace of our thought and our education there [in Europe]? Did not Peter I, tying us to Europe, reinforce our inheritance rights? Did we not take them ourselves, assimilating its issues, its grief, its suffering along with its accumulated experience and its accumulated wisdom? … Our past is poor; we do not want to invent heraldic tales; we have very few memories of our own, so what's so terrible if Europe's memories, its past, becomes our past?[46]

By contrast, in the consciousness of post-revolutionary émigrés, the disappointment with Europe, alongside the pain of separation from their homeland, rekindled the memory of Silver Age discourses about the imminent collapse of the Western world. Ideas about a universal confrontation between East and West, Vladimir Solovyov's concept of *panmongolism* popularized in Symbolist poetry, meditations on the crisis of humanism in Alexander Blok's 'Krushenie gumanizma' (The collapse of humanism, 1919) and Viacheslav Ivanov's 'Kruchi' (The heights, 1919),[47] and Andrei Bely's insights into the catastrophic closure of a civilizational cycle in his novel *Petersburg*, among multiple other factors, contributed to an apocalyptic perspective. Unsurprisingly, Oswald Spengler's book *Der Untergang des Abendlandes* (*The decline of the West*, 1918) was hugely popular in Russia, where its translation was released under the characteristic title *Zakat Evropy* (*The decline of Europe*). Even before the Russian translation was published in 1923, Spengler had become a cult author with broad Russian audiences, and in 1922 a collection of essays appeared containing detailed responses to the book from leading Russian philosophers.[48] Three of the four contributors to that volume, Fedor Stepun, Berdyaev and Semen Frank, were soon expelled from Russia on the infamous Philosophers' Ship. To a certain extent, their subsequent émigré writing was encrypted with Spengler's thoughts. What in the Russian readings and misreadings of Europe resonated most with Spengler was probably the German thinker's division between culture and civilization. For Spengler, civilization is the ultimate stage of the cultural cycle, when earlier organic creativity degenerates into mechanistic, egalitarian and artificial forms. This period of exhaustion prefigures the inevitable death of a particular culture. He argued that Western European culture (chronologically defined as the period between 1000 and 2000 CE) was then living through a decline characteristic of the civilization stage. With Spengler's idiosyncratic terminology in mind, Russian émigrés' encounter with Europe can be redefined as frustrated expectations: instead of the vital 'culture' that they had become so accustomed to cherishing, they found a stagnant 'civilization'.

In Russian narratives, critique of European civilization often morphs into exposing universal entropy and moral decay. Evil is no longer incarnated in the likes of Lenin, Stalin or Hitler but appears pervasive and omnipresent. It is significant that Georgy Ivanov intended to conclude 'Raspad atoma' with the following words: 'Heil Hitler; long live the father of nations Great Stalin; never, never will an Englishman be a slave!' Although Ivanov later regretted removing this coda (as he wrote in a 1955 letter to Roman Gul'), without this final line his text acquired more general connotations, reflecting 'the overwhelming hideousness of the world'[49] at large rather than localizing evil in specific dictators or political regimes.[50]

If we recall more recent anti-Western tirades of Russian émigrés, most famously those of Alexander Solzhenitsyn, as well as the rethinking of the European cultural legacy by Russian-Israeli intellectuals in the context of the Holocaust and the anti-Israel policies of contemporary European governments,[51] we find that the Russian diaspora had strayed far from the standpoint of Nikolai Turgenev and other nineteenth-century Westernizers. Nonetheless, this apparent departure serves to expand the notion of ambivalence that underlies the Russian exilic experience. The twentieth-century exile epitomizes an ambivalent stance not only towards the homeland, but also towards the entire amorphous 'West' as the primary destination of the Russian exodus.

What has remained practically unchanged through two centuries is the desire of the Russian diasporic elite to shape Russian cultural discourses, and the counter-reaction of all successive political regimes (Russian and Soviet), who routinely silenced exiles' voices and made their names taboo. Public life in numerous pockets of the post-revolutionary Russian diaspora was animated by intense debates about the future of the country. The multiplicity of émigré political factions mimicked the rich political scene in Russia before the Revolution, albeit on a diminished scale. The tragic assassination of Vladimir Nabokov's father in lieu of the targeted Pavel Miliukov is just one example of the seriousness that exiles attributed to their political activities. As the dream of a physical homecoming was undermined in the face of the strengthening of the Soviet state, the notion of 'return' was progressively reconfigured as textual. In the absence of immediate access to audiences at home, many writers, poets, philosophers and publicists wrote their works in the hope that eventually they would be read in Russia – something that actually happened only during perestroika. In a way, the dream of exercising an elite cultural role in the homeland from a foreign location has been realized in the twenty-first century. Today, some of the best-known Russian authors live abroad, but their works are published, read, reviewed and actively discussed in Russia. This is the case for Boris Akunin, Dina Rubina, Mikhail Shishkin, Vladimir Sorokin, Viktor Pelevin, Ludmila Ulitskaya and dozens of others. Ultimately, it does not matter much that some of them emigrated from the former Soviet Union, some chose to live abroad because of their distaste for the Russian political climate, and some belong to the growing category of globetrotters. All share a central aspiration to be successful and relevant in the country of their birth.

Finally, a few words need to be said about 'negotiation with the ruler', the fourth element in Schönle's paradigm. He writes,

> in Russia's heavily personalistic political culture, where the ruler is the ultimate arbiter of the fate of individuals regardless of the outward political system, exile has often taken the form of a personal falling-out with the ruler, sometimes prompting attempts on either side to open up a dialogue and engage in some form of negotiation, often through intermediaries.

This situation, as Schönle points out, is quite universal, and goes back to, for instance, Ovid's correspondence with Augustus, in which the poet tried to justify himself and regain favour in the eyes of the emperor. In the Russian context, the process of 'negotiation' with the ruler was enacted by Prince Andrei Kurbsky, a prototypical political exile who fled the court of Ivan the Terrible and sent long epistles to the tsar from his refuge in Lithuania. Later, this applied mostly to internal exiles, from Radishchev and Pushkin to Mandelstam, or quasi-exiles, like Gorky or Alexei Tolstoy, who contemplated return and needed to maintain a semblance of loyalty. But for the overwhelming majority of those who left 'for good', any form of 'negotiation' with Lenin, Stalin and their successors in the USSR was unthinkable. In his speech 'The mission of the Russian emigration', Ivan Bunin proclaimed that refusing to accept the Soviet state was the exile's chief mission.[52] Between the first wave of émigrés and the 1970s, such contacts with the cursed Communist regime would have been condemned as collaboration. That said, there were among 'White Russians' a number of actual Soviet collaborators and double agents. Some eventually had to be removed to the USSR 'for [their own] safety', only to be promptly executed, like Sergei Efron, but this situation is altogether different from 'negotiation'.

Perhaps Eurasianism can be viewed as a form of intellectual accommodation to Bolshevik rule. This important doctrine, developed in the 1920s and the early 1930s, attempted to bridge the gap between Bolshevik Russia and the diaspora; its ideologues advocated a 'third way' for their country, based on its semi-European/semi-Asian character, and looked to establish a utopian democratic-Orthodox-Soviet government. One of the leaders of the movement, Petr Savitsky, even made a secret trip to the USSR in 1927, trying to negotiate a Eurasianist political plan with the Bolsheviks. Ultimately, the Eurasianists' calls for reconciliation between exiles and Stalin's totalitarian regime fell on deaf ears on both sides of the Soviet border, and Eurasianism gradually withered (only to resurface in a new form in the post-Soviet metropolitan space).

Further insights into different modifications of the Russian exilic model are provided by other contributions to this volume. Most chapters deal with writers who found themselves abroad because of a specific political situation, their disagreement with the regime at home, and pressure from the Soviet authorities. Many among the artistic and literary intelligentsia continued to espouse firm political views throughout their years in exile, and these views often coloured their creative production.

What can be more natural for someone who wishes to play a significant cultural role for the sake of his fellow countrymen than to render the message in the language of prophecy? Pamela Davidson's chapter, 'Rewriting the Russian literary tradition of prophecy in the diaspora: Bunin, Nabokov and Viacheslav Ivanov', explores one of the central tropes in the Russian national canon – the cult of the writer as prophet – and its transformations after the Revolution in both the diasporic and Soviet contexts. The main research questions raised here concern the relationship between literary tradition, national identity and geographical location. Can a trope which has traditionally upheld the 'national' mission of a country's literature and set itself up in relation to the twin authorities of State and Church survive outside the homeland? If so, what happens to it and the literature it represents? Can the national become transnational? After a brief survey of prophetic interpretations of the Revolution in early Soviet writing, Davidson focuses on three main case studies: Bunin's speech 'The mission of Russian emigration', Nabokov's short story 'The storm' and V. Ivanov's cycle 'Roman sonnets', all composed in 1924 and each presenting a specific rendition of the literary tradition of prophecy. Her analysis demonstrates that the prophet metaphor remained central for the literary and political polemics of the post-revolutionary diaspora. Bunin adopted biblical language to define the mission of emigration in religious and political terms as the non-acceptance of Bolshevik Russia. In 'The storm', Nabokov literalized the metaphor of art as prophecy and translated Symbolist theurgic principles into a playful modernist narrative, thus casting the prophet theme in an ambivalent light. In his cycle of 'Roman sonnets', Viacheslav Ivanov expanded his already well-established prophetic inclinations into the broader space of Catholic humanism. Through his verse, non-fiction writing in several languages, conversion to Catholicism and strategies of self-presentation as a transnational European intellectual, Ivanov redefined the meaning of émigrés' geographical displacement as the fulfilment of Russia's providential mission to unify the Eastern and Western branches of Christianity.

Davidson's case studies invite an important question, although the answer lies beyond the scope of her chapter: which of these three 'actors', each playing (and playing with) the role of the prophet, presented a more generative model for future iterations of this canonical discourse? Arguably, with time fewer émigré authors tried on prophetic garb in earnest, preferring to reflect on the topic in a sceptical or ironic key. Commenting on David Markish's novel *Pes* (*The dog*, 1984), whose protagonist fails to re-establish himself as a moral authority in emigration and chooses to return to the USSR, Alice Nakhimovsky arrives at a categorical conclusion:

> [T]he myth of the Russian writer as 'beggar and prophet', the moral teacher of an audience who values and needs him, does not work in the West. It is a tradition that is meaningful only in non-freedom. ... Non-freedom permits certain knowledge of right and wrong. ... In the comfortable certitude of the totalitarian state, he [Vadim, protagonist of the novel *Pes*] had a clear identity as a nonconformist writer. ... In the West all these categories become confused.[53]

Yet, the figure of the (quasi-)writer-prophet kept resurging in the diaspora, with writers as diverse as Vasily Yanovsky, Elena Izwolskaya, Solzhenitsyn, Nicolas Bokov and Andreï Makine (to name just a few) seeking to integrate their Russian specificity, the pathos of spirituality and moral art with transnational literary patterns, and to address the 'comfortable certitude' of various totalitarian formations, which they found both inside and outside their homeland.

Understandably, for extraterritorial authors, whether their ambition is to stay relevant primarily in their homeland's cultural field or to break into a global literary scene, the target audience and the anticipated reception are crucial to defining the very nature of their writing and its linguistic medium. What role does self-translation play in the overall strategy of a bilingual diasporian? In his chapter, 'Translingual poetry and the boundaries of diaspora: the self-translations of Marina Tsvetaeva, Vladimir Nabokov and Joseph Brodsky', Adrian Wanner engages with the rapidly developing field of self-translation, to offer insight into the functioning of poetic creativity in different languages, the conundrum of translation and the vagaries of bilingual identity. Focusing on the bilingual oeuvre of three Russian exile poets – Marina Tsvetaeva, Vladimir Nabokov and Joseph Brodsky – who translated their own work into French or English, he addresses the problem of reception and reader response. Who is the intended, or the ideal, reader of self-translated texts? Does such an audience even exist? Is it growing today? Wanner's analysis demonstrates that despite their very different attitudes to the methodology and even the feasibility of adequate translation, these writers tested rather than 'maintained' (in Rogers Brubaker's sense) the linguistic boundaries of diaspora. Their self-translating practice prefigured a new kind of Russian diaspora, resulting from today's unprecedented global dispersion of russophone populations, whose members have not shed their original language and culture through assimilation, but transcend it in a form of transcultural polyglossia.

By considering self-translated texts of Tsvetaeva, Nabokov and Brodsky, Wanner develops and complicates Mikhail Epstein's concepts of 'interlation' and 'stereotextuality', which capture the practices of writing in two languages – and in between them. [54] As Epstein argues, in the contemporary globalized cultural reality, with a marked increase of multilingual competence among both writers and readers, the role of translation changes considerably: instead of creating a simulacrum of the original, it produces a variation, 'a dialogical counterpart to the original text'. Such contrastive juxtaposition of two apparently identical but in fact non-equivalent texts suspends the binary between 'source' and 'target' languages, making them interchangeable, and each variant allows the bilingual reader to perceive what the other language 'misses or conceals'. Interlation effectively cancels the idea that something can be lost in translation. It creates the effect of stereotextuality, as discrepancies between languages come to the fore, allowing a reader conversant in all of them to savour additional shades of meaning and layers of imagery. The 'same' text unfolds in alternative incarnations, providing a 'surplus of poetic value' but also pointing to more fundamental questions:

> Can an idea be adequately presented in a single language? Or do we need a minimum of two languages (as with two eyes or two ears) to convey the volume of a thought or symbol? Will we, at some future time, accustom ourselves to new genres of stereo poetry and stereo

philosophy as we have become accustomed to stereo music and stereo cinema? Will the development of translingual discourses … become a hallmark of globalization?[55]

As Wanner's analysis shows, this kind of implicit questioning informed the self-translating efforts of the leading poets from Russia Abroad throughout the twentieth century. Long before the translingual discourses became, in Epstein's words, 'a hallmark of globalization' they were instrumental for diasporic poetic consciousness, even if the reader (and scholar) attuned to the resulting 'stereo' effect is emerging only today.

In the following chapter, 'Evolutionary biology and "writing the diaspora": the cases of Theodosius Dobzhansky and Vladimir Nabokov', David M. Bethea taps into the logic and language of the rapidly developing evolutionary literary theory (also known as evocriticism)[56] to make larger points about the hundred-year history of the Russian diaspora and the processes of cultural adaptation over time. If evolution has produced the grand diversity of the living world, diaspora constitutes an environment that enhances progressive diversification in linguistic and cultural expression. Bringing together the intersecting biographies and life work of Vladimir Nabokov and geneticist Theodosius Dobzhansky, the author of the ground-breaking *Genetics and the Origin of Species* (1937), Bethea argues that their thinking as evolutionary biologists led both men on a path from the national to the transnational. Drawing on these specific examples, he suggests that the future of 'Russianness' in the literary realm, no longer described through the centre/periphery binary, points not only towards the hybrid identities of a multitude of authors, but also towards the concepts of 'hyper-personality', 'super-organism' and 'collective brain' discussed by Pierre Teilhard de Chardin, E. O. Wilson, Joseph Henrich and others.

The nexus between the canon, nationhood and the community's geographical position is approached from a different perspective in Katharine Hodgson's chapter, 'Repatriation of diasporic literature and the role of the poetry anthology in the construction of a diasporic canon'. Hodgson is interested not so much in how the inherited national tradition is preserved or transformed in diaspora, but how creative activities outside the metropolitan domain give rise to a new, diasporic literary canon, the sort of 'ambivalent otherness' such a canon represents, and what happens when the diasporic canon 'returns' to the metropolis. She starts with the premise that the emergence of diasporic canons in multiple locations outside the homeland inevitably challenges the idea that literary canons express the spirit of a nation, an idea that has persisted since the early nineteenth century. A diasporic canon creates a hyphenated collective identity for a community that attempts to maintain a distinctive culture while interacting with the host society. As Hodgson argues, when the diasporic canon is 'repatriated', its former role in maintaining the boundaries of the diasporic community often comes into conflict with a metropolitan viewpoint which may fail to recognize its otherness, preferring to assimilate it as a fragment that has been restored to the national canon. To test this tension, she concentrates on diverse anthologies of diasporic poetry published over the last century in different locations of Russia Abroad, and then compares their principles of composition, their objectives and their roles in asserting a diasporic identity with more recent anthologies published for readers inside Russia. She assesses the discrepancy in the presentation of diasporic poetry between these two types of anthologies targeting different audiences. This comparative analysis contributes to the ongoing inquiry into strategies for fashioning a distinct literary canon in the diaspora and to scholarship on canon formation more generally.

The last two chapters in the volume address the contemporary moment by considering how new virtual and geographical circuits of communication reframe the notion of the Russian literary diaspora. Mark Lipovetsky begins his chapter, 'Is there room for diaspora literature in the internet age?', by interrogating the relevance of the very distinction between diaspora and homeland writing in the era of global connectivity, when geographical distances and corresponding allegiances appear less important than discursive divides and cultural (or ideological) citizenships. Lipovetsky tests this hypothesis by analysing texts about the Siege of Leningrad, focusing on two poems, two plays and two novels, one in each category written by a diasporic author and the other by a homeland writer from the liberal milieu. This thematic choice is invested with special meaning in contemporary Russia, as the victory in the Great Patriotic War has become the cornerstone of post-Soviet identity making, and the Siege of Leningrad is the most sensitive and ideologized topic within this discourse, surrounded by many written and unwritten taboos.

Lipovetsky's analysis demonstrates that two types of narrative on the Siege remain distinctive, reflecting two typologically different approaches to the same historical event. Inclined to use the Siege as a rhetorical instrument in today's discursive wars, a liberal homeland author feels the need to deconstruct and de-realize this tragedy in order to connect it with his own, more recent, historical experience and memory. This triggers the accentuation of internal conflicts within the representation of the Siege of Leningrad in 'domestic' texts, 'cynical mockery of outdated humanistic principles allegedly devalued by the Siege', declarative 'modernization' and a lack of interest in historical documents. Conversely, for authors with extraterritorial experience the Siege is an example of the *unreal non-time*, which they strive to fill with the sense of the real through their attention to documentary evidence. For them, the Siege appears as the place outside the flow of history and offers an explosion of creative energy. This unreal non-time resonates with the construction of diasporic subjectivity around the central role of Home: the Siege, in Lipovetsky's opinion, emerges today as the new *diasporic myth of the Home*. The case studies provided in this chapter suggest that today 'diasporic' emerges as a typological category, reflecting a greater displacement in time and cultural context than just in geography. It can apply therefore in equal measure to authors within and without the homeland.

In the last chapter, 'The benefits of distance: extraterritoriality as cultural capital in the literary marketplace', Kevin Platt considers the economic and institutional networks operating in contemporary worldwide Russian literary geography and attempts to develop an analytical matrix appropriate to the steadily growing number of authors and texts that break out of the narrowly defined categories of national and global. He starts with an argument that in the current political climate we should not grant any ontological self-evidence to such ideologically exploited constructs as the presumably singular 'Russian world'. But the gist of this chapter transcends this political orientation and touches implicitly on the current crisis of professional language experienced by cultural and literary critics who reflect on creative writing at a time of extreme geographical, conceptual and linguistic diasporization. Indeed, after the collapse of the Soviet Union, with its rigid subdivision of cultural production into domestic and émigré, the Russian literary world has become so fragmented and dispersed that its multiplicity can only be captured through such pluralized neologisms as 'Russian literatures' and 'Russian cultures'. At the same time, Platt observes a counter-tendency: global Russian literary formations are becoming more systematically integrated through rapid circulation, cultural exchange, and numerous routes of textual dissemination. This paradox of unprecedented fragmentation and integration – a situation that Platt argues will be characteristic of the russophone global cultural scene for decades to come – requires the flexibility of 'mixed metaphors' that go beyond the established categories of World Literature as articulated by Pascale Casanova or Franco Moretti.

This is the only chapter in this book that deals with two primary kinds of currently evolving diasporic literary formations: one that has come into existence in Israel, and the other related to diverse russophone activities in the former Soviet republics. Focusing on contemporary extraterritorial writers who matured as authors outside Russia, but whose main audiences are within it, Platt's more detailed case studies address the best-selling Russian-Israeli prose writer Dina Rubina and the russophone Uzbek avant-garde poet Shamshad Abdullaev. Very different authors, they illustrate the benefits of being, in Platt's words, 'global yet national, Russian yet Jewish' (Rubina) or 'avant-garde yet peripheral' (Abdullaev). Contemplating a new kind of cultural capital that such shifting distances and blurred identities accrue today in the literary marketplace, Platt develops Pascale Casanova's conception of the World Republic of Letters, pointing out the growing instability of the structures of global literary life on which her analysis is based. Rather than studying the interrelationships between diverse national literatures in a world literary system, as per Casanova's model, he investigates the internal complexities of a single, ostensibly 'national' literature when it has itself become globalized and multiple.

The studies presented in this book test only some of many conspicuous and problematic issues of the centuries-long cross-border movements of texts and individuals. In a way, the fact that the chronological span of this particular volume extends from Nikolai Turgenev to Shamshad Abdullaev is a matter of our research contingency. Still, this configuration is instructive in itself. These two diasporians appear to differ in every possible way. One was deeply committed intellectually to his homeland, and contemplated its historical destiny in his writing in French from a distant land. The other has always resided in his place of birth on the periphery of the former Soviet empire and uses the Russian language as a pure code, effectively eliding Russian literary tradition, as he aims to join the cosmopolitan avant-garde. Nor does Abdullaev draw on local, provincial roots, the idiom of 'Uzbek Russian' recalling the cosy domesticity of more traditional diasporic enclaves. Is this 'writing from nowhere' in a sterile verbal code that triggers no particular cultural memories, and which doubtless lends itself more easily to translation, an extreme case or a trend prefiguring the near future of Russian global writing? Will this future resemble the fate of literary English, used by so many writers today with no tangible link to any specific cultural tradition within the anglophone world? Does this gesture of ultimate non-commitment represent the inflation of extraterritorial identities, reminiscent of the 'lightness' contemplated by Milan Kundera in his cult novel (Kundera once expressed a wish to move even further away from his Czech origins and his adopted French authorial guise and to write a novel in Spanish – had he only known the language better)? But it is worth recalling that Sabina, the chief incarnation of the concept of lightness in the novel, literally disappears into thin air, as her ashes are scattered over a Mexican volcano.

While it is impossible to capture the complex dynamic of Russian diasporic writing through any one set of analytical tools, one thing is clear enough: the story of the Russian diaspora is not a linear development. Between Nikolai Turgenev, as a chronologically earlier diasporian, and the currently active Shamshad Abdullaev, we have identified multidirectional vectors for constructing Russian identity within and between the national and transnational domains. The 'lightness' of diasporic existence is countered by a great deal of 'heaviness', even if the choice between these two modes of self-projection has gradually become more of a personal preference.

One hundred years ago, when two million Russians found themselves in emigration, diasporic communities were established out of historical necessity. Diaspora represented a refuge, a challenge, an opportunity, an opposition to the Soviet totalitarian regime, and also a site of freedom unavailable in the homeland. In today's globalized reality of porous borders, dual and triple nationalities, internet, international TV channels and increasing multilingualism, Russians who find themselves beyond the frontiers of the Russian Federation need only a limited support network constituted by their compatriots. And such networks are not crucial for their survival abroad, mostly offering additional amenities (a Russian cultural centre, an arts festival, extracurricular activities for russophone children, etc.). Unsurprisingly, today it is almost impossible to find tightly knit diasporic communities reminiscent of those of the interwar period (and paradoxically, if they still exist anywhere at all, it is in Israel). Does the decline of diaspora as a specific sociocultural network entail the deflation of the *idea* of diaspora?

Our present inquiry demonstrates that at least in the literary and cultural field diaspora remains relevant as a critical perspective, a creative practice and a typological category. And its relevance is likely to increase. Russia is an example of a country in which different temporal planes converge, from globalism to very archaic forms of mentality, ethics and governance. The twenty-first century has been marked so far by the recycling of symbols from the past, and by a burlesque and uneasy bricolage of incongruous elements lifted from the medieval, imperial,

Soviet and post-Soviet eras. A Communist crossing himself in front of an icon of the recently canonized Tsar Nicholas II is a fitting image for the present condition of mental confusion. Whether this illustrates the myth of an endless cyclical repetition of Russian history (predicted by Andrei Bely in his visionary novel), or the Kremlin ideological elite's lack of imagination, militant nationalist discourse once again dominates the official informational space. Numerous propagandistic talk shows, depending on the direction of the political weathervane, are at pains to endorse a uniform Russian national identity against the presumably monolithic 'Americans', 'Georgians', 'Ukrainians' or indeed dissenting Russians (labelled 'liberals', 'oppositionists' and 'foreign agents'). The current discussions of amendments to the Constitution have been marked by an aggressive reappropriation of culture as a symbol of Russian statehood and a 'genetic code of the nation'.[57]

In this specific historical situation, diaspora performs a different but vital function. It stands for a freely (and sometimes unconsciously) chosen identity and practice that facilitate a retreat from revived totalitarian rhetoric, state-sponsored patriotism, Orthodox 'spirituality' 'museified' cultural discourses, and all forms of monolingualism (in both a direct and a metaphorical sense). It also offers an option of maintaining a 'boundary' within a host society for those Russians abroad who feel constrained by certain Western social codes, dogmatic liberalism and political correctness. Diasporic double-coding represents a coveted ambivalence, a possibility of several alternatives, points of view, modes of living and narrating. And in this sense, the Russian diaspora endures both outside and inside the metropolitan borders.

## Notes

1  Brodsky 1988, 20.
2  See Rubins 2019, 21–47.
3  Gendelev 2003. Translations of quotations are mine unless otherwise indicated.
4  Zinik 2018.
5  Vrubel'-Golubkina 2016, 468.
6  Platt 2019, 6.
7  I examined the transnational creative practice of this émigré generation in my book, Rubins 2015.
8  Shishkin 2018–19, 41.
9  'I am speaking now of those of us who emigrated … and I suspect that there are times when the move seems wrong to us all, when we seem, to ourselves, post-lapsarian men and women. … Our identity is at once plural and partial. Sometimes we feel that we straddle two cultures; at other times, that we fall between two stools. But however ambiguous and shifting this ground may be, it is not an infertile territory for a writer to occupy. If literature is in part the business of finding new angles at which to enter reality, then once again our distance, our long geographical perspective, may provide us with such angles' (Rushdie 1991, 15).

10  Said, 2001, at 186.
11  See Moretti 2000.
12  See Livak 2003; Morard 2010; Trousdale 2010; Wanner 2011; Rubins 2015; Katsman 2016.
13  In this respect, literary scholarship has lagged behind sociological studies, which have engaged in theorizing the Russian diaspora for some time already. In particular, russophone Jewish communities that have formed over the last few decades in Israel, Europe and North America have become an object of a focused study on a number of occasions (see Remennick 2011, 2007; Fialkova and Yelenevskaya 2007; Ben-Rafael 2006).

In 2014, a special issue of the Moscow-based *New Literary Observer* was dedicated to the study of cultural mechanisms for constructing diasporic identities (*Novoe literaturnoe obozrenie* 127 (2014)). This issue provides a broad overview of the evolution of the field of diaspora studies, mostly referring to Western sources. It does not focus exclusively on the Russian diasporic experience, and articles on diasporic literature address mostly late Soviet emigration and contemporary Jewish writing in Israel, Germany and the United States.

14  Matich 1984, 182.
15  'Nina Berberova et Hubert Nyssen', 12 February 2012 (http://de-page-en-page.over-blog. com/article-nina-berberova-et-hubert-nyssen-99123565.html, accessed 29 August 2020).
16  This persistent association of exile with forced departure and banishment from the homeland is not even attenuated by the fact that the noun can be used with such adjectives as 'voluntary', 'involuntary' and 'internal'.
17  For more details on the etymology of the term 'diaspora' and its original connotations in the Greek translation of the Bible, see Pamela Davidson's chapter in this volume.
18  Tihanov 2015, 151.
19  See Davidson's and Hodgson's chapters in this volume for concrete examples of the use of the word diaspora.
20  McGuinness and McKay 2012, 231.
21  Brubaker 2005, 13.
22  Shackleton 2008, ix.
23  Maver 2009, xi.
24  Cohen 1997, 196.
25  Brah 1996, 209.
26  Gilroy 1993, 144.
27  Clifford 1994, 308.
28  Axel 2002.
29  Tölölyan 2007, 649.
30  Boym 2001, 256.
31  According to Khachig Tölölyan, the founder of *Diaspora: A Journal of Transnational Studies*, the nation state 'always imagines and represents itself as a land, a territory, a place that functions as the site of homogeneity, equilibrium, integration ... In such a territory, differences are assimilated, destroyed, or assigned to ghettoes, to enclaves demarcated by boundaries so sharp that they enable the nation to acknowledge the apparently singular and clearly fenced-off differences *within* itself, while simultaneously reaffirming the privileged homogeneity of the rest, as well as the difference *between* itself and what lies over its frontiers' (Tölölyan 1991, 6; emphasis in original).
32  Brubaker 2005, 5.
33  Moreover, as Mark Lipovetsky concedes in his chapter in this volume, contemporary liberal intellectuals experience a similar alienation from the domestic population in Russia, regardless of their position within or outside the country.
34  Brah 1996, 186.
35  This line of critique is represented in Galin Tihanov's contribution to this volume. I address this critique in more detail in the Conclusion.
36  See Soja 1996.
37  Brodsky 1988, 16.
38  See Burke 2005.
39  Brodsky 1988, 20.
40  Berdiaev 1934.
41  Berdiaev 1996, 183.
42  I examine the non-humanistic vector of twentieth-century Russian literature, including in émigré writing, in far more detail in Rubins 2020.

43 Berdiaev 1922.
44 Gazdanov 2009, 9, 191–2.
45 Gertsen 1905, 5.
46 Gertsen 1905, 11.
47 The full title of Ivanov's work is: 'Kruchi. Razdum'e pervoe: O krizise gumanizma. K morfologii sovremennoi kul'tury i psikhologii sovremennosti' (The heights. First meditation: on the crisis of humanism. towards morphology of contemporary culture and psychology of modernity).
48 *Osval'd Shpengler i Zakat Evropy*, 1922.
49 Ivanov 2002, 44.
50 The fact that patriotic salutes to Stalin and Hitler are featured alongside a quotation from the song 'Rule, Britannia!' adopted by the British Navy, is eloquent proof that Ivanov was not deluding himself with a naïve belief in Western democratic powers. (The actual refrain of the song, written by poet James Thomson and composer Thomas Arne, is: 'Rule, Britannia! Rule the waves: / Britons never will be slaves.')
51 Cf. Vrubel'-Golubkina 2016.
52 For a more detailed discussion of this speech and the concept of the mission, see Davidson's chapter.
53 Nakhimovsky 1992, 200, 206, 214.
54 Epstein, 2004, 42–60.
55 Epstein, 2004, 51.
56 Literary Darwinism is examined, inter alia, in Boyd 2009 and 2010.
57 'Popravki k Konstitutsii: Kul'tura – geneticheskii kod natsii i simvol strany' (Amendments to the Constitution: Culture – the genetic code of the nation and the symbol of the country). Murmanskii vestnik, 8 May 2020. https://www.mvestnik.ru/newslent/popravki-v-konstituciyu-kultura-geneticheskij-kod-nacii-i-simvol-strany/ (accessed 30 August 2020).

# Bibliography

Axel, Brian Keith. 'The diasporic imaginary', *Public Culture* 14(2) (Spring 2002): 411–28.
Ben-Rafael, Eliezer, Mikhail Lyubansky, Olaf Glöckner, Paul Harris, Yael Israel, Willi Jasper and Julius Schoeps. *Building a Diaspora: Russian Jews in Israel, Germany and the USA*. Leiden: Brill, 2006.
[Berdyaev] Berdiaev, Nikolai. 'Predsmertnye mysli Fausta'. In *Osval'd Shpengler i Zakat Evropy*. Moscow: Bereg, 1922.
[Berdyaev] Berdiaev, Nikolai. *Sud'ba cheloveka v sovremennom mire: k ponimaniiu nashei epokhi*. Paris: YMCA Press, 1934.
[Berdyaev] Berdiaev, Nikolai. 'Puti gumanizma'. In *Istina i otkrovenie: Prolegomeny k kritike otkroveniia*. St Petersburg: RKhGI, 1996.
Boyd, Brian. *On the Origin of Stories: Evolution, cognition, and fiction*. Cambridge, MA: Belknap Press of Harvard University Press, 2009.
Boyd, Brian, Joseph Carroll and Jonathan Gottschall, eds. *Evolution, Literature, and Film: A reader*. New York: Columbia University Press, 2010.
Boym, Svetlana. *The Future of Nostalgia*. New York: Basic Books, 2001.
Brah, Avtar. *Cartographies of Diaspora: Contesting identities*. London and New York: Routledge, 1996.
Brodsky, Joseph. 'The condition we call exile, or Acorns away', *New York Review of Books*, 21 January 1988: 16–20.
Brubaker, Rogers. 'The "diaspora" diaspora', *Ethnic and Racial Studies* 28(1) (January 2005): 1–19.
Burke, Peter. 'Performing history: The importance of occasions', *Rethinking History: The Journal of Theory and Practice* 9(1) (2005): 35–52.
Clifford, James. 'Diasporas', *Cultural Anthropology* 9(3) (1994): 302–38.
Cohen, Robin. *Global Diasporas: An introduction*. London: UCL Press, 1997.
Epstein, Mikhail. 'The unasked question: What would Bakhtin say?', *Common Knowledge* 10(1) (2004): 42–60.
Fialkova, Larisa and Maria N. Yelenevskaya. *Ex-Soviets in Israel: From personal narratives to a group portrait*. Detroit, MI: Wayne State University Press, 2007.

Gazdanov, Gaïto. *Night Roads*. Translated by Justin Doherty. Evanston, IL: Northwestern University Press, 2009.

Gendelev, Mikhail. *Nepolnoe sobranie sochinenii*. Moscow: Vremia, 2003.

Gertsen, A. 'Pis'ma iz Frantsii i Italii'. In *Sochineniia A.I. Gertsena i perepiska s N. A. Zakhar'inoi v semi tomakh*, vol. 5. St Petersburg: Tipografiia Iu.N. Erlikha, 1905.

Gilroy, Paul. *The Black Atlantic: Modernity and double consciousness*. London: Verso, 1993.

Ivanov, Georgii. 'The atom explodes'. Translated by Justin Doherty. *Slavonica* 8(1) (2002): 42–67.

Katsman, Roman. *Nostalgia for a Foreign Land: Studies in Russian-language literature in Israel*. Boston, MA: Academic Studies Press, 2016.

'Kto my segodnia?', *Zima* 6 (Winter 2018–19): 41. http://booknik.ru/today/directspeech/kto-my-segodnya/ (accessed 30 August 2020).

Livak, Leonid. *How It Was Done in Paris: Russian émigré literature and French modernism*. Madison: University of Wisconsin Press, 2003.

Matich, Olga. 'Is there a Russian literature beyond politics?' In *The Third Wave: Russian literature in emigration*, edited by Olga Matich and Michael Heim, 180–7. Ann Arbor, MI: Ardis, 1984.

Maver, Igor. 'Introduction: Positioning diasporic literary cultures'. In *Diasporic Subjectivity and Cultural Brokering in Contemporary Post-colonial Literatures*, edited by Igor Maver, ix–xiv. Lanham, MD: Lexington Books, 2009.

McGuinness, Aims and Steven C. McKay. 'Afterword: Diaspora and the language of neoliberalism'. In *New Routes for Diaspora Studies*, edited by Sukanya Banerjee, Aims McGuinness and Steven C. McKay, 229–32. Bloomington: Indiana University Press, 2012.

Morard, Annick. *De l'émigré au déraciné: La 'jeune génération' des écrivains russes entre identité et esthétique (Paris, 1920–1940)*. Lausanne: L'Age d'homme, 2010.

Moretti, Franco. 'Conjectures on world literature', *New Left Review* 1 (January–February 2000): 54–68.

Nakhimovsky, Alice Stone. *Russian-Jewish Literature and Identity: Jabotinsky, Babel, Grossman, Galich, Roziner, Markish*. Baltimore, MD: Johns Hopkins University Press, 1992.

'Nina Berberova et Hubert Nyssen', *De Page en Page: Littérature classique et contemporaine*, 12 February 2012. http://de-page-en-page.over-blog.com/article-nina-berberova-et-hubert-nyssen-99123565.html (accessed 16 September 2020).

*Osval'd Shpengler i Zakat Evropy*. Moscow: Bereg, 1922.

Platt, Kevin, ed. *Global Russian Cultures*. Madison: Wisconsin University Press, 2019.

Remennick, Larissa. *Russian Jews on Three Continents: Identity, integration and conflict*. New Brunswick, NJ, and London: Transaction Publishers, 2007.

Remennick, Larissa, ed. *Russian Israelis: Social mobility, politics and culture*. London: Routledge, 2011.

Rubins, Maria. *Russian Montparnasse: Transnational writing in interwar Paris*. Basingstoke: Palgrave Macmillan, 2015.

Rubins, Maria. 'A century of Russian culture(s) "abroad": The unfolding of literary geography'. In *Global Russian Cultures*, edited by Kevin Platt, 21–47. Madison: Wisconsin University Press, 2019.

Rubins, Maria. 'Negumanisticheskii vektor v russkoi literature XX veka', *Russkaia literatura* 2 (2020): 183–200.

Rushdie, Salman. *Imaginary Homelands: Essays and criticism, 1981–1991*. London: Granta Books in association with Penguin, 1991.

Said, Edward. 'Reflections on exile'. In *Reflections on Exile and Other Literary and Cultural Essays*, 173–86. London and New York: Granta, 2001.

Shackleton, Mark. 'Introduction'. In *Diasporic Literature and Theory – Where Now?*, edited by Mark Shackleton, ix–xiv. Newcastle upon Tyne: Cambridge Scholars Publishing, 2008.

Shishkin, Mikhail. 'Ia nikuda ne emigriroval, no emigrirovala Rossiia. Ona emigrirovala iz XXI veka v srednevekov'e', *Zima* 6 (Winter 2018–19): 41. https://zimamagazine.com/2018/10/mikhail-shishkin-emigratsija/ (accessed 30 August 2020).

Soja, Edward W. *Thirdspace: Journeys to Los Angeles and other real-and-imagined places*. Oxford: Blackwell, 1996.

Tihanov, Galin. 'Narratives of exile: Cosmopolitanism beyond the liberal imagination'. In *Whose Cosmopolitanism? Critical perspectives, relationalities and discontents*, edited by Nina Glick Schiller and Andrew Irving, 141–59. New York and Oxford: Berghahn, 2015.

Tölölyan, Khachig. 'The nation-state and its others: In lieu of a preface', *Diaspora: A Journal of Transnational Studies* 1(1) (Spring 1991): 3–7.

Tölölyan, Khachig. 'The contemporary discourse of diaspora studies'. *Comparative Studies of South Asia, Africa and the Middle East* 27(3) (2007): 647–55.

Trousdale, Rachel. *Nabokov, Rushdie, and the Transnational Imagination: Novels of exile and alternate worlds*. New York: Palgrave, 2010.

Vrubel'-Golubkina, Irina, ed. *Razgovory v Zerkale*. Moscow: NLO, 2016.

Wanner, Adrian. *Out of Russia: Fictions of a new translingual diaspora*. Evanston, IL: Northwestern University Press, 2011.

Zinik, Zinovy. 'Bol'shoe interv'iu 'Dissidenty i predateli sobstvennogo klassa menia zanimaiut bol'she, chem revoliutsionery i obshchestvennye deiateli', COLTA, 13 April 2018. http://www.colta.ru/articles/literature/17811 (accessed 30 August 2020).

Part two

# 'Quest for significance': performing diasporic identities in transnational contexts

# 2

# Exile as emotional, moral and ideological ambivalence: Nikolai Turgenev and the performance of political exile

Andreas Schönle

This chapter will analyse the case of one of Russia's first political exiles abroad, Nikolai Turgenev, a middle-ranking nobleman from a highly educated family, who found himself trapped in England (and subsequently France) after being sentenced to death in St Petersburg for alleged participation in the Decembrist conspiracy.[1] The case study will highlight a number of factors that make the performance of exile by Russian political and cultural elites distinctive. In particular, it will account for the ambivalence and complexities Russian political exiles in Western Europe experience as they come to terms with their position between two sociopolitical systems, which they perceive to be at different stages of civilizational development. My emphasis will be placed not on the socio-economic conditions of their existence outside their home country, but on the emotional, moral, cultural and ideological ambiguities and dislocations they experience as they adapt their worldview to their new interstitial existence, as well as the behavioural patterns they deploy in response. I will aim to show that Russia's position vis-à-vis Europe, as a country that defines itself as European yet sits geographically on the periphery of Europe and is a latecomer to Enlightenment-inflected thought and concomitant practices, lends added layers of ambivalence to the intrinsically ambivalent condition of exile, first and foremost because the 'homeland' is itself experienced as a fractured, non-homogeneous cultural territory. This chapter can hence serve to outline the paradigm of East–West exile.

By using the term *performance* of exile, I wish to capture several important factors. First, when members of the Russian (and indeed any) elite go into exile, they do not break hitherto untrodden behavioural ground, but deploy patterns of behaviour that they necessarily reference to the conduct of some famous predecessors, from Ovid to Dante to Pushkin. While the experience of predecessors does not necessarily present a *script* to fashion one's own behaviour, it nonetheless provides a repertoire of emotional responses and behavioural models against which one can evaluate one's own experience. Secondly, as we will see, exile is not a private act, but a series of gestures performed with an eye towards a public, who can range from the tsar to a community of reference (say the members of a circle), to the broader educated polity in both the home and adoptive countries. Thus it acquires a performative dimension in the sense of being in the limelight. Thirdly, and most importantly for my argument, performance captures the sense of acting in response to fluid, unexpected and changing circumstances, in line with what Peter Burke has called the 'occasionalist turn', which emphasizes the situational boundedness and improvisational reactiveness of historically relevant behaviour.[2] My contention will be that exile is less about draping oneself in the mantle of some glorious exceptionalism, than about muddling through contradictory pulls and ambivalent attachments that create inherently unstable positionings.

I have chosen the case of Nikolai Turgenev because before his exile he wrote a highly sophisticated and extensive diary, which gives access to his inner world and allows us to characterize how he felt about his public role and his responsibilities towards his country. He also wrote numerous treatises and pamphlets, notably a well-received volume on comparative systems of taxation in 1818, which sought to lay the groundwork for the abolition of serfdom. In exile he stopped writing his diary, and the source base for this chapter is somewhat less satisfactory. However, he engaged in extensive private correspondence with family and friends in Russia, only a small portion of which is published. He continued to write treatises, some of which were grouped in a three-volume edition entitled *La Russie et les Russes*, published in 1847 in Paris. The first volume of this publication, which he called 'Memoirs of an outcast', contains an extensive justification of his role in Russian society prior to exile and of his actions since he found himself abroad. The second volume is devoted to an analysis of contemporary Russian society, and the third to a project for Russia's future. After the publication of his magnum opus, he continued to intervene energetically in contemporary debates through various political pamphlets and proposals, writing both in French and in Russian, though publishing mostly in France and Germany, rather than in Russia. While not perfect, these sources allow us to develop a differentiated understanding of the ways in which he responded to the experience of exile and to evaluate the shifts in his self-identification. Turgenev was not a literary figure in the narrow, canonical sense, but he wrote at a time when the differentiation between genres of discourse was not yet fully operative and his diary has literary qualities. Although he penned some poetry in it, he deliberately published only political tracts because he thought that high literature, in particular because of the predominance of poetry, had failed to address the political and social concerns of his day.

I shall first attempt to describe his sense of self before his exile, focusing on the way he approached his role in society and the service he performed on behalf of Russia. Next I will trace how the experience of exile transformed his inner world. After focusing on the vagaries of his attempted and failed psychological disinvestment from Russia, I will evaluate subtle changes in his ideological position. This will allow me to broaden my discussion and draw some conclusions about what I have called the specific performance of Russian political exiles and to stake out, with due caution, distinctive elements in the way political exile is performed in the Russian context.

Born in 1789 into a noble family, Nikolai Turgenev, the son of a prominent Freemason, developed from the very beginning of his life a set of complex loyalties towards his country, which we can easily trace from the diary he started in 1806 and kept until he left Russia in 1824. His restlessness is first expressed in his continuous dissatisfaction and boredom with the present, which prompted dreams about a future in which he would dwell in perfect bliss. Of course this vision of an imaginary future, unstable in itself, only compounded his dissatisfaction with his present life, so that in time, to cope with the meaninglessness of his everyday life, he learned a form of stoic detachment and developed a practice of continuous self-reflection, which filled the perceived vacuity of his existence.[3]

This structure of feeling, however, changed once Turgenev found himself abroad. In 1808, he embarked on a journey to Göttingen, where he intended to study, following in the footsteps of his older brother Alexander. Much like Karamzin before him, Turgenev embraced travelling as a method of collecting memories for future enjoyment. But while still en route, he discovered that nostalgia for the fatherland elicited sweet tears, the typical sentimentalist mixed emotions, at once painful and pleasurable.[4] 'One needs to discover new countries, if only to become more attached to one's own', he concluded.[5] Stopping in Potsdam on his way to Göttingen, he longingly reminisced about his fatherland, forming the intention to sacrifice his life for it.[6] Suddenly his past existence in Russia came into view as a realm of belonging from which he was now severed. He also recognized that, in a few years, he would probably also feel nostalgic for his years in Göttingen. In short, he discovered the impermanence of his own self. Travel turned Turgenev into a different person, and so his past appeared in a new light. Even though it had been experienced as empty, it started to gain meaning precisely from the fact that it was different from the new present: 'Sometimes the thought of people whose company I had enjoyed brought joy to my despondent spirit. Now times are different, years are different, and I am myself different, with other new thoughts about people, about everything. But these memories will forever stay unforgettable.'[7] This discovery of his own historicity profoundly affected his experience of living abroad, giving rise to a complex reinvention of Russia itself, but also to the forming of new attachments, the adoption of new ideologies and the exploration of new identities.

From afar, in Germany, Turgenev looked back at Russia under Alexander I as a country engaged in rapid modernization. Encouraged by this thought, the blissful future he had always dreamt of took the form of a vision of a reformed country, one in which proximity to his loved ones was conflated with identification with the fatherland.[8] He even turned love for the fatherland into the one constant feeling that structured his identity:

> Я думаю, что долгое пребывание в чужих краях есть подлинно зараза для многих Русских: они неприметно переменяют образ мыслей о всем, даже и об отечестве. Но меня, кажется, таковые примеры тем более укрепляют в любви к этому божественному идеалу, усиливают высокое мнение мое о характере Русском и подтверждают справедливость этого мнения.

> I think that an extended stay abroad is a real plague for many Russians: they inevitably change their way of thinking about everything, even about the fatherland. But these examples only fortify me in my love for this divine ideal, strengthen my high opinion of the Russian character and confirm the justness of this opinion.[9]

Yet as he made ready to return to Russia in 1811 and embark on a career in public service, he developed anxieties about living in Russia, fearing the 'empty, unpleasant, difficult life' in the capital.[10] He experienced a hard landing in Moscow, where he was shocked at the coarseness of the people, at the 'stamp of slavery, vulgarity, heavy drinking' on their faces, which promptly kindled a desire to return to foreign lands.[11] He realized that 'he was deceived in the hopes his imagination had inspired in Göttingen'.[12] He became trapped in a disjunction between an ardent, if abstract, desire to contribute to progress in Russia and a profound distaste for everyday life in it. As he stated in 1822, 'I still love my compatriots, but I begin to realize that one can love the fatherland without respecting one's fellow countrymen'.[13] In short, while his political convictions militated for supporting the civilizing aims of the Russian state, relationally, he was unable to identify with the moral constitution of his countrymen and -women, let alone with everyday life in the Russian capital.

He eventually landed a post in the government that allowed him to influence official policy, and published treatises and pamphlets to further his vision of progress. Yet despite his energetic interventions in favour of civilizational reform, he bemoaned the uselessness of the civil service. He suffered from the clash between a romantic expectation that public life should somehow grow out of the aspirations of his innermost self and the sense of living like a soulless mechanism in an inert administrative system. In the early 1820s, his commitment to the Russian state, which he called his 'sole divinity', remained paramount, if entirely disembodied,[14] while he became ever more convinced that the thirst for freedom and inner peace was innate in him and could not be quelled in Russia.[15] To bridge this gap, he got involved with secret half-literary, half-political societies and tried to influence their objectives. His main concern was the abolition of serfdom, and he encouraged members of these societies to seek the release of their serfs. In his diary, bouts of depression inspired by the rigidities of Russian life and the uselessness of his service in the government coexist with brief moments of elation about future prospects. He kept thinking about moving abroad, or retiring to his estates, or settling in Crimea, fantasizing about what he called, in English, 'an independent life',[16] nurturing a vision of autonomous selfhood. Yet at the same time, the ethos of service to the ruler and his hopes for Russia's civilizational advance continued to command his loyalty. To evade his inner contradictions, he petitioned the tsar to send him abroad on a diplomatic posting, which would have allowed him to combine his patriotic commitment to Russia with an experience of the amenities and freedoms of life in Europe. His petition was turned down, yet, notwithstanding his profound disappointment, he thought he could not resign from the service, having received direct assurances from Alexander I that his contributions were highly valued. He felt trapped in a personal relationship with the tsar.

In April 1824, after his health began to deteriorate because of exhaustion, he was allowed to travel to Germany to visit spa towns there. While he was seeking a cure for his ailments, upon the sudden death of Alexander a small group of elite officers of the guard took advantage of the interregnum in December 1825 to attempt to overturn the government. The so-called Decembrists were crushed by regiments loyal to the regime and their leaders were put on trial. Five of them were executed and many others banished to Siberia. Although by the time of the uprising he had been abroad for more than a year and a half, Turgenev was seen as a co-conspirator, because of his role in secret societies before his departure. He was summoned to return to Russia to stand trial, which he refused, and as a result he was tried and convicted in absentia, earning himself a death sentence. So Turgenev became an exile, first in England and then in France, with little prospect of returning to Russia. The Russian government even made some attempt to have him extradited, but was rebuffed by the British authorities. Although partly serendipitous, these events capped a long process during which Turgenev continually wavered between his desire to move abroad or to retire to his estate and his commitment to state service and, more broadly, to Russia's political and moral progress.

The circumstances of his exile put Turgenev under considerable moral strain. Having heard that he was being investigated, he drafted a fairly casual self-justification in April 1826, which he sent to the authorities in St Petersburg. In it, he downplayed the significance of the society to which he belonged, the Union of Welfare, presenting it as all talk and no action. He also claimed to have had no ties with secret societies after the Union of Welfare was disbanded in 1821, and asserted that his sole concern had always been the amelioration or abolition of serfdom, rather than a change of political system.[17] At the time he wrote this he didn't know what he was charged with, nor did he realize that the Investigative Commission had a wealth of documents at its disposal and that some Decembrists had turned against him. So his self-justification was contradicted by the evidence gathered by the Commission. Combined with his refusal to stand trial, this evidence firmed up the conviction of the judges, who in the end sentenced him to capital punishment. Having heard the news and read the final report of the Investigative Commission, Turgenev drafted a second, much longer and more thorough justification. This was in effect a plea for pardon from the tsar, in which Turgenev had to adopt the rhetoric of the Investigative Commission, presenting the Decembrists in a sharply negative light as 'villains' and 'criminals' while trying to distance himself from them. Some of this was written under pressure from his brother Alexander and his friend the poet Vasily Zhukovsky, which he subsequently came to regret.[18] So he wrote to his brother, 'I can justify myself, but I should not write in this way about others who suffer incomparably more than I do.'[19]

Throughout this process, Turgenev faced several moral pitfalls. Not only had he to find a way of justifying himself without incriminating others and without completely trivializing the ideals the Decembrists had lived for and acted upon, but he also needed to make sure that his conviction and exile would not unduly harm his family and friends. In his letters to his brother Alexander, he agonized about the fact that while he enjoyed the freedoms of life in Britain, his brother's official career and his standing at court and in society had suffered irreparable damage, and he implored him to take every precaution. Alexander sold the family estate of Turgenevo in 1837 to support his brother's and his own lifestyle in Europe, as well as to pre-empt a possible expropriation. Concern for his brother also delayed Nikolai's publication of *La Russie et les Russes*, suggesting that his freedom of expression had been constrained by it.[20] On the one side, Nikolai encouraged his brother to move abroad or at least to take measures to protect his property should he be unable to return to Russia. But on the other, he also defended his own political freedoms, stating, 'I have the full right to speak about a country for which I am convinced that I have sacrificed everything and for which I desired sincerely, passionately to be useful.'[21]

His decision not to return to Russia to stand trial also created a moral predicament. While in his memoir he vigorously defended his decision and asserted his right to a retrial, in a letter to his brother from March 1827 he confided that his failure to appear in court was a stain on his conscience.[22] He wrote this in the context of discussions with his brother about whether he should petition the tsar directly for pardon. The sense of guilt resulting from his non-appearance reveals that he continued to see himself as a subject of the tsar and that his honour would have required that he trust in the tsar's justice. Yet in the same letter he also wrote that if he were now to be ordered to return to Russia and he obeyed, it would be a despicable act on his part.[23] How can we resolve this contradiction? The noble's oath of allegiance to the tsar, which continued to exert internal sway over him despite his exile, clashed with his Enlightenment-derived conviction that he had to stand first and foremost for the protection of his fundamental freedoms, and that returning to Russia and putting himself at the mercy of the tsar's favour would have meant a betrayal of his right to due process. In the end, the latter view prevailed and he decided not to write to the tsar directly, though he continued to send out feelers through intermediaries.

The issue flared up again in 1830, when through Zhukovsky, Turgenev was given to understand that the tsar would give him free passage to Russia to present his arguments in a court of law and try to clear his name. Turgenev immediately resolved to accept this offer and started frantically to prepare his return. As he put it in his memoir, against the advice of all his friends, 'I was keen to prove my innocence', although once successful he had no other desire but to return to England.[24] One gets a sense of his complex ambitions. He didn't care for a pardon from the tsar, only for the right to a retrial, through which he could obtain a legal confirmation of his innocence. Nor was he in any way interested in returning to Russia, only in being allowed to exercise his freedom to choose himself his place of residence. Not surprisingly, Zhukovsky clarified apologetically in a further letter that Nicholas had only proposed to improve his situation without rehabilitation, which Turgenev rejected out of hand. Turgenev denied that in this episode he also consciously intended to demonstrate civic courage, thus offsetting the original stain of non-appearance. He claimed that he acted primarily out of his sense of righteousness, although he also had in mind the destiny of others, who had suffered the consequences of his exile.[25] In another demonstration of his self-awareness, he also stated that he could not take pride in his condemnation, as he had not rendered sufficient service to his country. Not for him, he implied, the romantic exaltation of having sacrificed himself on the altar of patriotism and the love of freedom, although elsewhere in his memoir he did invoke the rhetoric of righteous self-sacrifice to justify his existence. Here, too, it seems, he was internally split.

Despite what he wrote, he took moral comfort from this episode, in that, his offer to return to Russia and stand trial having been rejected, he was now 'quits towards his country and his fellow citizens'.[26] He read this episode as a confirmation that his exile was in perpetuity, so he resolved to separate himself morally from his country. As he put it,

> Je m'efforçai d'y penser le moins possible, d'en effacer jusqu'au souvenir, et j'y serais peut-être parvenu si je pouvais oublier qu'il y a des infortunés en Sibérie et des esclaves dans tout l'empire. Par le fait même, d'ailleurs, je suis demeuré complètement étranger à tout ce qui se passe en Russie, comme à tout ce qui s'écrit sur elle à

l'étranger; je ne lis ni les journaux ni les livres russes, j'évite même les conversations où il peut être question de mon pays.[27]

This is contradicted by the second volume of *La Russie*, which shows familiarity with political events and legislative acts after his exile. In the preface to *La Russie*, Turgenev acknowledges, 'in vain did I hope to isolate myself from Russia: the fatherland retains over us an irresistible control'.[28] Towards the end of volume 1, he further confides that just as he had thought that his detachment from Russia was complete, the writing of his memoirs rekindled old memories, nearly extinct impressions, which flitted in his mind 'bright and throbbing'.[29] Years of conscious effort to divest himself from Russia had come to nothing. In a report addressed to Nicholas I, Mikhail Bakunin, who visited Turgenev in Paris in the 1840s, drew a portrait of a lonely man whose only wish was to return to Russia.[30]

From 1833, Turgenev lived near Paris, where he established a family with his wife Clara de Viaris. His daughter Fanni was born in 1835, his son Albert in 1843 and his son Pierre-Nicolas, a future sculptor of some renown, in 1853. While living in Paris, Turgenev had little interaction with Russians, who mostly avoided him, except for some émigrés like Bakunin and Herzen. But Turgenev cared enough about the public reception of *La Russie* to bring it actively to the attention of intellectuals in Britain and France, which resulted in two lengthy laudatory reviews in French magazines.[31]

The publication of his three-volume *La Russie et les Russes* is thought to have elicited a muted reaction and little repercussion in Russia, where the work was censored. The received view of the public indifference to Turgenev's works in France rests on the report of an agent of the Russian secret police, Ia. N. Tolstoy, who wrote, 'he describes Russia as it was 20 years ago ... and does not take account of Russia's enormous progress since then. On top of it, I'm convinced that this book will not attract fame: its verbosity, its paradoxes, and the boring first volume will inevitably turn off the readers.'[32]

This view needs to be qualified. In fact, the book made it all the way to Siberia, where several Decembrists reacted strongly and discordantly to it.[33] There were reviews in Britain and Germany, too, and a German translation appeared shortly after the French publication, suggesting international reach.[34] Turgenev himself was rather pleased with the reception of his work, noting in a letter to Zhukovsky, 'there are people here who read all three volumes from cover to cover without stopping ... It's true that these were not Russians ... for the simple reason that I don't see them.'[35] Reporting that many readers reproached him for being too moderate, Turgenev took comfort from the fact that the Polish poet Adam Mickiewicz had liked his book. He also added that a pirate edition in Belgium would save him the trouble of a second edition.[36] On the face of it, there is much exaggeration in the view that Turgenev led a secluded life, or failed to integrate himself into French public life, and that his magnum opus was ignored.

In 1856 Turgenev petitioned the new tsar Alexander II and in 1857 he received his pardon and the return of his rank and medals, though not his pension. He made three trips to Russia, in 1857, 1859 and 1864, but never considered settling there again, despite his professed inextinguishable love for the country. During his first journey, he travelled to an estate he had inherited in the Tula province and emancipated his four hundred serfs, applying the principles he had described in his theoretical works on serfdom. He had already undertaken an attempt to alleviate the predicament of his serfs in 1818, when he visited the family estate of Turgenevo. Then, he had written an instruction for managing the estate and, to stem the abuses of the steward, had introduced some degree of self-government by the serfs through elected elders, trying to instil self-interest, only to backtrack once he realized that this reform created all kinds of problems. Despite his theoretical views about the moral and economic advantages of quit-rent over corvée, he had been very hesitant to put his own serfs onto quit-rent, although in the end he did give instruction for this to be done.[37]

This time, in 1857, he more boldly granted a third of the land to his serfs in inalienable possession, while leasing the remainder to them at a relatively high price, equivalent to the quit-rent they would have paid on the entire estate if they had remained enserfed. A. N. Shebunin pointed out that while formally the serfs had been emancipated, the land they received in ownership was too small for subsistence, forcing them to accept the onerous conditions placed on the lease of the adjoining lands, which remained in Turgenev's ownership.[38] In his detailed description of his actions, Turgenev acknowledged that in the absence of an overall legal framework and while the soul tax and the recruitment levies remained unchanged, the peasant commune had a vested interest in all peasants staying put and discharging their obligations.[39] As a result, the reform did nothing to enable freedom of movement, and Turgenev concluded, 'I don't need to state how much I regret that the arrangement I made with my peasants had not been more beneficial to them in its results', yet he continued to argue that his method of emancipation was the 'least difficult'.[40] While it improved the serfs' legal position, this formula made no change to their economic livelihood, nor, in fact, to Turgenev's.

How can we characterize his political philosophy? Turgenev was a romantic nationalist. Despite his disdainful views of his urban compatriots, he idealized the Russian serfs and imputed Russia's deficiencies to an elite caste he described as foreign. In his analysis of Russian history, he pointed out that serfdom did not exist under the Tatar yoke, but was imposed by the ruling elite in subsequent centuries, a ruling elite that he saw as essentially foreign. He highlighted a profound historical irony whereby if in Western Europe it was the Barbarian invaders who introduced forms of slavery to dominate the vernacular populations, in Russia the vanquished Tatars remained free and many joined the ranks of the nobility, while the peasant victors were progressively enserfed.[41] As a result, as he put it, 'the Russian nobility resembles a race of conquerors which imposed itself by force upon the nation, introducing other instincts, other tendencies, and having other interests than those of the majority'.[42] Yet despite their centuries-long humiliating experience of serfdom, Russian peasants had remained surprisingly generous, faithful and devoted.[43] In fact, Turgenev maintains, 'servitude has not debased them; it seems, on the contrary, that the severity of their position has only elevated and ennobled them'.[44] By superimposing social, ethnic and geopolitical parameters, and despite his fraught dealings with his own serfs, Turgenev radicalized the gap between the elite and the people, laying the blame for Russia's dysfunctions at the feet of an exogenous elite, to which he himself belonged: 'it is the barbarian, egotistical and nonsensical politics of a usurper which has inflicted a wound on the entire nation, devouring it and thereby bringing shame on itself'.[45] In this way, the nation remains morally untainted by the deficiencies of Russian history, victimized as it was by foreign usurpers.

Turgenev identified himself wholeheartedly with the serfs, stating that he had always seen his compatriots, and his fatherland, in them.[46] Here we already see a subtle shift emerging from his exile. If, while he lived in St Petersburg and beheld the pathologies of urban life, he had to disassociate himself from his contemporaries, going so far as to say that one could love one's country without loving one's compatriots, in exile he was free to idealize the Russian serfs as the embodiment of an untainted Russian spirit.

Yet at the same time, despite this romantic affiliation with the people, Turgenev was a scion of the Enlightenment and a proponent of universalist values. To begin with, he was entirely committed to universal history, presenting England as the vanguard of history, and operating with a teleological paradigm, in which other nations are situated at various stages depending on the extent of delays in their modernization.[47] He defined the Enlightenment in civic, political terms as 'consciousness of one's rights and one's obligations'.[48] To him, there could be only one universal civilization, which manifests itself in respect for basic human rights, in what he called 'the feeling of justice, of equity, respect for life and the dignity of man'.[49] In other words, the goal of history resides in the ability to exercise civic and political freedoms, something he attempted to do, but struggled to maintain in his dealings with the tsar. His vision of world history was one of a continuous coming together and levelling of nations under the influence of the advance of civilization. So in this context, patriotism to him was a fraud, 'egoism on a large scale', while the expression of patriotic sentiments was nothing but some 'patriotic silliness' (niaiseries patriotiques).[50]

So how did he combine Enlightenment universalism with romantic nationalism? The main way in which he thought to bridge the intellectual gap between these two positions was by positing an intrinsic disposition towards progress among the people. To him, at least since the introduction of Christianity, the Russian people had always had a burning desire for progress, and this contention, or sleight of hand, allowed him to endow his romantic nationalism with a forward-looking, progressive politics, contrary to that of his Slavophile contemporaries, for whom the Russian peasants represented a repository of traditional values.[51]

Yet his view of Europeanization changed as a result of his exile. Before his exile and the repression that followed the Decembrist uprising, and despite his impatience with the maddeningly slow pace of government bureaucracy, he was convinced that under Alexander I Russia was on its way to catching up with Western societies.[52] Yet in exile he became much more sceptical about progress from above. One can see this in his evaluation of the reforms of Peter the Great. Before his exile, he had praised Peter for transforming Russian society: 'even if we make progress only slowly,' he wrote, 'then at least Peter closed off the road to the past. He burned the fleet that took us from the land of ignorance to the land of education.'[53] In contrast, after his exile, Turgenev blamed Peter for his focus on the superficial Westernization of the elite rather than on popular education, for his being more interested in the 'shiny than the solid'.[54] The result of the development of Russia in the eighteenth and early nineteenth centuries, to him, was the creation of a hybrid country, 'a mixture of enlightenment and obscurantism, of good and evil, of European inspirations and Asiatic instincts, in a word a hypocrisy of civilization'.[55] Russia had lost its intrinsic unity, it was split socially and historically, with some traces of a past unredeemed by 'civilization' lingering in the present and becoming the linchpin of some conservative nationalists' notion of national identity. And even though he understood that patriotic love for Russia can cling to these traces of the past, he stated unequivocally that nationalism should not stop progress.[56]

In his later political tracts, Turgenev attempted again to equivocate. While supporting the legitimacy of Alexander II, he articulated very forcefully the need to introduce constitutional order and representative government, which led him to propose the establishment of the *zemskii sobor* (an assembly of the land). Yet, strikingly, he argued less from the need to confer individual civil and political rights on the population, than as a way to solve the 'Polish question' and to enhance Russia's prestige and power in the international arena. He envisaged that the adoption of a constitution and the establishment of a representative assembly would give a voice to the Poles, who would hence realize that it was in their interest to remain within Russia. Progressively, other Slavic and Orthodox populations in Europe would likewise turn to the benevolent protection of Russia, which would then expand as a multinational empire underpinned by constitutional representative government, within which all nations could exercise political rights. Thus political rights were redefined as the rights of nations, rather than of individuals. Turgenev contrasted Russian tolerance of vernacular identities with the German drive to Germanize Slavic populations. And as proof that smaller nations could thrive within the Russian empire, he pointed to the Baltic provinces, whose elites assumed leading positions of influence in the government and in the army.[57] Thus, in keeping with his emphasis on legal structures, rather than ethno-cultural identities, he imagined that the 'ties of a wise constitution' would bind together all Slavic populations, hailing the day when 'we would see the children of constitutional Russia, all the Slavs fused in a fraternal embrace'.[58] While his construct had a veneer of supranationalism, it was firmly rooted in a primordialist definition of Slavdom and sought to tap into, if not co-opt, the Pan-Slavic ideology then on the rise in Central Europe and in the Balkans.

So what should we do with the multiple contradictions that underpin Turgenev's relations to Russia? He was a member of the elite disdainful of the elite, committed to Europeanization, but scathing about the superficial Europeanization of the upper nobility. He found justification for his life from his dedication to improving the lot of serfs in the abstract, but his initial attempt to endow the serfs he owned with a measure of freedom turned into a complete fiasco, while his second go at it made no material difference to them. He loved his country and wanted to sacrifice his life for it, but couldn't endure everyday life in the capital and buckled under the ignominies of a career in the civil service. Nor was he burning to return to Russia once he found himself in exile: he was more interested in defending his civil rights as a matter of principle than in exercising those rights in order to live in his home country. In exile he wanted to disinvest himself from Russia, yet discovered that he was unable to do so, either emotionally or intellectually. All his protestations that reading Shakespeare is more interesting than State Council protocols, that since he can no longer be of any use to Russia, he is no longer obligated to it for anything, that he enjoys the amenities and pleasantness of life in England and feels now alien to Russia, came to nothing.[59] Not only did he remain tied to Russia by family bonds, which weighed on him as he knew that his brothers had suffered administratively and financially from his becoming an outcast, he also continued implicitly to see himself as a subject of the tsar, bound to the ruler by an interiorized sense of honour, which was part of the compact between a noble and the monarch. He never fully resolved the contradictions between the somewhat demeaning ethic of chivalrous obedience and service to the ruler and his ideas of universal human rights and dignity. Yet eventually, after Alexander II pardoned him, he displayed no interest in returning to Russia or resuming service on behalf of his country. His political pamphlets, written more often in French than in Russian and published outside Russia, seemed aimed more at the French reading public than at his Russian contemporaries, even though he remained on the margins of public debates in France. And when he attempted to engage with topical political issues in Russian public life, he was reviled as a relic from another era. While residing in the vanguard of civilization, all of a sudden he found himself hopelessly *dépassé* in his own country.

This predicament reveals the complex temporality of exile. Despite significant accommodation to, and engagement with, public life in England and France, Turgenev could not cast off the weight of the past. Crossing the Russian border did not bring about a moral and existential rupture, as his bonds with Russian life endured despite his antagonistic relation to much in his home country, from its political structure, to everyday life, to the moral character of his compatriots. Much as he enjoyed the greater freedom of life in the West, including the opportunity to shore up his liberal, self-determining identity, Turgenev could not embrace diasporic existence as an exhilarating and subversive form of self-creation.[60] His tangled sense of self as a member of the elite performing a patriotic responsibility towards his country induced both guilt and despair at his powerlessness. While existentially he stood only to gain from his exile, the loss of political face prevented him from making peace with his new location.

It is important to recognize that his ambivalence regarding Russia pre-dated his exile. We saw that from his very first journey abroad in 1808, the experience of visiting another country paradoxically strengthened his love for Russia, while at the same time casting his home country in an unfavourable light, as the constant trampling of human dignity – the continuous moral debasement of the population, from serfs to aristocrats – came into view by comparison. In that sense, the experience of exile did not, in fact, create a radical rupture in his life, it only exacerbated what was already there, with contradictions becoming ever more difficult to reconcile. Similarly, as we saw, his noble habitus, his honour-bound loyalty to the tsar, did not evaporate after he was exiled. He continued very much to be plagued by thoughts about how he could justify himself in the eyes of the ruler without compromising his self-pride, despite being a free man in a free country. Ambivalence existed before and continued after the inception moment of exile.

Turgenev's contradictions result from Russia's distinctive position on the geopolitical map of Europe in the modern world. Despite being on the periphery of the continent, Russia found itself heavily engaged in European affairs, fighting several wars with European countries, but also playing the unstable game of power alliances. Peter the Great recognized that to strengthen its army and overcome its developmental gap with Europe, Russia required a caste of well-educated, Europeanized elites, who would contribute to administering the realm and serve the state in its modernization policies. Almost a century later, Turgenev represented the outcome of these policies, a highly educated Europeanized member of the noble and intellectual elite, who felt a strong bond of loyalty to his country, but whose cultural capital made him increasingly critical of its political system and, more broadly, of its unreformed, un-Europeanized values and practices. He experienced a form of moral hybridity, in which partial alienation from some spheres of Russian life competed with, or even reinforced, his overall identification with the destiny of Russia. This is how he could remain a patriot while despising much he saw in Russia.

Exile only reinforced the predicament of this moral ambivalence. On the one hand the commitment to Russia remained, although now tinged with a sense of powerlessness and inability to contribute meaningfully to its progress. On the other hand, the alienation from Russian values and practices only grew in the light of the experience of far more satisfactory British and then French behavioural norms, in particular with regard to the protection of individual freedom and dignity. The crux of the matter was that he had migrated from a country he described as a mixture of Enlightenment and barbarity, of Europe and Asia, to a country, Britain, that he saw as being at the apex of civilizational development, a unified, coherent, self-confident and holistic paragon of historical progress (he showed little interest in the specific conditions and limitations of British claims to civilizational pre-eminence). Thus, by the accidental circumstance of his exile, he had made a civilizational leap into the kind of future he wished for Russia. As a result, unlike his fellow countrymen, he enjoyed the protection of the rule of law, freedom of expression and the amenities of everyday life in a dynamic capital. How could he not at once feel relieved and guilty about that? He lived in the kind of future he had always dreamed about, and if he could only forget that he was once Russian, he could resolve all the tensions and contradictions he had confronted throughout his life. Exile offered the promise of internal reconciliation, if only he could suppress his memories of the past, which was, of course, impossible.

Edward Said famously maintained that exile is 'terrible to experience. It is the unhealable rift forced between a human being and a native place, between the self and its true home: its essential sadness can never be surmounted.'[61] The distinctiveness of Turgenev's performance of exile is that he never had a 'true home' in the untheorized sense in which Said uses the expression here. As we have seen, there was never a place that Turgenev felt to be entirely his own. Just as for Gogol and many others, it is only from the safe distance of abroad that Turgenev could fantasize about Russia being a home of sorts. Returning to it only produced a powerful urge to escape again. But does that mean that there was nothing tragic about Turgenev's experience of exile, and that we should count him as a forerunner of postmodern ex-territorial globetrotters who experience exile as a liberation from the repressive confines of exiguous national identity? Of course not. The bonds of memory and internalized responsibility were much too tight for that, and the result of exile only added a sense of guilt to the other confused feelings Turgenev confronted in his dealings with his native country.

We can now broaden the argument and risk some generalization. Mutatis mutandis, beyond the particulars of Turgenev's exilic situation, his experience is similar to that of twentieth-century émigrés and exiles from the Soviet Union, whether they belong to the first, second, third emigration, or beyond. I suggest that the performance of Russian exiles, conditioned by Russia's intrinsic dividedness and its ambiguous position at the periphery of the modern Western world, is one of profound ambivalence. For Russians, exile is both constricting and liberating, tragic and empowering, nostalgic and forward-looking, national and global. The critical antinomy between exile as tragic rupture and emancipatory reinvention needs to be overcome. Exiles from Russia experience both, in an uneasy and unstable overlayering, which itself goes back to the hybrid identities they had developed in their homeland before exile. Even those who negotiated an ostensibly 'successful' experience of exile, the Viacheslav Ivanovs and Vladimir Nabokovs of this world, continued to nurture complex bonds with their place of origin, sustained through their memories and their ambivalent use of the Russian language. At most, exile meant for Turgenev the displacement, exacerbation and reconfiguration of an alterity vis-à-vis the homeland that was always at the heart of his existence. But it also meant a loss of (imagined) political clout – the internalized habitus of a member of the elite – which was disconcerting and painful, and hence prevents us from trivializing Turgenev's experience as the manifestation of some diasporic normality.

Turgenev's case reveals several fault lines or pressure points in the performance of exile in the nineteenth and twentieth centuries in Russia. One important ingredient of Russia's distinctive historical performance of exile is that, until the late Soviet period, it is first and foremost a phenomenon specific to the intellectual and cultural elites. Furthermore, as a member of the elite, whose function, in a society defined by patronage structures, was to serve both the ruler and the country, Turgenev could not help experiencing exile as a forcible severing from the ruler, which precipitated a crisis of identity. Deprived of access to government and court, Turgenev lost not only all pragmatic means to weigh in on the course of state policy, but also participation in ceremonial rituals and access to the body of the emperor, something which in court culture was carefully calibrated and was expressive of social prestige. Turgenev had lofty ideas about political leadership, which he had honed while serving as personal secretary to Baron vom Stein, the Prussian statesman recruited by Alexander I to administer the provinces of East and West Prussia liberated from Napoleon. Stein was a progressive German nationalist who had instigated the emancipation of Prussian serfs and militated for the unification of Germany. Inspired by Stein to reflect on the nature of leadership, Turgenev noted in his diary that 'nothing can go by itself. One must and can direct [public] opinion. I didn't always think so forcefully, but recent events have demonstrated the justness of these words.'[62] This elite habitus, the internalized claim to act on behalf of the greater good of the nation, sometimes against its own will, is characteristic not only of Turgenev, but of much of the Russian intellectual elite across the ages, conditioned as it is by the drastic cultural gulf that separates it from the people.

In exile, of course, the means to discharge this political and cultural mission are sharply reduced. Turgenev's response to this loss of face was to attempt, or fantasize, a negotiation with the emperor, trying to navigate the contradictions between performing his emotional bond with, and dependence on, the tsar, while at the same time affirming his intrinsic dignity as an individual. This to-and-fro between a social, interactional definition of identity on one side, and a liberal, legal one on the other, is one that unfolded both within himself and in exchanges with the ruler and his agents. While his position may seem to occupy a transitional phase in the experience of exile – a progressive shedding of the mental habits of patronage and crystallization of identification with the nation and with legal and liberal definitions of the person and its dignity – the dialogue between the exile and the ruler (or the latter's agents) has remained a characteristic, if not ubiquitous, feature in Russian and early Soviet history, regardless of whether exiles left on a voluntary or forcible basis and whether they were consigned to internal or external exile. Suffice it to think of Radishchev in the 1790s, of Pushkin in the early 1820s, and of Mandelstam, Gorky, Kuprin, Alexei Tolstoi or Tsvetaeva in the early Soviet years.[63] Thus in Russia's heavily personalistic political culture, where the ruler is the ultimate arbiter of the fate of individuals regardless of the outward political system, exile has often taken the form of a personal falling-out with the ruler, sometimes prompting attempts on either side to open up a dialogue and engage in some form of negotiation, often through intermediaries. This state of affairs, of course, is hardly limited to Russia. It goes all the way back to antiquity, for example to Ovid's *relegatio* decreed by Augustus in 8 AD, of which writers, Pushkin first among them, were keenly aware and which they intensely romanticized.[64] In the Soviet Union, the situation changed in the 1970s and until the perestroika years, when the Soviet state was much more consistent in expelling dissidents and stripping them of their citizenship, while dissidents themselves took a principled view that any collaboration or accommodation with the Soviet state was both morally repugnant and politically impossible, which did not prevent them from intending to continue to influence political and cultural developments in Russia.[65]

More importantly, what this negotiation reveals is that claims to perform an elite political or cultural function in the polity of their homeland remained constitutive of the identity of many Russian exiles. The habit of shaping public discourse, acting as the 'conscience' of the nation, articulating the needs of the people, or representing the interests of the downtrodden – all these systems of legitimization crucial to the Russian intelligentsia – remained a latent aspiration throughout the experience of exile, even when the public forums to perform such roles became more restricted. As Pamela Davidson analyses in this volume, the prophetic mission many Russian authors assumed proved vital enough to adapt to conditions of exile and take new forms. And even those who frowned upon these forms of public validation, like Nabokov, ultimately gained much of their polemical edge and public resonance precisely from this rejection. Most exiles continued to enact a vicarious relationship with the public, audience or readers they had left behind in Russia, and this relationship continues to be based on an asymmetrical, hierarchical distribution of social roles, with the elite exiles arrogating to themselves some fiduciary function vis-à-vis the people. In that sense, the Russian experience of exile, perhaps at least until the collapse of the Soviet Union, never rose to the level of de-centring and de-territorializing which Paul Gilroy has associated with the diasporic experience.[66] Territory continued to determine identity even from a distance, as the asymmetric distribution of political and cultural capital endured beyond the border.

The second fault line we see in Turgenev's case is that between internal and external exile. It was largely fortuitous that Turgenev found himself abroad when the Decembrists rose up against the tsar, and the authorities wanted nothing more than to bring him back to Russia to stand trial. Writers had been exiled before him, notably, again, Radishchev and Pushkin, but their banishment was internal, to Siberia in Radishchev's case and to the South, the then Bessarabia, in Pushkin's. Decembrists who were not executed were likewise exiled beyond the Urals. Throughout Russia's imperial history, banishment to Siberia, from its conquest in the late 1500s, was a systematic policy, in part motivated by colonial and economic interests, and fostered by granting noble landowners the right to exile their troublesome serfs.[67] Of course, banishment was also a frequent, and milder, practice in court society. It could mean something as simple as losing favour and being cast out from the court and from the capital, which in practice meant banishment to the country estate. The case of A. B. Kurakin is instructive. Having fallen into disgrace in 1782 for a disrespectful comment he made in a private letter about G. A. Potemkin, then Catherine the Great's favourite, he was banished from court and from St Petersburg.[68] Although he was a protégé of Paul, Catherine's son, and could have stayed at Paul's 'small court' in Gatchina in the vicinity of St Petersburg, he preferred to retire to his distant country estate of Nadezhdino in the Saratov province, from where he engaged in an extensive correspondence with fellow aristocrats. As his correspondents exerted pressure on him to return to Gatchina and discharge his duties to Paul as was expected of a loyal courtier, Kurakin argued that in his voluntary retirement he sought to cultivate his knowledge, skills and civic virtues in preparation for future service, drawing on banished Romans as an example. At the same time, he undertook several attempts to negotiate his return to St Petersburg. Of interest here is the binary he established between access to ruler and court as a bona fide grandee on the one side, and, on the other, complete withdrawal from court life and absorption into the cultivation of moral virtues that would come in handy in changed political circumstances. Not content with assuming a reduced social role, he fell back on the cultivation of interiority as a compensation for his loss of prestige. His attitude reveals both the defining importance for an aristocrat of access to the ruler and the rise of notions of personal dignity that conflicted with the bowing and scraping required at court. What we see here is the foreshadowing of another prominent Soviet phenomenon, that of half-voluntary, half-forcible internal exile, the posture of individuals who, while residing in the homeland, actively disengaged themselves from public life in it and erected boundaries around their private spheres, living as if in a state of suspension until they could emigrate physically or until the regime changed. Internal migration thus became a form of exile without dislocation, yet no less self-alienating for it, in that it involved the rupture of networks of belonging and communication.

From the point of view of the state, as long as the empire was construed as a multinational and multilingual territory, banishment to its furthest corners, motivated largely by economic interests and the need to expand the reach of Russian culture, was deemed a sufficient form of punishment. It is only with the rise of a national conception of the state and of the printing press as a means of disseminating ideas that exile to a foreign country, i.e. complete rupture with the national fabric, could become a necessity in certain circumstances. However, here again, no consistent evolution can be discerned. Internal and external exile remained part of the arsenal of coercive measures at the disposal of the state throughout the course of Russia's history. And from the point of view of the individual, between exile to one's kitchen and exile to Paris there is a continuum in the severance of networks that sustained public performance, suggesting that the location of exile matters less than access to communicative circuits that facilitated the enactment of a public role.

The last fault line is that which emerges in the evolutionary gap between the home country and the country of refuge. This perceived developmental time lag is what significantly complicated Turgenev's performance of exile, as his emotional loyalty to Russia and its ruler conflicted with the sense that the European countries in which he resided during his exile – England and France – were significantly more advanced and more amenable to his liberal notions of personal dignity. The experience of exile as a leap in time, an abrupt propulsion into an imagined and desired future, yet in an alien territory and an alien culture, rested on the adoption of historical teleologies that ultimately go back to the Enlightenment. Yet it is only combined with Herder's notion of cultural nationalism that exile acquired its full disruptive force, as it now became not only a journey in time, but also a forceful tearing away from the organicist cultural fabric of the home country.

Of course this leap in time can be construed in various ways and can be both progressive and regressive. We can catch a glimpse of a similar, if inverted, dynamic in Alexander Herzen's performance of exile. After two periods of internal exile, Herzen (born in 1812, i.e. a full generation after Turgenev) had been seeking permission to leave Russia for a number of years, prompted primarily by his quest for freedom and the continuous trampling of his personal dignity under the regime of political surveillance to which he was subject. He finally obtained the right to travel abroad for medical reasons in late 1846 and bade farewell to his friends and his country in March 1847. His initial impressions from his travel through Germany and his life in Paris are expressed in his *Letters from the Avenue Marigny*, published immediately in *Sovremennik* and then republished in a redacted version as *Letters from France and Italy* in 1855 and 1858. From Cologne he writes about Europe as an old world buckling under its lengthy history: 'This country has lived long! Europe itself has lived long. Under every hewn stone, every constrained opinion, lie dozens of centuries.' 'Europeans', he goes on, 'cannot free themselves of the influence of the past. For them, the present is the roof of a multi-storeyed house, for us, as well as for North America, it is a high terrace, a foundation … We begin from their ending.'[69] As Aileen Kelly has explained in detail, under the influence of evolutionary science as well as the writings of Feuerbach, Herzen had by then rejected any ideas of teleology, yet without fully relinquishing the notion of progress, nor that of universal values.[70] To him Europe was a decaying world, an impression later strengthened by the failures of the 1848 revolutions.

Thus travel from Russia to the West was a journey in time, albeit in a reverse direction from that performed by Turgenev, from the future, if yet unrealized, potential of the Russian people to the obsolete and decaying achievements of Europe: 'It is enough to travel for an hour [from the Russian border] to land in a completely different world, in the world of the past, of losses, of memories and of widowhood', as he put it.[71]

Yet Herzen's position in this interstitial moment was no less ambivalent than Turgenev's. While he glorified the prospects of the rising Russian people – a new historical nation – he acknowledged the intellectual freedoms he enjoyed in France, Switzerland and then England, choosing, despite severe bouts of homesickness, to stay in the West when ordered to return home, and doing so in order to weigh in from abroad with his uncensored opinions on public debates in his home country. While he enjoyed the civil liberties offered by his host countries, he felt estranged from the vernacular elites, even though he also admitted that the reforms of Peter the Great had not only propelled the Russian elite into a successful embrace of Western forms of living, but also endowed it with a 'right of inheritance'. On the one hand, he would contend that 'sometimes people of our sort, the Scythians, feel uneasy among these inherited riches and bequeathed ruins. It is an awkward position for the stranger to be in a family hall where each portrait, each object, is precious to the heirs, but alien to him. He looks with curiosity at that which others remember fondly.'[72] Yet on the other hand, he felt enough kinship with Western elites to reject the Slavophile hostility towards Petrine reforms, arguing that the Russian nobility assimilated Western forms of behaviour without losing its unique Russian character, and expressing faith in the Russian people's ability to catch up with history, skipping over the Petrine era. Thus while living in Paris, Geneva and then London, bored to death yet strangely unwilling to join the intellectual debates raging in these cities, he fantasized a future communion with the Russian people, while admitting that 'the motherland of our thoughts, of our education, is here' and enjoying the legal freedoms in whose pursuit he had left Russia.[73] Kelly argued that his faith in the rise of the Russian people is not unlike the naïve faith in Providence that had helped him endure his previous two periods of internal exile.[74] Herzen, as it were, charted an evolutionary process whereby Russia inherited some traits acquired from its entanglement with Western cultures, yet without losing its own characteristics, thus propelling evolution into a different direction, leading to future socialism. The ambivalence of his exile stemmed from the transitional and incomplete nature of his historical moment.

The duality between Turgenev's and Herzen's performances of exile, between the leap into a desired future and a kind of déjà-vu return to a half-familiar past, illustrates that the temporal dislocations attendant on physical migration can assume divergent valences. Whether one migrates to or from the modern (or, later, postmodern) world (or a distortion of it), whether one returns to the traditional (if not 'eternal') homeland of European humanistic values or progresses from tyranny to democracy, whether one styles oneself as the guardian of national heritage in exile or the flag-bearer of a yet indistinct transnational future, whether one lands in a world of civilizational decay or embraces the arrogance of new beginnings (as in exile to Israel or the United States), the paradigm of East–West exile, conditioned by Russia's specific position on the outskirts of Europe and as a latecomer to Enlightenment thought and practice, easily takes on the shape of a shift, if not a leap, in time, yet one that can be performed in multifarious ways and through contradictory meanings. And as Maria Rubins reminds us in the introduction to this volume, this temporal dislocation also had to negotiate the gap between fixed, stereotypical views of the West formed on the turf of home culture and the specific experience of social, political and cultural realities made in the host country, which created an additional level of disruption. Thus, as Rubins details, in the wake of the devastation of the First World War, for many Russian émigrés of the Russian Revolution and its aftermath, the *expectation* of making a civilizational advance through exile exploded into a realization of the ubiquity of savage and unredeemable de-humanization, made only more traumatic by the collapse of lovingly hatched illusions about the West. This, in turn, robbed exile of any sort of incremental meaning, posing the question of whether a return to the homeland should not be contemplated or exacerbating the need for a justification of exile in spite of everything.

In an insightful essay, Galin Tihanov analysed, at a theoretical level, two different narratives of exile, the heroic narrative of creativity and the anguished narrative of suffering.[75] What unites the two, he submits, is the romantic valorization of the transcendence of everyday normality. Both narratives share the romantic stake in exceptionalism, whether connoted positively or negatively. Tihanov calls for a de-romanticization of the notion of exile, one that, as he concedes, is already happening de facto in the globalized conditions of multiple and frequent border crossings and with the rise of transnational history, even if the theoretical discourse of exile has not quite caught up with these developments yet. To further this de-romanticization, he draws attention to the degree of negotiation that takes place between citizen and state in the latter's deployment of indirect power. Ultimately, he proposes a de-liberalization of the person of the exiles, one that assumes not their autonomy as self-defining social agents, but their participation in various networks and communities and other forms of mediated solidarities that are not bound by the nation.

Contemplated in this light, the case of Nikolai Turgenev is instructive. We discern very clearly his attempt to negotiate his exile with the state, as well as within himself. We discover a continuous oscillation between creativity and anguish, between moments of liberal self-affirmation and moments of self-loathing, when he would hope for nothing more than to succumb to a nationally bound collective identity. In that sense, we can feel the everyday pulse of his exilic experience, a far cry from narratives of heroic exceptionalism. It is only in his dreams that he was a romantic in Tihanov's sense, as his identity was substantially dependent on the interactional dynamics of his relations with the tsar and his agents. In a sense, he never crossed the border. Liberal autonomy of selfhood is something he aspired to, but never realized. We can also see that the temporal projection of his performance of exile on a narrative of civilizational development reinforced the binary between Russia and the West from which he could not escape. Entangled within a social and cultural dependency on Russia and a liberal commitment to the West, he never succeeded in overcoming this contradiction and affirming who he was. The romanticism Tihanov disputes may have been a tenet of exilic theory, but it certainly did not define Turgenev's *performance* of exile, which better fits an occasionalist approach, as Burke defines it, namely an attention to the different ways in which the same person behaves in the light of different occasions or situations.[76] Whether Turgenev's case sets a model of what we can call the performance of East–West exilic border crossing is something that further historically grounded studies will have to ascertain, but it is clear that Turgenev's everyday performance casts serious doubt on the received theory of exile.

## Notes

1   I wish to express my gratitude to Maria Rubins, whose rigorous engagement with the theoretical issues raised by my article has helped me refine my argument considerably. Thanks are also due to the participants of the workshop on 'Redefining the Russian literary diaspora (1918–2018)' held at UCL in May 2018 for stimulating debates, and especially to the two discussants of my original paper, Mark Lipovetsky and Alexander Zholkovsky (in absentia), as well as the two anonymous peer reviewers of this chapter.
2   Burke 2005.

3   For a more detailed analysis of his emotional vagaries before his exile, see Schönle 2016, in particular 292–5.
4   Turgenev 1911–1921, vol. 1, 167.
5   Turgenev 1911–1921, vol. 1, 210. On the practice of travelling among the nobility, see Berelowitch 1993.
6   Turgenev 1911–1921, vol. 1, 167.
7   Turgenev 1911–1921, vol. 1, 223.
8   Turgenev 1911–1921, vol. 3, 12.
9   Turgenev 1911–1921, vol. 3, 143.
10  Turgenev 1911–1921, vol. 1, 305.
11  Turgenev 1911–1921, vol. 3, 190.
12  Turgenev 1911–1921, vol. 3, 191.
13  Turgenev 1911–1921, vol. 5, 316.
14  Turgenev 1911–1921, vol. 5. 220.
15  Turgenev 1911–1921, vol. 5, 309.
16  Turgenev 1911–1921, vol. 5, 315.
17  A. N. Shebunin analysed these claims, and while he concluded that Turgenev was on firm ground when he claimed that the loose talk in the secret societies to which he belonged did not legally amount to a conspiracy, some of his factual statements were incorrect. See Shebunin 1928.
18  On the basis of a comparison between the various drafts of this note, Shebunin demonstrated that Alexander partly rewrote the final version, in which he introduced this condemnation of Turgenev's former friends, while removing all the passages in which he incriminated himself. Contrary to Turgenev's request, Alexander didn't remove the negative characterizations of fellow Decembrists (Shebunin 1928, 126–7).
19  Quoted by Zhitomirskaia 2001, 629.
20  Writing to V. A. Zhukovsky in 1847, Turgenev claimed that the impact of his exile on his two brothers was such that it hastened their deaths, though he blamed the government for them (Lanskii 1975, 218). La Russie et les Russes was published only after the death of Alexander in 1845.
21  Zhitomirskaia 2001, 640.
22  Turgenev 1901, 274.
23  Turgenev 1901, 275.
24  Tourgueneff 1847, vol. 1, 398–9. His resolve in this might have been sharpened by his desire to clear his name so as to marry Harriet Lowell, the daughter of an English squire who had refused to give him her hand on account of the legal cloud hanging over him. See Mil'china 1997, 95–6. In the end, following his inability to obtain his rehabilitation, he moved to France in 1833 and married Clara de Viaris.
25  Tourgueneff 1847, vol. 1, 399.
26  Tourgueneff 1847, vol. 1, 403.
27  Tourgueneff 1847, vol. 1, 403.
28  Tourgueneff 1847, vol. 1, vii.
29  Tourgueneff 1847, vol. 1, 407.
30  Quoted by Shebunin 1925, 105.
31  Zhitomirskaia 2001, 640–2.
32  Zhitomirskaia 2001, 644.
33  Zhitomirskaia 2001, 647–9.
34  A review in The Daguerreotype (10(1) (25 December 1847): 433–6) managed to turn him into a serf who successfully obtained his emancipation. The German review (Blätter für literarische Unterhaltung 329 (25 November 1847): 1213–15) focused on his relations with Baron Heinrich vom Stein.
35  Lanskii 1975, 213.
36  Lanskii 1975, 225.
37  Turgenev 1911–1921, vol. 5, 136–48.
38  Shebunin 1925, 126.
39  Tourgueneff 1860, 107.
40  Tourgueneff 1860, 108–9.
41  Turgenev 1911–1921, vol. 5, 433.
42  Tourgueneff 1847, vol. 2, 31–2.

43  Tourgueneff 1847, vol. 2, 156.
44  Tourgueneff 1847, vol. 2, 94.
45  Tourgueneff 1847, vol. 2, 195. In this sense Turgenev's conclusions are substantially different from Chaadaev's, who articulated in his 'First Philosophical Letter' the notion that Russia had existed outside historical times and was lacking any traditions, having been only superficially Westernized as a result of the reforms of Peter the Great. Chaadaev neither idealized the Russian serfs, nor did he grant the elite much significance. See Raeff 1966, 162.
46  Tourgueneff 1847, vol. 2, 94.
47  In Britain, Turgenev had contacts with the intellectual elite, in particular with followers of Bentham, such as James Mill, and with the Whiggish circles around Lord Henry Holland. See Miliukov, 1932. In a draft written between 1817 and 1819, Turgenev contrasted the histories of France and Britain, praising the latter as the country of freedom, underpinned by a system of constitutional monarchy and the fostering of free trade, while France remained a despotic country until the Revolution. But at the end of the essay Turgenev also cryptically hints that the Declaration of the Rights of Man 'saved France' and should serve as an admonition to other countries in Europe (Beshenkovskii et al. 1971).
48  Turgenev 1911–1921, vol. 5, 370.
49  Tourgueneff 1847, vol. 1, 202.
50  Tourgueneff 1847, vol. 2, 2. In a long letter to V. A. Zhukovsky, who had blamed him for penning La Russie et les Russes in the language of hostility, rather than in the language of love, Turgenev answered that in it there is only indignation at Russian officials, but that he avoided expressing his love for Russian serfs for fear of lapsing into patriotism. He added, 'I don't object to patriotism when it consists of love towards one's land, but I'm against patriotism that hates everything that is not native and loves everything that is, even when it is bad' (Lanskii 1975, 215).
51  Tourgueneff 1847, vol. 2, 353.
52  Turgenev 1911–1921, vol. 5, 370.
53  Turgenev 1911–1921, vol. 5, 109.
54  Tourgueneff 1847, vol. 2, 355.
55  Tourgueneff 1847, vol. 3, 15.
56  Tourgueneff 1847, vol. 3, 9.
57  Tourgueneff 1848, 38–46; Turgenev 1868, 171–3.
58  Tourgueneff 1848, 45–6.
59  Turgenev 1901, in particular 245, 254, 261.
60  Unlike the liminal space inhabited by the black intellectuals Paul Gilroy describes in his Black Atlantic (1993, 111), Turgenev was unable to gain advantage from his dual position and enjoy something akin to the critical 'double consciousness' deployed by blacks in European exile.
61  Said 2000, 173.
62  Turgenev 1911–1921, vol. 3, 237. On Turgenev's relations with Stein, see Mohrmann 1956.
63  A famous example of such 'dialogue' is the correspondence between Prince Andrei Kurbsky and Ivan the Terrible in the sixteenth century. Kurbsky, a prominent and successful general, had defected to Lithuania for fear of repression at the hands of Ivan's oprichnina, initiating a lively exchange of letters with Ivan, which continued until 1579. The authenticity of the letters has been cast into doubt by Edward Keenan, although most historians of sixteenth-century Russia have rejected Keenan's thesis. See Keenan 1971 and Andreyev 1975.
64  Ovid's case, a relegatio, i.e. enforced exile from Rome with maintenance of civil and property rights, differed from previous instances of Roman exile, such as Cicero's, in which exile was a voluntary act chosen to avoid official prosecution, often understood to be irreversible, although not always. For exile in the time of the Republic, see G. Kelly 2006.
65  For a brief journalistic account of their moral posture after the collapse of the Soviet Union, see Mydans 1991.
66  Gilroy 2000, especially 122–9.
67  For a history of early modern exile to Siberia, see Gentes 2008 and Beer 2016.
68  See Schönle 2007, 164–217.
69  Gertsen [Herzen] 1955, 20–1.
70  A. M. Kelly 2016, 160–227.
71  Gertsen [Herzen] 1955, 25.
72  Gertsen [Herzen] 1955, 20–1.
73  Gertsen [Herzen] 1955, 21.

74   A. M. Kelly 2016, 285.
75   Tihanov 2015.
76   Burke 2005, 36.

# Bibliography

Andreyev, Nikolay. 'The authenticity of the correspondence between Ivan IV and Prince Andrey Kurbsky', *Slavonic and East European Review* 53(133) (October 1975): 582–8.

Beer, Daniel. *The House of the Dead: Siberian exile under the tsars*. London: Allen Lane, 2016.

Berelowitch, Wladimir. 'La France dans le "Grand Tour" des nobles russes au cours de la seconde moitié du XVIIIe siècle', *Cahiers du Monde russe et soviétique* 34(1–2) (1993): 193–209.

Beshenkovski, E. B, Bilinkis, M. Ia, and Pugachev, V. V. 'Neizvestnaia rukopis' N. I. Turgeneva "Sopostavlenie Anglii i Frantsii"', *Osvoboditel'noe dvizhenie v Rossii* 2 (1971): 108–40.

Burke, Peter. 'Performing history: The importance of occasions', *Rethinking History: The Journal of Theory and Practice* 9(1) (2005): 35–52.

Gentes, Andrew A. *Exile to Siberia, 1590–1822*. Basingstoke: Palgrave Macmillan, 2008.

Gertsen [Herzen], A. I. 'Pis'ma iz Frantsii i Italii, 1847–1852'. In A. I. Gertsen, *Sobranie sochinenii v tridtsati tomakh*, vol. 5. Moscow: Izdatel'stvo ANSSSR, 1955.

Gilroy, Paul. *The Black Atlantic: Modernity and double consciousness*. London and New York: Verso, 1993.

Gilroy, Paul. 'Identity, belonging, and the critique of pure sameness'. In Paul Gilroy, *Against Race: Imagining political culture beyond the color line*, 97–133. Cambridge, MA: Belknap Press of Harvard University Press, 2000.

Keenan, Edward L. *The Kurbskii-Groznyi Apocrypha: The seventeenth-century genesis of the 'correspondence' attributed to Prince A. M. Kurbskii and Tsar Ivan IV*. Cambridge, MA: Harvard University Press, 1971.

Kelly, Aileen M. *The Discovery of Chance: The life and thought of Alexander Herzen*. Cambridge, MA: Harvard University Press, 2016.

Kelly, Gordon. *A History of Exile in the Roman Republic*. Cambridge: Cambridge University Press, 2006.

Lanskii, L. 'Iz epistoliarnogo naslediia dekabristov: Pis'ma N. I. Turgeneva k V. A. Zhukovskomu', *Voprosy literatury* 11 (1975): 207–27.

Mil'china, Vera. 'Sed'mye eidel'manovskie chteniia', *Znanie-sila* 11 (1997): 93–7.

Miliukov, P. 'N. I. Turgenev v Londone', *Vremennik obshchestva druzei russkoi knigi* 3 (1932): 61–78.

Mohrmann, Heinz. 'Über die Beziehung des Dekabristen Nikolaj Turgenev zu Georg Sartorius und dem Freiherrn vom Stein'. In *Deutsch-slawische Wechselseitigkeit in sieben Jahrhunderten*, 378–98. Berlin: Akademie Verlag, 1956.

Mydans, Seth. 'Soviet turmoil; Exiled Russian writers, free to return, find visiting is enough', *New York Times*, 6 September 1991.

Raeff, Marc. *Russian Intellectual History: An anthology*. New York: Harcourt, Brace & World, 1966.

Said, Edward W. 'Reflections on exile'. In *Reflections on Exile: And other literary and cultural essays*, 173–84. London: Granta, 2000.

Schönle, Andreas. *The Ruler in the Garden: Politics and landscape design in imperial Russia*. Oxford: Peter Lang, 2007.

Schönle, Andreas. 'The instability of time and plurality of selves at court and in society'. In *The Europeanized Elite in Russia, 1762–1825: Public role and subjective self*, edited by Andreas Schönle, Andrei Zorin and Alexei Evstratov, 281–99. DeKalb: Northern Illinois University Press, 2016.

Shebunin, A. N. *Nikolai Ivanovich Turgenev*. Moscow: Gosudarstvennoe izdatel'stvo, 1925.

Shebunin, A. N. 'N.I. Turgenev v tainom obshchestve dekabristov'. In *Dekabristy i ikh vremia* 1: 109–46. Moscow: Vsesoiuznoe obshchestvo politicheskikh katorzhan i ssyl'no-poselentsev, 1928.

Tihanov, Galin. 'Narratives of exile: Cosmopolitanism beyond the liberal imagination'. In *Whose Cosmopolitanism? Critical perspectives, relationalities and discontents*, edited by Nina Glick Schiller and Andrew Irving, 141–59. New York and Oxford: Berghahn, 2015.

Tourgueneff, N. *La Russie et les Russes*. 3 vols. Paris: Comptoir des imprimeurs-unis, 1847.

Tourgueneff, N. *La Russie en présence de la crise européenne*. Paris: Comptoir des imprimeurs-unis, 1848.

Tourgueneff, N. *Un dernier mot sur l'émancipation des serfs en Russie*. Paris: A. Franck, 1860.

Turgenev, N. I. *Chego zhelat' dlia Rossii*. Leipzig: F. A. Brockhaus, 1868.

Turgenev, N. I. 'Nikolai Ivanovich Turgenev v pis'makh k svoim brat'iam', *Russkaia starina* 5 (1901): 235–75.

Turgenev, N. I. *Dnevniki i pis'ma Nikolaia Ivanovicha Turgeneva za 1806–1811 goda: Arkhiv brat'ev Turgenevykh*. 5 vols. St Petersburg: Tip. Imp. Akademii Nauk, 1911–1921.

Zhitomirskaia, S. V. '*Golos s togo sveta*: Kniga Nikolaia Turgeneva "Rossiia i russkie" – istoriia i sud'ba'. In Nikolai Turgenev, *Rossiia i russkie*, 623–54. Moscow: OGI, 2001.

# 3

# Rewriting the Russian literary tradition of prophecy in the diaspora: Bunin, Nabokov and Viacheslav Ivanov

## Pamela Davidson

Не устрашуся гибели,
Ни копий, ни стрел дождей, –
Так говорит по Библии
Пророк Есенин Сергей.

I shall not fear destruction,
Nor spears, nor rains of arrows, –
Thus speaks, as the Bible,
The prophet Esenin Sergei.[1]

Esenin, 1918

Миссия, именно миссия, тяжкая, но и высокая, возложена судьбой на нас.

A mission, precisely a mission, a hard but also a lofty one, has been laid upon us by fate.

Bunin, 1924

'Ты, Елисей?'
Я поклонился. Пророк цокнул языком, потирая ладонью смуглую лысину:
'Колесо потерял. Отыщи-ка.'

'That you, Elisha?'
I bowed. The prophet clucked his tongue, scratching the while his
bald brown spot.
'Lost a wheel. Find it for me, will you?'

Nabokov, 1924

Вновь арок древних верный пилигрим,
В мой поздний час вечерним 'Ave, Roma'
Приветствую как свод родного дома,
Тебя, скитаний пристань, вечный Рим.

Again, true pilgrim of your vaulted past,
I greet you, as my own ancestral home,
With evening 'Ave Roma' at the last
You, wanderers' retreat, eternal Rome.

Ivanov, 1924

This chapter explores a question of central relevance to the development of Russian literature in the diaspora. How did émigré writers relate to the well-established national tradition of literature as prophecy after the Revolution, when they found themselves displaced from their homeland?

Perpetuated by generations of writers, readers and critics, the cult of the writer as a figure of prophetic authority is widely recognized as one of the most distinctive and persistent tropes of Russian literature, setting it apart from other national literatures.[2] Although commonly associated with Pushkin and his generation, its literary roots go back much earlier, to two colourful churchmen in the second half of the seventeenth century. The learned Belorussian monk Simeon Polotsky (1629–80) became Russia's first professional court poet, while his vigorous opponent, the Old Believer archpriest Avvakum (1620–82), created an alternative model of prophetic authority, based on dissent and opposition rather than support of state and Church.[3] Simeon's influence dominated throughout the eighteenth century, but was supplanted by Avvakum's confrontational model in the second half of the nineteenth century, following the publication of his ground-breaking *Life* in 1861. Tellingly, when Iurii Nagibin assembled his short stories about writers in 1990, he included his tale about Avvakum (1974) in second place and chose the title *Prorok budet sozzhen* (The prophet will be burned) to characterize all the authors covered in the volume.[4]

Sustained by faith in the power of the word and dedicated to a national messianic mission, the image of the writer-prophet has generated a strong sense of unified literary tradition. Far from being a single, homogeneous entity, however, it is a remarkably flexible multifaceted construct, serving quite different agendas and aspirations. Its very elasticity has informed its central role as a driving force in the dynamics of cultural memory. It has acted as a potent force, easily manipulated by writers and the reading public, and capable of leading to various excesses. As Kundera reminds us, 'Metaphors are dangerous. Metaphors are not to be trifled with.'[5]

Given the powerful influence of this trope, it is of particular interest to examine how it was taken up by the first wave of émigré writers when they were faced with the double loss of their homeland – first through political revolution, then through emigration.[6] Did removal from the native land strengthen or weaken its importance? What, if anything, changed? What strategies were adopted by those who wished to maintain it? How did these developments relate to treatments of prophecy in post-revolutionary Russia? What role was played by religious belief? At the root of these questions lies a bigger one. What is the relationship between literary tradition, national identity and geographical location? Or, put another way, can a metaphor which has traditionally upheld the 'national' mission of a country's literature and set itself up in relation to the twin authorities of state and Church survive outside the homeland? If so, what happens to it and the literature it represents? Can the national become transnational?

Those émigrés who saw themselves and their work as an integral part or extension of the 'home' tradition most commonly invoked the prophetic mission of Russian literature. They were usually – but not always – members of the older generation, born in the 1860s to 1880s, and therefore in their thirties, forties or fifties at the time of the Revolution. Merezhkovsky (1865–1941), Viacheslav Ivanov (1866–1949), Shestov (1866–1938) and Gippius (1869–1945) were all born in the 1860s. Bunin (1870–1953), Sergei Bulgakov (1871–1944), Shmelev (1873–1950), Berdyaev (1874–1948), Remizov (1877–1957) and Osorgin (1878–1942) were born in the 1870s, followed by Zaitsev (1881–1972) and Khodasevich (1886–1939) in the 1880s. All these writers had completed their intellectual formation well before 1917. They had absorbed the prophetic ideas of Dostoevsky and Vladimir Solovyov into the heady, apocalyptic mood of the Silver Age and read the revolutions of 1905 and 1917 as the fulfilment of earlier prophecies. Naturally, they carried this legacy with them into emigration. They saw themselves as the guardians of this heritage, with a duty to transmit it to the next generation. Alongside the desire to preserve continuity with the past, they were also determined to create a new voice, distinct from the politically coloured messianic treatments of the Revolution emerging in Russia. Adopting (and adapting) the language of prophecy played an important function in maintaining the sense of a unified literary tradition, given direction by a common goal. It also catered to what Brodsky defined as the émigré writer's central concern: the 'quest for significance'.[7]

By contrast, émigré writers of the younger generation, born in the mid to late 1890s or early 1900s, were in their early twenties or even younger when they arrived in Europe and began to establish their literary reputations. Although authors like Otsup (1894–1958), Odoevtseva (1895–1990), Nabokov (1899–1977), Berberova (1901–93), Gazdanov (1903–71), Poplavsky (1903–35), Osorgina-Bakunina (1904–95), Ianovsky (1906–89), Varshavsky (1906–78) and Shteiger (1907–44) did not start from a clean slate, they were less burdened by pre-existent beliefs and expectations. Nor were they always willing to have these foisted upon them by the older generation. Rather than picking up the baggage of their elders, many of them preferred to satisfy their 'quest for significance' by building links with the host culture. As a result, they tended to underplay or subvert their relation to the native tradition. The close links between the work of the interwar writers of the Russian Montparnasse and their European contemporaries analysed by Maria Rubins in her illuminating book provide compelling examples of this trend.[8]

Émigré attitudes to the notion of the prophetic mission of Russian writers therefore coalesced around the struggle between different generations – always a powerful driving force in the dynamics of literary development, as noted by Tynianov. To illustrate this point, I shall consider three contrasting treatments of prophecy from 1924. I have chosen this year as a common denominator because it was a significant point of transition. Seven years after the Revolution, émigré life was beginning to assume a more settled form and a distinct identity.[9] Lenin's death in January marked the end of the first period of the Bolshevik experiment and invited reflection on future directions. The selected examples are drawn from three different cities and literary genres: Paris, where Bunin delivered a public lecture; Berlin, where Nabokov wrote a short story; and Rome, where Viacheslav Ivanov composed a cycle of sonnets. After comparing these responses, I will focus more closely on Ivanov's case. His example is an interesting one, I believe, as it reveals a sustained attempt, prompted by the diasporic condition, to inscribe the national tradition of prophecy into a new transnational context. In particular, I would like to test Nikita Struve's claim that Ivanov offers the best example among émigré writers of cultural symbiosis with Europe.[10]

First, however, a preliminary observation about the significance of the different terms used by these authors to describe the condition of emigration. The Russian-derived *izgnanie* (exile) puts the emphasis squarely on the idea of coerced expulsion from the motherland. The Latin-based *emigratsiia* (emigration) is more neutral, assuming the possibility of voluntary migration. Both terms define their members in relation to the place which they have left (*IZ-gnanie* / *E-migratsiia*) (EX-ile / E-migration). The same point can be made about words like *bezhentsy* (refugees) or *zarubezhnyi* (foreign). The Greek term *diaspora*, by contrast, focuses on the population of the new location. Its derivation from the verb σπείρω (*speirō*) (to scatter, to sow) lends itself to two readings: a neutral or negative one, associated with dispersion, and a positive one associated with sowing. These different uses, introduced into the Septuagint translation of the Hebrew Bible, are preserved in the Church Slavonic and Russian translations *ras-seianie* (dispersion). Before the Israelites enter the Promised Land, Moses warns them of the curses that will befall them if they fail to observe the divine commandments. The list includes the punishment of 'dispersion' or 'being removed' (זְוָעָה, *za'avah*, translated as διασπορᾷ, *diaspora*) to all the kingdoms of the earth.[11] This warning is reiterated in the prophetic books, most frequently by Jeremiah, who foretold the Babylonian exile.[12] In this context 'diaspora' carries the negative connotation of punishment. In the scriptural narrative, however, the 'punishment' of exile is but a stage on the way to redemption. Hence the second positive meaning, where 'scattering' becomes a form of 'sowing' for the future. This is the context in which the term 'diaspora' occurs in the Septuagint's version of Psalm 146 (147):2. In this song of praise, the psalmist exclaims, 'The Lord rebuilds Jerusalem, and gathers the dispersed of Israel' (נִדְחֵי, *nidhei*, also translated as διασπορᾷ, *diaspora*).[13] The vision of Jerusalem rebuilt marks not so much a geographical location as the creation of a community united in faith. Thus, the term 'diaspora' is associated not just with the historical *fact* of geographical displacement, but also with the *goal* of a *spiritual* homeland to be regained.

As far as I am aware, apart from Viacheslav Ivanov and Iurii Terapiano, Russian émigrés of the first wave did not generally use the term 'diaspora'.[14] They did, however, often apply the *idea* embodied in its biblical usage to their own situation. The Bible's understanding of the dual purpose of exile (corrective and redemptive) offered a clear framework for reviving the writer's prophetic message outside Russia.

# Early prophetic readings of the Revolution in Russia

Émigré writers developed a range of approaches to the prophetic tradition, prompted by its current manifestations in Russia as well as by its past history. To contextualize their responses, this section discusses a range of influential early readings of the Revolution in Russia.[15] Bunin's speech on the mission of the Russian emigration was clearly designed to counter some of these texts.

The pre-revolutionary Russian prophetic tradition took shape in relation to three main sources of power: state, Church and *narod* (people, nation). Some writers developed a prophetic voice in support of the ruling institutions (this approach dominated from Simeon Polotsky to Derzhavin). Others used the same voice to challenge these powers (Radishchev, for example, followed by the Decembrists and the radicals of the 1860s and 1870s); in compensation for the loss of support from the state or the Church, oppositional writers often sought or claimed validation by the *narod*. These different relationships were reinvigorated at the turn of the century under the influence of Vladimir Solovyov's belief in the theurgic and transformative properties of art. Although grounded in aesthetics, this empowering belief and its impact on the cult of *zhiznetvorchestvo* (life-creation) had strong religious and political ramifications, usually directed against the existing regime. Not surprisingly, the dissident dimension acquired a fresh intensity in the aftermath of the revolutions of 1905 and 1917.[16]

Several writers greeted the revolutions of 1917 as the realization of earlier prophecies, often building up a chain of 'predecessors' to buttress their own views. After the February uprising, for example, Viacheslav Ivanov recalled Khomiakov's prophetic warnings about the need for the state to build good relations with the *narod*. In a letter of July 1917, he took issue with Florensky's critique of the Slavophile philosopher, arguing that Khomiakov had delivered a timely 'prophetic warning' to the old regime, outlining the choice it faced: 'transcendentism towards the *narod*' would lead to its collapse, while a policy of 'carefully conducted immanentism, as an education to freedom' would ensure its survival. The February Revolution was a direct result of the state's failure to heed his prophecy: 'И вот, наша несчастная родина почти гибнет от того, что пророки втуне пророчествовали'[17] (And now, our poor motherland is almost perishing because its prophets prophesied in vain). This presentation of Khomiakov's views chimed well with Ivanov's long-standing desire to connect with the *narod* by creating new forms of 'bol'shoe, vsenarodnoe iskusstvo' (great, universal art) through myth and symbol.[18]

Revolution was therefore read both as the fulfilment of past predictions and as the prelude to a radiant future. Both approaches required the adoption of a prophetic voice. Poetry, which commanded a particular authority through its close association with prophecy, assumed a leading role in articulating initial responses to the upheavals of 1917. Voloshin, for example, in his collection of poems on war and revolution, Demony glukhonemye (Deaf-mute demons), published first in Kharkov (1919), then in Berlin (1923), followed Avvakum in presenting Russia's suffering at the hands of Satan as a God-given means of national purification.

The poema (long narrative poem), linked to the treatment of moments of historical transformation since Pushkin's 'Mednyi Vsadnik' (The bronze horseman), enjoyed a revival of popularity in this context. In the spring of 1918, Ivanov-Razumnik, the editor of the literary section of the newspaper of the Left Socialist Revolutionaries, published three long poems about the Revolution in Znamia Truda (The banner of labour). Blok's 'Dvenadtsat'' (The twelve), composed in January 1918, appeared on 3 March, followed by Bely's 'Khristos voskres' (Christ is risen), written in April and printed on 12 May. Both works juxtaposed the Revolution with the figure of Christ, but in different ways. Blok's poem follows the relentless forward march 'without a cross' of 12 destructive Red Guardsmen. At the very end of the poem, Christ appears in front of them; whether he is leading them or, as Voloshin claimed, being shot at by them, is left unclear.[19] Bely's poem reverses the order, opening with the crucifixion of Christ and closing with scenes from the Revolution. Both works invite a prophetic reading of recent events in the light of messianic Christianity.

A week later, on 19 May, extracts from Esenin's earlier poema 'Inoniia' (Otherland), conceived at the end of 1917 and completed in January 1918, also appeared in Znamia Truda. Raised by a religious grandmother in a peasant family, Esenin knew the Bible and Russian folklore intimately. In his adoption of a prophetic voice he was much more direct than Blok and Bely, but also far more heretical. After dedicating his work to Jeremiah, he introduced himself in the first quatrain as 'the prophet Esenin Sergei':

Не устрашуся гибели,
Ни копий, ни стрел дождей, –
Так говорит по Библии
Пророк Есенин Сергей.[20]

I do not fear destruction,
Nor spears, nor rains of arrows, –
Thus speaks, as the Bible,
The prophet Esenin Sergei.

The self-appointed prophet begins with a demonstrative rejection of traditional Christianity. He spits the body of Christ out of his mouth and declares that he will tear God's beard out with his teeth. He then promises to give the *narod* the utopian city of Inoniia:

Обещаю вам град Инонию,
Где живет Божество живых![21]

I promise you the city of Otherland
Where the God of the living lives!

The final section ends with a joyful song to the 'new faith, without a cross and suffering'; in this reborn Zion and Nazareth, man, not God, determines the truth:

Наша вера – в силе.
Наша правда – в нас![22]

Our faith is in strength.
Our truth is in us!

'Inoniia' provoked as much controversy as Blok's 'Dvenadtsat''. Ignoring the question of its aesthetic merits, critics argued endlessly about its political and religious orientation – was it pro- or anti-Bolshevik, Christian, pagan or atheist?[23] To clarify these polemics, Ivanov-Razumnik wrote a long essay, 'Rossiia i Inoniia' (Russia and Otherland), presenting all three narrative poems in the light of his own political ideal, based on a new synthesis of socialism and reformed Christianity. He first published his essay in 1918 alongside Bely's and Esenin's poems in *Nash put'* (*Our way*), the journal of the Left Socialist Revolutionaries which he edited.[24] In 1920 he reprinted the same three texts in book form in Berlin, leading to a fresh round of debate among émigré readers.[25]

To lend authority to his own views, Ivanov-Razumnik set his 'supporting' poems within the Russian literary tradition of prophecy: 'Поэмы Блока, Есенина, Белого – поэмы "пророческие", поскольку каждый подлинный поэт есть "пророк". И все истинные поэты всех времен – всегда были "пророками" вселенской идеи своего времени, всегда через настоящее провидели в будущем *Инонию*'[26] (The long poems of Blok, Esenin and Bely are 'prophetic' poems because every genuine poet is a 'prophet'. And all true poets of all times have always been 'prophets' of the universal idea of their time, they have always seen through the present to *Otherland* in the future). To forestall the objections of 'naïve people' to Esenin's self-designation as a prophet, Ivanov-Razumnik cited Pushkin's 'Prorok' (The prophet) as 'proof' and ultimate justification of this claim. A great distance lies between Esenin and Pushkin, but it is no greater than the distance between Pushkin and the prophet Isaiah, whose account of the seraph touching his lips with a burning coal is quoted at length (Isa. 6:1–2, 5–13). Although the voices of contemporary poets are undeniably weaker than the biblical prophet's word, they too must be heard.[27]

Ivanov-Razumnik's astonishing disregard for the profound difference between prophets and poets was driven by his desire to gain support for his own views. He repeats Isaiah's warning about those who have ears but cannot hear (Isa. 6:10) to rebut the 'enfeebled members of the intelligentsia' who cry out from the underworld that 'Russia has perished' and fail to recognize its rebirth in the world of 'Inoniia' with its 'god of the living'.[28] Given such forms of resistance, achieving the promised ideal will require a long period of struggle. The concluding part of the essay pointedly recalls the 'great prophet-poet' Goethe, who warned in *Faust Part II* of the Pygmies who tried to sabotage the transformation of the world by Seismos.[29]

The mechanism at work here is quite clear. First, the critic enlists poetry in support of his messianic ideal of political transformation. Then, to legitimize this ideal, he places the chosen texts (Bely, Blok and Esenin) within a 'validating' prophetic tradition, stretching back through its 'founding father' (Pushkin) to the original biblical precedent (Isaiah) and taking in a major European poet-prophet (Goethe) along the way. The resulting essay is a remarkable piece of persuasive rhetoric, a heady mix of revamped religion and political idealism, couched in the language of prophecy.

Other writers appropriated the same language but desacralized it. As had already happened in Russia during the 1860s, messianic ideals of religious origin were translated into secular political ideals. Building on their pre-war experiments in modernist innovation, the Futurists took up the Symbolists' faith in the theurgic power of the word and applied it to their own brand of earthly utopianism. With its firm focus on forging a glorious future, the Bolshevik project was well suited to this approach, pioneered by Maiakovsky. In his response to the February Revolution, 'Revoliutsiia: Poetokhronika' (Revolution: A poem-chronicle) (17 April 1917), after proclaiming the rebels' rejection of God ('Нам / До Бога / Дело какое?' (What do we need God for?)), he announced their new prophetic mission:

> Новые несем земле скрижали
> с нашего серого Синая.[30]

> We carry new tablets to earth
> From our grey Sinai.

In the original draft, Maiakovsky alluded even more explicitly to his rewriting of the old tradition of prophecy. After announcing the creation of a new religion ('Днесь созидается религия иная' (Today another religion is being created)), he first wrote:

> Сегодня скрижали нового пророчества
> сносим с нашего закоптелого Синая.[31]

> Today we carry down from our sooty Sinai
> the tablets of the new prophecy.

The old 'sooty Sinai' refers to Russia's long-standing prophetic history, now to be dusted down and renewed through a fresh covenant.

In 'My idem' (We march), written at the end of 1918 and first published in 1919, Maiakovsky continued to speak fervently for the 'разносчики новой веры, / красоте задающей железный тон' (bearers of the new faith, / that sets an iron tone for beauty).[32] Within a few years, however, he had lost faith in this new direction and satirized it in 'O poetakh' (On poets) (1923). The epigraph paraphrasing the divine command from the end of Pushkin's 'Prorok' – 'Глаголом жги сердца людей' (With the word burn the hearts of people) – signals his ironic attitude to the misappropriation of this injunction:

> Всем товарищам по ремеслу:
> несколько идей
> о 'прожигании глаголами сердец людей'.

> To all fellow craftsmen:
> A few ideas
> About 'burning the hearts of people with words'.

He conjures up a grotesque picture of some twenty thousand poets, bent over their work, striving to carry out this command:

От жизни сидячей высохли в жгут.
Изголодались.
С локтями голыми.
Но денно и нощно
жгут и жгут
сердца неповинных людей 'глаголами'.
Написал.
Готово.
Спрашивается – прожёг?
Прожёг!
И сердце и даже бок.
Только поймут ли поэтические стада,
что сердца
сгорают –
исключительно со стыда.[33]

From a lifetime of sitting they've dried up into wisps.
They're starving.
With bare elbows.
But day and night
they burn and burn
the hearts of innocent people 'with words'.
He's finished writing.
It's ready.
The question is – did he burn them?
He did!
Both the heart and even the flank.
Only will the poetic herds understand
That hearts
Burn out –
Only from shame.

The hack prophets and 'poetic herds' have missed the point. As indicated by the reference to shame, the starting point of Isaiah's prophetic vocation was the awareness that he was 'a man of unclean lips', dwelling 'among a people of unclean lips' (Isa. 6:5). To be meaningful, the prophetic tradition must be grounded in an understanding of the moral underpinnings of speech; the mechanical repetition of messages couched in the external language of prophecy is an absurdity, well captured in the 'recipe' for prophetic verse which concludes the satire.

With his reference to the 'poetic herds', Maiakovsky touched on the crucial role of the prophet's need for an audience. The same problem was raised on a deeper level by the mystically inclined Futurist, Velimir Khlebnikov. Towards the end of his short life he was deeply engrossed in composing 'Doski sud'by' (Tables of fate), constructing elaborate historical prophecies based on numerology. In 'Odinokii litsedei' (The lone performer) (1921–2), he lamented the prophet's isolation and lack of audience. The poem opens with a tired and lonely actor, who drags himself through a wilderness like Pushkin's 'Prorok': 'Как сонный труп, влачился по пустыне' (Like a sleepy corpse, I dragged myself through a wilderness). This blind seer confronts and overcomes a Minotaur-like monster. When he holds its head up in front of the crowd, however, nobody can see him; new eyes must be sown for the 'воин истины' (warrior of truth) to be visible:

И с ужасом
Я понял, что я никем не видим,
Что нужно сеять очи,
Что должен сеятель очей идти![34]

And with horror
I understood that I was seen by no one,
That it was necessary to sow eyes,
That a sower of eyes must come forth!

From the mid-1920s onwards, writers who remained in Russia came under the increasingly centralized control of the state and its ideology. They tried to deal with the problem of being 'seen' and understood in different ways. As Zamiatin observed in his prescient essay 'Ia boius" (I am afraid) (1921), the 'nimble' (*iurkie*) new court poets (members of Proletkult and certain Futurists) learned how to adapt and survive, while the 'non-nimble' (including Blok and Bely) fell silent. If this state of affairs continued, he concluded, the only future of Russian literature would be its past.[35] By 1924, the first wave of prophetic responses to the Revolution had dried up. In the same year, countering the relentless forward march to the glorious future, Akhmatova composed 'Lotova zhena' (Lot's wife), a poignant tribute to the woman whose backward glance cost her her life.[36]

The notion of writers as engineers of the human soul popularized by Stalin and Zhdanov in the early 1930s was a direct outgrowth of the pre-revolutionary view of the prophetic mission of literature, harnessed in support of the state. For those who did not wish to play this role, silence, exile or repression was the likely outcome. Difficulties also faced those who tried to toe the party line. Soon after the Revolution the peasant poet Nikolai Kliuev wrote a cycle of prophetic poems in praise of Lenin; in 1921 he bound them in a booklet, inscribed it with a personal dedication to the leader and had it delivered to the Kremlin.[37] But by the summer of 1924 he was already complaining to Esenin and a friend about being forced to produce ideologically driven optimistic verse; significantly, the two examples he cited to ridicule this requirement were both dissenting prophets burnt at the stake (the Czech reformation preacher Jan Hus and Avvakum). As his friend noted in his diary: 'Клюев жалуется, что его заставляют писать "веселые песни", а это, говорит, все равно что Иоанна Гуса заставить в Кельнском соборе плясать трепака или протопопа Аввакума на костре петь "Интернационал". Кстати, Аввакума он числит в ряду своих предков'[38] (Kliuev complains that he is being forced to write 'jolly songs' and this, he says, is tantamount to forcing Jan Hus to dance a trepak in Cologne cathedral, or Avvakum to sing 'The Internationale' at the stake. By the way, he counts Avvakum among his ancestors.).

By the end of the decade, Kliuev had expressed shame over his cycle of poems to Lenin:

Я книжку <'Ленин'> намарал,
В ней мошкара и жуть болота.
...
И не сковать по мне гвоздя,
Чтобы повесить стыд на двери!..
В художнике, как в лицемере,
Гнездятся тысячи личин[.][39]

I scribbled the booklet ['Lenin'],
It is full of midges and the terror of the swamp.
...
And no nail can be forged for me
To hang my shame on the door!..
In the artist, like a hypocrite,
Lodge a thousand masks[.]

In the summer of 1934, from exile, he composed the *poema* 'Kreml" (Kremlin), an ambivalent address to the seat of power, replete with echoes of Pushkin's 'Prorok'.[40]

In sum, therefore, as demonstrated by these examples, writers who remained in Russia after 1917 continued to develop the existing prophetic tradition with renewed vigour. As before, invoking different predecessors, they pulled it in contradictory directions: to serve the state or to oppose it, to promote or to undermine a religious approach to historical change, to gather supporters or to lament the lack of an audience. The genre of poetry (short and long) remained the most authoritative, supplemented by a blend of literary commentary and political feuilleton. Satire and irony were deployed alongside messianic seriousness. This complex medley of voices and different ways of performing the role was the background against which émigré writers negotiated their approach to the tradition. Like their counterparts in Russia, they also faced the problem of finding a receptive audience. As we shall see in the next sections, Bunin, Nabokov and Ivanov tackled this challenge in different ways.

## Bunin's 'Missiia russkoi emigratsii' (The mission of the Russian emigration)

My first example comes from a member of the older generation. On 16 February 1924 Bunin delivered his famous speech 'Missiia russkoi emigratsii' at a large gathering convened in Paris's Salle de Géographie – a fitting venue for a geographically displaced population coming together to define its mission.[41] Bunin gave the opening address, followed by five other speakers, including Merezhkovsky and Shmelev.[42]

Addressing his audience as 'sootechestvenniki' (compatriots), i.e. as members of a single common fatherland, Bunin began by describing them as 'emigranty' (émigrés), not 'izgnanniki' (exiles): 'Мы эмигранты, – слово "émigrer" к нам подходит, как нельзя более. Мы в огромном большинстве своем не изгнанники, а именно эмигранты, то есть люди, добровольно покинувшие родину'[43] (We are émigrés – the word 'émigrer' suits us better than anything else. In our overwhelming majority we are not exiles, but precisely émigrés, that is to say people who have voluntarily left their homeland). Why did this distinction matter? Because voluntary emigration implies a sense of mission. In defining this term, Bunin turned to a French dictionary, evidently because it linked the idea of mission with power: 'Миссия – это звучит возвышенно. Но мы взяли и это слово вполне сознательно, памятуя его точный смысл. Во французских толковых словарях сказано: "миссия есть власть (pouvoir), данная делегату идти делать что-нибудь"… . Миссия, именно миссия, тяжкая, но и высокая, возложена судьбой на нас'[44] (A mission – this sounds elevated. But we have also chosen this word quite deliberately, remembering its exact meaning. In French explanatory dictionaries, it says: 'a mission is the power (*pouvoir*) delegated to someone to go and do something' ... . A mission, precisely a mission, a hard but also a lofty one, has been laid upon us by fate).

His essential point was quite simple – the émigré 'mission' is the 'non-acceptance' ('*nepriiatie*') of the Bolshevik regime, which he condemns in the roundest terms, together with its recently deceased leader. To lend authority and passion to his message, he frames the mission of the Russian diaspora in the context of the prophetic tradition, saturating his speech with biblical images. He compares the millions of Russian souls in emigration to the Exodus of the Jews, suffering all the Egyptian plagues. He reads recent Russian history as the fulfilment of Joseph's prophetic explanation of Pharaoh's dream about the seven lean cows who eat up the seven fat cows but do not become any fatter. He deplores the destruction of Moses's tablets at Sinai and of Jesus's Sermon on the Mount, now replaced by Lenin's 'seven commandments'. 'Moral foundations' have been shaken, the world is like Tyre and Sidon, Sodom and Gomorrah.[45] The Bolshevik regime has given the crowds a golden calf to worship instead of God. Lenin on his 'bloody throne' is likened to the Babylonian king Nebuchadnezzar. The Russian Cain must be hated, for the holy city of St Peter has been renamed Leningrad. Divine wrath will fall on all the 'Leningrads', just as it destroyed Sodom and Gomorrah. At the end of his speech, Bunin invokes something even greater than Russia – God and his soul – reminding his audience that a loyal Jew would never abandon the faith of his fathers. His message – delivered on French soil – was intended for a broad audience. As he explained, the Bolsheviks' internationalist agenda provoked 'a truly biblical fear, not just for Russia but also for Europe'.[46]

After all this rousing rhetoric, the actual content of the proposed mission ('non-acceptance' of the new regime) seems somewhat inadequate.[47] Given the fundamentally Christian nature of Bunin's vision of suffering Russia, one might well also wonder why he uses so many images from Hebrew scriptures. The answer is twofold. First, to assume the authoritative voice of the biblical prophet, he needed to tap into the well-established trope of Russia as the new Israel (he had already done this in verse written before and after the Revolution, before his emigration).[48] Second, as an effective strategy to rebut the messianic readings of the Russian Revolution discussed in the previous section, he took up the language of prophecy and redeployed it against the very poets and critics who had misused it, peppering his speech with scathing quotations from Esenin's 'Inoniia', Blok's 'Dvenadtsat'' and Mariengof's verse.[49] His focus on the Hebrew prophets resonated with his antipathy to these poets' facile blending of the Revolution with Christ. The message was blunt: all these constructions, together with the Revolution, were to be rejected; it was high time to abandon 'this heartless and abusive word game, this political rhetoric, these literary vulgarities'.[50] In other words, his argument was not just with the Revolution as a *political* phenomenon – it was also with its *literary* representations.[51]

In a follow-up essay, 'Inoniia i Kitezh' (Otherworld and Kitezh) (1925), Bunin expressed his contempt for such poets even more forcefully. After quoting the same lines from Esenin, Blok and Mariengof, as well as verses by Bely, Maiakovsky and the proletarian poet Gerasimov, he pauses to ask whether it is in fact worth paying any attention to these hackneyed old forms of 'missionism' (*missianstvo*). Unfortunately, it is necessary, he concludes, because these texts are treated so seriously as a guide to Russia's future. He is particularly irritated by the way poets of the Revolution, like the Bolsheviks, claim a monopoly on the discourse of Russian messianism: 'Теперь, революция в поэзии выродилась, как в жизни, в большевизм и, достигая своего апогея, притязает, как и большевизм, на монопольный руссизм и даже на мессианство' (At the present time, revolution in poetry, as in life, has degenerated into Bolshevism and, reaching its peak, just like Bolshevism, lays claim to a monopoly on Russianness and even to messianism). In response to Esenin's grand pledge 'Я обещаю вам Инонию!' (I promise you Otherland), he retorts: 'не дыши на меня своей мессианской самогонкой! А главное, все-то ты врешь, холоп, в угоду своему новому барину!' (Don't breathe all over me with your messianic home-brewed vodka! But the main thing is, all the while, you're lying, you lackey, to please your new master!).[52]

Bunin's adoption of an elevated religious tone in his speech, steering clear of any specific political programme, was supposed to promote unity and pre-empt polemical squabbles.[53] The result was the opposite; his talk unleashed a torrent of conflicting responses, published in at least 16 different periodicals from all over the Russian diaspora and even from Moscow.[54] P. N. Miliukov, the liberal politician and editor of *Poslednie Novosti* (The latest news), started the ball rolling by writing a highly critical leading article with the rousing title of 'Golosa iz groba' (Voices from the grave), printed immediately before a negative report on the gathering, 'Vecher strashnykh slov' (An evening of terrifying words).[55] As a historian, he held a rather different view of the forces driving revolution. Although he was also against the Bolshevik regime, he was optimistic that it would soon come to an end and enthused about the 'many germs of new life' that would blossom in the ruins.[56] As a politician, he was evidently annoyed by Bunin's substitution of rhetorical verbiage for any form of action.

To refute the misrepresentations (*krivotolki*) of his lecture and the evening as a whole, Bunin arranged for his original speech to be printed in the Berlin émigré newspaper *Rul'* (The rudder) on 3 April, together with a postscript in which he summarized the attacks against him. It is clear from his comments that he was particularly stung by the central accusation that he (and the other speakers) were posing as prophets, claiming the role of 'teachers' (*uchitelia*). First, he tackled the report: 'Отчет … вполне исказил меня, приписал мне нелепый призыв "к божественному существованию" и претензию на пророческий сан, сообщил как мало я похож на пророка … , и весьма глумился и над всеми прочими участниками вечера, тоже будто бы желавшими пророчествовать, но оказавшимися совершенно неспособными "подняться на метафизические высоты"'[57] (The report … completely distorted me, attributed to me a ridiculous call 'to divine existence' and a claim to prophetic rank, noted how little I resemble a prophet … and made a great mockery of all the others who took part in the evening, who apparently also wished to prophesy, but turned out to be completely unable to 'rise to metaphysical heights'). Then he recounted the contents of the leading article: 'Писатели, принадлежащие к самым большим в современной литературе, те, кем Россия по справедливости гордится … выступили с проповедью почти пророческой, в роли учителей жизни, в роли, отжившей свое время'[58] (Writers counted among the greatest in contemporary literature, those of whom Russia is justifiably proud … delivered a sermon that was almost prophetic, adopting the role of life-teachers, a role which has outlived its time). Finally, he described the article which had appeared in the Soviet press on 16 March under the macabre title 'Maskarad mertvetsov' (A masquerade of corpses), recycling the critical opinions published in *Poslednie novosti* and claiming that Bunin 'позирует теперь под библейского Иоанна' (is now posing as the biblical John [of Revelation]).[59]

The publication of Bunin's speech and postscript was followed on 18 April by a particularly vicious attack entitled 'Razoblachennyi prorok' (The prophet unmasked). The article poured scorn on the 'émigré Jeremiah' and his 'prophetic wrath'. Bunin had concluded his speech with a prayer that he would be able to continue howling with the same 'holy hatred' as a dog whose master had been murdered by Red

Guardsmen. As the details of the dog's ownership turned out to be false, the critic gleefully pounced on this error to undermine Bunin's prophetic credentials: '"Святая собачья ненависть..." В этом слышится железный голос пророка Иеремии. В этом есть пророческий пафос. Но... На всякого мудреца довольно простоты. Собачонку Бунина, с которой он хотел брать пример, разоблачили, и с лица эмигрантского Иеремии сошли румяна пророческого гнева'[60] ('The holy hatred of a dog ...'. In this phrase we can hear the iron voice of the prophet Jeremiah. In it there is prophetic pathos. But ... Every wise man has a fool in his sleeve. Bunin's little dog, which he wanted to take as an example, has been unmasked and the face of the émigré Jeremiah has lost its flush of prophetic wrath). If Bunin still wants to bark like a dog, the critic concluded, he should be packed off to join the 'parshivyi pes' (mangy dog) from Blok's 'Dvenadtsat''. Strangely enough, the close association of a writer-prophet with a barking dog reappears in Nabokov's story, discussed below.

Two themes stand out from all these reviews. One is the attack on Bunin's alleged claim to prophetic status (not entirely unjustified since he did indeed adopt such a stance in his speech). The other is the depiction of all the speakers, Bunin included, as dead men, relics from a distant past who had outlived their time and would not gain any followers among the younger generation (this observation also contained more than a grain of truth). Some of these negative responses may have stemmed from an uncomfortable sense that Bunin (an 'absolute and inveterate atheist', according to Nina Berberova) was adopting the *language* of prophecy as an oratorical pose, without sharing its foundation in religious faith.[61] Other reviewers may have objected to Bunin's cavalier debunking of sacred 'prophetic' texts, which had already entered the nascent canon of revolutionary verse. It is certainly ironic that Bunin fell victim to the very accusations which he had levelled against the 'false prophets' of the Revolution. Much energy was expended on arguing who had the right to lay claim to the status of prophetic authority. The circular round of attacks and counter-attacks demonstrates just how central the metaphor of the writer as prophet was to the literary and political polemics of the time, both in Russia and in the diaspora.

## Nabokov's 'Groza' (The thunderstorm)

Bunin's speech captured the urgent *desire* for an alternative prophetic mission (if not its precise content) shared by many Russian émigré writers of his generation. What about the so-called younger generation? Did they pick up the baton? Some did and some did not. And some took up the tradition and toyed with it in a playful manner. Nabokov's short story 'Groza' can be read as an interesting example of the latter approach. Written in Berlin in July 1924, it was first published in an émigré newspaper in September of that year and then included in his collection of stories and poems, *Vozvrashchenie Chorba* (*The return of Chorb*) (1930).[62] My claim is that this story offers an oblique – and entirely different – response to the same challenge that Bunin addressed in his speech. Could the prophetic mission of Russian literature cross national boundaries and inspire writers of the emigration? If so, how might this process of transmission be imagined?

'Groza' belongs to a group of early stories which combine symbolism with realism, embedding myth in the prose of everyday life.[63] The story opens on a windswept evening in the city. The narrator returns to his rented room. He looks down into the courtyard, from which the 'blind wind' rises. He falls asleep and then awakens (whether this is a 'real' awakening or still part of his dream is left unclear). The night is alive with a thunderstorm – flashes of lightning, peals of thunder and pelting rain. Intoxicated, he watches the scene from his window. The prophet's chariot approaches through the clouds. The 'Thunder-god' (*gromoverzhets*) appears, driving his fiery chariot. This mighty bearded giant is a 'flustered prophet' (*rasteriannyi prorok*), who struggles to control his steeds. When they hit the rooftop, a wheel comes off and the prophet, now identified by name as Il'ia (Elijah), merged in folk tradition with the Slavic thunder-god, is thrown out of his chariot. Evidently, this is not for the first time. He cautiously climbs down into the yard. The narrator runs down the steep staircase and meets Elijah in the yard. The prophet, reduced to a 'lean, stoop-shouldered old man', greets him as his successor (Elisha) and instructs him to search for the wheel:

'Ты, Елисей?'
Я поклонился. Пророк цокнул языком, потирая ладонью смуглую лысину:
'Колесо потерял. Отыщи-ка.'

'That you, Elisha?'
I bowed. The prophet clucked his tongue, scratching the while his bald brown spot.
'Lost a wheel. Find it for me, will you?'

Under a lilac bush the narrator finds a rusty wheel from a child's pram and gives it to Elijah, who is delighted. The narrator, together with a dog, watches the prophet ascend to heaven, now restored to his former grandeur. The unusual appearance of the dog, first described as a 'staraia lokhmataia sobaka' (shaggy old dog), then as a barking 'driakhlyi pes' (decrepit dog), evokes the 'pes parshivyi' (mangy dog) from Blok's 'Dvenadtsat'' and the 'khudaia sobachonka' (scrawny little dog) whose howling Bunin wished to emulate.[64] Still in his dressing-gown and wet slippers, the speaker runs to catch the first tram to recount the story of his vision to an unidentified 'ty' (you).

The thunderstorm and downpour of rain which accompany Elijah's fall into the yard provoke the narrator's sudden epiphany, linked with artistic inspiration.[65] This is made plain by two details. Before falling asleep and having this experience, the storyteller is unable to write about his happiness: 'В этой тишине я заснул, ослабев от счастия, о котором писать не умею, – и сон мой был полон тобой' (In this silence I fell asleep, exhausted by the happiness of my day, a happiness I cannot describe in writing, and my dream was full of you). After the visitation, he runs to catch the first tram, imagining how he will 'relate' the story: 'воображая, как сейчас приду к тебе и буду рассказывать о ночном, воздушном крушении, о старом, сердитом пророке, упавшем ко мне во двор' (I imagined how, in a few moments, I would be in your house and start telling you about that night's mid-air accident, and the cross old prophet who fell into my yard).

Elijah's gift of artistic inspiration to the narrator is presented as an act of prophetic succession. Elijah is the perfect choice for a dramatization of this subject, as Hebrew scriptures record in unmatched detail the precise way he transfers his prophetic power to his pupil Elisha, who witnesses his ascent to the heavens. Nabokov's story plays upon Russian literature's traditional invocation of the myth of prophetic succession, recasting it in a modern urban setting and incorporating disconcerting shifts from the real to the imagined, from the register of high language to everyday diction. In constructing his story around a series of vertical ascents and descents, he appears to be echoing (and perhaps parodying) Viacheslav Ivanov's celebrated account of artistic creation as a transformative process involving two stages. The first stage of spiritual ascent ('voskhozhdenie') starts with Dionysiac agitation and culminates in an epiphany, followed by catharsis. The second stage of descent ('niskhozhdenie') moves through the Apollonian dream, captured in memory, to the artistic incarnation of the original experience.[66] Nabokov's narrator experiences the first stage of spiritual 'ascent'. Intoxicated by the storm (Dionysiac agitation), he encounters

Elijah who greets him as his successor (the epiphany), and finally finds the wheel for him (the act of catharsis). The story closes with the hero looking forward to the second stage of 'descent', embodying his experience in artistic form, i.e. recounting the story which we have just read. The circle is closed. Nabokov has provided a humorously literal enactment of the Symbolists' agenda to reveal the action of 'higher realities' on this world and to transmit the prophetic gift of inspiration to the next generation.

Given the many other parodic references in the story (to Pushkin's 'Prorok' and 'Mednyi Vsadnik', Tiutchev's 'Vesenniaia groza' (Spring thunderstorm), Blok's 'Dvenadtsat'), it is difficult for the reader to disentangle the serious from the humorous.[67] Does the sparkling narrative convey the writer's genuine engagement with art as prophecy? Or has the older generation's serious treatment of this tradition become a purely aesthetic plaything in the hands of the younger generation? What can this story tell us about Nabokov's famed interest in *potustoronnost'* (otherworldliness)? How does it relate to Maksim Shrayer's conclusion that Nabokov is 'always a lyrical visionary, a modern version of the prophet in Pushkin's programmatic poem "Prorok"'?[68] Obliquely and provocatively, the story poses a key question: can a literary trope central to Russian national identity be sustained and survive in the diaspora? Its profound ambivalence is the secret of its charm.

## Viacheslav Ivanov's 'Rimskie sonety' (Roman sonnets)

Against this background of earnest exhortation versus playful engagement with the prophetic tradition, Viacheslav Ivanov's 'Roman sonnets' (1924) strike a very different note. Perhaps this is not altogether surprising, given his cosmopolitan background. Educated in Moscow and Berlin, resident in England, France, Germany, Italy and Switzerland, multilingual and fluent in all the main cultures of classical antiquity and modern Europe, he was already a true Russian European well before he emigrated. In *Perepiska iz dvukh uglov* (A correspondence from two corners), a sequence of letters exchanged with Gershenzon in a Moscow sanatorium during the summer of 1920, he offered an interesting definition of his hybrid identity: 'я наполовину – сын земли русской, с нее однако согнанный, наполовину – чужеземец, из учеников Саиса, где забывают род и племя' (I am half a son of the Russian land, albeit exiled from it, and half a foreigner, one of the novices of Sais, where kith and kin are forgotten).[69] As we shall see, this independence from conventional territorial definitions of selfhood later enabled him to develop a new approach to prophecy within the broad transnational community of Catholic humanists.

After Ivanov's first application to travel abroad was turned down, he spent four years teaching at the University of Baku. When he finally got permission from Lunacharsky, he set off for Rome in September 1924, aged 58.[70] The choice of destination was highly significant. Rather than joining one of the established centres of the Russian emigration, he chose to settle in the Eternal City, once the capital of the Roman empire, now the heart of Catholic Europe. By the end of the year he had completed his remarkable cycle of 'Roman sonnets', comprising nine poems, echoing the number of the Muses.[71] Following four years of poetic silence, the fountains of inspiration had opened up once more. In tribute to this, the middle seven sonnets all describe different fountains in Rome; for Ivanov as for Nabokov, water serves as a metaphor for the creative process. The first and final sonnets frame this renewal of inspiration in a broad historical context associated with prophecy, starting with the point of departure – the abandoned city (Moscow, the 'third Rome', burns like ancient Troy) – and culminating in the closing image of St Peter's dome.

The first sonnet, 'Regina Viarum', opens by making it clear that the poet's return to Rome is an act of spiritual pilgrimage:

> Вновь арок древних верный пилигрим,
> В мой поздний час вечерним 'Ave, Roma'
> Приветствую как свод родного дома,
> Тебя, скитаний пристань, вечный Рим.
>
> Мы Трою предков пламени дарим;
> Дробятся оси колесниц меж грома
> И фурий мирового ипподрома:
> Ты, царь путей, глядишь, как мы горим.[72]

> Again, true pilgrim of your vaulted past,
> I greet you, as my own ancestral home,
> With evening 'Ave Roma' at the last,
> You, wanderers' retreat, eternal Rome.
>
> The Troy of your forebears we give to fire;
> The chariots' axles crack from furious churning
> In this hippodrome of the world entire:
> Regina Viarum, see how we are burning.

Instead of the language of emigration and displacement (used by Bunin and Nabokov), Ivanov uses the language of homecoming, welcoming Rome 'kak svod rodnogo doma' (as my own ancestral home), as a final resting place, 'skitanii pristan'' (wanderers' retreat). He plays on the city's names in Latin and Russian. The masculine rhymes of the two quatrains all end in 'rim' (Rome),[73] while the feminine rhymes echo 'Roma', significantly paired with 'doma' (home). The reversible anagrams 'rim' / 'mir' (Rome / world) and 'Roma' / 'amor' (Rome / love) encapsulate the poet's deep love of Rome as a city of the world and place of peace where all roads meet.

In the second quatrain the poet's voice expands into a communal 'we', which has offered up Moscow, compared to ancient Troy, to the flames of destruction. This acknowledgement of responsibility for destruction echoes the opening lines from Ivanov's earlier poem of December 1919:

> Да, сей костер мы поджигали,
> И совесть правду говорит[.][74]

> Yes, we lit this bonfire,
> And conscience speaks the truth[.]

The city of Rome witnesses this destruction. It embodies both the experience and the memory of survival from destruction, of new life emerging stronger from the ashes:

> И ты пылал и восставал из пепла,
> И памятливая голубизна
> Твоих небес глубоких не ослепла.

> И помнит в ласке золотого сна,
> Твой вратарь кипарис, как Троя крепла,
> Когда лежала Троя сожжена.

> And you went down in flames and rose from embers;
> The mindful blueness could not blind the eye
> Of space in your unfathomable sky.

> Your cypress, standing sentinel, remembers
> In the caresses of a dream of gold
> How strong was Troy in ashes lying cold.

In this opening sonnet Ivanov presents exile in an entirely different way from Bunin and Nabokov. He inscribes his personal experience and his understanding of recent events in his native country into a much broader transnational – or even supranational – framework. By weaving together different historical eras, geographical locations and languages, he transcends the limitations of time and place and adopts a long-term prophetic view of history as a cycle leading through destruction to rebirth. Aeneas's mission to found the new city of Rome was sustained by promises received from the gods and prophetic visions revealed to him in the underworld. By echoing the narrative of the *Aeneid*, Ivanov associates himself with Virgil, the foremost messianic poet of ancient Rome. In this way he writes himself into a long-standing tradition of prophetic art linked with exile.

In the middle (fifth) sonnet, he extends this tradition to take in two Russian prophetic artists who lived for many years in the Eternal City, toiling on their masterworks. His wanderings from his home on Via Quattro Fontane take him past the place where the painter Aleksandr Ivanov used to visit Gogol:

> Бернини, – снова наш, – твоей игрой
> Я веселюсь, от четырех Фонтанов
> Бредя на Пинчьо памятной горой,
>
> Где в келью Гоголя входил Иванов[.][75]

> Bernini – ours anew – your playful skill
> Makes me rejoice as from Four Fountains' knoll
> I wander to the Pincio, [along] memory's hill,
>
> Where Ivanov to Gogol's cell would stroll[.]

By inserting this tongue-in-cheek reference to his namesake, the poet establishes his place as a successor to the tradition of prophetic artists living in Rome, the city where Ivanov completed his monumental canvas *Iavlenie Khrista narodu* (*The appearance of Christ to the people*) (1833–57) and Gogol worked on his epic novel *Mertvye dushi* (*Dead souls*) (1835–52).[76]

The final sonnet of the cycle, 'Monte Pincio', draws on imagery of water and golden sunlight to convey the sense of spiritual plenitude which the poet finds in Rome in the evening of his life:

> Пью медленно медвяный солнца свет,
> Густеющий, как долу звон прощальный;
> И светел дух печалью беспечальной,
> Весь полнота, какой названья нет.[77]

Slowly I savor the sun's honeyed glow
Thickening like the valley's farewell chime;
With careless care the spirit is aglow,
All plenitude, whose name is paradigm.

In the last tercet he contemplates the view of the dome of St Peter's, silhouetted against the gold of the sun. The capitalized closing word of the cycle, *Kupol* (Dome), serves as a fitting image of the eternal realm the poet seeks to access:

Ослепшими перстами луч ощупал
Верх пинии, и глаз потух. Один,
На золоте круглится синий Купол.

With dazzled fingers groping, the last beam
Felt pine-top and its eye went out. Left there
In liquid gold the blue Dome circles air.

While Bunin addressed his fellow émigrés with a public speech, defining their mission in religious and political terms as the non-acceptance of Bolshevik Russia, and Nabokov toyed in prose fiction with the notion of artistic inspiration as prophetic, Ivanov chose the much shorter and more private form of lyrical verse to express his relation to the prophetic tradition, following the practice he had initiated at the start of his literary career.[78] And yet, despite the compression of the sonnet form, the range covered is immeasurably greater. The upheaval of revolution is presented as part of the grand sweep of history, reflected in prophetic word and image and mirrored in eternity. His orientation in emigration is not political, nor purely literary; it is religious, but unlike the Russian Orthodox focus of Bunin's 'mission', it moves from ancient Troy and Rome through the Renaissance and the baroque fountains of Rome to the Eternal City's symbol as the capital of Christendom – the dome of St Peter's.

Ivanov sent off his sonnets to Gorky and Khodasevich for publication in their new journal *Beseda* (*Conversation*).[79] In his response, Khodasevich began by sharing his inner despair over the state of Russian literature, both at home and in emigration: 'Россия раскололась пополам, и обе половины гниют, каждая по-своему. Мучительно то, что никаким *словом* здесь не поможешь: происходит "исторический процесс", а это вроде дурной погоды: ее надо переживать, пересиживать. А пересидим ли? Боюсь, что процесс не только русский, а всемирный, затяжной, лет на триста' (Russia has split into two, and both halves are rotting, each in its own way. It is painful that in this situation you cannot help with any *word*: a 'historical process' is taking place, and it is like bad weather: you have to live through it, sit it out. But will we sit it out? I am afraid that the process is not just Russian, but universal, drawn out, for about three hundred years). Against this background, Ivanov's sonnets had lifted his flagging spirits by reminding him that 'настоящая поэзия, тонкая мысль, высокое и скромное, некрикливое мастерство' (true poetry, subtle thought, lofty and modest unshowy mastery) were still possible.[80]

In his reply, sent at the end of December, Ivanov tried to counter Khodasevich's pessimism over the word's impotence in relation to the 'historical process' by invoking hope for the renewal of prophetic art. He compared himself to Saul, longing for the 'magical song' of David: 'Саул во мне стосковавшись по все чаще и слишком надолго пропадающем Давиде, сам пытается перебирать пальцами струны его заброшенной арфы, да не налаживается волшебная песня' (The Saul inside me that longs for David, who disappears with increasing frequency and for too long, tries himself to finger the strings of the abandoned harp, but the magical song does not take shape). Anticipating that Khodasevich might claim that a poet cannot live a full life outside his own country, he pointed out that the Moscow he saw before his departure from Russia was a dead city, devoid of any life-giving Spirit. He summed up his present state in emigration with a pithy allusion to Pushkin's 'Prorok': 'и вот влачусь в пустыне мрачной. Остается обратить пустыню в пустынь, чего бы я и желал' (and now I drag myself through a gloomy wilderness. All that remains is to transform the wilderness into a hermitage, which is what I would like to do).[81]

## Ivanov's path from the national to the transnational

Transforming the '*pustynia*' (wilderness) of Europe into a '*pustyn'*' (hermitage), a place of spiritual meditation and creativity, was an internal, religious task, not a political one. In March 1926 Ivanov made an important move in this direction by joining the Catholic Church. Using the formula devised by Vladimir Solovyov, cited in *La Russie et l'Eglise universelle* (1889), he took this step as an act of ecumenical unification, renouncing the schism but not Russian Orthodoxy.[82] As he explained in his letter of 1930 to the French critic Charles Du Bos, this was his radical response to the question posed to man's conscience by the Revolution: 'Est-on avec nous ou avec Dieu?' Neither nostalgia for the past nor loyalty to the 'mother-Church' could sway his decision.[83] He recognized that he had chosen a very different path from the rest of emigration: 'Aussi mon attitude sous ce rapport était-elle diamétralement opposée à celle de l'émigration russe (j'allais dire plus significativement *diaspora*), qui s'attache avec un zèle particulier à la conservation des formes confessionelles dans lesquelles la vie religieuse de la nation est moulée depuis neuf siècles.'[84]

Ivanov's use of the word 'diaspora' is highly unusual and deserves attention. As he pointed out, every word in his letter was carefully weighed in terms of meaning and psychological nuance.[85] Why, then, would 'diaspora' have been a 'more significant' term than 'emigration'? No doubt because its biblical connotations, derived from the Septuagint, offered a religious perspective on exile, allowing for the possibility of sowing while in dispersion. If so, why did he prefer to speak of 'l'émigration russe'? Evidently, he found this term more fitting to describe a community that was looking backwards, to the country it had left behind, rather than focusing on the 'more significant' religious opportunities afforded by its new location. He used the rhetorical figure of paralepsis to signal this difference, offering the thought as only half-said to soften its controversial impact.

A few lines earlier, Ivanov had described Russian Orthodox émigrés as a 'troupeau dispersé, errant autour du bercail que je savais paternel et l'évitant par méfiance séculaire'.[86] By maintaining the 'ancient error of separation', they were following a course which he found unjustifiable and damaging to Christianity, as it placed the 'national' and the state above religion. They failed to grasp their true calling, which Ivanov identified as 'la mission de servir la cause de l'unité en rôle d'intermédiaires entre l'Orient et l'Occident, – tâche qui paraît indiquée par la Providence aux chrétiens en exil mis en contact intime avec d'autres chrétiens qui professent la même foi'.[87]

According to Ivanov, therefore, the geographical displacement of emigration was providentially ordained to enable the Russian diaspora to carry out its prophetic mission and bring about the reunification of the Eastern and Western branches of Christianity. Once Ivanov himself had taken this step, he felt that he could at last breathe fully with both lungs, content in the knowledge that he had finally carried out his 'personal duty' and his nation's duty.[88] Although he wanted the message of his letter to Du Bos to be heard by the Russian emigration, his refusal to allow Gleb Struve to publish a Russian translation in *Rossiia i slavianstvo* (Russia and Slavdom) confirmed his detachment from narrow definitions of Russianness (whether territorial, linguistic, political or confessional) and deliberate orientation towards his new European audience.[89]

In a less formal letter to his children, written at the end of the year, Ivanov explained how right he felt to have joined the Catholic Church, as it is not a national body: 'Никакой духоты нет, – ни эллина, ни иудея, – в национальной церкви как-то человека в религиозном смысле не чувствуешь, нет простора, в котором говорят друг с другом Бог и Человек' (There is no stuffiness – neither Greek nor Jew; in a national church you somehow cannot feel a person's religious significance, there is no space in which God and Man can talk to each other). In a postscript he shared his daughter's scepticism about the existence of 'inherent or intrinsic Russianness' – this cannot be found in anyone, just as one can never find a 'core' artichoke inside an artichoke. Everything is shared and universal: 'Нужно быть самим собой и делать общее – личность тут и скажется… . Кто теряет душу свою в *общем* деле (забывает о своей личности), тот и находит ее; а кто бережет, потеряет'[90] (You have to be yourself and work for the common good – this is where the self reveals itself… . Whoever loses his soul for the *common* good (forgets about his self), that person finds it; while whoever conserves it will lose it).

This understanding of the dependence of the national on the universal informed Ivanov's perspective on what constituted his true homeland. In 'Zemlia' (Earth) (1928), part of a poetic dialogue with his friend and fellow émigré, Il'ia Golenishchev-Kutuzov, he defined his extraterritorial sense of home through paradox:

Повсюду гость, и чуженин,
И с Музой века безземелен,
Скворешниц вольных гражданин,
Беспочвенно я запределен.[91]

Everywhere a guest and alien,
And landless with the Muse of the age,
A citizen of free starling-nests,
Groundless, I transcend limits.

The poet's belief that his inner creative self existed '*bespochvenno*' in the transnational space offered by the Muse was quite different from the view of émigré critics such as Mark Slonim, who claimed that Russian literature could not flourish outside the homeland because of its '*glubokaia pochvennost*'' (deep rootedness / attachment to the soil).[92] Ivanov tried to influence others to share his point of view. In 1935, responding to a request for spiritual guidance from a Russian deacon serving in Milan, he advised him not to lament the 'destruction of Russian culture', for 'it is not destroyed, but called to new challenges, to a new spiritual awareness'. Citing Dostoevsky, he explained that a 'truly Russian person is first of all a "universal man"' ('*vsechelovek*') and is therefore 'more of a European' in Europe than a French, English or German person. For this reason, an émigré who wants to be true to the Russian spirit must break out of the closed mindset of Russian 'colonies' and share the life of Western nations.[93]

This was the goal which Ivanov set himself in the diaspora. He pursued it single-mindedly, deploying a range of strategies to reach his new audience. These tactics included:

- Arranging for the translation of his works into all the major European languages. He acted as translator, co-translator or editor, constantly revising his original texts to bring their meaning closer to foreign readers. His reputation outside Russia took off after the publication of *Perepiska iz dvukh uglov* in German, French, Italian and Spanish translations.[94]
- Writing essays in French, German and Italian for leading European journals (the French Catholic *Vigile*, the Swiss *Corona*, the German Catholic *Hochland* and the Italian *Il Convegno*).
- Choosing topics like Virgil's messianic poetry (1931) and the laurel in Petrarch's verse (1933) to consolidate his position in the transnational humanist tradition.
- Cultivating a network of key contacts among the leading humanists of Europe and establishing close links with them through extensive correspondence. This strategy, developed by him in emigration, corresponded to his view of dialogue as the ideal method for clarifying ideas and forging solid bonds.[95] In this way he joined the company of many prominent European intellectuals, including Ernst Curtius, Martin Buber, Charles Du Bos, Jacques Maritain, Gabriel Marcel, Alessandro Pellegrini, Karl Muth, Herbert Steiner and Maurice Bowra (to whom he wrote in Greek, Latin, English and French). In parallel, he maintained long correspondences with Russian émigrés such as Stepun, Shestov, Zelinsky, Frank and Evsei Shor.

These strategies were highly successful. Ten years after his arrival in Italy, the fruits were already visible. In 1933 he was invited to give a speech on the orientations of the contemporary spirit at the prestigious

'Literary Mondays' held at Sanremo. April 1934 saw the publication of a special issue of the cultural periodical *Il Convegno*, entirely devoted to his work. It included his speech, his open letter to Pellegrini on Christian humanism and his Italian prose translations of the first and last 'Roman sonnets' (under the title 'La cupola'). Contributions from like-minded Russian émigrés (Zelinsky, Stepun, Ganchikov, Ottokar) sat alongside essays by his European correspondents (Curtius, Steiner, Marcel, Pellegrini).

In his brief but heartfelt contribution, Curtius hailed Ivanov as a member of the 'spiritual brotherhood' of European humanists, drew attention to his *prophetic* talent and described the homage to Ivanov represented by the journal as a 'vinculum amoris' (bond of love) – a phrase originally coined in connection with humanism.[96] In a similar vein, when reading the proofs of Ivanov's letter on 'Docta pietas', Pellegrini was moved to pen a letter, saluting him as a humanist of the fifteenth century. In his reply Ivanov thanked him once more for this 'vinculum amoris', enabling the 'obscure work' of an old man in exile, forbidden in his homeland, to become known in his 'beloved Italy'.[97] Thus, the image that Ivanov had built up for himself as a transnational Catholic humanist was mirrored back to him by his European admirers.[98]

## Conclusions

What conclusions can we draw from the examples of these three writers? How did their development of the existing tradition of literary prophecy differ from that of their compatriots who remained in Russia? Although rooted in common origins, the two paths diverged over time, shaped by differences in many areas, including political and religious beliefs, relations with the host culture, audience receptivity and freedom of expression.

At first, the émigré 'mission' continued to define itself along familiar lines; opposition to the power of the state was extended – from afar – to the new rulers of Russia. Bunin serves as a prominent example of this trend. Exile changed the context of his prophetic message, enabling him to adopt a public voice exhorting a large audience to embrace his vision of their 'mission', but it did not change its essential parameters: 'non-acceptance' of the Bolshevik regime perpetuated the long-standing tradition of prophetic dissidence.

As time moved on, it became increasingly difficult to sustain a mission based on opposition to a distant and inaccessible regime. A few years after Bunin's speech, Nina Berberova signalled a shift of focus. She took up the form of the *poema* but redefined it. Instead of using it to dramatize a moment of historical transformation, following the pattern set by Pushkin, Blok, Bely and Esenin, she created a new lyric version of the genre as a vehicle to explore the exile's relation to the homeland from a more universal perspective, closer in spirit to Lermontov. The poem is narrated by a female émigré, living in Paris in 1920, who comes to the realization that she need not pine for Russia, since her true home, like Adam's, is God's universe. This understanding comes to her through a dream 'like a vision' of the creation of the world and of Adam's state before the Fall and his exile. The phrase 'Я не в изгнаньи, я в посланьи' (I am not in exile, I am on a mission) is used twice in the poem, first by Adam in Paradise, then by the female narrator.[99]

This line has often been quoted out of context. Rephrased in the first person plural, the original formulation of the individual's existential freedom was turned into a collective mission statement for the emigration. When Gippius first read the poem in 1926, she informed Berberova that it interested her because she was working on a 'letter to Russia', 'где главное вот это: "не изгнаны, а посланы"' (where the main point is this: 'not exiled, but on a mission').[100] In her resulting article, 'Nashe priamoe delo' (Our immediate task) (1930), she took Berberova's line in a new direction. Russian émigrés should no longer focus on 'territorial Russia' and its political situation; instead, they should regard themselves as part of a single *narod*, formed like the Jewish diaspora by the experience of exodus, and cultivate a new sense of mission on this basis: 'Зарубежная Русь ... должна сознать свое посланничество' (Rus' in the diaspora ... must recognize that it is *on a mission*).[101] Although the goal was no longer Bunin's 'non-acceptance' of the Bolshevik regime, it remained undefined.

Others were not convinced of the need to believe in a special calling. Slonim, writing in 1931, was particularly outspoken on this subject. He regarded the 'illusion about the greatness and salvational significance of émigré literature' as one of the main myths created by the diaspora imagination, maintained in Paris and Berlin as an 'obligatory article of faith', which it would be an act of betrayal not to believe in. As examples of the perpetuation of this myth, he cited Bunin's speech, Berberova's line (rewritten in the first person plural) and Gippius's essays. For Slonim, the reality was quite different. Émigré literature was not carrying out any mission, it was dying. Why? Because it had failed to generate any new ideas. At the same time, he pointed out that writers like Nabokov, Gazdanov, Fel'zen or Sharshun who tried to become Russian Europeans by cultivating Western influences, risked losing all traces of Russianness and merging altogether with European literature.[102]

Khodasevich shared Slonim's bleak view of the current state of émigré literature, but differed in his understanding of the root causes. For him, the idea of prophetic mission remained central to the identity of the Russian literary diaspora. As he noted in his essay of 1933 on literature in exile, 'Без возвышенного сознания известной своей миссии, своего посланничества – нет эмиграции, есть толпа беженцев, ищущих родины там, где лучше' (Without an elevated awareness of its avowed mission, of being sent on a mission – there is no emigration, there is a crowd of refugees, looking for a homeland wherever is best). Although the younger generation embraced Berberova's maxim 'Мы не в изгнаньи, мы в посланьи!' (We are not in exile, we are on a mission!), it had not been able to find adequate teachers. The older generation had failed to pass on its sense of mission; instead, it looked to the past, substituting comfort and stability for a true sense of tragedy and innovation. As a result, the younger generation had turned to the imitation of foreign writers.[103] Ironically, in a letter to Gleb Struve apologizing for his pessimistic predictions, Khodasevich himself took on the mantle of prophet: 'Если я окажусь плохим пророком, то, Боже мой, как буду я рад сам первый объявить, что ошибся!' (If I turn out to be a bad prophet, then, my God, how happy I will be to be the first to announce that I was mistaken!).[104]

Unlike Slonim, Khodasevich argued that 'national' literatures were often at their best in exile, citing as proof a series of prophetic writers whose works were strongly coloured by their sense of messianic mission: Hebrew poets from the Middle Ages to Bialik, Dante and the three national prophets of Polish Romanticism, Mickiewicz, Słowacki and Krasiński. The names on this list suggest that he was influenced by his own Jewish and Polish heritage in taking their prophetic traditions as a model for Russian literature in the diaspora.[105]

Although the award of the Nobel Prize to Bunin in 1933 temporarily rekindled faith in the 'mission' of Russian literature in exile (prompting the reprinting of his original speech), the tide was turning. Gippius had made a good point: facing backwards, whether in space (towards Russia) or in time (towards the past) was not the way to sustain or build a forward-looking prophetic mission. As Brodsky noted, the exiled writer should not be 'like the false prophets of Dante's *Inferno*', whose 'head is forever turned backwards'; he must combat the retrospective tendency and seek instead to 'play at causes'.[106]

Nabokov and Ivanov both 'played at causes', but in very different ways. Emigration gave Nabokov the opportunity to reinvent the metaphor of art as prophecy. By literalizing it, he recast Symbolist theurgic principles into an entirely new form. The assimilation of the religious aspect of prophecy into the aesthetic dimension of artistic inspiration enabled him to 'play God' in the construction of complex narratives, guiding the reader's search for meaning. Given the seriousness with which the prophetic strain was treated by writers in Russia (whether dissident or official), the ambivalent, playful tone adopted by him in relation to prophecy could only have flourished in the diaspora. Unique and original, his contribution in this respect was significant. As Berberova pointed out, 'Nabokov alone with his genius was able to bring in a renewal of style' and, in this way, to solve the fundamental problem faced by émigré writers of the younger generation.[107] This problem was nothing to do with the choice of subject matter or language, it concerned the creation of a new style, capable of generating fresh ideas.

Ivanov took the prophetic tradition in an entirely new direction. Returning to Europe and redefining his religious views allowed him to expand his already well-established prophetic inclinations into the broader space of transnational Catholic humanism. He signalled this upon his arrival in the Eternal City with his cycle of 'Roman sonnets', merging present with past, personal and national dimensions with the universal. The position which he carved out for himself through verse, self-translation, publications in several European languages and an extensive chain of correspondence, meant that by 1933 the self-image he had constructed was reflected back on him by his European circle of like-minded Catholic humanists. In this way he extended the Russian tradition started by two seventeenth-century churchmen beyond national borders to embrace a wider community of believers.

Nikita Struve's claim that Ivanov offers the best example among émigré writers of cultural symbiosis with Europe therefore seems amply justified. In fact, in Ivanov's view, he was at home in Europe and it was those who had remained in Russia who were 'abroad'. As he wrote in a private letter, referring to the recently widowed Nadezhda Chulkova: 'Мученики все они там, за рубежом… ведь за рубежом-то они, а не мы' (They are all martyrs there, abroad … for they are the ones who are abroad, not us).[108] Ivanov was able to reverse the idea of exile in this way because he defined his sense of home not by geography but by spiritual community.

Returning now to our opening questions, we can propose a few answers. The condition of exile was undoubtedly productive for the development of the prophetic tradition by both generations of émigrés. All the writers discussed in this chapter successfully transplanted this tradition to new European settings, often drawing on foreign languages to facilitate its absorption. When declaiming his prophetic speech in Paris, Bunin turned to French, citing the link between '*pouvoir*' and 'mission' to empower his audience and extend the import of his message. Nabokov brought a thoroughly Russian Elijah to life on the streets of émigré Berlin. Ivanov conjured up the image of burning Troy to justify his move from Moscow to Rome, using the classical Latin phrase 'Ave, Roma' to buttress his position. Later, he articulated his reasons for embracing Catholicism in French; significantly, he would not allow Struve to translate and publish this key text in Russian.

Life in the diaspora gave rise to new modes of writing which would not have been possible in Soviet Russia. These included the rousing public speech, the development of dialogic correspondence to foster a new sense of spiritual community, and the experimental reworking of existing traditions. Exile also altered the relationship between literary tradition, national identity and geographical location, showing that a metaphor which had traditionally upheld the 'national' mission of a country's literature could survive and even be reinforced outside the homeland, and that (in the case of Ivanov), the national could become transnational.

With hindsight, it becomes clear that the most important factor ensuring the perpetuation of the prophetic tradition in the diaspora after the Revolution was not its transmission from one generation to the next, as was so often claimed, but the writer's own creative originality and orientation. Bunin and Ivanov were both members of the older generation but faced in opposite directions. Bunin looked back to Russia; he used the language of prophecy to oppose the ruling power of the state, following the well-trodden path of predecessors. By contrast, Ivanov and Nabokov, although members of different generations, were both oriented towards the future; they rewrote the existing trope of prophecy to create new possibilities, either in the realm of transnational religious and cultural exchange or in the field of radical stylistic experimentation. Ultimately, the survival of the prophetic tradition in exile depended more on the individual writer's ability to look forward and 'play at causes', as Brodsky put it, than on any mechanical process of handover between generations.

How do these varied responses to exile relate to other perspectives explored in this volume? In the preceding chapter, Andreas Schönle argues that nineteenth-century Russian political exiles such as Nikolai Turgenev always remained psychologically and emotionally bound to the ruler of their home country, even when living abroad and professing different ideals. In their attempts to navigate these contradictions, they embraced ambivalence. He further suggests that their experience was similar to that of twentieth-century exiles from the Soviet Union. While this observation is certainly correct in the case of political exiles, it requires some qualification in relation to other types of émigré. Literary writing offered exiles of a creative disposition more fluid opportunities for self-expression than the realm of social action. Bunin's example is instructive in this respect. When he defined the mission of the Russian emigration as non-acceptance of the Bolshevik regime in his public speech, he necessarily remained bound to the rulers of his homeland, like the dissident exiles of the previous century. When he turned to imaginative writing, however, he was able to achieve independence from this bond. Nabokov and Ivanov, who preferred to steer clear of political engagement, shaped new hybrid identities in prose and verse, free of any connection with Russia's rulers. By drawing on powerful existing tropes and adapting them to their situation, their performance of exile was more flexible and open to different readings.

What about these examples' relation to the outlook at the end of the first century of post-revolutionary diasporic existence? In the introduction to this volume, Maria Rubins states that all master narratives concerning the romantic myth about the mysterious 'Russian soul' and the notion of an essential 'national character' have lost their former lustre. The deeply ingrained habits of writers and their readers, however, resist being dislodged by academic discourse. Well-established literary tropes such as the cult of the writer as a prophetic authority continue to proliferate in contemporary Russian writing, both within and without the nation's geographical boundaries. It is always in the nature of the literary process to engage with past traditions. Moreover, recent developments in the political arena show that the more 'global' the world becomes, the greater the desire to invoke existing tropes that reinforce a sense of national identity. In his closing remarks, Galin Tihanov suggests that the notion of diaspora, closely associated with the nation state, may lose its relevance in today's 'increasingly globalized and interconnected world'. While this may be true in the geopolitical and economic spheres, it is unlikely to apply to literary and cultural traditions, where diasporic communities will continue to play a crucial role, mediating between the national and the transnational and facilitating their cross-fertilization.

# Notes

1 Translations are the author's, unless indicated otherwise.

2 This chapter forms part of a wider project on 'Prophecy and power in the Russian literary tradition (1650–1930)', generously supported by the Leverhulme Trust with the award of a two-year research fellowship. I would like to thank Maria Rubins and the participants of the workshop she convened in May 2018 on 'Redefining the Russian literary diaspora (1918–2018)' for their stimulating papers and thoughtful comments; particular thanks are due to the two discussants of my paper, Adrian Wanner and Lada Panova.

3 See Davidson 2017.

4 'Ognennyi protopop' (1974), first published in *Druzhba narodov* 1975(4), in Nagibin 1990, 19–42. The story's concluding words, 'С этого пустозерского пламени возжегся костер великой русской прозы' (p. 42), link the prophet's martyrdom to the genesis of Russian prose.

5 Kundera 1995, 11.

6 For a stimulating introduction to this period, see Slobin 2013.

7 Brodsky 1988, 16.

8 Rubins 2015, 2017.

9 The return to Russia in 1923 of several prominent expatriates (Alekei Tolstoi, Bely, Shklovsky) marked the end of the first open-ended period of the emigration. According to Slonim (2002, 116), the last threads linking émigré literature with the home tradition were broken off in 1922–4.

10 N. Struve 2003, 15.

11 Deut. 28:25: ἔσῃ ἐν **διασπορᾷ** ἐν πάσαις ταῖς βασιλείαις τῆς γῆς (*esē en **diaspora** en pasais tais basileiais tēs gēs*), translated as 'thou shalt be a **dispersion** in all kingdoms of the earth' or '[thou] shalt be **removed** into all the kingdoms of the earth' (AKJV).

12 Jer. 15:4, 24:9, 29:18, 34:17.

13 Translation from the New American Bible (revised edition). In the Septuagint translation of these two examples, the same Greek word *diaspora* is used to translate two different Hebrew words: *za'avah* (Deut. 28:25) and *nidhei* (Ps. 147:2). By conflating these two terms, the Septuagint translation obscures an important difference in the Hebrew original and associates the curse of scattering from Deuteronomy with the psalmist's promise of being gathered together by God.

14 The term 'diaspora' is relatively new in the Russian literary language. It does not appear in standard dictionaries until the Soviet period. Almost all the titles of twentieth-century anthologies of émigré literature published in the West and in Russia refer to the literature of '*russkoe zarubezh'e*'. A prominent exception, combining the terms 'diaspora' and 'zarubezhnyi', was the anthology *Muza Diaspory: izbrannye stikhi zarubezhnykh poetov, 1920–1960* (Terapiano 1960). A more lasting shift of terminology occurred in 2003 when Novoe literaturnoe obozrenie launched the series *Russkaia poeziia diaspory*. A comparative analysis of the Russian terms *izgnanie, emigratsiia* and *diaspora* conducted on Google Books Ngram Viewer shows a steep rise in the use of the first two terms after 1917 (*izgnanie* was initially in the lead, and was then overtaken by *emigratsiia*). The term *diaspora* became more frequent after 1986, but still lags behind the other two.

15 For a useful introduction to this topic, see Pyman 1990.

16 See, for example, the doctrine of mystical anarchism promulgated by Georgii Chulkov (1906) (with an introductory essay by Viacheslav Ivanov).

17 See Ivanov's letter of 12 July 1917 to P. A. Florensky, in Isupov and Shishkin 2016, 2:632. Ivanov was responding to Florensky's review article about Khomiakov. Florenskii 1916.

18 See, for example, Ivanov's essays 'Kop'e Afiny' (1904), 'Poet i Chern'' (1904), 'Predchuvstviia i predvestiia' (1906).

19 See the entry of 17 February/2 March 1919 in V. N. Muromtseva-Bunina's diary, reporting Voloshin's view and Bunin's disagreement (Grin 1977–82, 1:210).

20 Esenin 1995–2000, 2:61. The manuscript draft of the poem was dedicated to 'Z. N. E. <senina>', the actress Zinaida Raikh (Esenin's wife at the time, later married to Meierkhol'd). The versions published in *Znamia Truda* and *Nash put'* did not carry any dedication. Esenin 1995–2000, 2:223. The dedication to Jeremiah first appeared in Esenin's collection *Preobrazhenie* (Esenin 1918).

21 Esenin 1995–2000, 2:62. See the lines 'Тело, Христово тело, / Выплевываю изо рта' and 'Даже Богу я выщиплю бороду / Оскалом моих зубов' (2:61–2).
22 Esenin 1995–2000, 2:68.
23 For an overview of contemporary critical responses in the Russian and émigré periodical press, see the notes in Esenin 1995–2000, 2:346–5.
24 *Nash put'* 2, May 1918, 134–51 (the issue appeared on 15 June). Blok's 'Dvenadtsat'' had previously appeared in *Nash put'* 1, April 1918, 1–12.
25 Ivanov-Razumnik 1920.
26 Ivanov-Razumnik 1920, 28.
27 Ivanov-Razumnik 1920, 22–3. According to the critic, Pushkin escaped censure because readers mistakenly thought that he was just writing about the biblical prophet, not about the poet within himself.
28 Ivanov-Razumnik 1920, 28.
29 Ivanov-Razumnik 1920, 28–31. See Goethe's *Faust, Part II*, Act II, scene iv.
30 Maiakovskii 2013–, 1:106. After its first publication in *Novaia zhizn'*, 21 May 1917, the poem was twice reprinted in 1918 (1:496).
31 Maiakovskii 2013–, 1:374.
32 Maiakovskii 2013–, 1:135.
33 Maiakovskii 2013–, 1:212.
34 Khlebnikov 1986, 166–7. The poem takes up Pushkin's treatment of the parable of the sower (Matt. 13:1–23) in 'Svobody seiatel' pustynnyi …' (1823).
35 Zamiatin 2004, 120–4.
36 In his earlier essay 'Zavtra' (1919), Zamiatin had censured Lot's wife for not taking part in the struggle for the 'great human tomorrow': 'Тот, кто нашел свой идеал сегодня, – как жена Лота, уже обращен в соляной столп, уже врос в землю и не двигается дальше. Мир жив только еретиками'. Zamiatin 2004, 114.
37 For the poems of the cycle and its history, see Kliuev 1999, 310, 328–36, 899 (note).
38 I. A. Oksenov, 'Iz dnevnika', in Poberezkina 2010, 180. Oksenov's diary entry of 20 July 1924 refers to a meeting with Kliuev and Esenin on the previous day. Jan Hus's death at the stake in 1415 was well known in Russia from Tiutchev's anti-Catholic poem 'Gus na kostre' (1870).
39 'Pesn' o velikoi materi' (written between 1929 and 1934), in Kliuev 1999, 752.
40 'Kreml'. Poema', first published in *Nash sovremennik*, 2008, 1: 135–57, in Kliuev 2015, 215–38.
41 Bunin's speech and his postscript, written to counter attacks that appeared in the press after his lecture, were first published in the Berlin émigré newspaper *Rul'* (Bunin 1924). The date of 29 March 1924 appeared after the postscript. For both texts, see Bunin 1998b, 148–57, 535–41 (notes). A newspaper cutting of the article with Bunin's manuscript annotations, held in Bunin's papers at the Leeds Russian archive (MS 1066/1114), is reproduced in Bakuntsev 2014b, 283. Bunin's speech was reprinted with cuts twice in his lifetime, soon after he won the Nobel Prize (Bunin 1933, 1934). See Bakuntsev 2014b, 289–90. The next émigré publication took place 40 years later (Bunin 1975). In post-Soviet Russia, the speech has frequently been anthologized, sometimes as an example of patriotic, nationalist feeling. A recent anthology (Bunin 2014) opens with Catherine the Great's speech against Old Believers, includes two wartime speeches by Stalin and rounds off with two speeches by Putin, including his 'Crimean speech' of 2014. The editor comments: 'В этом сборнике, который должен стать настольной книгой каждого русского патриота, представлены лучшие речи государственных деятелей России XIX–XX вв.'
42 The other three speakers were A. V. Kartashev, Professor N. K. Kul'man and I. Ia. Savich, a student. The titles of the talks reveal the speakers' orientation. Kartashev: 'Smysl neprimirimosti'; Shmelev: 'Dusha rodiny'; Merezhkovsky: 'Slova nemykh'; Savich: 'Vestniki vozrozhdeniia'; Kul'man: 'Kul'turnaia rol' emigratsii'. See Bakuntsev 2014b, 270–1. For details of the preparations for the evening and its aftermath, see the entries in Bunin's diary from 23 December 1923/5 January 1924 to 27 February 1924, in Grin 1977–82, 2: 121–3.
43 Bunin 1998b, 148.
44 Bunin 1998b, 148.
45 Hebrew scriptures contain several prophecies against Tyre and Sidon, predicting their complete overthrow (Isa. 23; Jer. 25, 27, 47; Ezek. 26–8; Joel 3; Amos 1:9–10; Zech. 9:1–4). Sodom and Gomorrah were destroyed for their immorality (Gen. 19:1–29).
46 Bunin 1998b, 153.

47 'Миссия русской эмиграции, доказавшей своим исходом из России и своей борьбой, своими ледяными походами, что она не только за страх, но и за совесть не приемлет Ленинских градов, Ленинских заповедей, миссия эта заключается ныне в продолжении этого неприятия.' Bunin 1998b, 153.

48 On an earlier use of this trope, see Davidson 2018. Bunin was inspired by his honeymoon trip to Jerusalem in 1907 to write a series of travel notes and poems on Jewish history and the Holy Land. After the Revolution, still in Russia, he wrote 'Iz knigi proroka Isaii' (1918), predicting (through the voice of Isaiah) God's removal of prophet, judge, leader and advisor from the nation, the mocking of elders by youth, the open glorification of sin as in Sodom and the eventual ruin of the nation. In emigration he wrote a remarkable prose poem, 'Plach o Sione' (1925), using midrashic sources to illuminate the causes of exile.

49 Bunin cites Esenin's promise to tear out God's beard from 'Inoniia' and Blok's march 'without a cross' from 'Dvenadtsat''. He also quotes Mariengof's image of Jesus on the cross from 'Oktiabr'' and his plan to pray with curses from 'Krov'iu pliuem zazorno …' (1918). See Bunin 1998b, 153–4.

50 Bunin 1998b, 154.

51 In his diary entry of 17/30 April 1918, Bunin criticized Blok and Bely for their Bolshevik sympathies, describing them as 'два сукина сына, два набитых дурака'. For evidence of his dislike of the Symbolists, culled from his essays, letters and diaries and from memoirs about him, see the notes in I. A. Bunin, *Publitsistika 1918–1953 godov*, edited by O. N. Mikhailov, Moscow: Nasledie, 1998, 536–7, and his 'anti-obituary' of Blok, 'Muzyka', written in 1921 (Bakuntsev 2014a). In 1932 Bunin summarized his negative view of the prophetic rhetoric surrounding Voloshin and other writers who dealt with the Revolution: 'возвели и его в пророки, в провидцы "грядущего русского катаклизма", хотя для многих из таких пророков достаточно было в этом случае только некоторого знания начальных учебников истории.' See his essay 'O Voloshine', first published in *Poslednie novosti*, 8 September 1932, Bunin 1998c, 386.

52 'Inoniia i Kitezh', first published in *Vozrozhdenie*, 12 October 1925, Bunin 1998a, 163, 171. Bunin continued to attack Esenin and Mariengof in a later essay, 'Samorodki', first published in *Vozrozhdenie*, 11 August 1927, Bunin 1998d, 253–8.

53 See his diary entry of 15/28 January 1924 about plans for the gathering: 'Было постановлено, что все речи должны быть, так сказать, в религиозном плане, а потому не важно, каковы политические убеждения говорящего' (Grin 1977–82, 2:122).

54 For a detailed account of the press coverage and Bunin's response, see Bakuntsev 2014b, 282, 292–5, 299–336, and his shorter article, Bakuntsev 2015, 11–21.

55 Miliukov's leading article 'Golosa iz groba' and the report by R. S. [Slovtsov] (N. V. Kalishevich) were published four days after the gathering at which Bunin spoke, in *Poslednie novosti*, 20 February 1924, 1–2. Miliukov had previously published a critical article about Bunin's controversial 'Literaturnye zametki' (1922).

56 Miliukov 1922, 262–3. This work expresses a more positive view of the future than his earlier book on Bolshevism (Miliukov 1920).

57 Bunin 1998b, 155.

58 Bunin 1998b, 156.

59 Bunin 1998b, 157. Bunin incorrectly states that the article was published in *Pravda*. In fact, it appeared on the same date in *Izvestiia*, signed 'N. S.<mirnov>. See Bakuntsev 2014b, 313.

60 Treplev 1924. For details, see Bakuntsev 2014b, 332–3. The author's pseudonym may allude to Konstantin Treplev, the young writer in Chekhov's *The Seagull* who challenges the work of his elders. 'На всякого мудреца довольно простоты' is the title of a comedy by Ostrovsky, featuring an unprincipled careerist, Glumov, whose true nature is eventually unmasked.

61 Berberova 1969, 256. Berberova's comment only considers one side of the picture; for a more nuanced view of Bunin's approach to religion, see Shraer 2014, 100–1.

62 'Groza', dated 22–5 July 1924, first appeared in Nabokov 1924. In a note accompanying its English translation (first published in *Details of a Sunset and Other Stories*, 1976), Nabokov incorrectly states that it first appeared in *Rul'* in August 1924. See Nabokov 1997, 646. *Vozvrashchenie Chorba: Rasskazy i stikhi* appeared in December 1929. The story (Nabokov 1930, 76–80) is cited from the online version of this collection. The translations are taken from 'The thunderstorm', Nabokov 1997, 86–9.

63 On 'Groza' and its context, see Naumann 1978, 75–81; Shrayer 1999, 22–3; Moteiunaite 2016.

64  A dog, described as '*nishchii pes golodnyi*', '*pes parshivyi*', '*pes kholodnyi* – *pes bezrodnyi*', '*golodnyi pes*', reappears in the final section of Blok's 'Dvenadtsat'' (1918). It drags itself along behind the Red Guardsmen, who are led by Christ, and is associated with the old world, to be destroyed. At the end of his speech, Bunin introduces the image of the howling '*khudaia sobachonka*'. At the end of 'Groza', Nabokov introduces a '*staraia lokhmataia sobaka*' looking upwards, '*kak chelovek*', together with the narrator, watching Elijah climbing up the roof. The arrival of morning is heralded by the barking of a '*driakhlyi pes*'. In a later letter, of 26 April 1934, to Khodasevich, Nabokov compared himself directly to a dog, intoxicated by the smells of springtime Berlin: 'Берлин сейчас очень хорош, благодаря весне, которая в этом году особенно сочная, – и я, как собака, шалею от всяких интересных запахов' (Babikov and Shruba 2017, 233).

65  Nabokov associated creative inspiration with rain or a storm in a number of poems. The story 'Groza' reworks some of the images from his earlier poem 'Groza' (Nabokov 1923), including the blinding wind, banging window frames, downpour, thunder and the 'gods' leaving when the storm is over ('Уходят боги, громыхая, / стихает горняя игра'). The absent person addressed as '*ty*' in the story is present in this poem as the poet's beloved. Later, in a letter to his wife of 7 June 1926, Nabokov describes in detail how he wrote the poem 'Tikhii shum' (Nabokov 1926), commenting on the state of '*grozovoe napriazhenie*' which preceded its composition. See the notes on this poem in Nabokov 2015. 'Tikhii shum' was included by Nabokov in *Vozvrashchenie Chorba* (Nabokov 1930, 210–11), alongside the story 'Groza'.

66  'O granitsakh iskusstva', delivered as a lecture in 1913, was first published in Ivanov 1914, and included in Ivanov 1916, 187–229.

67  The narrator's retreat from the elements to his rented room and subsequent dream evoke Pushkin's Evgenii in 'Mednyi Vsadnik'; the storm recalls Tiutchev's 'Vesenniaia groza' and his vision of man caught up in the chaos of the nocturnal world; the setting, the presence of the dog and the incorporation of a biblical figure into the modern urban landscape echo Blok's 'Dvenadtsat''. On echoes of Pushkin's 'Prorok', see Iukhnova 2018.

68  Shrayer 1999, 320.

69  Ivanov 1971–87, 3:412. Sais was a legendary centre of religious knowledge in ancient Egypt, visited by many philosophers of the ancient world. The phrase '*iz uchenikov Saisa*' refers to Novalis's philosophical fragment 'The novices of Sais' (1798–9).

70  Ivanov first applied to travel abroad in the spring and summer of 1920. See his letter of 18 July 1920 to N. G. Krupskaia in Berd 1999, 309–11. His wife, Vera Shvarsalon, died in August 1920. In the autumn he left with his children for the Caucasus and then for Baku, where he was elected professor of classical philology on 19 November 1920. He returned to Moscow in June 1924 to take part in the Pushkin celebrations and stayed till the end of August. During this visit he received permission from Lunacharsky to travel to Italy to set up a Russian academy or institute of archaeology, history and history of art in Rome – on condition that he would not contribute to émigré publications. Ivanov left Moscow on 28 August, arriving in Italy in early September. After being granted Italian citizenship in 1935, he did not renew his Soviet passport. From 1936, starting with 'Rimskie sonety' in *Sovremennye zapiski*, he began to publish in the émigré press.

71  On 25 November 1924 Ivanov sent seven sonnets to Gorky for publication in the journal *Beseda*, founded with the aim of publishing the work of authors living in Russia and abroad, and edited by Gorky and Khodasevich. On 10 December 1924 he sent two more sonnets describing fountains, noting in his accompanying letter that his 'first' cycle now mirrored the number of the Muses. See Kotrelev 1995, 193, 195.

72  Ivanov 2011, 29. In this essay the cycle is cited in its first version of 1924, reproduced in facsimile and typescript in the above edition. The second version published in *Sovremennye zapiski* (1936), *Svet vechernii* (1962) and Ivanov 1971–87, 3:578–82, includes several changes, such as the replacement of the original titles of the sonnets by the roman numerals I–IX. The translations cited in this chapter are by Lowry Nelson, in Ivanov 2011, 48–64.

73  The opening rhyme 'piligrim' / 'Rim' is echoed in the closing rhyme 'Rima' / 'piligrima' of the eighth sonnet, 'Aqua Virgo' ('Vest' moshchnykh vod i v veian'i prokhlady …'), originally positioned as the closing sonnet.

74  Ivanov 1971–87, 4:81. Ivanov wrote his poem in response to G. I. Chulkov's address to him, 'Poetu' (15 August 1919), which contained the lines: Мы, буйства темного предтечи. / Ведь вместе мы сжигали дом, / Где жили наши предки чинно ' (Chulkov 1922, 39). Chulkov was recalling their cooperation in developing the idea of mystical anarchism in 1906.

75 'Il Tritone', in Ivanov 2011, 37. I have amended the translation of the line 'Бредя на Пинчьо памятной горой' from Lowry Nelson's version 'I wander to the Pincio, memory's hill' to 'I wander to the Pincio along memory's hill' as 'memory's hill' refers to the Quirinal Hill on Ivanov's walking route, not to the Pincio.

76 On Gogol's and Ivanov's prophetic 'rivalry' in Rome, see Davidson 2013.

77 Ivanov 2011, 45. This sonnet was originally placed second in the cycle, as a companion piece to the opening sonnet, 'Regina Viarum'.

78 For an overview of Ivanov's cultivation of the image of the poet as prophet throughout his life, see Davidson 2002.

79 Although Ivanov was paid a royalty, *Beseda* folded before his sonnets appeared. The cycle nevertheless became well known in Russia where it circulated in bound, typescript copies. After Ivanov became an Italian citizen and was no longer bound by his promise to Lunacharsky not to publish in the émigré press, the full cycle appeared in *Sovremennye zapiski* (Ivanov 1936). Before 1936, a few of the 'Roman sonnets', including the first and the ninth, were quoted in Golenishchev-Kutuzov 1930, 466–8, 470. Italian verse translations of the first and ninth sonnets appeared in *Il frontespizio* (September 1930), 5, and a German translation of the third sonnet in *Russische Dichter*, trans. D. Hiller von Gaertingen (Leipzig: Kommissionsverlag Otto Harrassowitz, 1934), 77; Ivanov's own prose translations of the first and ninth sonnets appeared in *Il Convegno* 14(8–12) (1933–4), 369. The first and ninth sonnets were included in the pioneering anthology of Russian émigré verse, *Iakor'* (Adamovich and Kantor 1936, 4–5); the ninth appeared in *Muza Diaspory* (Terapiano 1960, 46). On the significant role of these two anthologies in the process of canon formation in the diaspora, see Katharine Hodgson's contribution to this volume.

80 Khodasevich, Letter of 28 November 1924 to V. I. Ivanov, in Shishkin 2002, 110.

81 Ivanov, Letter of 29 December 1924 to V. F. Khodasevich, in Berberova 1960, 285. On the metaphor of exile as a *'pustynia'*, see the lines from Khodasevich's poem 'Pered zerkalom' (1924): 'А глядишь – заплутался в пустыне, / И своих же следов не найти.'

82 For two perspectives on Ivanov's conversion, see Shishkin 2003; Iudin 2008.

83 'Mon adhésion devait être ma réponse radicale à la question posée par la Révolution aux consciences: "Est-on avec nous ou avec Dieu?" Eh bien, si je ne préférais pas le parti de Dieu, ce n'est pas la nostalgie du passé qui me séparerait des énergumènes de la religion universelle à rebours' ('Lettre à Charles Du Bos', in Ivanov 1971–87, 3:424). After his return to Catholicism in 1927, Du Bos became editor of the Catholic review *Vigile*, where he published a French translation of *Perepiska iz dvukh uglov* after having read the German translation published in Buber's *Die Kreatur* in 1926. Ivanov's letter was written in July 1930 in response to Du Bos's request to him to clarify his current position in relation to the views expressed 10 years earlier. For the full correspondence, see Zarankin and Wachtel 2001.

84 Ivanov 1971–87, 3:426.

85 See Ivanov's letter of 24 June 1931 to I. N. Golenishchev-Kutuzov, explaining why he would not find it easy to translate his letter into Russian or allow anyone else to undertake this task, in Shishkin 1989, 503.

86 Ivanov 1971–87, 3:426.

87 Ivanov 1971–87, 3:426.

88 Ivanov 1971–87, 3:426, 428.

89 See Ivanov's letter of 24 June 1931 to I. N. Golenishchev-Kutuzov, in Shishkin 1989, 502–3.

90 See Ivanov's letter of 26 December 1926 to D. V. and L. V. Ivanov, in *Simvol* 53–4 (2008): 508–9. Ivanov is alluding to Paul's description of Christianity in which 'There is neither Jew nor Greek' (Gal. 3:28).

91 Ivanov 1971–87, 3:508. Ivanov's play on two meanings of *'zemlia'* (earth, land) is lost in translation.

92 Slonim 2002, 119.

93 See Ivanov's letter of 7 December 1935 to A. G. Godiaev, in Isupov and Shishkin 2016, 2:676. Dostoevsky would have recoiled in horror at the notion of a Russian writer embracing Catholicism.

94 For full details of Ivanov's multilingual publications and translations of his works in emigration, see Davidson 2012.

95 On this point, see the introduction to Zarankin and Wachtel 2001, 503–4.

96 See Curtius 1933–4, 270–1. Curtius first used the phrase 'amicitiae vinculum' in his letter to Ivanov of 5 February 1934; Ivanov expanded on this phrase in his reply of 12 February. See their correspondence in Ivanov 1995, 62–3.

97  See Pellegrini's letter of 3 March 1934 and Ivanov's reply of 19 April 1934, in Shishkin 2015, 154–5.

98  On Ivanov's relation to the debate surrounding the national and transnational dimensions of humanism, see Wang 2016.

99  Berberova 1927, 227, 230. In section 2, in the narrator's dream, Adam says: 'И если здесь я средь других, – / Я не в изгнаньи, я в посланьи / И вовсе не было изгнанья, / Падений не было моих!' (227–8). In the closing lines of section 3, the narrator applies this idea to herself: 'Я не в изгнаньи – я в посланьи, / Легко мне жить среди людей. / И жизнь моя – почти простая – / Двойная жизнь. И умирая / В каком-то городе большом, / Я возвращусь в селенья рая, / В мой нерушимый, древний Дом, / К дверям которого порою, / Я приникаю, может быть, / Какъ к ветке лист перед грозою – / Чтоб уцелеть, чтоб пережить' (230) (emphasis added). The same issue of *Sovremennye zapiski* included the last section of Merezhkovsky's second prophetic Egyptian novel *Messiia* and Nabokov's story 'Uzhas'.

100  In a letter of 12 November 1926 to N. K. Berberova, Gippius (1978, 14) wrote: 'Ваша поэма меня интересует еще по одному поводу: у меня есть давно начатое и неоконченное "письмо в Россию", где главное вот это: "не изгнаны, а посланы" и вы даже не знаете, м.б., какая тут реальность.'

101  Gippius is echoing the view of her co-author, the economist Kocharovsky. See Gippius 1930, 13. See also her comment on the relation of the Russian emigration to the Jewish diaspora: 'Напрасно сравнивать ее даже с "еврейским рассеянием". Но одно есть у них общее: "исход" евреев был исходом *народа*; русские, ушедшие из своей земли, тоже есть *народ*.' For a detailed discussion of her use of the concepts of exile and mission, see Solivetti and Paolini 2003.

102  Slonim 2002, 115–6, 118–9, 125–6.

103  Khodasevich 1982, 214, 220.

104  Letter of 18 August 1933 to G. P. Struve, in G. Struve 1970, 398.

105  Khodasevich 1982, 212–3. Khodasevich also worked on anthologies of Hebrew verse and of Bialik's poetry. In his poem 'Moisei' (1909–15), he compared the poet to the 'great prophet' Moses, condemned to remain in exile from the Promised Land (Khodasevich 1989, 237–8).

106  Brodsky 1988, 16, 20.

107  Berberova 1969, 351.

108  Ivanov, Letter of 28 March 1939 to B. K. Zaitsev, in Isupov and Shishkin 2016, 2:682.

# Bibliography

Adamovich, G. V. and M. L. Kantor, eds. *Iakor': antologiia russkoi zarubezhnoi poezii*. Berlin: Petropolis, 1936.

Babikov, Andrei and Manfred Shruba. 'Pis'ma V. V. Nabokova k V. F. Khodasevichu i N. N. Berberovoi (1930–1939)', *Wiener Slavistisches Jahrbuch* n.s. 5 (2017): 217–48.

Bakuntsev, A. 'Neizvestnaia "zametka" Bunina na smert' Bloka'; Iv. Bunin, 'Muzyka', *Novyi zhurnal* 277 (2014a): 218–40. https://magazines.gorky.media/nj/2014/277, accessed 2 September 2020.

Bakuntsev, A. V. 'Rech' I. A. Bunina "Missiia russkoi emigratsii" v obshchestvennom soznanii epokhi (po materialam emigrantskoi i sovetskoi periodiki 1920-kh godov)'. In *Ezhegodnik Doma russkogo zarubezh'ia imeni Aleksandra Solzhenitsyna – 2013*, 268–337. Moscow: Dom russkogo zarubezh'ia imeni Aleksandra Solzhenitsyna, 2014b.

Bakuntsev, A. V. 'Polemika vokrug rechi I. A. Bunina "Missiia russkoi emigratsii"'. In *Metropoliia i diaspora: dve vetvi russkoi kul'tury*, compiled by I. Iu. Beliakova, 11–21. Moscow: Dom-muzei Mariny Tsvetaevoi, 2015.

Berberova, Nina. 'Liricheskaia poema', *Sovremennye zapiski* 30 (1927): 221–30.

Berberova, N. N. 'Chetyre pis'ma V. I. Ivanova k V. F. Khodasevichu', *Novyi zhurnal* 62 (1960): 284–9.

Berberova, Nina. *The Italics Are Mine*. Translated by Philippe Radley. London and Harlow: Longmans, 1969.

[Bird] Berd, Robert. 'Viacheslav Ivanov i sovetskaia vlast' (1919–1929). Neizvestnye materialy', *Novoe literaturnoe obozrenie* 40 (1999): 305–31.

Brodsky, Joseph. 'The condition we call exile', *New York Review of Books*, 21 January 1988, 16–20.

Bunin, I. A. 'Missiia russkoi emigratsii (Rech', proiznesennaia v Parizhe 16 fevralia)', *Rul'* 1013, 3 April 1924, 5.

Bunin, I. A. 'Missiia russkoi emigratsii', *Rossiia i slavianstvo* 227 (December 1933): 1.

Bunin, I. A. 'Missiia russkoi emigratsii'. In *Den' Russkoi Kul'tury*, 6–8. Kharbin, 1934.

Bunin, I. A. 'Missiia russkoi emigratsii'. In I. A. Bunin, *Pod serpom i molotom: sbornik rasskazov, vospominanii, stikhotvorenii*, edited by S. P. Kryzhitskii, 209–17. London, ON, Canada: Izd-stvo 'Zaria', 1975.

Bunin, I. A. 'Inoniia i Kitezh'. In I. A. Bunin, *Publitsistika 1918–1953 godov*, edited by O. N. Mikhailov, 158–71. Moscow: Nasledie, 1998a.

Bunin, I. A. 'Missiia russkoi emigratsii'. In I. A. Bunin, *Publitsistika 1918–1953 godov*, edited by O. N. Mikhailov, 148–57. Moscow: Nasledie, 1998b.

Bunin, I. A. 'O Voloshine'. In I. A. Bunin, *Publitsistika 1918–1953 godov*, edited by O. N. Mikhailov, 386–94. Moscow: Nasledie, 1998c.

Bunin, I. A. 'Samorodki'. In I. A. Bunin, *Publitsistika 1918–1953 godov*, edited by O. N. Mikhailov, 253–8. Moscow: Nasledie, 1998d.

Bunin, I. A. 'Missiia russkoi emigratsii'. In *Velichaishie rechi russkoi istorii: Ot Petra Pervogo do Vladimira Putina*, edited by A. Iu. Klimenko, 191–9. Moscow: Algoritm, 2014.

Chulkov, G. I. *O misticheskom anarkhizme*. St Petersburg: Fakely, 1906.

Chulkov, Georgii. *Stikhotvoreniia*. Moscow: Zadruga, 1922.

Curtius, Ernst Robert. 'Venceslao Ivanov'. Translated by Bruno Revel. *Il Convegno* 14(8–12) (1933–4): 270–1.

Davidson, Pamela. 'Viacheslav Ivanov's ideal of the artist as prophet: From theory to practice', *Europa Orientalis* 21(1) (2002): 157–202.

[Davidson] Devidson, Pamela. *Bibliografiia prizhiznennykh publikatsii proizvedenii Viacheslava Ivanova: 1898–1949*. Edited by K. Iu. Lappo-Danilevskii. St Petersburg: Kalamos, 2012.

Davidson, Pamela. 'Aleksandr Ivanov and Nikolai Gogol': The image and the word in the Russian tradition of art as prophecy', *Slavonic and East European Review* 91(2) (April 2013): 157–209.

Davidson, Pamela. 'Simeon Polotskii and the origins of the Russian tradition of the writer as prophet', *Modern Language Review* 112(4) (October 2017): 917–52.

Davidson, Pamela. 'Leading Russia as the new Israel: Authorship and authority in Fedor Glinka's *Letters of a Russian Officer* and *Experiments in Sacred Verse*', *Russian Review* 77(2) (April 2018): 219–40.

Esenin, Sergei. *Preobrazhenie: Stikhotvoreniia*. Moscow: Moskovskaia trudovaia artel' khudozhnikov slova, 1918.

Esenin, Sergei. *Polnoe sobranie sochinenii*. Edited by Iu. L. Prokushev, 7 vols. Moscow: Nauka-Golos, 1995–2000.

Florenskii, Pavel. *Okolo Khomiakova (Kriticheskie zametki)*. Sergiev Posad: Tip. Sv.-Tr. Sergievoi lavry, 1916.

Gippius, Z. N. 'Nashe priamoe delo'. In *Chto delat' russkoi emigratsii: Stat'i Z. N. Gippius i K. R. Kocharovskogo s predisloviem I. I. Bunakova*, 10–18. Paris: Rodnik, 1930.

Gippius, Zinaida. *Pis'ma k Berberovoi i Khodasevichu*. Edited by Erika Freiberger Sheikholeslami. Ann Arbor, MI: Ardis, 1978.

Golenishchev-Kutuzov, Il'ia. 'Lirika Viacheslava Ivanova', *Sovremennye zapiski* 43 (1930): 463–71.

[Greene] Grin, Milatsa, ed. *Ustami Buninykh: Dnevniki Ivana Alekseevicha i Very Nikolaevny i drugie arkhivnye materialy*. 3 vols. Frankfurt am Main: Posev, 1977–82.

Isupov, K. G. and A. B. Shishkin, eds. *Viach. Ivanov: Pro et contra. Lichnost' i tvorchestvo Viacheslava Ivanova v otsenke russkikh i zarubezhnykh myslitelei i issledovatelei. Antologiia*. 2 vols. St Petersburg: Izd-stvo Russkoi khristianskoi gumanitarnoi akademii, 2016.

Iudin, Aleksei. 'Eshche raz ob "obrashchenii" Viach. Ivanova v katolichestvo: formula prisoedineniia ili formula otrecheniia', *Simvol* 53–4 (2008): 631–42.

Iukhnova, I. S. 'Pushkinskii "Prorok" v rannei proze V. Nabokova i G. Gazdanova', *Novyi filologicheskii vestnik* 2(45) (2018): 191–201.

Ivanov, Viacheslav. 'O granitsakh iskusstva', *Trudy i dni* 6 (1914): 81–106.

Ivanov, Viacheslav. *Borozdy i Mezhi: Opyty esteticheskie i kriticheskie*. Moscow: Musaget, 1916.

Ivanov, Viacheslav. 'Rimskie sonety', *Sovremennye zapiski* 62 (1936): 178–83.

Ivanov, Viacheslav. *Sobranie sochinenii*. Edited by D. V. Ivanov and O. Deschartes. 4 vols. Brussels: Foyer Oriental Chrétien, 1971–87.

Ivanov, Vjačeslav. *Dichtung und Briefwechsel aus dem deutschsprachigen Nachlass*. Edited by Michael Wachtel. Mainz: Liber Verlag, 1995.

Ivanov, Viacheslav. *Ave Roma. Rimskie sonety*. Edited by A. B. Shishkin. St Petersburg: Kalamos, 2011.

Ivanov-Razumnik, *Rossiia i Inoniia*. Andrei Bely, *Khristos voskrese*. Sergei Esenin, *Tovarishch; Inoniia*. Berlin: Skify, 1920.

Khlebnikov, Velimir. *Tvoreniia*. Edited by V. P. Grigor'ev and A. E. Parnis. Moscow: Sovetskii pisatel', 1986.

Khodasevich, Vladislav. 'Literatura v izgnanii'. In Vladislav Khodasevich, *Izbrannaia proza*, edited by N. Berberova, 210–24. New York: Russica, 1982.

Khodasevich, V. *Stikhotvoreniia*. Leningrad: Sovetskii pisatel', 1989.

Kliuev, Nikolai. *Serdtse edinoroga: Stikhotvoreniia i poemy*. Edited by V. P. Garnin. St Petersburg: Izd-stvo Russkogo Khristianskogo gumanitarnogo universiteta, 1999.

Kliuev, Nikolai. *Izbrannoe*. Edited by A. P. Kazarkin. Tomsk: Tomskaia pisatel'skaia organizatsiia, 2015.

Kotrelev, Nikolai. 'Iz perepiski Viach. Ivanova s Maksimom Gor'kim: K istorii zhurnala "Beseda"', *Europa Orientalis* 14 (1995): 183–208.

Kundera, Milan. *The Unbearable Lightness of Being*. Translated from the Czech by Michael Henry Heim. London: Faber and Faber, 1995.

Maiakovskii, V. V. *Polnoe sobranie proizvedenii v dvadtsati tomakh*. Edited by V. N. Terekhina et al. Moscow: Nauka, 2013–.

Miliukov, Paul N. *Bolshevism: An international danger, its doctrine and its practice through war and revolution*. New York: Charles Scribner's Sons, 1920.

Miliukov, Paul N. *Russia To-day and To-morrow*. New York: Macmillan, 1922.

Moteiunaite, I. V. 'Bibleiskaia alliuziia v rasskaze V. V. Nabokova "Groza"', *Vestnik Cherepovetskogo gosudarstvennogo universiteta* 2 (2016): 38–41.

Nabokov, V. 'Groza', *Rul'* 767, 10 June 1923, 2.

Nabokov, V. 'Groza', *Segodnia*, 28 September 1924, 6.

Nabokov, V. 'Tikhii shum', *Rul'* 1676, 10 June 1926, 4.

[Nabokov] Sirin, V. *Vozvrashchenie Chorba: Rasskazy i stikhi*. Berlin: Slovo, 1930. https://imwerden. de/pdf/nabokov_vozvrashhenie_chorba_1930.pdf (accessed 2 September 2020).

Nabokov, Vladimir. *The Collected Stories*. London: Penguin Books, 1997.

Nabokov, Vladimir. *Stikhi*. Edited by M. Malikova. St Petersburg: Azbuka, 2015. https://profilib.net/ chtenie/52794/vladimir-nabokov-stikhi-35.php (accessed 2 September 2020).

Nagibin, Iurii. *Prorok budet sozzhen*. Moscow: Kniga, 1990.

Naumann, Marina Turkevich. *Blue Evenings in Berlin: Nabokov's short stories of the 1920s*. New York: New York University Press, 1978.

Poberezkina, P. E., compiler. *Nikolai Kliuev: Vospominaniia sovremennikov*. Moscow: Progress-Pleiada, 2010.

Pyman, Avril. 'Russian poetry and the October revolution', *Revolutionary Russia* 3(1) (1990): 5–54.

Rubins, Maria. *Russian Montparnasse: Transnational writing in interwar Paris*. Basingstoke: Palgrave Macmillan, 2015.

Rubins, Maria. *Russkii Monparnas: Parizhskaia proza 1920–1930-kh godov v kontekste transnational'nogo modernizma*. Translated by M. Rubins and A. Glebovskaia. Moscow: Novoe literaturnoe obozrenie, 2017.

Shishkin, Andrei. 'Perepiska V. I. Ivanova i I. N. Golenishcheva Kutuzova', *Europa Orientalis* 8 (1989): 489–526.

Shishkin, Andrei. '"Rossiia raskololas" popolam": neizvestnoe pis'mo Vl. Khodasevicha', *Russica Romana* 9 (2002): 107–14.

Shishkin, A. B. '"Rossiia" i "Vselenskaia tserkov"' v formule Vl. Solov'eva i Viach. Ivanova'. In *Viacheslav Ivanov – Peterburg – mirovaia kul'tura*, 159–78. Tomsk and Moscow: Vodolei Publishers, 2003.

Shishkin, Andrei. '"Legate intorno alla profonda realtà dell'anima umana": Iz perepiski A. Pellegrini, T. Gallarati Skotti i P. Treves s Viach. Ivanovym (1932–1943)'. In *Archivio russo-italiano X*, edited by Daniela Rizzi and Andrej Shishkin, 135–82. Salerno: Europa Orientalis, 2015.

Shrayer, Maxim D. *The World of Nabokov's Stories*. Austin: University of Texas Press, 1999.

[Shrayer] Shraer, Maksim D. *Bunin i Nabokov: Istoriia sopernichestva*. Moscow: Al'pina non-fikshn, 2014.

Slobin, Greta N. *Russians Abroad: Literary and cultural politics of diaspora (1919–1939)*. Edited by Katerina Clark, Nancy Condee, Dan Slobin and Mark Slobin. Boston, MA: Academic Studies Press, 2013.

Slonim, Mark. 'Zametki ob emigrantskoi literature'. In *Kritika russkogo zarubezh'ia*, edited by O. A. Korostelev and N. G. Mel'nikov, vol. 2, 115–26. Moscow: Olimp, 2002.

Solivetti, K. and M. Paolini. 'Paradigmy "izgnaniia" i "poslannichestva": evropeiskii opyt russkoi emigratsii v 20-e gody', *Europa Orientalis* 22(2) (2003): 145–70.

Struve, Gleb. 'Iz moego arkhiva: 1. Pis'ma i stat'ia V. Khodasevicha', *Mosty* 15 (1970): 396–403.

Struve, Nikita. 'Vstrecha pervoi russkoi emigratsii s Evropoi', *Europa Orientalis* 22(2) (2003): 15–20.

Terapiano, Iurii, ed. *Muza Diaspory: izbrannye stikhi zarubezhnykh poetov, 1920–1960*. Frankfurt am Main: Posev, 1960.

Treplev, K. 'Razoblachennyi prorok', *Nakanune* 89, 18 April 1924, 4.

Wang, Emily. 'Viacheslav Ivanov in the 1930s: The Russian poet as Italian humanist', *Slavic Review* 75(4) (2016): 896–918.

Zamiatin, Evgenii. *Sobranie sochinenii: Litsa*. Moscow: Russkaia kniga, 2004.

Zarankin, Julia and Michael Wachtel. 'The correspondence of Viacheslav Ivanov and Charles du Bos'. In *Archivio italo-russo III: Vjačeslav Ivanov – Testi inediti*, edited by Daniella Rizzi and Andrej Shishkin, 497–540. Salerno: Europa Orientalis, 2001.

## Part three

# Evolutionary trajectories: adaptation, 'interbreeding' and transcultural polyglossia

4

# Translingual poetry and the boundaries of diaspora: the self-translations of Marina Tsvetaeva, Vladimir Nabokov and Joseph Brodsky

Adrian Wanner

## Diasporic identity and self-translation

In his seminal article 'The "Diaspora" Diaspora', Rogers Brubaker lists 'boundary maintenance' as one of the three necessary core elements for a definition of diaspora (together with 'dispersion' and 'homeland orientation'). At the same time, he notes that there is 'a tension in the literature between *boundary-maintenance* and *boundary-erosion*', which is reflected in the increasing scholarly focus on 'hybridity, fluidity, creolization and syncretism'.[1] Which criteria allow us to decide who belongs to a putative diasporic community and who doesn't? Russia is a country that hovers uneasily between a nation state and an empire. For that reason, ethnicity and religion have been less than satisfactory yardsticks in delineating the contours of the Russian diaspora. Instead, language is usually seen as the determining factor. In that view, what we call the 'Russian' diaspora is really a russophone diaspora. Kevin Platt, in his introduction to a recent volume on global Russian cultures, places the study of extraterritorial Russian cultures into dialogue with such related and rapidly expanding subdisciplines as global anglophone, francophone and sinophone studies.[2] Given the key role of the Russian language in defining 'Russianness', can there be such a thing as a non-russophone Russian diaspora? I have looked at this question in an earlier monograph dealing with Russian-born émigré writers working in languages other than Russian. As I argued in that book, if these authors do qualify as 'Russian writers', it is not because of their place of birth or their Russian native language, but because of a conscious choice. When Gary Shteyngart titled his first novel *The Russian Debutante's Handbook*, he positioned himself quite consciously as a 'Russian' writer even though he was writing in English.[3]

Rather than defining diaspora as an objectively existing bounded group based on essentialist criteria, Brubaker argues that it should be understood as a 'category of practice, project, claim and stance'.[4] In other words, personal intentions play a key role in how authors place themselves within diasporic formations. With the poet Marina Tsvetaeva we are looking in some respects at the opposite position to the one taken by Shteyngart. In a 1926 letter to Rainer Maria Rilke, Tsvetaeva wrote, rather startlingly perhaps: 'I am not a Russian poet and am always astonished to be taken for one and looked upon in this light. The reason one becomes a poet … is to avoid being French, Russian, etc., in order to be everything.'[5] In spite of this declaration of poetic universalism that distanced her from membership in the Russian diaspora, Tsvetaeva is usually taken for a monolingual Russian poet who wrote little of significance outside her native tongue. The fact that she ended up returning to the Soviet Union from her Western European exile reinforced the narrative of a potentially cosmopolitan writer who opted nevertheless to remain within the fold of the native culture. Vladimir Nabokov, on the other hand, is regarded as someone who successfully crossed the linguistic boundary to become a bona fide American writer and thus managed to propel himself outside the boundaries of the Russian diaspora. Joseph Brodsky, finally, occupies an intermediate position: even though he was made the Poet Laureate of the United States in 1991 and received high praise for his English-language essays, his English-language poetry has been largely disparaged. A preliminary conclusion one might draw from this fact is that it seems to be easier to cross the language boundary as a prose writer than as a poet.

Analysing and comparing the bilingual and self-translated oeuvre of these three prominent Russian émigrés will allow us to probe the shifting boundaries of the Russian diaspora over the course of the twentieth century.[6] Such an approach interrogates the 'monolingual paradigm' still prevalent in contemporary criticism, according to which, in Yasemin Yildiz's formulation, 'individuals and social formations are imagined to possess one "true" language only, their "mother tongue", and through this possession to be organically linked to an exclusive, clearly demarcated ethnicity, culture, and nation'.[7] In such a view, poetic writing outside the mother tongue and self-translation into a non-native language appear as eccentric anomalies that fall through the cracks of a taxonomy in which, despite evidence to the contrary, 'mononational constructions of modern and contemporary poetry' are still largely posited as the norm.[8]

Poetry plays a particularly important role in ideologies of linguistic identity and national belonging. Some of this thinking goes back to German romantic ideas of the national soul rooted in the native idiom, of which poetic masterpieces provide the most exemplary illustration. In reality, composing poetry in a non-native language or in multiple languages is less rare than one may think. As Leonard Forster has shown in his pioneering monograph *The Poet's Tongues*, multilingual poetry was a widespread practice in medieval and early modern Europe, when authors routinely switched between Latin and a vernacular language, and increasingly also between individual vernacular languages. Creativity in non-native languages can also be found among more recent poets, such as Stefan George, Rainer Maria Rilke or members of the twentieth-century avant-garde.

If there are no a priori reasons that would preclude a poet from composing verse in a foreign language, the stakes are raised considerably when it comes to the issue of self-translation. The problem now is not only to create a poetic text in a non-native idiom, but to reproduce an artistic concept that has already received a concrete shape in the native tongue. While the practice of literary self-translation has only relatively recently begun to attract serious scholarly attention, 'self-translation studies' has now developed into a booming academic subfield of its own.[9] In spite of the substantial and ever-growing volume of research devoted to self-translation, many issues remain unresolved. One difficulty in coming to terms with this phenomenon is the challenge that it presents to received notions of translation theory and textual authority. As Jan Hokenson and Marcella Munson have pointed out, self-translation 'escapes the binary categories of text theory and diverges radically from literary norms, [given that] the translator *is* the author, the translation is an original, the foreign is the domestic, and vice versa'.[10] In collapsing the roles of author and translator, self-translations tend to acquire in the eyes of the reading public a more authoritative status, given that the writer-translator, compared to an extraneous translator, is supposed to be closer to the original text. At the same time, somewhat paradoxically, it is assumed that the author-translator, as the intellectual owner of the text, 'can allow himself bold shifts from the source text which, had it been done by another translator, probably would not have passed as an adequate translation'.[11]

It should be noted that the term 'self-translation' is in itself ambiguous, depending on whether we see the 'self' as the subject or the object of the translational process. If the self is perceived as the object, self-translation literally involves a 'translation of the self'. Seemingly 'saying the same thing twice' in two different languages becomes a test case for larger questions of cultural allegiance and diasporic identity. Juxtaposing Tsvetaeva's self-translated poetry with that of Nabokov and Brodsky allows us to probe how different poets have approached the thorny issue of translation and what it tells us about their self-positioning within the Russian diaspora. At the same time, the question arises for whom self-translated poems are ultimately written. Does a poet cross the linguistic boundary to gain a different audience, or to create a new artistic experience? In other words, is the poet looking outward or inward?

In his book on translation and the making of modern Russian literature, Brian Baer has argued that the notion of translation lies at the core of Russia's self-definition as a multilingual and multi-ethnic empire, in which 'imperial realities produced an enormous number of bilinguals and a culture marked by hybridity'.[12] Given the number of writers forced into exile after the Bolshevik Revolution, the history of Russia in the twentieth century was particularly propitious for the flowering of bilingual and self-translated literature. Tsvetaeva and Nabokov share the experience of a multilingual upbringing in Russia before being forced out of their native country. Both were trilingual from childhood – Tsvetaeva in Russian, German and French, and Nabokov in Russian, French and English. By contrast, Brodsky grew up as typical monolingual Soviet child. He learned English only as an adult and spoke it with a heavy accent even decades after moving to the United States. The three authors have very different reputations with regard to their non-Russian writings as well. While Nabokov's name has become almost synonymous with multilingual shape-shifting, Brodsky is considered to be a major Russian poet with a secondary and flawed English-language career. Tsvetaeva's French-language oeuvre has suffered almost complete neglect. Why is that so? In what follows, I will address each poet in turn before arriving at some more general conclusions.

## Tsvetaeva's double creation of *Mólodets*

Living in multiple languages was an important feature of Tsvetaeva's biography from the very beginning. As the daughter of a Russian father and a half-German half-Polish mother she grew up in a multilingual home. In an autobiographical sketch of 1940 she wrote: 'First languages: German and Russian, by age seven – French.'[13] As a child and an adolescent, she wrote poetry not only in Russian, but also in German and French.[14] None of these texts seems to have survived, but it becomes clear that the idea and practice of writing poetry in a non-native language was certainly not alien to Tsvetaeva. She later furnished a theoretical and philosophical justification for translingual poetry in her correspondence with Rainer Maria Rilke during the summer of 1926. On 6 July 1926, she wrote to Rilke (in German):

> Goethe says somewhere that one can never achieve anything of significance in a foreign language – and that has always rung false to me. ... Writing poetry is in itself translating, from the mother tongue into another. Whether French or German should make no difference. No language is the mother tongue. Writing poetry is rewriting it [*Dichten ist nachdichten*]. That's why I am puzzled when people talk of French or Russian, etc., poets. A poet may write in French; he cannot be a French poet. That's ludicrous.[15]

If, according to Tsvetaeva, writing poetry is always already a translation from a spiritual into a material realm, interlingual transposition between different idioms presents a lesser challenge. For her, contrary to popular assumptions, poetry is in principle always translatable. She explained this thought in a letter to the French poet Paul Valéry in 1937 (in French):

> One says that Pushkin cannot be translated. Why? Every poem is a translation from the spiritual into the material, from feelings and thoughts into words. If one has been able to do it once by translating the interior world into external signs (which comes close to a miracle), why should one not be able to express one system of signs via another? This is much simpler: in the translation from one language into another, the material is rendered by the material, the word by the word, which is always possible.[16]

One may object that the logic behind this statement is somewhat dubious. If we follow Tsvetaeva's argument, a successful translation of Pushkin would entail the intuition of the spiritual 'interior world' behind the Russian text and its recasting into a different language, which surely is more complex than a horizontal transposition between equivalent external signs. How can the form be separated from the spiritual content if they are both extensions of each other? Whatever its validity, though, Tsvetaeva's belief in the fundamental translatability of poetry facilitated her own self-translation of the fairy-tale poem *Mólodets* (usually called in English *The Swain*).

Written in 1922 and published in 1924 in Prague, *Mólodets* is based on a story in Afanasiev's classic collection of Russian fairy tales. Tsvetaeva's poem preserves the basic plot outline of Afanasiev's tale, but it significantly expands the text and gives it a radically different ending. The heroine, a village girl named Marusia, is seduced by a handsome stranger who turns out to be a vampire and ends up killing her brother, her mother, and finally herself. After her death, Marusia is reincarnated in a red flower, which is found by a nobleman who becomes her husband after she metamorphoses back into a woman. They live together for five years and have a son. One day, the vampire confronts Marusia again during a church service. In Afanasiev's tale, Marusia manages to destroy her tormentor by sprinkling him with holy water. In Tsvetaeva's version Marusia abandons husband and child to reunite with the vampire and fly off with him 'into the blue fire'. Tsvetaeva's revision thus turns the fairy tale into a story of passionate love and all-consuming obsession. In her correspondence with Boris Pasternak, who became the poem's dedicatee, Tsvetaeva stressed the autobiographical significance of the poem, claiming a kinship between herself and the female protagonist Marusia.[17]

In 1929, Tsvetaeva became acquainted with the painter Natalia Goncharova, who offered to do a series of illustrations for *Mólodets*. This gave Tsvetaeva the hope of publishing her poem in France, and, since no other translator was available, she decided to translate the text herself, giving it the title *Le Gars*. Her attempts to find a publisher remained unsuccessful, however. After lying dormant for many decades in Tsvetaeva's Moscow archive, the manuscript was finally published in France in the early 1990s.[18] A decade later *Le Gars* also appeared in Russia. A 2003 edition of *Mólodets* published in St Petersburg includes the French text with a literal Russian translation printed *en face*, while a 2005 bilingual Moscow edition presents Tsvetaeva's Russian and French versions on facing pages. Both of these editions also include Natalia Goncharova's illustrations. These publications didn't do much to establish a reputation for Tsvetaeva as a French-language poet, however. Even among Tsvetaeva specialists, *Le Gars* has thus far received only minimal attention.[19]

Given the idiosyncratic language and style of *Mólodets*, Tsvetaeva faced formidable challenges in recasting her poem in French. In order to reproduce the archaic and folkloric features of the text, she resorted to the pre-classic French language of Villon and Rabelais. Tsvetaeva's archaic French pertains not only to vocabulary, but to grammar and syntax as well. It also features her trademark nominal style. Both in Russian and in French, Tsvetaeva routinely omits subject pronouns with conjugated verbs. Likewise, the frequent omission of articles creates an alien effect in French that could perhaps be interpreted as a 'foreignizing' element pointing to the Russian source, but is also meant to evoke an archaic or folkloric register.

In Tsvetaeva's approach to translation, the rendition of structural and formal features trumps semantic accuracy. Remarkably, this formal faithfulness pertains not only to rhyme, but also to metre. Theoreticians of verse maintain that an equimetrical translation between Russian and French is impossible, given that the two languages use different systems of versification: syllabotonic in Russian, syllabic in French. However, Tsvetaeva simply chose to ignore this fact. The polymetric twists and turns of the Russian original are replicated in the French translation, as demonstrated by the description of the nobleman's palace:

| | |
|---|---|
| Впрочем – Богу ли соврем? – | By the way – why lie to God? – |
| Столб как столб и дом как дом: | A column and a house like any other: |
| С башнями, с банями: | With towers, with baths: |
| Нашего барина. (vv. 872–5) | Of our nobleman. |

| | |
|---|---|
| Pic sur pic et bloc sur bloc. | Peak above peak and block above block. |
| – A qui fillette ce roc | – To whom, girl, [belongs] this rock |
| De marbre? | Of marble? |
| – Pardine! | – Goodness! |
| A notre barine. (71) | To our nobleman. |

In Russian, the first two lines are written in four-foot trochees (a predominant metre in *Mólodets*) before the stanza unexpectedly switches to two-foot dactyls in lines three and four. In French, the text shifts from trochees to amphibrachs if we read it 'à la russe', so to speak, by emphasizing the stressed syllables in accordance with the metre (and also by counting the silent 'e muet' as a full syllable, as is indeed the norm in French poetic scansion).

Remarkably, the French translation retains *not a single word* of the original stanza aside from the closing 'barin' (nobleman), an expression that entered the French language in the nineteenth century as a Russian loan word. Instead of the semantics, Tsvetaeva attempts to replicate the form of the Russian original as closely as possible. Aside from the metrical shift in mid-stanza, this includes the paired masculine and dactylic rhymes. Since, strictly speaking, no dactylic endings exist in French, the latter are replaced by feminine rhymes, but the sonic structure of 'Pardine–barine' nevertheless suggest a trisyllabic rhyme. The rhythm of the second line in Russian with its repetition of the monosyllabic words 'stolb' (column) and 'dom' (house) finds an exact equivalent in the first line of the French stanza, which repeats the words 'pic' and 'bloc'. Furthermore, the alliteration 'bashniami–baniami–barina' is echoed by the repetition of the 'ar'-sound in 'marbre–Pardine–barine'.

Given the identity of author and translator, *Le Gars* is not only a translation, it also functions as a sort of self-exegesis. The Russian original is not an easy text. Its idiosyncratic language and form create an impediment to smooth reading, and the action remains at times rather obscure. The French translation, by comparison, is somewhat more reader-friendly. Whereas the Russian text shifts abruptly between various voices, which can belong either to one of the fictional characters or to the narrator, in the French version the speaker of an utterance is usually identified. As far as the plot is concerned, the French version sometimes provides more details and explanations, even though the translation is overall somewhat shorter than the original (2,146 lines in French versus 2,227 in Russian). The French version also reinforces implicit symbolic links built into the Russian text. As the German scholar Christiane Hauschild has observed, Tsvetaeva blasphemously identifies the consummation scene between Marusia and the vampire with the ritual of Holy Communion. The scene turns into a literal, cannibalistic consumption of blood, in which Marusia offers herself to her lover as the sacramental 'cup'.[20] In the French text, this connection is made much more explicit by the mention of bread and wine. The French version is also more explicit with regard to colour symbolism, which relies on the contrast between white and red. In fact, 'rouge' is the most frequently used adjective in *Le Gars*. This coloration is reflected in Tsvetaeva's statement at the end of her preface: 'Et voici, enfin, la Russie, rouge d'un autre rouge que celui de ses drapeaux d'aujourd'hui' ('And here, finally, is Russia, red with a different red than the one of her present-day banners') (130).

In rewriting her poem in a new language seven years after its original composition, Tsvetaeva could not help becoming aware of how she herself, and therefore also her relation to the original text, had changed over time. Interestingly, the reworking of her Russian poem in French seems to have made Tsvetaeva more aware of her Russian roots. The French version contains numerous allusions to Russia that are absent in the Russian original. The vampire refers to 'saintly Russia' (47), he tells Marusia that she should be buried 'a hundred versts from the temple ... in the vast land, the Russian land' (60), snow is called 'Russia's manna' (68), Marusia has 'Russian braids' (76), the nobleman's valet asks him reproachfully 'Are you Russian?' (92), the nobleman's guests abuse him with 'Russian curses' (96), and the nobleman boasts about his spouse that '[she is] mine – Russian' (105). In addition there are other clichéd 'Russian' elements that exist only in the French text: Marusia's mother orders 'a litre of eau de vie' (i.e., vodka) for the brother's funeral (43), the wind is blowing 'in the steppe' (46), Marusia's grave is haunted by wolves (60), midnight is personified as a 'tsarina' (73 and 74).

A possible explanation for these additions may be that Tsvetaeva, in transplanting the poem from a Russian to a French linguistic medium, was trying to compensate for the loss in 'Russianness' by asserting it discursively. As Efim Etkind has noted, the language of the Russian version is intimately rooted in Russian folklore, whereas the French version displays more of a 'neutral' folkloric style that cannot be located in a specific national tradition.[21] If Tsvetaeva wanted to signal to her French readers the Russian nature of her poem, she had to do it by other means. Interestingly, she does so by deploying Western stereotypes about Russia, be it in order to make the text more readable to a presumptive French audience, or perhaps with the subversive intent of undermining these clichés with a self-ironic overemphasis of Russian exoticism.

It is important to note that Tsvetaeva's heroine herself is intimately connected to a personification of Russia. The very name 'Marusia' contains the root 'Rus''. In addition it contains the hair colour 'rusyi' (dark blond). These connotations work somewhat differently in French. The name 'Maroussia' can be linked with 'rousse' (red-haired) as well as with 'russe' (Russian), a similarity exploited in the tongue-twisting juxtaposition 'rousses russes tresses' (red Russian braids) (76). To be sure, in spite of the phonic similarity, 'rousse' is not the same colour as 'rusyi'. One could argue that the French 'rousse' works even better than the Russian 'rusyi' in the colour symbolism of the poem, since it associates the female character more explicitly with the theme of 'redness'. In calling Marusia a 'krasnaia devitsa', Tsvetaeva is not only using a folkloric cliché for 'beautiful girl', but also pointing to the inherent 'redness' that links her to her male partner. If Tsvetaeva persisted in seeing the female heroine of her poem as a self-portrait, the 'Maroussia' of the French version gains additional poignancy as a rebellious 'redhead' and as a 'Russian' living in an alien environment.

In sum, we see that in rewriting her poem in French, Tsvetaeva had no intention of becoming a French poet (she explicitly rejected such mononational labels, as we have seen). Somewhat paradoxically, the French version seems to reaffirm her own Russian identity. We may read this as proof of the impossibility of shedding one's own national roots in spite of all declarations of poetic universalism. More likely, though, Tsvetaeva's double self-portrait as Marusia/Maroussia illustrates a translingual metamorphosis evoked symbolically in the fairy-tale heroine's shape-shifting between woman and flower. By stepping out of her native idiom, Tsvetaeva comes closer to her proclaimed ideal of being a poet outside the confines of a nationally or monolingually defined literature. By retaining at the same time some key elements of Russian prosody such as syllabotonic verse as well as a discursively stated 'Russianness', *Le Gars* exists in a hybrid transnational domain that cannot be associated unequivocally with either Russian or French poetry. To some extent, Tsvetaeva's cosmopolitanism overlaps with Viacheslav Ivanov's 'independence from conventional territorial definitions of selfhood' and his 'scepticism about the existence of inherent or intrinsic Russianness', discussed by Pamela Davidson in an earlier chapter of this volume, as long as we substitute for Ivanov's supranational framework of Christian humanism Tsvetaeva's more idiosyncratic notion of the 'spirit of poetry'. Both Ivanov and Tsvetaeva believed in the 'transnational space offered by the Muse', even though Tsvetaeva, an instinctive rebel rather than a synthesizer, never succeeded in finding a spiritual home in her places of exile.

## Nabokov's problems with *Poems and Problems*

We will now turn to the poetic self-translations of another prominent Russian émigré. Nabokov belongs to the same generation as Tsvetaeva, but he recast his Russian poems in English a few decades after Tsvetaeva wrote *Le Gars*. While Nabokov's Russian-to-English and English-to-Russian translations of his own novels and memoirs have garnered a fair amount of critical attention, very little has been written about his self-translated poetry.[22] The majority of Nabokov's poems in English (39 out of 62, to be exact) are self-translations of texts that he had originally written in Russian between 1917 and 1967. The English version of these poems first appeared in the 1970 volume *Poems and Problems*. In his preface to this book, Nabokov drew an explicit connection between his method of self-translation and the literalist theory he developed while preparing his English edition of Pushkin's *Eugene Onegin*, which had appeared six years earlier. As he put it,

> For the last ten years, I have been promoting, on every possible occasion, literality, i.e., rigid fidelity, in the translation of Russian verse. Treating a text in that way is an honest and delightful procedure, when the text is a recognized masterpiece, whose every detail must be faithfully rendered in English. But what about faithfully englishing one's own verse, written half a century or a quarter of a century ago? One has to fight a vague embarrassment; one cannot help squirming and wincing; one feels rather like a potentate swearing allegiance to his own self or a conscientious priest blessing his own bathwater. On the other hand, if one contemplates, for one wild moment, the possibility of paraphrasing and improving one's old verse, a horrid sense of falsification makes one scamper back and cling like a baby ape to rugged fidelity.[23]

The fact that both Tsvetaeva and Nabokov were poetic self-translators allows for a comparison of their theory and praxis of bilingual creation. Tsvetaeva, as we have seen, embraced poetic creation outside the mother tongue and believed in the fundamental translatability of poetry. Nabokov, even though he is considered a paragon of bilingual virtuosity, expressed scepticism on both of these counts. His apprehension about writing outside the native tongue is captured in his well-known lament, in the afterword to the American edition of *Lolita*, of having to abandon his 'untrammeled, rich, and infinitely docile Russian tongue for a second-rate brand of English'.[24] Moreover, Nabokov exhibited a radical scepticism about the translatability of poetry. His literalist version of *Eugene Onegin* is ultimately meant to demonstrate the impossibility of translating Pushkin's verse. Not surprisingly, then, self-translation becomes for Nabokov a form of self-torture. As early as the 1930s Nabokov complained that translating his own work was like 'sorting through one's own innards and then trying them on for size like a pair of gloves'.[25]

Nabokov made it quite clear that the literalist method of translation he championed in the preface to *Eugene Onegin* and other related publications did not only apply to his English rendition of Pushkin's verse, but was meant as a prescription for the translation of poetry *tout court*. One might wonder, then, to what extent he adhered to his literalist credo when it came to translating his own work. A closer look at Nabokov's self-translated poetry reveals a rather inconsistent picture. Many translations deviate from his publicly proclaimed literalist doctrine by retaining vestiges of rhyme and metre. Clearly, for Nabokov translating his own poetry was different from translating Pushkin. 'Killing' the original text and replacing it with a hypertrophied commentary, as he did with *Eugene Onegin*, was not a viable solution when his own work was at stake. Instead, he resorted to a somewhat haphazard approach, with the decision to reproduce or ignore the formal features of the original poem determined on a case-by-case basis. With their mixture of rhymed and unrhymed lines, and the presence or absence of metre, Nabokov's self-translated poems differ markedly from his originally composed poetry in Russian and English. They also differ from the translations he did of the work of other poets.

The rigid fidelity that Nabokov demanded of verse translators becomes problematic in the context of self-translation, given that it would imply fidelity to a self that evolved over time. As is the case with all self-translators, revisiting and translating his earlier work would have offered Nabokov, at least theoretically, a chance for rewriting and improvement. However, for Nabokov this urge for revision came into conflict with his self-imposed ethos of translational fidelity, according to which any improvement or paraphrase would amount to falsification. It is important to note that his obsession with 'fidelity' only applied to the translation of poetry – it did not carry over to his self-translated prose, where we find a wide spectrum of approaches ranging from relative literality to creative rewriting and fundamental transformation. This is particularly visible in his memoirs, which he first wrote in English under the title *Conclusive Evidence*, then translated into Russian as *Drugie berega* (*Other shores*), and then re-Englished as *Speak Memory*, each time with added layers of new detail and significant alterations.[26] It also bears mentioning that earlier in his career, and even occasionally *after* his conversion to literalism, Nabokov had no qualms producing the kind of 'paraphrastic', rhymed translations that he so vehemently attacked in others.[27]

Given that, in comparison with Tsvetaeva, Nabokov was a rather average poet, his hesitancy and over-theorizing of the process of translation could perhaps be explained by his general insecurity about poetic composition. But the differences between Nabokov's conflicted self-translations and Tsvetaeva's virtuoso performance in *Le Gars* stem not only from a discrepancy in poetic talent, but also from a different stylistic pedigree. As a Russian poet, Nabokov was a post-Symbolist attached to classic forms. He was also in his bones a 'pictorial' and visual image-oriented poet who cared about finding the *mot juste* or exact phrasing in the poetic line rather than creating a sense of sweeping musicality. As a poetic self-translator, Nabokov's efforts were hemmed in by his theoretical rigidity about the only 'correct' method of translation and his pessimism about bridging the linguistic gap in poetic creation. His belief in the impossibility of translating poetry, which hardened with his long labour over *Eugene Onegin*, seems to have turned into a self-fulfilling prophecy in *Poems and Problems*, even though he deviated from his own literalist credo by smuggling occasional vestiges of rhyme and metre into the English text.

## Brodsky's self-translated poetry

We will now 'triangulate' our discussion of poetic self-translation by introducing a third prominent Russian exile poet and self-translator.[28] Brodsky's method of self-translation has more in common with Tsvetaeva than with Nabokov. This is probably no accident, given that Brodsky was a lifelong admirer of Tsvetaeva. In fact, he considered her to be the greatest poet of the twentieth century in any language,[29] even though, not knowing French, he was not in a position to evaluate her French-language oeuvre. Tsvetaeva and Brodsky both believed in the fundamental translatability of poetry, partly because, in their opinion, a poem is always already a translation. As Brodsky put it in his essay 'In the shadow of Dante', 'Poetry after all in itself is a translation; or, to put it another way, poetry is one of the aspects of the psyche rendered in language.'[30] The technique, and to some extent the critical reception, of Tsvetaeva's and Brodsky's self-translations followed a similar trajectory. Both poets opted for a 'foreignizing' approach that infuses the target text with prosodic features borrowed from the source language. This technique clashed with the conventions of the target culture and marked them as outsiders within their adopted linguistic milieu.

Brodsky's status as an American poet, or a bilingual poet, is far from a settled question. His decision as a non-native speaker of English to take the translation of his poems into his own hands, or – perhaps even worse – to edit and 'correct' the work of prominent anglophone poets who had agreed to translate his work was bound to raise eyebrows. To many critics, such behaviour seemed, at best, presumptuous, and at worst, self-destructive in terms of Brodsky's reputation in the anglophone world. In actuality, Brodsky's knowledge of English was better than his accent suggested. Unlike Nabokov and Tsvetaeva, he was essentially a self-made bilingual. A key moment in his appropriation of the English language was his discovery of John Donne and other poets of the

English metaphysical school during his exile in Norenskaia, the small village near the Arctic Circle to which he had been banished on charges of 'social parasitism'. We should not forget that his Anglophile leanings preceded Brodsky's actual residence in an English-speaking environment. Motivated by literary and poetic considerations rather than biographic happenstance, Brodsky's appropriation of the English language was essentially a labour of love.

Nevertheless, when questioned by interviewers in the late 1970s, Brodsky denied that he had any ambition to write serious poetry in English. This is how he answered a question (in Russian) by John Glad, who asked Brodsky whether he wanted to become a bilingual poet:

> You know, no. This ambition I do not have at all, although I am perfectly capable of writing entirely decent poems in English. But for me, when I write verses in English, this is rather a game, chess, if you want, putting bricks together. But I frequently realize that the psychological, emotional-acoustic processes are identical. The same mechanisms are mobilized that are active when I compose verses in Russian. But to become a Nabokov or a Joseph Conrad, such ambitions I do not have at all. Even though I imagine that this would be completely possible for me, I simply don't have the time, energy or narcissism for this. However, I fully admit that someone in my place could be one and the other, i.e., write poems in English and in Russian.[31]

Brodsky's answer is strangely coy and self-contradictory. Almost every sentence begins with a hedging word – 'no' (but), 'khotia' (even though), 'odnako' (however). Essentially, Brodsky seems to be saying that, even though he has no plans to become a bilingual poet, there would be no real impediment to his being a great poet in more than one language. The only thing that stops him is his alleged lack of ambition, or his unwillingness to become another Nabokov (which, as far as Brodsky is concerned, is not a flattering comparison). Writing poetry in English looks at first sight like a mere 'game' devoid of serious artistic value. However, at second sight it turns out to be not all that different from writing poetry in the native language after all. It is not surprising, then, that Brodsky began to write poems in English more and more often. As Eugenia Kelbert has pointed out, '[w]hile Brodsky only published one original English poem in the 1970s, fifteen were published in the 80s and this number almost doubled (28) in the short half-decade before the poet's death in 1996. These numbers speak for themselves: clearly,

Brodsky's English career, cut short at the age of fifty-five, was only just unfolding.'[32]

Brodsky and Nabokov were antipodes in their approach to poetic translation. While they shared a contempt for 'smooth' translations, Brodsky's formal absolutism is the polar opposite of the semantic absolutism that Nabokov propagated in his later years. In their translational practice, both of them adopted a stubborn 'in-your-face' attitude, presenting the translation as a challenge to the philistine tastes and prejudices of the presumptive audience. Like Nabokov, Brodsky was not willing to make any concessions to public preferences and established practice in his pursuit of what he considered to be the only legitimate and 'true' translation method. As Valentina Polukhina put it, 'He was willing to sacrifice rhetorical figures to rhyme, syntax to prosody – everything, including meaning, to form. And he did.'[33] This method of self-translation comes close to that of Tsvetaeva. Neither Tsvetaeva nor Brodsky had any patience for free verse in the translation of formal poetry. Like Tsvetaeva in her French version of *Mólodets*, Brodsky introduced significant semantic alterations in his self-translated poems for the sake of preserving the formal energy of the original text. Moreover, both Tsvetaeva and Brodsky were ready to violate the norms of the target language when it suited their purpose, creating a 'Russified' version of French and English that left some of their readers baffled or indignant.

Many of Brodsky's self-translations are a tour de force seemingly designed to prove the presupposition that formal equivalence between Russian and English is an achievable goal. Rather than picking 'easy' texts, he gravitated towards poems that presented a particular formal challenge. Thus, the first poem that he translated on his own in 1980, 'December in Florence', is written in triple-rhymed tercets, a feature preserved in the English version.[34] The poem 'Portrait of Tragedy', first published in 1996, presents an even greater tour de force, featuring 12 stanzas with AAAABBB rhymes.[35] The English text not only maintains the rhyme scheme of the Russian original, it even preserves the feminine nature of all the rhymes, a feat not easily achieved in English. A listing of the words that form the end rhymes in the English translation of the poem demonstrates Brodsky's verbal creativity (words in italics correspond semantically to the analogous rhyme word in the Russian text):

Stanza 1:   '*creases*-rhesus-rises-wheezes', 'lately-lazy-lady'
Stanza 2:   'senseless-lenses-else's-pretenses', 'heroes-eras-chorus'
Stanza 3:   'gnashes-flashes-ashes-blushes', '*surprise us*-devices-crisis'

| Stanza 4: | '*Gorgon*-golden-burden-broaden', 'fashion-ashen-crush on' |
| Stanza 5: | 'ardor-under-fodder-founder', 'cartridge-courage-garbage' |
| Stanza 6: | 'feces-faces-save this-laces', 'cheer up, *cherub*, stirrup' |
| Stanza 7: | 'hidden-heathen-mitten-smitten', 'decent-distant-*instant*' |
| Stanza 8: | 'statues-much as-catch is-matchless', 'martyrs-starters-tatters' |
| Stanza 9: | 'evening-beginning-being-grieving', 'vowels-bowels-ovals' |
| Stanza 10: | 'gargle-ogle-ogre-goggle', 'of us-sofas-surface' |
| Stanza 11: | 'stir it-Spirit-serried-buried', 'badly-buggy-ugly' |
| Stanza 12: | 'torrent-warrant-weren't-worried', 'oven-cloven-open' |

Aside from occasional slant rhymes, the consistent 'femininity' of the rhyming is produced more than once by means of compounds. Such rhymes have a tendency to sound comical in English, although several compound rhymes also occur in the Russian original, with similar implications. The scansion of 'weren't' as a two-syllable word possibly betrays the peculiarities of Brodsky's oral performance in English. The potentially comic implication of the compound rhymes is not necessarily a distraction here – they serve to underline Brodsky's tragicomic representation of tragedy as a grotesque female character. In terms of phonetics, some of the English rhymes manage to reproduce the hissing sound characteristic of the Russian original ('creases-rhesus-rises-wheezes' corresponds to '*morshchiny-muzhchiny-chertovshchiny-prichiny*'). The reproduction of form in translation, especially such a challenging one as a stanza consisting of quadruple and triple feminine rhymes, necessitates semantic shifts. Natalia Rulyova, in her detailed comparison of the Russian and English versions of the poem, has observed that the autobiographical references to Brodsky's Soviet past are toned down in English, where tragedy is represented more in abstract than historically concrete terms and the irremediability of tragedy is less pronounced than in the Russian original.[36]

## From translingual poetry to 'stereotextuality'

How successful are Tsvetaeva's, Nabokov's and Brodsky's self-translations? If we judged them by their critical or popular resonance, we would probably have to conclude that they were failures. Tsvetaeva's reading of *Le Gars* at a Paris literary salon turned out to be a fiasco: as we know from the memoirs of E. A. Izvol'skaia, the audience reacted with 'deadly silence'.[37] More devastatingly, Tsvetaeva was unable to get her translation into print. As she reported in a 1931 letter, 'About the French *Mólodets* there is only one refrain: "*Too* new, unusual, outside of any tradition, not even surrealism" (NB! God save me from the latter!). Nobody wants to *courir le risque.*'[38] Even when *Le Gars* was finally published half a century after Tsvetaeva's death, it attracted little attention.

The situation was different for Nabokov and Brodsky, of course. By 1970, when he published *Poems and Problems*, Nabokov had long been a literary celebrity, which meant that finding a publisher for his self-translated poems presented no difficulties. However, *Poems and Problems* received only a lukewarm reception. Contemporary reviewers were aware of Nabokov's literalist theory of translation and blamed it in part for the shortcomings of his book. Richmond Lattimore, the celebrated translator of Homer, noted in his review that Nabokov's insistence on 'strict fidelity' led to various 'oddities' such as inverted phrases or, in the poem 'To Russia', a bumpy metre that feels like 'driving on a flat'.[39] Konstantin Bazarov, a reviewer who did know Russian, opined that Nabokov's 'translations often turn moving Russian poems into banal and embarrassing English ones' whose 'obscurity can often only be clarified by reference to the original lucid Russian', thus implying that Nabokov's literal method not only did a disservice to Pushkin's poetry but to his own as well.[40]

As for Brodsky, his prominent status as Nobel Prize winner and American Poet Laureate also meant that he easily found a publisher for his self-translated poetry. However, the critique of Nabokov's *Poems and Problems* was rather mild compared to the vitriol poured on Brodsky's self-translations. The most vociferous attacks against his English-language writings came from two well-established British poets and critics, Christopher Reid and Craig Raine. The titles of their reviews – 'Great American disaster' and 'A reputation subject to inflation' – speak for themselves. Even among critics sympathetic to Brodsky who acknowledge his capability to write compelling poetry in English, one can find a certain apprehension about his self-translations. David M. Bethea leaves no doubt that, in his opinion, Brodsky was able to write great poetry in English.[41] Yet, when discussing the poem 'May 24, 1980', one of Brodsky's most famous texts, Bethea adds the following qualifier: 'It is an exceptionally powerful poem in Russian, especially if one has heard Brodsky read it aloud. Sadly, much of that power is lost in translation (the author's own).'[42] Bethea does not elaborate in what ways he considers the translation deficient. Others have done this job for him. In their anti-Brodsky sallies, Reid and Raine (neither of whom knew

Russian) homed in on that particular text as an especially egregious example of Brodsky's mishandling of the English language. Sceptical assessments of Brodsky's self-translation also came from more nuanced critics who were able to compare the English version with the Russian original, such as Charles Simic and Valentina Polukhina.[43]

The difficulties that Tsvetaeva, Nabokov and Brodsky faced in finding a sympathetic audience for their self-translated poetry stem in part from the fact that none of them was willing to make concessions to the taste and expectations of their target readership. Tsvetaeva's and Brodsky's insistence on preserving metre and rhyme in translation was bound to appear outlandish and artificial to a public accustomed to free verse, while Nabokov's awkward literalism flew in the face of established notions of poeticity. Furthermore, a reader attuned to syllabic verse cannot be expected to appreciate the subtleties of syllabotonic prosody, which may come across as monotonous to a French ear. The eminent émigré critic Vladimir Weidlé, who had a solid understanding of both Russian and French versification, described his reaction to Tsvetaeva's translations of Pushkin as follows: 'Tsvetaeva unwittingly exchanged French for Russian metrics. To a Russian ear these translations are superb, but as soon as I mentally switched to the French system, I noticed myself that for the French they will not sound good.'[44] Significantly, the few positive appreciations of Tsvetaeva's French translations have generally come from native speakers of Russian, i.e., from readers who do not *need* a translation. The same holds true for Brodsky's English self-translations. The most positive assessments of his English-language poetry and self-translations come from Russian-born scholars (Ishov, Berlina, Kelbert) rather than native speakers of English.

In her PhD thesis devoted to Brodsky's self-translations, Natalia Rulyova – another Russian native speaker – concludes that Brodsky's English texts should not be read as if they originated in English, but 'with an awareness of the value of their foreignness'.[45] Perhaps the secret of appreciating Tsvetaeva's and Brodsky's self-translations is that one has to read them together with the Russian original. In other words, the ideal reader of these translations may not necessarily be a monolingual French or English speaker, but someone familiar with both versions of the text. The native language of such a person is less important than the ability to read and compare both linguistic incarnations of the poem.

Mikhail Epstein, drawing on the dialogical philosophy of Mikhail Bakhtin, has theorized such an approach as 'interlation'. In Epstein's words:

With the spread of multilingual competence, translation will come to serve not as a substitute but as a dialogical counterpart to the original text. Together they will comprise a multidimensional, multilingual, 'culturally curved' discourse. Bilingual persons have no need of translation but they can enjoy an 'interlation', a contrastive juxtaposition of two apparently identical texts running simultaneously in two different languages – for example, a poem by Joseph Brodsky in the Russian original and in English autotranslation. Interlation is a multilingual variation on the same theme, where the roles of 'source' and 'target' languages are not established or are interchangeable, and one language allows the reader to perceive what another language misses or conceals.[46]

Perhaps it was this 'stereoscopic' effect created by parallel texts in two different languages that made Tsvetaeva a fertile translator and self-translator, but impeded her writing of self-standing poetry in French. As we have seen, Tsvetaeva defined the essence of poetry as translation. It is not surprising, then, that she realized her ideal of transnational and translingual poetry first and foremost as a self-translator.

Brodsky's bilingual practice shows a similar concern with 'stereo-textuality'.[47] Clearly, he came to see his existence in two linguistic spheres as a gain rather than a curse. Writing in English was more than a pragmatic decision prompted by the exigencies of living in an anglophone environment – it fulfilled a genuine creative need. Having two languages at his disposal became an existential and psychological necessity that he was unwilling to part with. In conversation with Solomon Volkov, Brodsky described his bilingualism as 'a remarkable situation psychically, because you're sitting on top of a mountain and looking down both slopes. ... [Y]ou see both slopes, and this is an absolutely special sensation. Were a miracle to occur and I were to return to Russia permanently, I would be extremely nervous at not having the option of using more than one language.'[48]

Tsvetaeva and Brodsky both shared a belief in the fundamental translatability of poetry. Nabokov's attitude was quite different, as we have seen. Even though he published his self-translated poems in a bilingual edition, the intent was hardly to achieve an Epsteinian 'interlation'. Rather, the juxtaposition of source and target text underlines the unbridgeable gap between the two versions. Following Nabokov's own theory of translation, the Russian original can never be truly recovered in the English rendition. In its inevitable failure, the 'ruined' English text validates the primacy and canonical sanctity of the Russian original.

When comparing Nabokov with Tsvetaeva and Brodsky, we arrive at a paradoxical conclusion. At first glance, Nabokov seems the most cosmopolitan of the three. Polyglot since childhood and a suave and urbane resident of multiple countries, he achieved a splendid career outside the mother tongue by turning himself in mid-life into an American writer. And yet, by declaring the adequate translation of poetry to be an impossible endeavour, and by insisting that writing in a language other than Russian was painful and problematic for him, Nabokov seemed bent on protecting his status as a bona fide Russian author, perhaps in an effort to make amends for his 'betrayal' of the native language. By contrast, Tsvetaeva is taken to be a monolingual Russian poet, and Brodsky is seen as a Russian poet with only a minor career in English. Yet Tsvetaeva and Brodsky took a more expansive position than Nabokov with regard to their linguistic identity. While the label 'Russian-American' seems fitting for Nabokov inasmuch as it indicates a conjunction of two identifiable and distinct nationalities, Tsvetaeva and, to a lesser extent, Brodsky strove to transcend a nationally circumscribed identity. Rather than being Russian *and* French, in the same way as Nabokov was Russian and American, Tsvetaeva's ambition was to be *neither* Russian *nor* French, 'in order to be everything'.

To be sure, there is something utopian about such a project, akin, perhaps, to Walter Benjamin's proclaimed messianic aim of achieving the 'hitherto inaccessible realm of reconciliation and fulfillment of languages' through the act of translation.[49] The risk in such an endeavour is of becoming unreadable to the target audience. Tsvetaeva's lack of recognition as a French poet may to a significant degree be explainable by the fact that she created for herself an ideal readership so attenuated as to be 'not of this world', as David M. Bethea has pointed out:

> Who is Tsvetaeva writing for *in this world* when late in life she translates her own *poema-skazka The Swain* (Molodets), a work already strangely inverted vis-à-vis the original, into French that, if grammatically correct, syntactically resembles Russian? Her voracious poetic appetite having exhausted the semantic, prosodic, and generic resources of her native speech, she moved into a linguistic no-man's land. By the same token, who is Brodsky writing for when he smuggles into his Russian verse extended scholastic arguments and elaborate English metaphysical conceits that can only be perceived as profoundly alien to the native tradition?[50]

Bethea's remark also shows that there is more than one way to become a translingual poet. Brodsky's translingualism manifests itself not only in his self-translations into English, but also in his later Russian-language poems, which depart significantly from the formal regularity and even the spirit of his earlier Russian verse.

Does an audience for such writings exist today? The answer to this question lies perhaps in Epstein's notion of the multilingually competent reader produced by the forces of globalization, a reader attuned to 'interlation' and 'stereotextuality'. Over the past 30 years, we have witnessed an unprecedented global dispersion of Russian speakers over three continents, leading to the emergence of a new generation of bilingual or multilingual diasporic Russians dwelling in the countries of the so-called 'Near Abroad' as well as in Israel, Germany, the United States, and elsewhere. The 'postmonolingual condition' that is affecting a growing number of today's global population and creative writers has ushered in an era of transnational mobility and linguistic mixing.

In the contemporary intellectual climate, 'innocent' self-translation has become problematic in the same way as the concept of equivalence has been met with increasing suspicion by translation theorists. Nabokov's scepticism about translatability has become a tenet of translation studies, albeit without Nabokov's gloomy conclusions. Rather than as the impossible creation of a transparent simulacrum of an original text, translation is now understood as the creative rewriting and multiplying of potential meanings. In that sense, a self-translator is forced to grapple with his or her own multiple identities, which may not always be reducible to a common denominator. Epstein explains the sea change in attitude towards language and translation as follows:

> Translation as the search for equivalence has dominated the epoch of national cultures and monolinguistic communities, which needed bridges of understanding more than rainbows of cocreativity. ... With the globalization of culture and the automatization of literal translation between languages, it is untranslatability (and nonequivalencies among languages: truly Bakhtinian polyglossia) that reach the foreground.[51]

The contemporary generation of Russian-American immigrants offers a case in point. *Vid s mosta / View from the Bridge*, a volume of self-translated poems by the bilingual poet Andrey Gritsman, presents the Russian and

English versions as 'parallel poems' rather than as bona fide translations.[52] Printed *en face*, the two texts invite the reader to discover the gaps between them. If in Nabokov's *Poems and Problems* the juxtaposition of source and target text served to underline the unbridgeable difference between them and thus to highlight the primacy of the Russian original, Gritsman's versions exist as parallel poems on an equal footing. The difference between original and translation becomes a fully intended and welcomed embodiment of transnational fluidity. In other words, the boundary, whose maintenance, according to Rogers Brubaker, is supposed to be a defining element of diasporic culture, turns here into something like a porous membrane.

As David M. Bethea argues (in this volume), by 'gradually morph[ing] from a speaker exiled from Russia to a peripatetic expat tourist' and by 'splicing together' or 'interbreeding' different national traditions, Brodsky, with his linguistic hybridity, may be 'revealing of new "genre-less" versions of authenticity'. As Bethea shows, this move was to some extent prefigured by Nabokov's aesthetically tinged scientific interest in the evolution and diversity of the natural world, although the notion of exile, and thus of 'loss', coloured his aporetic understanding of poetic translation. Tsvetaeva's more expansive notion of a disembodied 'spirit of poetry', resembling to some extent Viacheslav Ivanov's religiously grounded ecumenicity, comes closer to an ideal of universality beyond any national incarnation. Does this mean that Tsvetaeva's utopian quest for a poetry untethered from any national embodiment is about to become a reality? Probably not in the absolute form that Tsvetaeva imagined. Nevertheless, we seem to be witnessing the emergence of a new kind of diaspora whose members do not shed the original language and culture through assimilation, but transcend it in a new form of transcultural polyglossia, rendering obsolete the traditional dichotomies between '*svoi*' and '*chuzhoi*', the 'native' and the 'foreign'. It has to remain an open question whether the term 'diaspora', according to Galin Tihanov an archaic and dated notion dependent on the concept of national immutability and tribal solidarity, will still apply to this new formation.[53]

## Acknowledgements

I would like to thank the participants of the workshop on 'Redefining the Russian literary diaspora (1918–2018)' in May 2018 for their stimulating feedback. I am particularly indebted to David M. Bethea and Maria Rubins for their thoughtful reading of my original draft and helpful suggestions for improvement.

# Notes

1   Brubaker 2005, 6 (Brubaker's emphasis).
2   Platt 2019, 4.
3   See the chapter 'Gary Shteyngart: The New Immigrant Chic' in Wanner 2011, 95–133.
4   Brubaker 2005, 13.
5   Rilke and Zwetajewa 1992, 76 (English translation cited from *Letters*, 221).
6   A more detailed discussion of Tsvetaeva's, Nabokov's and Brodsky's self-translations, including the close reading of concrete parallel texts in two languages, can be found in Wanner 2020, 76–153.
7   Yildiz 2012, 2.
8   See Ramazani 2009, 24.
9   There has been a steady stream of recent conferences, special issues of journals, monographs and edited volumes devoted to self-translation. The bibliography on self-translation maintained by Eva Gentes at Heinrich Heine University in Düsseldorf has reached the impressive length of 212 pages in its latest iteration, containing over 1,000 entries of published and over 200 entries of unpublished items.
10   Hokenson and Munson 2007, 161.
11   Perry 1981, 181.
12   Baer 2016, 14.
13   'Avtobiografiia', in Tsvetaeva 1994–5, 5:6.
14   See Tsvetaeva's statements in 'Otvet na anketu' (1926), Tsvetaeva 1994–5, 4:622, and 'Avtobiografiia', 5: 6–7.
15   Rilke and Zwetajewa 1992, 76 (English translation cited from *Letters*, 221). The quote imputed to Goethe is nowhere to be found in Goethe's works. Perhaps Tsvetaeva is referring to an entry in Goethe's diary in 1770: 'Wer in einer fremden Sprache schreibt oder dichtet, ist wie einer, der in einem fremden Haus wohnt' ('He who writes or composes poetry in a foreign language is like someone who lives in a house not his own'). See Rilke and Zwetajewa 1992, 235, note 134.
16 ·   Cited in Etkind 1996, 237. Unless otherwise noted, all English translations of French, German or Russian quotes are my own.
17   See the letters to Pasternak of 22 May and 10 July 1926 in Tsvetaeva 1994–5, 6:249, 264 (English translation in *Letters*, 137, 232).
18   *Le Gars* appeared in two different editions in 1991 and 1992. Page references given in the text refer to the 1992 edition. The Russian quotes from *Mólodets* are identified by line numbers.
19   Neither of the two existing monographs on *Mólodets* (Hauschild 2004 and Lane 2009) discusses the French version of the poem. The most extensive comments on *Le Gars* are provided by Etkind 1992 and 1996. A brief discussion (based on only a partial knowledge of the text, which was then still unpublished) can also be found in Makin 1993, 309–15. Gasparov 1997, 267–78, discusses Tsvetaeva's Franco-Russian metrical experiments. French Slavists, with the exception of a 2019 essay by the Russian-born Anna Lushenkova Foscolo, have shown no interest in *Le Gars*.
20   Hauschild 2004, 146.
21   Etkind 1992, 271.
22   The only exception thus far is Wanner 2020, 112–34.
23   Nabokov 1970, 14.
24   Nabokov 1991, 316–17.
25   Cited in Shakhovskaia 1991, 22.
26   Nabokov's self-translated fiction and memoirs have been discussed by a number of scholars (see, in particular, Grayson 1977, Beaujour 1995 and García de la Puente 2015). None of these critics addresses Nabokov's self-translated poetry.

27 See the chapter 'Beyond *Eugene Onegin* (1965–1977)' in Shvabrin 2019, 311–38.
28 Brodsky's self-translated poems have attracted more critical interest than those of Tsvetaeva and Nabokov. Berlina 2014 offers close readings of the Russian and English versions of multiple key poems. Useful information can also be found in Ishov 2008.
29 See the testimony by Kudrova 1998, 154.
30 Brodsky 1986, 104.
31 'Nastignut' utrachennoe vremia' (*Vremia i My* 97, 1979), in Brodskii 2007, 123.
32 Kelbert 2016, 146.
33 Polukhina 1998, 52.
34 Brodsky 2000, 130–32. For a detailed comparison of the English self-translation with the Russian original, see Berlina 2014, 9–45.
35 Brodsky 2000, 414–16.
36 Rulyova 2002, 112–17. A discussion of Brodsky's self-translation of 'Portrait of Tragedy' can also be found in Nesterov 2001, 251–3.
37 Cited in Tsvetaeva 2005, 297.
38 Letter to Nanny Wunderli-Volkart, 6 March 1931, in Tsvetaeva 1994–5, 7:361.
39 Lattimore 1971, 506–7.
40 Bazarov 1972, xii.
41 See Bethea's analysis of Brodsky's English-language poem 'To my daughter' in Loseff and Polukhina 1999, 240–57.
42 Bethea 1994, 13.
43 See Simic 2000 and Polukhina 2007.
44 'O poetakh i poezii', quoted in Gasparov 1997, 278.
45 Rulyova 2002, 144.
46 Epstein 2004, 50.
47 The term is Epstein's. See Epstein 2004, 51.
48 Volkov 1998, 185–6.
49 Benjamin 1992, 76.
50 Bethea 1994, 290–1 (Bethea's italics). Tsvetaeva's self-translation of *Mólodets* was not really 'late in life', but a similar argument could perhaps be made for her French translations of Mikhail Lermontov's poems written in 1941 shortly before her death.
51 Epstein 2004, 51.
52 For a discussion of Gritsman, see Wanner 2020, 155–61.
53 See Tihanov's afterword to this volume.

# Bibliography

Baer, Brian James. *Translation and the Making of Modern Russian Literature*. New York: Bloomsbury Academic, 2016.
Bazarov, Kostantin. 'Poet's problems', *Books and Bookmen* (October 1972), xi–xii.
Beaujour, Elizabeth. 'Translation and self-translation'. In *The Garland Companion to Vladimir Nabokov*, edited by Vladimir E. Alexandrov, 714–24. New York: Garland, 1995.
Benjamin, Walter. 'The task of the translator'. Translated by Harry Zohn. In *Theories of Translation: An anthology of essays from Dryden to Derrida*, edited by Rainer Schulte and John Biguenet, 71–82. Chicago: University of Chicago Press, 1992. (Originally published 1923.)
Berlina, Alexandra. *Brodsky Translating Brodsky: Poetry in self-translation*. New York: Bloomsbury Academic, 2014.
Bethea, David. *Joseph Brodsky and the Creation of Exile*. Princeton, NJ: Princeton University Press, 1994.
Bibliography: Autotraduzione / autotraducción / self-translation (XXXIX edition: July 2020), edited by Eva Gentes. https://www.self-translation.blogspot.com (accessed 3 September 2020).
Brodsky, Joseph. *Less than One: Selected essays*. New York: Farrar, Straus and Giroux, 1986.
Brodsky, Joseph. *Collected Poems in English*, edited by Ann Kjellberg. New York: Farrar, Straus and Giroux, 2000.
Brodsky, Joseph [Brodskii, Iosif]. *Kniga interv'iu*, edited by V. Polukhina. Fourth edition. Moscow: Zakharov, 2007.

Brubaker, Rogers. 'The "diaspora" diaspora', *Ethnic and Racial Studies* 28(1) (2005): 1–19.

Epstein, Mikhail. 'The unasked question: What would Bakhtin say?', *Common Knowledge* 10(1) (2004): 42–60.

Etkind, Efim. '"Molodets" Tsvetaevoi: Original i avtoperevod', *Slavia* 61(3) (1992): 265–84.

Etkind, Efim. 'Marina Cvetaeva, poète français'. In *Un chant de vie: Marina Tsvétaeva. Actes du Colloque international de l'Université Paris IV*, 237–62. Paris: YMCA Press, 1996.

Forster, Leonard. *The Poet's Tongues: Multilingualism in literature*. London: Cambridge University Press, 1970.

García de la Puente, Inés. 'Bilingual Nabokov: Memories and memoirs in self-translation', *Slavic and East European Journal* 59(4) (2015): 585–608.

Gasparov, M. L. 'Russkii Mólodets i frantsuzskii Mólodets: Dva stikhovykh eksperimenta'. In M. L. Gasparov, *Izbrannye trudy*, vol. 3: O stikhe, 267–78. Moscow: Iazyki russkoi kul'tury, 1997.

Grayson, Jane. *Nabokov Translated: A comparison of Nabokov's Russian and English prose*. Oxford: Oxford University Press, 1977.

Gritsman, Andrey. *Vid s mosta / View from the Bridge*. New York: Slovo-Word, 1998.

Hauschild, Christiane. *Häretische Transgressionen: Das Märchenpoem 'Molodec' von Marina Cvetaeva*. Göttingen: Wallstein Verlag, 2004.

Hokenson, Jan Walsh and Marcella Munson. *The Bilingual Text: History and theory of literary self-translation*. Manchester: St Jerome, 2007.

Ishov, Zakhar. '"Post-horse of civilisation": Joseph Brodsky translating Joseph Brodsky: Towards a new theory of Russian-English poetry translation'. PhD dissertation, Free University of Berlin, 2008.

Kelbert, Eugenia. 'Joseph Brodsky's supralingual evolution'. In *Das literarische Leben der Mehrsprachigkeit: Methodische Erkundungen*, edited by Till Dembeck and Anne Uhrmacher, 143–63. Heidelberg: Universitätsverlag Winter, 2016.

Kudrova, Irma. '"Eto oshelomliaet...": Iosif Brodskii o Marine Tsvetaevoi'. In *Iosif Brodskii: tvorchestvo, lichnost', sud'ba. Itogi trekh konferentsii*, 154–60. St Petersburg: Zhurnal 'Zvezda', 1998.

Lane, Tora. *Rendering the Sublime: A reading of Marina Tsvetaeva's fairy-tale poem The Swain*. Stockholm: Acta Universitatis Stockholmiensis, 2009.

Lattimore, Richmond. 'Poetry chronicle', *Hudson Review* 24(3) (1971): 499–510.

*Letters: Summer 1926. Boris Pasternak, Marina Tsvetayeva, Rainer Maria Rilke*, edited by Yevgeny Pasternak, Yelena Pasternak and Konstantin M. Azadovsky. Translated by Margaret Wettlin, Walter Arndt and Jamey Gambrell. New York: New York Review of Books, 2001.

Loseff, Lev and Valentina Polukhina, eds. *Joseph Brodsky: The art of a poem*. New York: St. Martin's Press, 1999.

Lushenkova Foscolo, Anna. 'L'Autotraduction dans la poésie de Marina Tsvetaeva'. In *Plurilinguisme et autotraduction*, edited by Anna Lushenkova Foscolo and Malgorzata Smorag-Goldberg, 137–58. Paris: Éditions EUR'ORBEM, 2019.

Makin, Michael. *Marina Tsvetaeva: Poetics of appropriation*. Oxford: Clarendon Press, 1993.

Nabokov, Vladimir. *Poems and Problems*. New York: McGraw-Hill, 1970.

Nabokov, Vladimir. *The Annotated Lolita*. Edited by Alfred Appel, Jr. New York: Vintage Books, 1991.

Nesterov, Anton. 'Avtoperevod kak avtokommentarii', *Inostrannaia literatura* 7 (2001): 249–55.

Perry, Menakhem. 'Thematic and structural shifts in autotranslations by bilingual Hebrew-Yiddish writers: The case of Mendele Mokher Sforim', *Poetics Today* 2(4) (1981):181–92.

Platt, Kevin M. F. 'Introduction: Putting Russian cultures in place'. In *Global Russian Cultures*, edited by Kevin M. F. Platt, 3–17. Madison: University of Wisconsin Press, 2019.

Polukhina, Valentina. 'Angliiskii Brodskii'. In *Iosif Brodskii: Tvorchestvo, lichnost', sud'ba: Itogi trekh konferentsii*, 49–59. St Petersburg: Zhurnal 'Zvezda', 1998.

Polukhina, Valentina. 'Literaturnoe vospriiatie Brodskogo v Anglii', *Storony Sveta* 9 (2007). http://www.stosvet.net/9/polukhina/ (accessed 3 September 2020).

Ramazani, Jahan. *A Transnational Poetics*. Chicago: University of Chicago Press, 2009.

Rilke, Rainer Maria and Marina Zwetajewa. *Rainer Maria Rilke und Marina Zwetajewa: Ein Gespräch in Briefen*, edited by Konstantin M. Asadowski. Frankfurt am Main: Insel Verlag, 1992.

Raine, Craig. 'A reputation subject to inflation', *Financial Times*, 16 November 1996, 19.

Reid, Christopher. 'Great American disaster', *London Review of Books*, 8 December 1988: 17–18.

Rulyova, Natalya. 'Joseph Brodsky: Translating oneself'. PhD thesis, University of Cambridge, 2002.

Shakhovskaia, Zinaida. *V poiskakh Nabokova: Otrazheniia*. Moscow: Kniga, 1991.

Shteyngart, Gary. *The Russian Debutante's Handbook*. New York: Riverhead Books, 2002.

Shvabrin, Stanislav. *Between Rhyme and Reason: Vladimir Nabokov, translation, and dialogue*. Toronto: University of Toronto Press, 2019.

Simic, Charles. 'Working for the dictionary', *New York Review of Books*, 19 October 2000. http://www.nybooks.com/articles/2000/10/19/working-for-the-dictionary/ (accessed 3 September 2020).

Tsvetaeva, Marina. *Le Gars*. Sauve: Clémence Hiver, 1991.

Tsvetaeva, Marina. *Le Gars*. Préface de Efim Etkind. Paris: Des femmes, 1992.

Tsvetaeva, Marina. *Sobranie sochinenii v semi tomakh*. 7 vols. Moscow: Ellis Lak, 1994–5.

Tsvetaeva, Marina. *Mólodets*. Edited by Natal'ia Teletova. St Petersburg: DORN, 2003.

Tsvetaeva, Marina. *Mólodets/Le Gars*. Moscow: Ellis Lak, 2005.

Volkov, Solomon. *Conversations with Joseph Brodsky: A poet's journey through the twentieth century*. Translated by Marian Schwartz. New York: Free Press, 1998.

Wanner, Adrian. *Out of Russia: Fictions of a new translingual diaspora*. Evanston, IL: Northwestern University Press, 2011.

Wanner, Adrian. *The Bilingual Muse: Self-translation among Russian poets*. Evanston, IL: Northwestern University Press, 2020.

Yildiz, Yasemin. *Beyond the Mother Tongue: The postmonolingual condition*. New York: Fordham University Press, 2012.

# 5
# Evolutionary biology and 'writing the diaspora': the cases of Theodosius Dobzhansky and Vladimir Nabokov
David M. Bethea

Вопрос о том: *что есть* известный предмет? – никогда не совпадает с вопросом: *из чего* или откуда *произошел* этот предмет?

The question '*What is* a certain subject?' never coincides with the question '*Whence arose* that subject?'

Solovyov, 'Krasota v prirode' (Beauty in nature), 1889

'It is not in their germinal state that beings manifest themselves but in their fluorescence.'

Teilhard de Chardin, *Phenomenon of Man*, 1955

'We are right in saying quite literally, in the human, cerebral sense, that nature grows wiser as time passes.'

Nabokov, 'Father's Butterflies'
(unfinished continuation of *Dar*, late 1930s)

'Nothing in biology makes sense except in the light of evolution.'

Dobzhansky, paraphrasing Teilhard de Chardin,
addressing the National Association of
Biology Teachers, 1972

# Introduction

The very idea of diaspora begins with the notion of mass and force: the expulsion of a people from their homeland. In the Russian context we can refer to historical examples of exiles, individuals like Andrei Kurbsky, Nikolai Turgenev, and Alexander Herzen and Nikolai Ogarev, but we can't speak accurately of diaspora until we come to the mass expulsions (self- or state-imposed) that arrived in the wake of the Russian Revolution. In the century that has passed since 1917 the conceptual binaries that so starkly defined one's existential choices at the time, most notably centre/periphery and Soviet/exile, have gradually morphed, blurred and otherwise interspersed into different linguistic and cross-cultural combinations. Furthermore, as the process has evolved and as the cultural forces on the ground have helped stimulate different relationships between author and audience, the tension between national and transnational – between preserving an accent on the values of the native tradition and taking a position that acknowledges the native tradition but also sees itself as moving beyond it – has oscillated accordingly.

My chapter takes a different tack on what Maria Rubins calls the 'emancipation of the diasporic "periphery" from the metropolitan "center"'. I propose to use terminology and logic from the discipline of evolutionary biology to make an argument about where this emancipation is going in the cultural realm. In the first part of the chapter I focus on two Russian exiles, Theodosius Dobzhansky (1900–75) and Vladimir Nabokov (1899–1977), who grew up in the shadow of 1917 and went on to establish careers of international distinction. These exemplars had their origins, which I examine, and their career arcs, which project a certain momentum – a momentum that I'd like to suggest points beyond their individual achievements. Where that momentum appears to be pointing is the real subject of the chapter, which is the primary focus of the second part. The reasons I compare and contrast these two Russian exiles are that they were almost exact coevals who were strongly influenced by the great Russian writers and thinkers of the pre-revolutionary period and that evolutionary biology lies at the core of their personhoods alongside their 'Russianness'. In a not trivial way it was their thinking as evolutionary biologists that led both of them on a path from the national to the transnational. Also, their work on such concepts as speciation, adaptive landscape and genetic drift turns out to have useful implications for understanding the cultural patterns observable in 'writing the diaspora'.

Before we start it might be well to identify a few of the more salient cutting-edge issues in contemporary evolutionary biology that will shape our discussion as we attempt to navigate the crowded path from strict biological evolution in primitive organisms to advanced-stage cultural evolution in *Homo sapiens*, including how literary works are produced in diasporic conditions. Obviously, the scientific literature is vast here and the shorthand needed to address a non-specialist audience threatens to cause a kind of intellectual vertigo by what it is forced to leave out. Be that as it may, we should at least try to get the organizing principles right. It all begins with 'biological relativity', which is defined by Denis Noble as the idea 'that there is no privileged level of causation in biology; living organisms are multi-level open stochastic systems in which the behaviour at any level depends on higher and lower levels and cannot be fully understood in isolation'.[1] Thus, organisms are *multi-level* in that regardless of which level we are observing – molecule, cell, tissue, organ – there are initial and boundary conditions that serve to regulate, in a functional way, the lower-level components by higher-level properties. And they are *open* and *stochastic* because they react to stimuli from the outside in order to adapt to their surroundings and because these reactions are not predetermined, i.e. they are random. In other words, at every level we encounter feedback loops that make it possible for the level to function properly. These feedback loops apply all the way up the line into the realm of cultural evolution, only at some point their purposiveness (higher regulating lower) shifts from strictly 'neo-Darwinian' (chemistry, molecular biology, DNA coding for amino acids) to 'Lamarckian' (social learning, construction and transmission of information through symbolic systems).

Next, language, human beings' special domain, is no longer thought of, or only thought of, in Chomskyan terms, as something inherent to the human mind, a universal grammar 'organ' waiting to be turned on. Rather it can now be seen, as Daniel Dor has recently argued, as a 'communication technology', the very first, that grew out of our social nature. (Although Dor insists on the idea of 'technology' as a way of linking archaic humankind with later developments like the printing press and social networks, in its original instantiation language might be better conceptualized as 'technique' or social orientation, a precursor of technology.) The techniques of social communication (gestures, sounds, touching, 'body language', etc.) allowed us, *before* individual speakers were adapted for a specific language and while we were still living in pre-linguistic societies, to begin to bridge the gap between experiential, sensory perceptions (what we are seeing in the here and now at the campfire or on the savannah and communicating non-linguistically) and the imagination (what is not directly in front of us but can be pictured in the mind's eye). Plans and strategies for hunting and gathering began to be communicated socially. Dor calls this linguistically based functional capacity the 'instruction of imagination'. 'First we invented language. Then language changed us.'[2]

Finally, as modern-day scientists have studied the shift from the purely chemical/biological to the cultural/learned, two additional areas of interest central to our discussion have emerged. First, there is the birth of the aesthetic in nature, which is inextricably linked to female choice in sexual selection and which, as the inflection point where the idea of the attractive/beautiful emerged, created the neuronal and social pathways that led to our interest in art, in this case literary art. We will look at how aesthetic desire *coevolves* in a loop involving the aroused subject and the ever more flamboyantly desired object that is not only about the passing on of healthy genes or the attracting of a protective male (i.e. the neo-Darwinist view) but is also, and more directly, about the arbitrary, non-utilitarian allure of the object per se, and here again we come to the cognitive edge of the birth of artistic representation. Second, while considerable attention has been paid to the parallels between how the genetic (supposedly 'non-thinking') and symbolic (supposedly 'thinking') systems work, the fact that these parallels already appear 'linguistically organized' without being established scientifically as such cries out for further examination. If a gene's nucleotides can be seen as 'letters', and if the gene itself can be looked at as a 'word' (i.e. it 'codes' for a certain function – 'make x molecule'), and if the gene in connection with other genes can produce, 'sentence-like', a complex cellular function, then is this set of parallels an analogy or something more organically joined at the hip, so to speak? How is it that the latent information in gene sequences and the implied meaning in a literary text can be stored and activated in the future?[3] Are these linguistic metaphors only words or are they also somehow bodies?

## Dobzhansky and Nabokov

The *Weltanschauung*, some components of which are sketched in the pages that follow, was nurtured, modified, and corrected for something close to half a century. Its germs arose when the author was in his teens, and became naively enraptured with evolutionary biology. The intellectual stimulation derived from the works of

Darwin was pitted against that arising from reading Dostoevsky, to a lesser extent Tolstoy, and philosophers such as Soloviev and Bergson. Some sort of reconciliation or harmonization seemed necessary. The urgency of finding a meaning of life grew in the bloody tumult of the Russian Revolution, when life became insecure and its sense least intelligible.[4]

Thus opens Dobzhansky's preface to his book *The Biology of Ultimate Concern* (1967), as he sets the stage for making a case for biology as the discipline underpinning all disciplines, any flexing of our intellectual muscles towards issues of 'ultimate concern' (i.e. philosophy and metaphysics) necessarily growing *organically* out of a basic understanding of biology. In order to create a worldview for his anxious teenage self beset by the threat of social and political upheaval, he engaged in a cognitive tug-of-war between the 'hard science' of Darwin, which 'enraptured' him, and the literary and philosophical works of Dostoevsky and Solovyov, which he 'pitted against' the laws of evolution with equal passion.

Nabokov's origins nest in telling ways within Dobzhansky's. Not only was his engagement with modern evolutionary biology under the influence of Darwinian thought by the time he became smitten with butterfly hunting and collecting, it too was embedded from the start in alternate strivings between the worlds of art and science.[5] The common denominator here is Vladimir Solovyov, Russian Symbolism's polymath *predtecha* ('precursor'). In 1885, the Moscow Psychological Society, principal hatchery of Russian neo-idealist thought, was founded at Moscow University. Solovyov's ideas played a seminal role in the movement's inception and his articles featured prominently in its leading journal *Questions of Philosophy and Psychology*. In a real sense, Solovyov, originally trained as a naturalist, was the filter through which Russian philosophy absorbed Darwinian science. The philosopher's long essay entitled 'Beauty in nature' ('Krasota v prirode', 1889), which examines the emergence of the beautiful (design, coloration, euphony, etc.) in different species all the while parsing meticulously, and approvingly, Darwin's findings, appeared simultaneously with the Society's early flowering. Furthermore, with its implied Symbolist message of another force ('Sophia') working through matter to spiritualize it and with its interest in beauty or form as a catalyst of nature 'thinking itself forward', this is a text that the early-career Nabokov would have found congenial. For Solovyov, the nightingale's song and the randy tomcat's urgent cries contain a difference: both involve a call to mating but in the former that urge is transformed into an 'excess' of enchanting sound that is more than it needs to be for mere reproduction and survival.

Now let us look at Nabokov and Dobzhansky at mid-career, once they have fully established themselves and followed their unique talents and interests beyond their nativist origins. In both cases, their love of pure science, lepidoptery and genetics respectively, grounds them and provides a direction out of the parochial as they extend their career arcs. Nabokov's passion for beauty in language and artistic composition are natural extensions of his attraction to compositionist or organismic beauty in butterflies; likewise, Dobzhansky's internationally recognized expertise in the more non-standard aspects of speciation with regard to population genetics leads him eventually to take up questions of a philosophical and moral character.

One of the most powerful theories in the history of evolutionary study involves a metaphor, Sewall Wright's notion of 'adaptive landscape'. In Edward Larson's telling,

> Natural selection should drive populations up toward peaks of fitness … but could not fully account for one species branching into many. Branching would require subpopulations of organisms to travel down from their current peaks of fitness, across valleys of relative unfitness, and back up other peaks of fitness – all through a process of incremental genetic variation… . If the subpopulation were small enough and subject to intense inbreeding (which stimulates genetic interactions and brings out recessive traits), then selection might not operate to maximize its adaptive fitness. In his [Wright's] metaphor, the subpopulation would move downhill and begin wandering across the valley. Wright called the phenomenon 'genetic drift'.[6]

Clearly, Wright is not suggesting that something other than natural selection is drawing these subpopulations into valleys where there is less chance of future group survival. Nor is he implying that increased inbreeding along with the production of more recessive traits is in any way purposeful. But his main conclusion, new at the time, was that 'genetic drift functioned in a "shifting balance" with natural selection to generate new species through alternating periods of genetic restriction (or "bottlenecks") and expansion'.[7] The question seemed to ask itself: why don't the fit simply become more fit? Why don't those trending to the less fit *automatically* disappear?

Wright's theory is pertinent to our discussion in the following way. Before emigrating to America in 1927 Dobzhansky had been heavily influenced by the great Moscow geneticist Sergei Chetverikov, pioneer of the principle that 'recessive mutations create hidden reservoirs of genetic diversity within populations on which selection can act when conditions warrant'.[8] Once in the States, Dobzhansky became enamoured of Wright's adaptive-landscape metaphor when hearing him at a genetics congress in 1932. Clearly he was making the connection between Chetverikov's principle that recessive mutations can contribute in unpredictable ways ('hidden reservoirs') to a population's genetic diversity and Wright's seminal metaphor involving hills and valleys of viability. Thereafter, Dobzhansky collaborated with Wright and developed the latter's ideas further. His first major book, *Genetics and the Origin of Species*, appeared in 1937, as Nabokov was completing *The Gift* but before he wrote 'Father's butterflies'. Not only was Dobzhansky one of the major players (the so-called 'four horsemen') in the great Darwin–Mendel synthesis of the 1930s–1940s – a synthesis which brought into fruitful contact Darwinian natural selection with the rediscovery and application of modern Mendelian genetics – he was also a world leader in refining the concept of species, which became one of Nabokov's keenest interests once he joined the Museum of Comparative Zoology (MCZ) at Harvard in 1941. Indeed, the geneticist's definition of species, one of the most complicated concepts in all of biology, is still a tour de force of precise denotative phrasing. In the words of his biographer,

> It [Dobzhansky's work on the genetics of translocations and his study of sex determination] led in 1935 to a formulation of the concept of (sexually reproducing) species still accepted today: 'That stage of the evolutionary process at which the once actually or potentially inter-breeding array of forms becomes segregated in two or more separate arrays which are physiologically incapable of inter-breeding.'[9]

Thus, Dobzhansky's signature stance of foregrounding the vast genetic diversity within a given species, so that recessive genes and alleles become potentially significant in their own right in determining aspects of speciation, surely appealed to the Nabokov who opposed the domination of the predictably unfit by the predictably fit. Intriguingly, however, Dobzhansky's use of the latest microscopy in the lab, his method of counting genes on chromosomes and marshalling statistics to identify new species, did *not* appeal to Nabokov during his MCZ tenure because it 'remov[ed] the morphological moment' – an understandable objection when we take into account Nabokov's painstaking, indeed one might say lovingly laborious, efforts to track intermediate steps in speciation by studying the tiny genitalic features of his butterflies.[10] Nabokov followed Dobzhansky's work with some interest and corresponded with him in 1954. Dobzhansky was nominated for the Nobel Prize in 1975, shortly before his death, but did not receive it.

For his part, Nabokov by mid-career has shed any Symbolist pretensions of 'life-creation' / *zhiznetvorchestvo* (Blok for him is a kind of demonic revenant), but the idea of *potustoronnost'* (some sort of mind 'out there') is still very much with him. What he also hasn't shed are his earlier notions of a Solovyovian compositionist beauty (and its incompletely formed twin 'ugliness' or 'lack of form' / *bezobrazie*), which become, as Nabokov's work matures, the organic world's expression of 'intelligence', but an intelligence now complicated by contemporaneous discoveries in biochemistry, microbiology and population genetics.

Recall that what overarches species development for the Solovyov of 'Beauty in nature' are three impulses: 1) the 'internal essence or *prima materia* of life, that is, the urge or desire to live, to feed oneself and to reproduce oneself'; 2) 'the form [*obraz*] of that life, that is, the morphological and physiological conditions according to which each species' feeding and reproduction (along with other secondary functions) are determined'; and 3) 'the biological goal – not in the sense of an external teleology, but as an aspect of comparative anatomy, which determines with regard to the whole of the organic world the place and significance of those particular forms which in each species are sustained by food and perpetuated via reproduction'.[11] It is this third, 'mereological' factor, which is simultaneously aware of form and function, biological need and morphological response, and of how the parts relate to the whole and the whole to the parts, that most intrigues Solovyov. Here one could argue, by the way, that Solovyov was ahead of his time, his conceptual framework (purposiveness without 'external teleology') essentially anticipating the 'biological relativity' position of leading contemporary scientists like Denis Noble.

To return to the example of the nightingale's song, Solovyov fully acknowledges that the utilitarian impulse (mating) is still present in the material result, but it is precisely the fact that the biological need is *transformed* along the way into something of genuine aesthetic value, and not just for the human listener, but, as Solovyov would have us believe, *for the bird itself*, that shows the philosopher-poet to be, once again, prescient. As Richard Prum has lavishly demonstrated in his book *The Evolution of Beauty* (2017), the females of different bird species base their choice of mate on the *aesthetic* traits of the males' plumage, wing ornamentation, bower construction and mating movements, all of which emerge over time *arbitrarily* (i.e. not as a result of adaptive/genetic health in the male or his potential offspring); that is to say, the trait of a certain bower construction and the female's receptiveness to that construction *coevolve* according to aesthetic rather than utilitarian criteria. 'Culture' begins to happen at the point when the female is not coerced but actively chooses the male she fancies. Or, as Solovyov formulates it more than a century before Prum,

> In the nightingale's song the matter-based [*material'nyi*] sexual instinct is clothed in the form of lovely sounds. In this instance the objective acoustic expression of sexual desire completely occludes its material origin; it acquires an independent meaning and can be abstracted from its most immediate physiological motivation... . This song is the transfiguration of the sexual instinct, the freeing of it from crude physiological fact – it is the animal's sexual instinct realizing in itself the *idea of love*, while an amorous tomcat's cries on a roof are simply the expression of the physiological effect – of not being able to control itself. In the latter example it is the matter-related impulse that completely predominates, while in the former that impulse is brought into balance through ideal form.[12]

Hence beauty in the natural world, whose appreciation has long been presumed to be a wholly human construct, is, according to Solovyov, 'the transfiguration of matter through its embodiment [*voploshchenie*] of another, supra-material element'.[13] The philosopher will not allow something of natural beauty to be flattened out into the sex drive, which is the only way the neo-Darwinians will explain the mating impulse; he recognizes that drive as a starting point, but he refuses to rely on it as an explanation of the thing in and of itself.

Nabokov, I suggest, is both a direct descendant of Solovyov and an uncanny precursor of Prum in his reasoning about the presence of compositionist (parts to whole, whole to parts) beauty in nature. What is uniquely Nabokovian, however, and what is a key ingredient of his transnational fame, is *the way he aligns nature's 'aesthetic wisdom' to the artistic process in humans*. Let us now look at one of Nabokov's well-known statements in favour of what today would be termed, in most cases pejoratively, as 'intelligent design' (ID). Here, in *The Gift*, he describes how Konstantin Kirillovich passes down to Fyodor his special knowledge of mimicry in butterflies:

He told me about the odours of butterflies – musk and vanilla; about the voices of butterflies; about the piercing sound given out by the monstrous caterpillar of a Malayan hawkmoth, an improvement on the mouselike squeak of our Death's Head moth …. He told me about the incredible artistic wit of mimetic disguise, which was not explainable by the struggle for existence (the rough haste of evolution's unskilled forces), was too refined for the mere deceiving of accidental predators, feathered, scaled and otherwise (not very fastidious, but then not too fond of butterflies), and seemed to have been invented by some waggish artist precisely for the intelligent eyes of man.[14]

Even Nabokov's biographer suggests that the author is overplaying his hand in passages such as this, that he is giving too much credit to nature's intricate design and not enough credit to the predator's ability to detect the prey behind the camouflage:

One of his [Nabokov's] main props for still retaining, a century after Darwin, his deep conviction that there was some form of Mind or Design behind life was the case of mimicry. He was convinced mimicry could not be accounted for by its protective role because it exceeded predators' powers of perception and seemed almost designed by some waggish artist for human discovery. But research from the 1950s to the present on many facets of the subject and in many species has presented conclusive evidence for the protective advantage of mimicry, the extraordinary perceptual discrimination of predators, and the power of natural selection to account completely for even the most complex instances of mimicry.[15]

True, nature may not exactly be a 'waggish artist' and a predator's skill at perceiving may still come down to 'the struggle for existence (the rough haste of evolution's unskilled forces)', but with recent research like Prum's it seems indisputable that there is an aesthetic impulse in evolutionary development, that this impulse has to do with choice (the rudiments of 'mind'), and that Nabokov was not wrong about that.

As we know, Nabokov's core interest as a scientist was more in the accurate naming of biological form, especially the microscopically observed genitalic features of his beloved Blue butterflies, than in entering into metaphysical debates about an 'intelligence' that put that form there in the first place. 'Harvard's lepidopterists [at the MCZ in the 1940s] complained that he prioritized "description" over "synthesis".'[16]

It could be argued, however, that it was the 'reverse engineering' situations, where the function of something is understood only after the fact of its appearance, and where that appearance could not be predicted beforehand, that most fired Nabokov's imagination. According to this line of thought, there are phenomena of resemblance in nature that are not explainable strictly in terms of adaptation and directionality. These are those knight's moves ('nature's rhymes') that so appealed to Nabokov the artist. To take an example from 'Father's butterflies', a natural selection process that does *not* take place when we expect it to but still eventuates in survival is the caterpillar of the Siberian owlet moth found on the chumara plant: the colouring of the insect's fetlocks and dorsal shape appears at the end of summer, while the lookalike shrub blooms in May. Following the logic of adaptation, 'nature [has] defrauded one of the parties'.[17]

But more to our point, how is nature's ability to create patterned surprises 'mimicked' in Nabokov's play with ingenious feedback loops in his greatest art, including *The Gift*? To start with, the very structure of the novel, its blurring in and out of the 'I' and 'he' narrators, its tying-up of the plot with an Onegin stanza, itself a pseudo-genetic map for creating infinite meanings out of a single string (rhyme scheme), its merging of personal and literary history ('from Pushkin Avenue to Gogol Street') – all this challenges the reader to understand such patterning as 'open' or 'closed', or somehow both (i.e. a feedback loop). Might this complex layering not be the representation in words of that same biological relativity detailed by Denis Noble, only in this instance the multi-level dance is the movement of biological life as it becomes *cultured, conscious, authored*? Likewise, do we explain the spirals and spheres that embed themselves in Nabokov's speculations about time by tracing them back to Symbolists' notions of cosmic return, to Bergson's cloud of 'creative evolution', or to some deep-seated biological-cum-cognitive intuition? 'The spiral is a spiritualized circle. In the spiral form, the circle, uncoiled, unwound, has ceased to be vicious; it has been set free... . A colored spiral in a small ball of glass, this is how I see my own life.'[18]

Here Nabokov again joins hands with Dobzhansky, who describes the compositionist evolution of the individual organism in spiral-shaped terms thus:

> An individual begins its existence as a fertilized ovum, and proceeds to develop through a complex series of maneuvers. Body structures and functions that are formed fit together not because they are contrived by some inherent directiveness named 'telos', but because

the development of an individual is a part of the cyclic (*or, more precisely, spiral* [emphasis added]) sequence of the developments of the ancestors. Individual development seems to be attracted by its end rather than impelled by its beginning [NB *reverse engineering*]; organs in a developing individual are formed for future uses because in the evolution they were formed for contemporaneous utility. Individual development is understandable as a part of the evolutionary development of the species, not the other way around.[19]

Fyodor says of his father's prose, which he gets closer to by reading Pushkin, that

the very body, flow, and structure of the whole work [*Butterflies and Moths of the Russian Empire*] touches me in the professional sense of a craft handed down. I suddenly recognize in my father's words the wellsprings of my own prose: squeamishness toward fudging and smudging, the reciprocal dovetailing of thought and word ... and I doubt that the development of these traits under my frequently willful pen was a conscious act.[20]

The process is presented here as virtually *physiological*, which again recalls Solovyov and his 'spiritualization of matter' and of nature, even human nature, 'thinking itself forward'. Perhaps the 'body, flow, and structure' of a cultural construct are not simply figures of speech. As animal behaviourist N. K. Humphrey puts it,

Memes should be regarded as living structures, not just metaphorically but technically. When you plant a fertile meme in my mind you literally parasitize my brain, turning it into a vehicle for the meme's propagation in just the way a virus may parasitize the genetic mechanism of a host cell. And this isn't just a way of talking – the meme for, say, 'belief in life after death' is actually realized physically, millions of times over, as a structure in the nervous systems of individual men the world over.[21]

This is what we mean in modern parlance by 'going viral'. Nabokov, for his part, was trying to get at this idea *avant la lettre*, but in his own writing, in a deeply personal, deeply cultural sense.

In 'Father's butterflies' we learn further that Fyodor is fascinated by the exceptional flora and fauna of Russia that *gets left out* ('the unfit') of popular German editions of butterfly atlases. The fact that Konstantin Kirillovich fills this lacuna with *The Butterflies and Moths of the Russian Empire*, itself a fiction, is Nabokov's attempt to reverse the dumbing-down of history that was the Soviet regime and the tragedy that was the death of Fyodor's (and Nabokov's) father. 'Father's butterflies' ends with Fyodor's voice saying 'The bitterness of interrupted life is nothing compared to the bitterness of interrupted work: the probability that the former may continue beyond the grave seems infinite when compared to the inexorable incompletion of the latter.'[22] *The future is secretly embedded in one's work: that is why the latter is so crucial.* In Fyodor's reading Pushkin and Konstantin Kirillovich sense the future ('fate') in their lives and through their work. Thus, the difference between a meme à la Dawkins and the pattern Nabokov is invoking revolves around what Dawkins calls 'imitation', the cultural version of replication, and what the hero of *The Gift* experiences as artistic growth and innovation, as culture's flow in and through him, as an explosion of new and powerful energy.[23] 'Imitation', 'meme', 'memeplex' may be sufficient from the scientific side to explain the clusters of meaning in *The Gift*, but from the artistic side they are woefully inadequate when it comes to under-standing, or measuring, the 'personality', the 'aura', responsible for the cultural creation. The multiple and interlocking feedback loops formed in *The Gift* (Pushkin + poetry + Konstantin Kirillovich + butterflies + science + fatedness + art-in/as-life) are not ones that can be simply 'copied'. To be authentic they must be *lived* in a new way.

## Diaspora and the big picture

What then could the intersecting biographies and scientific (or scientifi-cally themed) work of two famous Russian émigrés have to do with the hundred-year history of 'writing the diaspora'? First, the complementary aspects of Dobzhansky's and Nabokov's thought *and* the manner in which that thought matured over their lifetimes suggest a way of looking at the history of Russian writing beyond the bounds of the geographical entity known as Russia. The 'big picture' begins with an a priori acceptance that we, as literature scholars, do not run from biology as a starting point; that we are ourselves primates who with the help of enlarged brains and the ability, in time, to make tools, socialize with others and, especially important, deploy symbolic logic and ultimately language, became conscious, able to self-reflect; and that the key to providing a framework for analysing cultural products needs to have an evolutionary basis. Next, species concept, adaptive landscape and genetic drift can be seen as useful heuristics when applied to other domains of the living world, including the 'bottlenecks' and 'valleys' of decreasing fitness in human cultural production. Yes, these are metaphors, but they are embedded deeply in cultural decision-making, so deep as to appear actually 'embodied' and predictive of cultural life forms and life spans. The fact that Dobzhansky's definition of species comes in wholly abstract, non-metaphorical language ('the once actually or potentially inter-breeding array of forms' sounds like a mathematical set), while Nabokov's attempts to get at the transition between species and subspecies reveal a dense weave of morphological detail and metaphorical shading, should give us pause.[24] We can't really 'get here from there'. What we are examining is a moving target. The good news, however, is that the same principles that underlie evolutionary growth in the natural world also fuel change, mutatis mutandis, in the cultural realm, including the history of the Russian diaspora.

The first of those principles involves the role of coercion. If the idea of diaspora invoked to describe the outpouring of refugees from Russia as a result of 1917 had as its core meaning the notion of expulsion, then over time the magnitude or intensity of that original force decreased. Evolutionary time works slowly, in fits and starts, and the Leninist-Stalinist era was clearly one marked by exceptional carnage and social repression, but it is still fair to say that the psychological dislocation facing someone like Khodasevich was different from the quandary of language and lifestyle facing a later iteration of the exiled poet, like Brodsky. Khodasevich was trying, inter alia, to preserve the Pushkinian legacy in an alien francophone context he had no intention of domesticating and hybridizing into his own art. Scenes from Paris and Berlin serve only to show how alienated the speaker of a poem is from that backdrop. Brodsky, on the other hand, who certainly experienced coercion at the hands of the Soviet state before his expulsion and who portrayed himself as being on the social margins while still living in the Soviet Union, gradually morphs from a speaker exiled from Russia to a peripatetic expat tourist drawn to exotic locales around the globe into which he never fits and which afford him an occasion to meditate. His supreme success at making his way in the anglophone world of letters and his manner of mixing heroes and themes from Anglo-American and Russian poetry would be unthinkable to a first-generation émigré like Khodasevich. For Khodasevich there could be no 'interbreeding' between the species marked 'Soviet' and the species marked 'Russian'.

Here the idea of force or coercion is a necessary consideration, because it lies at the evolutionary origins of the aesthetic. Recall again the female birds who, after generations of coevolving with the objects of their desire, actively 'shop for' a mate on the basis of the allure of the male's ornaments. What in human terms is rape cancels out that choice and any possible 'culture of courtship', just as the either/or binaries of centre/periphery and homeland/exile suppress Khodasevich's desire to artistically 'mate' (share what is most 'his') with his adoptive context, while Brodsky creates space between those binaries for additional aesthetic effects. And whereas both Khodasevich's and Brodsky's fates as poets are filled with their own version of tragedy, what Khodasevich senses is that his kind, his 'species' of lived poetic values and connections to the past, is dying out, has reached a 'European night'; what Brodsky feels, on the contrary, is that he has fulfilled some higher mission (the splicing together, or 'interbreeding', of different traditions) and expresses gratitude on the occasion of his 1980 birthday poem: 'Что сказать мне о жизни? Что оказалась длинной. / Только с горем я чувствую солидарность. / Но пока мне рот не забили глиной, / из него раздаваться будет лишь благодарность' (What shall I say about life? That it's long and abhors transparence. / Broken eggs make me grieve; the omelette, though, makes me vomit. / Yet until brown clay has been crammed down my larynx, / only gratitude will be gushing from it).[25] These uses of 'species' and 'interbreeding' are metaphorical, of course, but not entirely so, or – which may be the same thing – no less meaningful for being so. As Adrian Wanner shows in his chapter on the poetic self-translations of Tsvetaeva, Nabokov and Brodsky in this volume, *what is self* (which self to which self?) and *what is translation* (which language/tradition to which language/tradition?) are not always so obvious when the idea of source and target has become problematized by shifting social, political and cultural norms. If the 'choric' basis of Tsvetaeva's translations of herself into stilted French or Brodsky's renderings of himself into doggerel English require a reader who knows the *Russian sound* of the poet's verse before it can be understood what he or she is trying to do in the target language, is this a reader/listener who represents the future (the idea of translation moving to another level) or one so stranded on a 'fitness downslope', to use Sewell Wright's metaphor for genetic drift, as to be destined to die out? A stereoscopic 'interlation' (Mikhail Epstein) or a unidirectional translation?

As scholars we know there are connections between the biological and cultural realms. We just don't know how to talk about them in a manner intellectually acceptable to both the scientific and the non-scientific communities. When we move from the genetic plane to the symbolic-linguistic plane, and when the new information conveyed 'jumps' from vertical transmission (genotype-phenotype) to horizontal transmission (social learning), we bump up against the thorny problem of identifying and measuring agency. Is it really still the metaphor of water running downhill – are the opportunities being taken advantage of in a niche environment ones that are actively created by the exploring organism or ones that are simply available, or a combination of the two?

> But an even bigger problem is that the transmission of ideas, patterns of behaviors, skills, and so on involves several types of concurrent and interacting learning processes. Focusing on one aspect will not lead us very far. It is the non-automatic and nonrote aspects of symbolic transmission – those aspects that involve directed, actively constructed processes – which are the most dominant and interesting in the generation and construction of cultural variations.[26]

The 'interacting learning processes' that guided the different generations of émigré writers always had built into them the idea of where the force/coercion was coming from and how to deal with it in order to adapt and survive. Thus while Bunin, Tsvetaeva, Nabokov and Gazdanov may have considered different artistic survival mechanisms when thinking about audience and publisher, they all still understood the reality of the Soviet force that was defining their work as outside the centre's mainstream. Today the world of 'global Russian cultures' does not really have a centre; it is more of an 'archipelago' (Maria Rubins's terms), and the idea of force has more to do with markets and identity shape-shifting than with Nansen passports and border guards.[27] It can be a world in which Gary Shteyngart writes in hilariously inflected English about a Jewish-Russian-American hero and his madcap adventures (*The Russian Debutante's Handbook*) or it can be a world in which Dina Rubina describes, in Russian, the lives of Soviet Jews who have migrated to the Zionist homeland and have trouble shedding their diasporic identities (*Vot idet Messiia*).

Along with the gradual easing of force/coercion as a factor in the experience of writing as a Russian abroad comes the idea that global culture(s) is/are becoming more and more democratized and national 'essences' dispersed. The 'post's in 'postcolonialism', 'poststructuralism' and 'postmodernism' all point to the same thing: the structures and narratives that defined Empire, poetic artefact and high modernist myth have been superseded, their dominance hierarchies undermined by irony, verbal play, and ultimate suspicion towards the human project. In shorthand, Pushkin's *Onegin* becomes Prigov's *Onegin*. What this democratization also means in conceptual terms is that religious myth, which had still functioned as a substrate of high modernism (think Yeats, Blok, Mandelstam, etc.), is replaced by cybernetics, artificial intelligence and the attempt to construct a simulacrum of the human mind and personality technologically. This, I would say, is the greatest challenge of Russian-language authors freed from the curse of exile but still keen to draw on their heritage in a world of increasingly hybridized voice zones. The classics of the nineteenth century and the great modernist poets and novelists of the twentieth century lived in a world that was not completely secularized, a world in which literature took a position between the sacred and the profane, 'the Book' and *byt*, and where authors did battle with God's creation, with being itself. Now something else is needed, and it is here that figures like Dobzhansky and Nabokov might also be seen to come to the rescue.

One of Dobzhansky's early heroes and mentors was the eminent geochemist and public man Vladimir Vernadsky, who had ties to the neo-idealist movement in pre-revolutionary Russia and who wielded his immense authority as a scientist to argue for the legitimacy of non-scientific worldviews. Along with Pierre Teilhard de Chardin, Vernadsky is considered a discoverer of the 'noosphere', although there is some confusion about who employed the term first (there is even a third possibility, Édouard Le Roy). In 1922, Teilhard de Chardin wrote an essay entitled 'Hominization', in which he stated: 'And this amounts to imagining, in one way or another, above the animal biosphere a human sphere, the sphere of reflexion, of conscious invention, of the conscious unity of souls (the Noosphere, if you will).'[28] Teilhard de Chardin was a famed palaeontologist, co-discoverer of Peking Man, but also a Christian mystic and philosopher. Vernadsky, equally celebrated but as an earth scientist, described the planet as evolving in layers, beginning with the geosphere, progressing to the biosphere, and culminating in the noosphere, the sphere of human knowing and communication (cf. Lotman's 'semiosphere'). Furthermore, it turns out that Teilhard de Chardin was Dobzhansky's favourite philosopher, someone who was not only brilliant as a scientist but also possibly prescient with regard to the direction Darwin's natural selection was taking on the human cultural level.

Teilhard de Chardin argues in *The Phenomenon of Man* that movement in the noosphere, which has been accelerating at greater and greater speed in recent centuries and now decades, is poised to reach a tipping point, an 'Omega'. The noosphere's 'enormous layers, followed in the right direction, must somewhere ahead become involuted to a point which we might call *Omega*, which fuses and consumes them integrally into itself'.[29] Note that one of Teilhard de Chardin's favourite words is 'involuted', which is his way of describing the mind turning back on itself and digging deeper into the expanding folds of consciousness. And when this tipping point is reached the 'thinking skin' of the world will become 'hyper-personal',[30] that is, it will retain the personal in each consciousness but also radiate a kind of super-consciousness that unites the individual in something more (cf. Solovyov's *vseedinstvo*).

> [T]he concentration of a conscious universe would be unthinkable if it did not reassemble in itself *all consciousnesses* as well as all *the conscious*; each particular consciousness remaining conscious of itself at the end of the operation [i.e. the mental act], and even (this must absolutely be understood) each particular consciousness becoming still more itself and thus more clearly distinct from others the closer it gets to them in Omega.[31]

To be sure, Teilhard de Chardin's formulations can be a bit woolly and too optimistic (especially the part about 'each particular consciousness becoming still more itself'), and for that reason they have attracted over the years some strenuous criticism from the scientific community, but as heuristic shorthand they serve a purpose.

As it happens, these ideas of the Omega point, hyper-consciousness and the noosphere feed suggestively into the work that celebrated entomologist/myrmecologist (ant specialist) E. O. Wilson has been doing for decades with 'eusocial' insect communities like beehives and ant and termite colonies. These latter are viewed as 'super-organisms' because their collective activities model a 'mind' that, seemingly located everywhere and nowhere, operates over and above the roles of the different insects. What we see as nascent social roles – worker bees or soldier termites – that look like insect squads on missions are actually manipulated (as in turned on and off) when something happens in the environment to trigger the release of pheromones. To take another example, originally solitary wasp species produced larvae, which were consumed by their adult mothers when the food supply became depleted (in human terms, 'infanticide'). In order to save themselves the larvae started to excrete saliva which the mothers found nutritious. Eventually, the solitary wasp species 'learned' sociality when the adult wasps that grew up from the larvae preferred to stay in the nest rather than fly off and reproduce elsewhere. It was at this point that the 'solitary' wasps began to *cooperate* among themselves to form a community nest. In effect, in David Wilson's apt phrasing, the larvae became the 'group stomach for the colony'.[32]

While we don't know what it 'feels like' to be an ant or a wasp, their behaviour can at this moment in our history be explained fully enough by science. There is not yet rudimentary 'consciousness' taking place, although the social aspect of their behaviour is crucial for our final thoughts. It still all starts with genes (again as 'data banks' rather than as 'command centres'), but what happens as we reach the process of hominization and then the advent of *Homo sapiens* some two hundred thousand years ago is a different story. Knowing genetics or microbiology is not enough once we attain the boundaries of consciousness. The termite soldier does not attack its adversary because it is thinking of something else, say the sanctity of its home, but the female bowerbird that spends time at different bowers until she finds the one that attracts her enough to pause there and allow the bower's male architect to mate with her – can we call that conscious decision-making or ant-like behaviour? I would say the former.

Insect colonies and human beings are the only known species whose eusocial behavioural patterns show the ability of cooperation to outmanoeuvre brute force. There is also a big difference, however: the evolution towards 'mind' in *Homo sapiens* is not a trending towards the unification, zombie-like, of all individual mental operations into one super-consciousness (the ant colony model), but, as Teilhard de Chardin projects, an Omega, where a hyper-awareness *includes* the necessary condition that each individual's self-reflective capacity is also moving towards a higher inflection point. 'By its structure Omega, in its ultimate principle, can only be a *distinct Centre radiating at the core of a system of centres*; a grouping in which personalization of the All and personalization of the elements reach their maximum, simultaneously and without merging, under the influence of a supremely autonomous focus of union.'[33]

The problem, which all of our heroes – Solovyov, Vernadsky, Teilhard de Chardin, Dobzhansky and Nabokov – were supremely interested in, is that the appearance of consciousness in human beings cannot be pinpointed in time and space. 'No photograph could record upon the human phylum this passage to reflection which so naturally intrigues us, for the simple reason that the phenomenon took place inside that which is *always* lacking in a reconstructed phylum – the peduncle [the main stalk bearing flowers] of its original forms.'[34] Thus, that which is emerging from its organic whole (the compositionist view) is not yet discernible as that which has emerged and is separate. As a default position we have ceded authority to the materialist (physico-chemical) argument, which despite its gaps, has the prestige of the scientific method behind it and the rhetorical flair of neo-Darwinian atheists like Dawkins and Sam Harris. But if Solovyov and Teilhard de Chardin were Christian mystics (though mystics who got into serious trouble with their respective churches for their unorthodox views), Dobzhansky and Nabokov do not appear to have believed in a personal God, nor did they ever try to explain their understanding of meaning or design in the universe with reference to the Christian deity. Their science was too rigorous and chaste for that. They attempted to chart a third way in their work between deism (some intelligence outside the immanence of biology) and mechanical reductionism. In this they anticipated the modern-day philosopher Thomas Nagel, author of *Mind and Cosmos*, who endeavours to retain the original, still tentative in places, Darwin of *Origin* and *Descent* without the monologic hectoring of the neo-Darwinians:

> What explains the existence of organisms like us must also explain the existence of mind. But if the mental is not itself merely physical, it cannot be fully explained by physical science… . A genuine alternative to the reductionist program would require an account of how mind and everything that goes with it is inherent in the universe… . My guiding conviction is that mind is not just an afterthought or an accident or an add-on, but a basic aspect of nature.[35]

And so, when we think about the hundred-year history of the diaspora and how the classificatory terms of our subject form a picture of ever-increasing foreshortening and hybridization the closer we get to the present moment, we face a problem. *What exactly does this momentum mean?* Is there a connection between the internet, social networks, artificial intelligence and the perception that the latter are shrinking geography and accelerating time, on the one hand, and the fact that literature qua literature is becoming harder and harder to define, becoming something other than itself, on the other? While acknowledging the immense prestige of the Nobel Prize, can we still call Alexievich's psyche-impersonating witness accounts and Dylan's whimsical 'bardish' lyrics belles-lettres? The sticking point here is that the form of the writing has no specified rules, no genre constraints, other than it be perceived as 'authentic', itself a vague, affect-laden, essentially undefinable term.

Which brings us back to Teilhard de Chardin's Omega and the crucial factor of *lichnost'* ('personhood'), a term more culturally freighted in the Russian context. Both Dobzhansky and Nabokov were highly distinct *lichnosti*, persons whose work could not be separated from their very being in the world. They did not simply copy or imitate (Dawkins's memetic model), they built obsessively on past mental achievements (first others', but then their own), using their special talents and intelligence in intensely lived feedback loops, to produce work that was recognized not only for its brilliance, but – which for our purposes is the same thing – its *future* orientation. For example, Dobzhansky's ideas about equality and fair play began with what biology taught him but then went far beyond that: 'There is more genetic variation within any human race than there are genetic differences between races. It follows … that individuals should be evaluated by what they are, not by the race to which they belong.'[36] This, by the way, is a distinct echo of the quote from Solovyov we took as one of the epigraphs to launch the present essay: 'The question "*What is* a certain subject?" never coincides with the question "*Whence arose* that subject?".'

Likewise, while Nabokov's interest in the diversity of the natural world always had an aesthetic tinge, Dobzhansky's deep understanding of genetics had a more philosophical, ethically coloured one. 'It is the adaptive level of individuals heterozygous for various chromosomes which is most important.'[37] Here what Dobzhansky is saying is that a 'homozygous' situation (i.e. where the same alleles are selected) can be deleterious for the individual or the population when the alleles are lethal, while a heterozygous situation (i.e. the alleles are different) translates into better adaptive potential. Thus, the diversity that comes from 'genetic drift' turns out ultimately to be a good thing, both at the chromosomal level and at the human social one. As his writings continually underscore, Dobzhansky was again, like Nabokov, intensely interested in the *creative* character of biological evolution. According to his biographer,

Dobzhansky was a religious man, although he apparently rejected fundamental beliefs of traditional religion, such as the existence of a personal God and of life beyond physical death.[38] His religiosity was grounded on the conviction that there is meaning in the universe. He saw that meaning in the fact that evolution has produced the stupendous diversity of the living world and has progressed from primitive forms of life to mankind. Dobzhansky held that, in man, biological evolution has transcended itself into the realm of self-awareness and culture. He believed that somehow mankind would eventually evolve into higher levels of harmony and creativity.[39]

I would like to close by suggesting that, while different temperamentally, Nabokov and Dobzhansky were almost perfectly aligned in their views regarding humanity's role in the evolutionary process. It is about us and it is not about us and these two statements, read in tandem, encapsulate the co-evolutionary spiral. Nabokov writes in 'Father's butterflies', 'We are right in saying quite literally, in the human, cerebral sense, that nature grows wiser as time passes.'[40] But this 'grows wiser', as Nabokov with his personal history knew as well as anybody, does *not* take into account the viability of the individual or the species. The random happens in natural selection and in human history. Nabokov's way of writing 'adaptive landscape' into his novels is to show that creativity and morality come together when they 'drift away' (are allowed by circumstances to drift away) from brute coercion and migrate into the 'valleys' where something like, in Stanislav Shvabrin's wonderful phrase, 'the survival of the weakest' takes place.[41] Luzhin, Cincinnatus, Sineusov, Pnin – these are the figures in Nabokov's fiction who survive long enough to remind us what it looks like, but more accurately what it feels and thinks like (again, the *mind*), to be a unique species on the verge of extinction. Mortality brings out their creativity, their (and their creator's) spectacular displays of mind.

If biology teaches us anything, it is that species change and adapt or they disappear. One reason that Dobzhansky's and Nabokov's legacies have not disappeared but remain burnished is that their thinking always involved a complex straddling, and not just of any disciplines, but precisely those subject areas – evolutionary biology and imaginative literature/philosophy/ethics – that are arguably crucial for the future development of *Homo sapiens*. At the same time, and no less important, Dobzhansky and Nabokov did not force evolution's hand, did not distort the 'what is' of science. This is what makes their life's work 'hyper-personal', something that can be built upon. When Nabokov writes

Smoothly a screw is turned; out of the mist
two ambered hooks symmetrically slope,
or scales like battledores of amethyst
cross the charmed circle of the microscope.

I found it and I named it, being versed
in taxonomic Latin; thus became
godfather to an insect and its first
describer – and I want no other fame.[42]

he is telling, but also showing through the *frisson* of metre and rhyme, how
the passion of the scientist *feels like* the creative inspiration of the artist.
Refinement in consciousness, the involutions of which Teilhard de Chardin
speaks, do reveal 'in a human, cerebral sense', nature 'growing wiser'.

Although personality, style and quality of mind matter most to us
as readers we need to try to move beyond the idea of the *poet bozh'ei
milost'iu* (the romantic 'poet by the grace of God'). Nabokov and
Dobzhansky are possibly unique to their moments, but they are more
useful heuristically when studied as something more than solitary
geniuses *tout court*. Perhaps their trajectories are telling us something
now about a movement towards 'collective brains' and 'hyper-personality'?
Perhaps diasporic instances of linguistic hybridity are revealing of
new, 'genre-less' versions of authenticity, opportunities for consciousness
to extend the brain/mind frontier, regardless of where that frontier
is located geographically or phenomenologically. We are no longer
Descartian dualists. We are more and more embodied minds. The 'craft
handed down' that Fyodor feels as physiological when he is writing about
Pushkin and his father is simply a later, but now much more conscious,
more aware in myriad cultural ways, more 'involuted' version of the same
mental toolkit that helped archaic man learn how to make spears
straighter.[43] If scientists can compare the way a gene operates in the
chemical realm to how a word operates in a language, and if individual
cells can show how they are responding to environmental stresses, and if
magnetic resonance imaging of the brain can show how subjects'
neuronal pathways fire at the mention of certain metaphors, and if
contemporary thinkers can refer to 'ideas having sex' (Matt Ridley), then
perhaps Solovyov with his androgyn ('The meaning of love') and Nabokov
with his art as incest (*Ada*) were onto something. The texts of the diaspora
that bring this momentum into view and update it are, I would submit,
our quarry now.

## Notes

1  Noble 2017, 160.
2  Dor 2015, 4.
3  Jablonka and Lamb 2014, 220–2.

4   Dobzhansky 1967, 1.
5   See Nabokov 1996, 462–65.
6   Larson 2004, 230.
7   Larson 2004, 230.
8   Larson 2004, 232.
9   Ayala 1985, 171.
10  Nabokov, Boyd and Pyle 2000, 353–4; cited Mallet 2016, 239–40.
11  Solov'ev 1911–14, 55. Translations are the author's.
12  Solov'ev 1911–14, 41.
13  Solov'ev 1911–14, 41.
14  Nabokov 2001, 108.
15  Boyd 2011, 104–5.
16  Nabokov, Boyd and Pyle 2000, 63.
17  Nabokov 2001, 390.
18  Nabokov 1996, 594.
19  Dobzhansky 1967, 25.
20  Nabokov 2001, 377.
21  Cited Dawkins 2006, 192.
22  Nabokov 2001, 402.
23  Dawkins 2006, 192.
24  See, e.g., Konstantin Kirillovich's description of a 'species circle' in Nabokov 2001, 384, and Nabokov's own thoughts on the topic as a practising scientist at MCZ, in Nabokov, Boyd and Pyle 2000, 207–8, 226–30, 238–41, 301–3.
25  Brodsky 1987, 177; 1992, 3.
26  Jablonka and Lamb 2014, 222.
27  See Platt 2019, 3–17.
28  Teilhard de Chardin 1967, 63.
29  Teilhard de Chardin 2008, 259.
30  Teilhard de Chardin 2008, 260.
31  Teilhard de Chardin 2008, 261–2 (emphasis original).
32  Wilson 2011, 74; see also 70–3.
33  Teilhard de Chardin 2008, 262–3.
34  Teilhard de Chardin 2008, 187.
35  Nagel 2012, 14–16.
36  Cited Ayala 1985, 169. Also, Ayala 1976, 5–6: 'Dobzhansky was a warm and compassionate man who had little patience with obscurantism, racial prejudice, or social injustice. In the 1940s and 1950s he published several articles criticizing Lysenko's biological quackery.... He relentlessly denounced what he called [the] "bogus 'science' of race prejudice".'
37  Dobzhansky 1942, 487; cited Ayala 1985, 173.
38  Others, like Ernst Mayr, have reported that he was a 'firm believer in a personal God', so the record is not clear on this point.
39  Ayala 1985, 179.
40  Nabokov 2001, 387.
41  Shvabrin, 'Berlin', 93, in Bethea and Frank 2018.
42  Nabokov, 'A discovery', 155–6, in Nabokov 1969.
43  Henrich 2016, 323.

# Bibliography

Ayala, Francisco J. 'Theodosius Dobzhansky: The man and the scientist', *Annual Review of Genetics* 10 (1976): 10–16.
Ayala, Francisco J. 'Theodosius Dobzhansky (1900–1975): A biographical memoir'. In *Biographical Memoirs*, 161–213. Washington, DC: National Academy of Sciences, 1985. http://www.nasonline.org/publications/biographical-memoirs/memoir-pdfs/dobzhansky-theodosius.pdf (accessed 4 September 2020).
Bethea, David M. and Siggy Frank, eds. *Vladimir Nabokov in Context*. Cambridge: Cambridge University Press, 2018.

Boyd, Brian. *Stalking Nabokov: Selected essays*. New York: Columbia University Press, 2011.

Brodsky, Joseph. *Uraniia*. Ann Arbor, MI: Ardis, 1987.

Brodsky, Joseph. *To Urania*. New York: Noonday Press, 1992.

Dawkins, Richard. *The Selfish Gene*. Oxford: Oxford University Press, 2006. (First published in 1976.)

Dobzhansky, Theodosius. *Mankind Evolving: The evolution of the human species*. New Haven, CT: Yale University Press, 1962.

Dobzhansky, Theodosius. *The Biology of Ultimate Concern*. New York: New American Library, 1967.

Dobzhansky, Theodosius, A. M. Holz and B. Spassky. 'Genetics of natural populations. VIII. Concealed variability in the second and fourth chromosomes of *Drosophila pseudoobscura* and its bearing on the problem of heterosis', *Genetics* 27(5) (1942): 463–90.

Dor, Daniel. *The Instruction of Imagination: Language as a social communication technology*. Foundations of Human Interactions series. Oxford: Oxford University Press, 2015.

Henrich, Joseph. *The Secret of Our Success: How culture is driving human evolution, domesticating our species, and making us smarter*. Princeton, NJ: Princeton University Press, 2016.

Jablonka, Eva and Marion J. Lamb. *Evolution in Four Dimensions: Genetic, epigenetic, behavioral, and symbolic variation in the history of life*. Cambridge, MA: MIT Press, 2014. (Revised edition.)

Larson, Edward J. *Evolution: The remarkable history of a scientific theory*. New York: Modern Library, 2004.

Mallet, James. 'Nabokov's evolution'. In *Fine Lines: Vladimir Nabokov's scientific art*, edited by Stephen H. Blackwell and Kurt Johnson, 235–42. New Haven, CT: Yale University Press, 2016.

Nabokov, Vladimir. *Poems and Problems*. New York: McGraw-Hill, 1969.

Nabokov, Vladimir. *Speak Memory: An autobiography revisited*. In *Novels and Memoirs 1941–1951*, 359–638. New York: Library of America, 1996.

Nabokov, Vladimir. *Nabokov's Butterflies: Unpublished and uncollected writings*. Edited by Brian Boyd and Robert Michael Pyle. Boston, MA: Beacon Press, 2000.

Nabokov, Vladimir. *The Gift*. Translated by Michael Scammell and Dmitri Nabokov in collaboration with the author. London: Penguin, 2001.

Nagel, Thomas. *Mind and Cosmos: Why the materialist neo-Darwinian conception of nature is almost certainly false*. Oxford: Oxford University Press, 2012.

Noble, Denis. *Dance to the tune of Life: Biological relativity*. Cambridge: Cambridge University Press, 2017.

Platt, Kevin M. F., ed. *Global Russian Cultures*. Madison: University of Wisconsin Press, 2019.

Prum, Richard O. *The Evolution of Beauty: How Darwin's forgotten theory of mate choice shapes the animal world – and us*. New York: Doubleday, 2017.

Ridley, Matt. *The Rational Optimist: How prosperity evolves*. New York: HarperCollins, 2010.

Skipper, Robert A. and Michael R. Dietrich. 'Sewall Wright's adaptive landscape: Philosophical reflections on heuristic value'. In *The Adaptive Landscape in Evolutionary Biology*, edited by Erik Svensson and Ryan Calsbeek, 16–25. Oxford: Oxford University Press, 2012.

Solov'ev, Vladimir Sergeevich. 'Krasota v prirode'. In *Sobranie sochinenii*, vol. 6, edited by S. M. Solov'ev and E. L. Radlov, 33–74. St Petersburg: Prosveshchenie, 1911–14.

Teilhard de Chardin, Pierre. *The Phenomenon of Man*. New York: Harper Perennial, 2008. (Original French edition, *Phénomène humain*, 1955.)

Teilhard de Chardin, Pierre. *The Vision of the Past*. London: Collins, 1967.

Wilson, David Sloan. *The Neighborhood Project: Using evolution to improve my city, one block at a time*. New York: Little, Brown, 2011.

Part four
# Imagined spaces of unity and difference

# 6
# Repatriation of diasporic literature and the role of the poetry anthology in the construction of a diasporic canon

Katharine Hodgson

This chapter explores how far the 'rhetoric of a unified literary canon', which has dominated discussions of the relationship between twentieth-century Russian literature in the metropolitan centre and the diaspora, is adopted by anthologies of poetry.[1] All the anthologies under scrutiny include only poetry written in Russian. Most of them are dedicated to the work of poets living in diaspora, and are made up only of texts written while their authors were living outside Russia. These anthologies fall into two groups: those published between the 1930s and the 1970s outside Russia, and those published during and after the 1990s, mainly, though not solely, in Russia. In addition, the chapter will consider two substantial anthologies of twentieth-century poetry, both published in Russia in the 1990s, which bring together poetry written in Russia, both official and underground, and poetry written outside the country, with the aim of providing a comprehensive picture of the century's poetry. The selected anthologies will be investigated in order to explore the different ways in which they construct, through their composition and apparatus, the relationship between literary canon, community and nationhood.

The discussion will be informed by consideration of two aspects of diaspora. The first, most relevant to the earlier anthologies, is boundary maintenance, explained by Rogers Brubaker as 'the preservation of a distinct identity vis-à-vis a host society', which supports cohesive community within the country of residence and across borders, wherever members of the diaspora are to be found.[2] The second is an aspect of the diaspora journey identified by Avtar Brah: the fact that 'home' can mean the Russia of memory and origin, 'a mythic place of desire in the diasporic imagination', but also the present location.[3] As Brah points out, diasporic journeys are 'essentially about settling down, about putting roots "elsewhere"'.[4] Diaspora entails traumatic separation and dislocation, but also the start of a new community in 'contested cultural and political terrains where individual and collective memories collide, reassemble and reconfigure'.[5] Diaspora studies draw attention to the ambivalence inherent in the word 'home'. As this chapter shows, however, the ambivalence of 'home' risks being erased when poetry is brought from the diaspora to the metropolis, a journey that is frequently represented within the metropolis as a return, even though the work was created elsewhere.

A diaspora poetry anthology which brings together a body of texts written by authors living in different locations but using a common language and drawing on a shared cultural heritage expresses a collective identity based on the sense of ambivalent otherness described above. It traces a scattered community's attempts to maintain a distinctive culture, but may also reveal the effects of interactions between its own culture and that of the host societies, which contribute to the development of a literary culture that is distinct from that of the metropolis. The Soviet-era anthologies provide a shared space and meeting point for both poets and their readers that makes visible at least some of the range and variety of the work produced in diaspora. They also act as a building block in the process of canon formation, and so challenge the idea that literary canons necessarily express the spirit of a nation. The post-Soviet anthologies show what can happen when the diasporic canon arrives in the metropolis: its former role in maintaining the boundaries of a diasporic community may come into conflict with a metropolitan viewpoint which may fail to recognise the otherness of this body of work.

The case study in this chapter informs current approaches to the legacy of diaspora by providing a dual perspective on how poetry anthologies function as a way of shaping a diasporic canon, both in diaspora and in the metropolis. The chapter explores the extent to which anthologies compiled principally for readers inside Russia, and those aimed at readers in the diaspora, differ in their presentation of diasporic poetry. It traces the emergence of a tentative diasporic canon outside Russia, comparing anthologies published in different places and at different times to see how far they assert an identity understood primarily in national terms, or a distinct diasporic identity. The earlier volumes published outside Russia are examined with a view to showing how far they present themselves as statements of intent to preserve a collective identity rooted in Russian literary culture rather than making room for works which transcend national, linguistic and cultural boundaries. The chapter then compares anthologies published both in Russia and elsewhere since 1991, to discover whether they are shaped principally by a discourse of repatriation which presents diaspora poetry as an expression of a national tradition now restored to its homeland and to its proper place in a reunified Russian poetry canon, or whether there are signs of a revised understanding of poetry written in Russian which is connected to, but extends beyond, the national.

Before proceeding to a discussion of the anthologies themselves, the chapter will examine the relationship between anthologies, the literary canon and the concept of nation, and consider how appropriate it might be to apply this model to diasporic literature. A literary canon is a body of texts that is given exemplary status by being widely reproduced and circulated, made the subject of scholarly commentary and analysis, and included in educational curricula as well as anthologies and literary histories. The selection and reproduction of texts in anthologies contributes to the process of canon formation. Repeated inclusion of a particular text, or of works by a particular author, marks them out as worthy of being remembered, and suggests that they express ideas or qualities that are valuable to a culture. While the publication of a limited number of anthologies over several decades does not in itself create a literary canon, successive anthologies do offer a picture of continuity, as certain authors and texts are reproduced, which consolidates their position in a developing canon. Anthologies also reflect changes by registering the appearance of new poets and revising the selection of previously anthologized authors and their works.

The concept of canon that was prevalent in European literature before the nineteenth century came from classical antiquity and was understood as a set of standards by which a work of art could be judged. It was modified in response to romantic ideas of a nation's unique 'spirit', so that by the early nineteenth century it was widely accepted that there was a close relationship between literary canon and nation, and that literature should express the qualities that were associated with its nation of origin. The involvement of literary canons in nation-building projects, and of anthologies in shaping those canons, is shown, for example, by Alan Golding's analysis of the part played by eighteenth- and nineteenth-century American poetry anthologies in reinforcing a sense of cultural and moral distinction between the United States and England.[6]

The counter-canonical artistic movements in early twentieth-century Russia, however, were open to forming transnational connections which took little account of borders and national tradition. When revolution and civil war led to the creation of a Russian diaspora which, as it soon became clear, was going to last into the foreseeable future, it was not a given that anthologies created in diaspora would model a straightforward relationship between the literary canon and the national. Even before the twentieth century the concept of nation in relation to Russia, with its long history as a multi-ethnic empire, presented difficulties. Russian writers and thinkers in the nineteenth century were preoccupied by the attempt to characterize Russia specifically as a nation, while the state continued to pursue its project of imperial expansion. Yet it was Russia's imperial experience that arguably informed ideas about the universality of Russia as a nation, popularized by Fedor Dostoevsky in his speech on the occasion of the unveiling of the first statue to Pushkin in Moscow in 1880. Dostoevsky spoke of Russia's unique capacity to absorb elements from other cultures, and then give them back to the world in a new, universal form.[7] This declaration of Russia's openness to other cultures created a flattering self-image with messianic overtones, but without the chauvinism that revealed itself in some of the state's treatment of others within the empire.

The move into diaspora opened up new possibilities for compilers of anthologies to imagine poetry written outside Russia in terms of connections to and interactions with other literary cultures. Some poets, such as Valerii Pereleshin, did indeed engage with the literature and language of their host countries, as translators, and also as authors whose work showed a creative response to their environment. Yet what happened in practice was that anthologies' selections and paratextual apparatus tended to emphasize a distinctive Russian community whose members were connected across national borders but not especially involved with the cultures of their host countries. It was not necessarily the case, however, that the anthologies were put together with the intention of representing the diasporic community specifically in terms of nation. During the 1920s, according to Greta Slobin, 'The separation from the homeland forced the émigré community to try to formulate its identity as a national entity without a nation.'[8] What this paradox might mean in relation to the five anthologies produced in diaspora to be considered in this chapter is difficult to establish, unless 'national entity' is to be understood as a community that identifies itself not in terms of social and political structures, but through a collection of shared experiences and memories connected with childhood, traditions and landscapes that could be identified as specific to Russians, together with a common language and literary heritage. Perhaps Dostoevsky's model of Russia's 'all-humanity' (*vsechelovechnost'*) that inspired the reception and transformation of foreign culture, worked more effectively within the metropolis than in diaspora. To judge from the anthologies under consideration here, Russians living in diaspora may have found themselves recast as the Other rather than the receptive, transformative Self, and so felt themselves drawn to a collective identity project that foregrounded distinctive attributes of Russian community. Yet, when it came to the 'return' of diaspora poetry, the model of Russia's universality may have played a part in the process of repatriation of literary works that could be understood in some sense as a foreign Other that was to be enfolded within the Self. This act of appropriation involves more than a hint of the neo-imperialist attitudes inherent in the project of constructing a 'Russian world', where difference is marginalized or erased.

One reason why compilers of anthologies published outside Russia between the 1930s and the 1970s tended to include works that suited the task of boundary maintenance may be found by looking at the principal and conflicting impulses, as identified by Golding, which inform the process of creating an anthology. One is preservation, the gathering of a broad range of texts from disparate, often ephemeral, sources to ensure that they are protected from being forgotten. The other is selection, a focus on applying criteria in order to draw from the available texts those works which can be presented as most worthy, or most representative of a particular quality. An anthologist guided mainly by the impulse to preserve is likely to contribute to the creation or extension of what Alastair Fowler terms the 'accessible canon'; Golding notes that if an accessible canon already exists, anthologists are more likely to move away from preservation to selection.[9] Editors of poetry anthologies published in diaspora tended to come down in favour of preservation, a choice that may well have been made in response to the fragmented nature of the Russian diaspora, which severely restricted the size and range of the accessible canon. The anthologies' contributors and potential readers were scattered across many countries; they had access to journals, newspapers, and almanacs of poetry or individual collections of poems that were mainly local and ephemeral. In the absence of a system of publishing and literary criticism that spanned the diaspora, anthologies offered a rare opportunity to make the range and extent of poetry in the diaspora visible to readers, providing them with a representative picture of poetry written outside Russia, and evoking a sense of a shared cultural community.

These anthologies did succeed in showing readers that poetry was being created across the diaspora, but they had varying levels of success in reflecting the full extent and variety of locations where Russian poets were active. It was particularly challenging for the compilers of the earlier anthologies to include work by contributors located outside the main European and, later, American centres of diaspora, especially during the immediate post-war period when many potential contributors faced an uncertain future as 'displaced persons'. In the foreword to the 1948 anthology *Estafeta* the editors note that some poets had been unable to send their work to them because of 'purely technical reasons or the lack of communications' between countries in which émigrés were living.[10] While the limited nature of the accessible canon meant that anthologists were focused on the task of preservation, their work helped to lay the foundations for a broader accessible canon, and, indeed, to provide the resources for later anthologists in Russia who were looking both to establish a canon of Russian poetry abroad, and to integrate it with the metropolitan canon.

Like their predecessors abroad, the compilers of anthologies of diaspora poets' work published in Russia in the 1990s and into the early years of the new century also tended to favour preservation over selection. In the first decade and a half of post-Soviet existence the twentieth-century poetry canon was going through a phase of considerable revision. New anthologies of diaspora poetry contributed to this process by making available to readers in Russia a large amount of previously unfamiliar material in the form of 'anthologies of the whole' (to use Dmitry Kuz′min's term *antologiia tselogo*).[11] While these anthologies might subsequently provide the basis for a selective canon, their primary aim was to demonstrate a commitment to the preservation of a mass of material through breadth and inclusivity. The 'anthologies of the whole' which presented diaspora poetry to readers in the metropolis are too large to serve as clearly articulated statements on national identity or nation building, or to draw readers' attention to elements of interaction and dialogue with other cultures. These are questions which might be addressed more readily in more narrowly defined thematic anthologies, or in textbooks and literary histories, where there is a focus on the selection and interpretation of texts. The ambitious scale and scope of these anthologies do, however, provide the opportunity for their compilers to appeal to 'literary nationalism', claiming to play their part in the restoration of a temporarily disunited national canon. Their anthologies, while acknowledging the distinctiveness of diaspora poetry and making the effort to include poets from every part of the diaspora, seem more concerned with the extension of the boundaries of Russian literature so as to encompass and perhaps assimilate it as material that rightfully belonged within a national canon, part of a national Self that had been temporarily detached.

For those setting out in earlier decades to produce anthologies outside Russia, the project was not one of restoration and reconnection, but of establishing some kind of collective identity which lay outside the framework of a nation, but within the framework of a literary canon. More precisely, the developing diasporic canon was envisaged in terms that set it apart from the canon that was being constructed inside the Soviet Union. Soviet poetry was understood as an aberration from the Russian literary tradition which was being maintained and furthered outside Russia, beyond the distorting effects of state-imposed censorship. Diaspora authors could derive a sense of identity and purpose by insisting on what Slobin describes as 'the autonomy of national culture and its separation from the state'.[12] While some anthologies of diaspora poetry may have included work by poets who had returned to the Soviet Union after a period in emigration, they all excluded work by Soviet poets who never established themselves abroad. Released from the ambiguous embrace of the state (that might nurture culture or seek to control it), the diaspora could rely instead on a shared language and cultural heritage as a way to establish an identity but also create the possibility of independent development and renewal outside the territory of the Soviet Union.

The anthologies in question were far from being iconoclastic in the way they positioned themselves in relation to the canon. Those who had left the country understood their role as guardians of Russia's cultural heritage, living outside national territory but inside Russian cultural space. Their anthologies risked being backward-looking museums exhibiting the legacy of a culture before diaspora, and lacking any response to and engagement with the new environment. Some early anthologies were largely given over to reproducing the classical poetry canon of the nineteenth century, with only limited space for more recent work.[13] The question of the relationship between the contents of these early anthologies and a national canon was not considered; implicitly, they simply reaffirmed an established canon. The first anthologies to present only work written by poets outside Russia were beginning to outline, whether implicitly or explicitly, a new relationship with the literary canon. Their compilers are careful to avoid making claims that their work is to be understood as a statement of any kind of canon. Yet the work of early diaspora anthologists does represent the first steps towards a canon which would stand independently from the contemporary canon of Soviet Russian poetry as a 'viable alternative to the Soviet cultural tradition'.[14] It also serves as a necessary preliminary to some future work of canon reconstruction, when poetry rooted in Russian literary tradition but written outside national boundaries would reach Russia and be reintegrated. The compiler of the 1950 anthology *Na Zapade* makes a comment to this effect in his foreword: 'A complete evaluation of this work will fall to Russian readers in the future, far away, people we can hardly imagine.'[15]

Canon formation in the Russian diaspora presented particular challenges precisely because the diaspora community was dispersed and fragmented. There are various models of canon formation which rely on highly developed institutions and networks as the agents through which canons are produced; such structures are harder to establish outside the framework of a nation. Simone Winko's 'invisible hand' model of canon formation envisages a process of numerous, simultaneous and spontaneous decisions made by many agents: readers, booksellers, publishers, critics and scholars.[16] The small and scattered community of diaspora is likely to struggle because of fragmented and underdeveloped networks; its lack of overarching educational institutions backed by government is also a hindrance, if canon formation is understood largely in terms of institutional power engaged in the distribution of cultural capital.[17] Models of canon formation which depend on poets – in competition with one another, or as the highest arbiters of artistic merit – do at least fit in with the value of cultural autonomy that was embraced as a feature distinguishing diaspora culture from that of the metropolis.[18] Yet in diaspora the capacity of isolated individuals to exert influence beyond their immediate surroundings is likely to be restricted, making this model of canon formation difficult to apply.

If we understand a canon as 'a register of how our historical self-understandings are formed and modified' or as 'a construct, like a history text, expressing what a society reads back into its past as important to its future', canon formation can be seen as part of the work of boundary maintenance for a diaspora community.[19] After the upheaval of revolution, civil war and emigration, the impulse to make a statement through compiling a body of poetry that could provide the makings of a canon could be seen as an attempt to create something distinctive, stable and enduring, evidence of cultural continuity. An anthology offered the possibility of creating a diasporic 'imagined community' by assembling a geographically dispersed entity in the pages of a book and in the minds of its readers.[20]

## Anthologies of diaspora, 1930s–1970s

The first major anthology of Russian poetry written abroad was published in the mid-1930s at a time when, according to Slobin's periodization of the Russian diaspora, the focus had shifted to 'self-affirmation and consolidation of the diaspora's legacy' as well as increasing 'accommodation' with host countries.[21] In Slobin's view, by this point the diaspora had become increasingly cosmopolitan in its outlook, as those who had left Russia as children came of age and identified more strongly with European modernism than with their elders' allegiance to Russian tradition.[22] Since the compilers of the earlier anthologies came largely from the older generation, born in the 1890s and emigrating between 1917 and the early 1920s, this shift did not necessarily find itself reflected in their selections and the criteria, implicit or explicit, behind them.

This section considers five anthologies produced in diaspora during the Soviet period. The first one, *Iakor'*, appeared in 1935, comprising work by poets in France (61 per cent of contributors), with small numbers of poets in Czechoslovakia, Estonia, China, Poland, Finland, Latvia, Germany, Italy, Serbia, the United States, Belgium and Lithuania. The compilers were the poet and critic Georgii Adamovich, the leader of the 'Paris Note' movement in poetry, and Mikhail Kantor, who had trained as a lawyer but in emigration worked as an editor for Paris-based Russian literary journals. The anthology was published by Petropolis, a publishing house set up in Petrograd which moved first to Berlin, and then, by the mid-1930s, to Brussels. *Iakor'* has six sections: the first comprises poets who were already established before they left Russia; the others are devoted to poets who became known only after emigrating, and are arranged by geographical location: France, Prague, Berlin, the Far East, and a final section for the rest. The second anthology to appear, *Estafeta*, was published in 1948 by Dom knigi. It was printed in Paris, where the bookshop Dom knigi had operated a publishing enterprise between 1938 and 1940; I have not been able to establish whether the publisher of *Estafeta* was connected to this business.[23] *Estafeta* was edited by three poets: Irina Iassen, Vadim Andreev and Iurii Terapiano. Iassen would go on to found the publishing house *Rifma* in Paris in 1949; she had considerable experience as an editor of émigré journals. *Estafeta* is made up of work by poets in France (66 per cent of contributors), poets in the USA (32 per cent) and one poet in the United Kingdom.

In 1953 came the third anthology, *Na Zapade*, compiled by the poet Iurii Ivask. The anthologies that had preceded it had to contend with considerable financial constraints. As Marc Raeff points out, publishing in the pre-war diaspora presented difficulties at every stage, including the high costs of distributing books to customers who were widely dispersed and who could not afford to pay high prices for them.[24] In contrast to preceding anthologies, *Na Zapade* had solid financial backing: it was published by the New York-based Chekhov publishing house, founded in 1951 with finance from the East European Fund, a CIA front organization funded largely by the Ford Foundation. This new publishing house, directed by Nicholas Wreden, was created to assist Russian émigrés and oppose the USSR and Communism.[25] In *Na Zapade*, diaspora poets based in France remained well represented, numbering just over half of contributors, while a little over 25 per cent were based in the United States. The rest represent mainly the pre-war diaspora in Germany, Estonia, Finland, Czechoslovakia, Belgium, Italy and Israel. The poets are divided into categories similar to those in *Iakor'*: those established before emigration, Paris poets, those based in 'small centres' of emigration, for example Prague and Berlin, and poets who had emigrated in the last decade or so, living mostly in the United States. The fourth anthology under discussion, *Muza Diaspory*, was published in 1960 by Posev, a publishing house that originated in 1945 in a displaced persons camp in Germany. Posev played an important role in re-establishing Russian émigré publishing in Europe; it took a clearly anti-Soviet line, producing *tamizdat* – editions of manuscripts banned in the Soviet Union to be smuggled back across the border. Just over half the poets in *Muza Diaspory* (1960), edited by Terapiano, were based in France, 27 per cent in the USA, with small numbers of contributors from Germany, Italy, Finland, Belgium and Israel. The way this anthology is structured does not foreground geographical location. Its first section is made up of work by poets already well known before they went abroad; the second brings together all the rest.

The final Soviet-era diaspora anthology to be considered is *Vne Rossii* (1978), published by Wilhelm Fink, a Munich-based publisher with a strong track record of producing books on Russian literature and reprinting rare works of Russian literature and criticism. The anthology was edited by H. William Tjalsma, an American scholar specializing in Silver Age modernism, including poetry of the interwar emigration. Of the 32 poets in *Vne Rossii*, 20 are from France (62 per cent), eight from the United States (25 per cent), and one each from Estonia, China, Germany and Israel. The four sections, to judge from the introductory essay by George [Iurii] Ivask, group the poets together by generation. This brief overview shows that while these anthologies managed to give some sense of the geographical extent of the diaspora and the post-war shift to the United States, they provided only a limited picture of what poets had produced in some parts of the world, particularly in China. The task of creating a more comprehensive view of diaspora poetry would be taken up by the compilers of anthologies that appeared in the 1990s and later.

The process of sourcing texts for anthologies in diaspora, particularly from the 1930s to the 1950s, involved painstaking work. The editors of *Iakor'*, Adamovich and Kantor, who had already worked together editing journals, placed a newspaper advertisement in September 1934 inviting poets whose work had appeared in periodicals or in separate collections to send in a selection of poems to be considered for inclusion.[26] Correspondence between the editors shows that they also trawled through journals to come up with their final list of poems. Neither *Estafeta* nor *Muza Diaspory* offers clues about the sources its compilers might have drawn on. More helpfully, after the table of contents *Na Zapade* gives an alphabetical list of contributors, with information on the collections published by each poet, and *Vne Rossii* prefaces each poet's work with a list of their published collections.

As far as criteria for selection are concerned, Adamovich's foreword to *Iakor'* announces that the compilers' individual preferences had been set aside as far as possible in order to create a representative picture: 'Personal taste, which cannot be excluded altogether, did of course play its part, guiding us in selecting work that would be most representative of each author.'[27] The balance between preservation and selection was a delicate one, as letters from Adamovich to Kantor show. In a letter of 12 September 1934 Adamovich showed confidence that it would be possible to reconcile quality with representation: '"the best or the most representative?" In my view, the best is also the most representative. In any case, if there is any doubt, then I am on the side of the best.'[28] Writing a year later, as the final version of the anthology was almost complete, Adamovich evidently felt that in some instances the demands of compiling a representative selection had required him to make compromises on matters of taste and quality: 'there are lots of bad poems (Bal'mont! Bunin! etc.)'.[29] Adamovich's foreword makes a case for a balance between selection and preservation, placing emphasis on the compilers' responsibility to create a book that would be an enduring monument to its age; they have an eye to the future and to a sense of perspective that will develop with the passage of time: 'this collection is aimed more at the future than at the present day, and perhaps the future will discover an overall justification for our work where the majority of contemporaries, who so readily talk of "missions" of all kinds, see nothing but frivolity, indulgence and boredom.'[30] Leonid Kostiukov, reviewing the facsimile reprint of *Iakor'* in 2007, described it as being 'like a message in a bottle', a simile that implies that the compilers were sending their book out on an uncertain journey into the unknown.[31]

As the first comprehensive anthology of diaspora poetry, *Iakor'* was, of course, addressed to a contemporary diaspora readership as well as to unknown inhabitants of a remote future world. Present-day concerns were, understandably, prominent in the foreword to *Estafeta*, which reflects the difficult contemporary conditions that the anthology aimed to overcome. Its editors wished to provide the fullest possible picture of the current state of Russian poetry abroad, and to help poets who would otherwise struggle to publish their work, 'given the almost complete lack of literary publications'.[32] Like their predecessors, the compilers of *Iakor'*, the compilers of *Estafeta* declare that they have set aside personal preferences in order to present work by the largest possible number of poets of all tendencies, though they acknowledge that this aim may not have been fully realized owing to the considerable practical difficulties in obtaining contributions from poets scattered across the world.[33] Iurii Ivask's foreword to *Na Zapade* sets out the task for the anthology in the present day: to present readers with a sense of Russian poetry abroad 'as a whole' (*v tselom*), rather than the fragmented and arbitrary picture created by poetry published in journals.[34] Like Adamovich in 1935, Ivask looks to the distant future for an eventual assessment of the merits of this body of work.[35] Iurii Terapiano states his aims in compiling his 1960 anthology, *Muza Diaspory*, in a brief preface. He sets aside any claim that his anthology might present a detailed picture of 40 years of Russian diaspora poetry, stating that it provides 'just the main tendencies in poetry abroad, their style, and their general ideology'.[36] According to Greta Slobin, this anthology's title marks the first use of the word 'diaspora' by a member of the Russian émigré community.[37]

H. W. Tjalsma's preface to *Vne Rossii* is preoccupied with the nature of émigré experience, offering no thoughts on the process of compilation or the criteria for selection. Unlike the compilers of the four earlier anthologies discussed here, Tjalsma was not himself a Russian emigrant. Starting with the proposition that 'the age of alienation' turns all people into émigrés of a kind, he suggests that there is nevertheless something unique about the predicament of émigré poets who must live outside the place where their native language is spoken. This may not, he reflects, be a major problem, 'judging by what Russian émigré poets have achieved since 1917'. The only thing the poets in his anthology have in common, writes Tjalsma, is that they wrote the poems collected in it while living outside Russia. And yet he identifies the specific plight of emigration as something that forms a common thread in their writing: 'More than occasionally ... they share a natural preoccupation with the loss of homeland and the rootless existence of exile. For whatever can be said of the alienation of our world, which makes us all kin, it ignores the practical matters of deprivation and guilt which are the émigré's lot.'[38]

The remainder of this section is concerned with the way these five anthologies handle the question of the relationship with Russia, nation and identity. The title of Tjalsma's anthology defines his selection of poetry in terms of exclusion: it has been created outside Russia, and is at least to some extent defined by loss. The titles of the other anthologies also signal their acknowledgement of the diasporic situation. They reflect to a much greater degree a concern with boundary maintenance in terms of distinctiveness and community. The choice of *Iakor'* (Anchor) certainly suggests an intention of staying put, at least for a time. The metaphor of the anchor assigns agency to Russians in diaspora: they are free to decide when and where they end their voyage. While offering the hope of stability, the anchor metaphor may also imply a certain degree of separation and a reluctance to put down roots. The ship may be at anchor, but the passengers remain on board, constituting some kind of temporary community. Adamovich himself glossed the title as 'a symbol of hope', citing lines by Baratynskii.[39] The title *Estafeta* (Baton) implies the process of passing on the cultural legacy of the diaspora to a new generation, suggesting a mixture of continuity, movement and change. The early years of Russian cultural life abroad gave rise to fears among some that poetry would dwindle and vanish. These fears were recognized by the compilers of *Estafeta* in the foreword, only to be rejected: 'In spite of the indifference and the at times hostile attitude of writers of the older, pre-revolutionary generation, the absence of readers and the huge difficulties of a material nature ... poetry did not die, but a whole set of new names, unknown before the war, has appeared – both in Paris and in New York.'[40] Tellingly, the subtitles of both *Iakor'* and *Estafeta* use the word 'zarubezhnyi' (abroad) rather than 'emigrantskii' (émigré) to describe the poetry they contain, downplaying the moment of departure from the place of origin in favour of acknowledging the present location and shifting the focus from the loss of homeland to the encounter with other places and cultures, and the changing relationship of successive generations to these places and cultures. In diaspora an anthology may function as a surrogate and virtual home, a statement of community and identity based on a shared linguistic and cultural heritage. The title *Na Zapade* similarly emphasizes location and acknowledges the post-war shift towards the United States. The compiler, Ivask, somewhat disingenuously claims that the title of the anthology 'is a simple statement of fact, the interpretation of which is handed over to readers'.[41] The significance of the title, as will be discussed below, is in fact developed in the foreword: location in the West is not to be understood as a dilution of the national in Russian poetry; the contrast between Russia and the West is emphasized.

Unlike the other four, the title of Terapiano's anthology *Muza Diaspory* foregrounds not geographical location, but poetic inspiration. The diaspora is implicitly credited with its own, distinctive creative possibilities, having not only survived but evolved over decades of separation from the metropolis. *Muza Diaspory* and *Na Zapade* use their forewords to address in detail questions of the relationship between Russian poetry abroad and Russia as a source of collective identity. Ivask's foreword to *Na Zapade* identifies three main themes of poetry in emigration: Russia, '*chuzhbina*' (foreign or alien lands) and loneliness, which he declares to be an inevitable part of émigré life but also something common among artists in the West. Ivask states 'The main theme is, of course, Russia', before going on to announce that in the present day, while Western literatures are national in terms of language alone, Russian poetry is 'the most national poetry in Europe'. What precisely is meant by the quality of being 'national' is left vague. Ivask is ready to assert the ubiquity of Russia as a theme: 'Even if the name of Russia is not stated, Russia is present as a hidden motif.'[42] This echoes what Adamovich says in his foreword to *Iakor'*: 'Russia is present as a background or accompaniment.'[43] Foreigners, writes Ivask, tend to see a certain provincialism in the orientation towards Russia, but 'we' are bound by tradition and conscience to the theme. '*Chuzhbina*' repulses some, attracts others, while some are both repelled by and attracted to it. All, however, are enriched by the new experience that it offers. Ivask insists that while poetry reflects the new experiences offered by the world abroad it remains faithful to what he calls the traditional theme of 'Russia and the West'.[44] Nevertheless Ivask is willing to admit that the very fact of emigration has actually enriched Russian poetry.

In his introductory essay to *Muza Diaspory*, Terapiano repeatedly draws parallels between the development of poetry abroad and in the Soviet Union, seeing, for example, in the move away from formal experimentation signs of a fundamental connection between the diaspora and the metropolis that transcends state borders. Nevertheless, the essay establishes a trajectory of development for Russian poetry abroad that was not available to poetry in the Soviet Union: 'The question of man in the new era – not the theoretical "man" as in the Soviet Union, but about man *existing in reality*, and preserved, as if by a miracle, abroad – became the main focus as the theme for the new era and could only be discussed in an atmosphere of freedom, that is, because of the conditions of the time, – abroad.'[45] Terapiano lauds the 'Paris' poets of the 1930s in heroic terms: 'In isolation, in the harsh conditions of émigré life, where each person can rely exclusively on his own individual material and spiritual resources, faced with the complete indifference towards him of both "his own people" and "others", the new man, the Poor Knight, the man of the 1930s was able to achieve great insight and measure thanks to his own spiritual and moral initiative.'[46] The possibility that contact with another culture might have contributed to this generation's insight and creativity is not entertained. When considering the post-war situation, Terapiano continues to take his bearings from a comparison between poetry in the Soviet Union, constrained by lack of freedom, and poetry abroad, which for him embodies creative freedom.

An investigation of the contents of these five anthologies offers a way of testing the claims made by their compilers about the persistence and prevalence of Russia as a theme in diaspora poetry, and of comparing the way each anthology constructs a sense of community and identity in relation to Russia and to nation. What is immediately apparent is that none of these anthologies contain an overwhelming number of poems that are explicitly dedicated to Russian themes such as nostalgia, memories of former homes, a sense of loss of homeland and roots, or a sense of continued connection with the homeland. The majority of poems in all cases are lyrical explorations of emotions such as love or loneliness, momentary moods and impressions, responses to the natural world or evocations of urban and interior scenes. A count of the number of poems explicitly concerned with themes connected to Russia, whether as lost homeland or fondly remembered home, shows that the proportion of poems on such themes actually becomes larger in the anthologies that appeared later on. In *Iakor'* they amount to 12 per cent of the content; in *Estafeta* the proportion is 10 per cent, and in *Na Zapade* 16 per cent. Then the proportion rises to 21 per cent in *Muza Diaspory* and 24 per cent in *Vne Rossii*.

A further examination of the poems that explicitly address Russia-related themes shows considerable variety. Some express a sense of irretrievable loss, or describe an existence that is marked by a sense of being out of place. It is perhaps not surprising that in *Iakor'*, the first anthology to appear, almost 40 per cent of the Russia-themed poems evoke this aspect of the émigré experience. One poem by Raisa Blokh expresses a profound feeling of loss with restraint and a display of stoicism reminiscent of early, pre-revolutionary poems by Anna Akhmatova. The speaker is caught between the need to live in the present and the impossibility of dismissing the memory of her past life, irretrievably lost. The poem begins:

> Принесла случайная молва
> Милые, ненужные слова:
> Летний Сад, Фонтанка и Нева.
>
> Вы, слова залетные, куда?
> Здесь шумят чужие города
> И чужая плещется вода.[47]

Talk, overheard by chance, brought to me dear, unnecessary words: Summer Garden, Fontanka and Neva. Where are you going, you unexpected words? Here is the noise of alien cities and the ripple of alien water.

Not surprisingly, perhaps, the poems in *Iakor'* that evoke feelings of loss and alienation are more frequent among the works of the older generation of poets. At the same time, *Iakor'* contains the largest proportion of poems which express an enduring attachment to Russia and hopes of an eventual return (32 per cent). No subsequent anthology comes even remotely close to this. *Iakor'* is also an outlier as far as poems are concerned which embrace the possibilities of the new place in which the poets now find themselves (25 per cent). With the journey into diaspora still prominent in the memories of the compilers and contributors, it is to be expected that the first diaspora anthology will be more concerned with questions of departure, the attempt to put down new roots, and pondering connections with what has been left behind. After *Iakor'*, the next-highest proportion of poems concerned with emigration as loss is to be found in *Na Zapade* (31 per cent), including Ivan Bunin's 'Poteriannyi rai' (Lost paradise),[48] Dmitri Merezhkovskii's 'Inogda byvaet tak skuchno' (Sometimes it is so dull),[49] and Irina Knorring's bleak vision of her present as an émigré in 'Ia uzh ne tak moloda, chtoby ekhat' v Rossiiu' (I am no longer young enough to go to Russia):

Жизнь прошаталась в тумане – обманчиво серым,
Где даже отблеск огня не сверкал вдалеке.
Нет у меня ни отчизны, ни дружбы, ни веры, –
Зыбкое счастье на зыбком и мертвом песке.[50]

Life has stumbled by in a fog which is deceptive and grey, where not even a reflection of light sparkles in the distance. I have no fatherland, no friendship, no faith, – a fragile happiness on dead and shifting sand.

The future offers no more hopeful prospect than a hospital bed and a simple wooden cross. One of Lidiia Chervinskaia's poems in *Na Zapade* compares the certainties of the past with the unreliable existence of the present day:

Когда-то были: родина, семья,
Враги (или союзники), друзья…
Теперь остались только ты и я.
Но у тебя и в этом есть сомненье.[51]

Once there was a motherland, family, enemies (or allies), friends … Now you and I are all that is left. But you have your doubts even about that.

Poems that consider the loss of homeland and alienation in the present are least numerous in *Estafeta*. This post-war anthology has no poems at all which express a continued emotional attachment to Russia, except through nostalgic reminiscences of childhood and landscape, or through evocations of Russia as a literary construct, represented not through place but through language and the imagination. While nostalgia does feature in poems in which the remembered past is a painful reminder of what has been lost, it appears more frequently in the later anthologies in poems in which memory provides a reassuring sense of identity and continuity. Anthologies of diaspora poetry are unable to recreate a homeland or replace it, but they can provide a space for what Svetlana Boym terms 'reflective nostalgia' (a counter to 'restorative nostalgia' which is focused on a 'national past and future'). Reflective nostalgia is concerned with 'individual and cultural memory'; it 'lingers on ruins, the patina of time and history, in the dreams of another place and another time'.[52] It is, perhaps, reflective nostalgia that informs the insistent attachment to the 'other place and time' of Russia in the foreword to *Na Zapade*, and the deep-rooted cultural memory of the contrast between Russia and the West as a mainstay of Russian identity.

*Na Zapade* is the most nostalgic of the five anthologies. It contains the second-highest proportion of Russian-themed poems that recall moments from childhood or youth in Russia (15 per cent), including recollections of peasant nannies by both Konstantin Bal'mont and Vladislav Khodasevich.[53] There are far more poems offering nostalgic evocations of particular places or landscapes than in any other anthology (37 per cent of the poems that are connected to themes of Russia and home). It finds room for Don Aminado's 'Uezdnaia siren'' (Provincial lilac), recalling the inimitable scent of springtime in Russia (p. 16),[54] Galina Kuznetsova's portrayal of winter sleigh rides, 'Takoe nebo byvaet nad snegom' (p. 161),[55] and a modest domestic Petersburg street scene in Sofiia Pregel''s 'Stalo v ulitsakh dymno i shumno', evoking sights, sounds, scents and sensations, every detail of which is familiar:

Талый лед под перилами булькал,
На мостах врастали горбы.
На ходу обломала сосульку,
У кривой водосточной трубы.[56]

Melting ice gurgled below the railings, the bridges grew into humps.
As I walked I snapped an icicle off the crooked drainpipe.

What is perhaps the most striking feature of the anthologies is that, with the passage of time, references to the Russian literary tradition become more numerous. Russian literature seems to have acted as a shared resource which played an important role in collective identity for members of a diaspora who could see no realistic prospect of a future in the metropolis. As might be expected in *Muza Diaspory*, given the title, such poems make up a significant proportion of poems about Russia and home (29 per cent), but this is far exceeded in *Vne Rossii*, in which 44 per cent of such poems draw on literature to create a sense of belonging. Aleksandr Pushkin is a recurring reference point, whether he is mentioned in passing in Dovid Knut's 'Kishinevskie pokhorony' (Kishinev funeral) (pp. 108–10), or made the centre of attention in Marina Tsvetaeva's 'Stikhi k Pushkinu' (Verses to Pushkin) (pp. 40–4). Other authors who feature include Mikhail Lermontov, Nikolai Gumilev and Alexander Blok.[57] Perhaps the fact that the compiler of *Vne Rossii* was a scholar of Russian literature might help to explain the shift in emphasis.

One of the poems included in *Vne Rossii* offers an example of the way material from the Russian literary tradition may be woven together with the language and literary heritage of other cultures in a creative response to the experience of diaspora. In the form of poetry known as a *cento*, which has its roots in Latin literature, quotations from existing poems by one single author or several different authors are combined to create a new work. The *cento* carries associations of parody and postmodernity, but Nikolai Morshen's playful poem 'Ia svoboden, kak brodiaga' (I am as free as a vagrant) seems to revel in multiple layers of language and allusion, rather than expose the inability of literary texts to transcend their inherent second-hand quotedness. The poem begins with an allusion to Longfellow's 'Song of Hiawatha' which places the poet in America, 'where once Minnehaha sailed past in her boat', but quickly moves on to the question of language. English is not rejected as alien, but Russian remains the most familiar and the most inspiring language. The speaker wanders through a multilingual landscape, where nature once spoke to Minnehaha in 'the Indian language', and speaks to the poet now in English, but, if he listens attentively, he can also make out Russian phrases. The phrases that make up the poem's final stanza are all taken from works that are firmly part of Russia's poetic tradition:

"Вы откуда собралися
"Колокольчики мои?
"В праздник, вечером росистым
"Дятел носом тук да тук
"Песни, вздохи, клики, свисты
"Не пустой для сердца звук.
"Шепот. Робкое дыханье.
"Тень деревьев, злак долин.
"Дольней лозы прозябанье.
"Колокольчик дин-дин-дин…?"[58]

Where have you come from, my little bells? On a holiday, in the evening dew the woodpecker went knock knock with his nose. Songs, sighs, calls, whistles, a sound not without meaning for the heart. A whisper. Timid breathing. The shadows of trees, the grain of the valleys. The growing of the vine in the valley. The little bells go ting-ting-ting …?

Morshen's poem reveals the discovery of something indelibly Russian that is woven into the experience of diaspora. The increasing prevalence in the later anthologies of Russian literary allusions, and of references to the Russian language as an intangible, but enduring, source of identity and continuity may simply reflect the preferences of individual compilers. Or it may be an indication that as the diaspora becomes more established, with increasingly tenuous connections to Russia as a place that could be called 'home', and with an ever more extensive repertoire of poetry created in diaspora, the locus for a sense of collective identity shifts to a shared culture which supplements the roots laid down in a new home by embracing an entire community, wherever it happens to be located.

The analysis of these five anthologies suggests that whatever some compilers might wish to claim in their forewords about an enduring sense of Russia as some kind of national entity, the poetry that they assemble points towards a more personal, less sharply delineated sense of what poets in the diaspora understood about their relationship with the Russian home made up of memories and a common culture.

## Post-Soviet anthologies

It was in the 1990s that the diaspora's literary legacy came to Russia, part of the avalanche of little-known twentieth-century texts that threatened to overwhelm readers. This was a time when the literary canon was up for revision in the wake of the ending of censorship. The mass emergence of texts from abroad, the underground and the archives played its part in demanding a reassessment of Russian identity in the new post-Soviet world. Literature from the diaspora was initially received with nostalgia as a survival from a pre-revolutionary 'originary tradition', and claimed by conservative nationalists as an expression of imperial Russia.[59] The belated encounter with diaspora poetry could be seen as an opportunity to reconnect with a branch of literary tradition that had not been scarred by Soviet oppression, to encounter some kind of authentic pre-revolutionary Russian identity. This last idea rested on the belief that Russian poetry abroad had existed in some sterile and unchanging environment where it had been preserved for use on its eventual return. Vadim Kreid, in the foreword to his 1995 anthology, *Vernut'sia v Rossiiu – stikhami* (*Return to Russia – in poems*), described the predicament of émigré poetry in exactly these terms, declaring that it 'existed in conditions of absolute creative freedom and in an absolutely indifferent alien environment, lacking external stimuli' but nevertheless continued to be 'inspired, inspiring and fruitful!'.[60]

As it turned out, the discovery of diasporic poetry may have had a particular resonance for post-Soviet Russian readers not because of its assumed connection with an 'authentic' but vanished Russia, but because of its origins in sudden change and deprivation. Like émigrés who left Russia after the 1917 October Revolution, readers in post-1991 Russia faced the traumatic loss of their country and of a familiar way of life. Serguei Oushakine identifies loss as the defining characteristic of the post-Soviet experience: 'the sharp disruption of once stable institutions resulted in poverty, a loss of status, or professional disorientation.'[61] The predicament of Russian émigrés after 1917, as described by Natalia Starostina, might have entailed coping with a new language, but otherwise involved many uncertainties similar to those confronting the Russian population in the early 1990s: 'Emigration brought the world of poverty, even misery, an alien linguistic milieu, an uncertain future, and, worst of all, the realization that there was no return to the past life.'[62] It should not be forgotten, either, that some ethnic Russian inhabitants of other former Soviet republics did themselves experience enforced emigration from a familiar environment to a place that both was, and was not, their home.

Slobin describes the encounter between the Russian homeland and diaspora writing as 'a tale of competing cultural monopolies, incongruous resemblances, and matching nostalgias'.[63] The process of 'repatriation' involved a certain amount of misrecognition by the receiving party; the sheer quantity of unfamiliar texts created over several decades made it difficult to gain a rapid overview of the work of diaspora poets. Slobin notes a tendency of authors attempting to assimilate the legacy of diaspora literature to focus on continuities between writers in the Soviet Union and writers abroad, and to give little attention to the fact that the legacy of diaspora went beyond the preservation and continuation of a national culture, to active engagement with other cultures.[64] This engagement left its mark in hybrid work that, like Morshen's poem discussed above, maintained distinctive Russian elements but was also open to the environment in which it was produced. The rush to assimilate diaspora poetry into a revised national canon, part of a literary heritage energetically claimed as undivided, meant that the ways in which this poetry responded to other cultural traditions, while also asserting its distinctiveness in relation to Russian poetry written in the Soviet Union, were largely disregarded.

An essential stage in the process of integrating diaspora literature consisted of efforts to make texts available to readers, many of them for the first time. Here the role of the anthology was potentially significant as a way of acquainting readers with a broad overview of poets' work across several decades. The 1990s saw a boom in the production of substantial anthologies which announced themselves as comprehensive reflections of the century's poetry, or as exhaustive representations of the hitherto largely unknown works of poets who wrote in the diaspora. The two largest anthologies of twentieth-century poetry that appeared in the 1990s each offer their readers works by a considerable number of diaspora poets. *Strofy veka* includes around 150 of them, while *Russkaia poeziia: XX vek* includes just over 100 names. There is a significant overlap in the selection of poets, but far less overlap in the poems chosen to represent them, suggesting some differences in the agenda pursued by each anthology, beyond their shared commitment to providing readers with breadth of coverage.[65] Both, unsurprisingly, include Ivan Bunin. In *Strofy veka* he is represented entirely by poems written before his emigration. In *Russkaia poeziia: XX vek* there are poems addressing directly the poet's suffering arising from being exiled, and a prophecy of doom issued to the nation that has been led, apparently willingly, to its own downfall.[66] The anthologies' treatment of Dmitrii Klenovskii also suggests a greater preoccupation shown by the compilers of *Russkaia poeziia: XX vek* with the theme of exile and a nostalgic attachment to the Russian homeland. Their selection of poems by Klenovskii is rather more extensive than the one put forward in *Strofy veka* and includes nostalgic references to sites connected with Russia's cultural heritage, and with Pushkin in particular, as well as a yearning to remember the voice of someone lost, or left behind, in his home country;[67] *Strofy veka* presents just two poems by Klenovskii, neither of which address themes so explicitly linked with the poet's separation from Russia.

Ol'ga Demidova, writing in 2000 about the process of canonization of émigré literature with particular reference to female authors, offers the following comment about recent anthologies of émigré poetry:

> During the last ten years the literature of the emigration 'has returned to its homeland', which may be considered in itself a process of particular importance for Russian culture. However, speaking of the current perception of émigré literature in Russia, one must acknowledge that it is in fact a perception of a perception. The compilers of contemporary anthologies of émigré literature either aim to take account of all literary facts as far as possible, or base their work on anthologies published in the diaspora from the 1930s to the 1960s.

As a result, Demidova continues, recent anthologies put forward forgotten or little-known poets, or reproduce texts published many times before. In her view, both the critical reception of diaspora literature and the 'material canon' have barely changed over a number of decades.[68]

The 1995 four-volume anthology 'My zhili togda na planete drugoi...' (We lived on a different planet then ...) may be seen as an example of an anthology focused on providing broad coverage of poetry from the first and second waves of emigration, combining some familiar names and texts with others barely known. A further volume dedicated to the third wave of emigration had been in preparation, but financial difficulties prevented its publication.[69] The anthology takes its title from a poem by Georgy Ivanov, 'Nad rozovym morem' (Over the rosy sea).[70] This line of verse frames the anthology's entire project as one of return from somewhere almost impossibly distant and alien, and emphasizes its role in acquainting readers in Russia with a more or less unknown body of work. The fact that it was this poem in particular that was chosen to give the anthology its title actually hints at a more complicated relationship between diaspora and metropolis, as it provided the lyrics for a song by Aleksandr Vertinskii which he recorded in Moscow in the year following his return from Shanghai to the Soviet Union in 1943. A poem that asserted an absolute, unbridgeable distance between 'here' and 'there', 'now' and 'then', was brought to the author's country of origin and became part of Stalin-era culture, while the author remained in France.[71] In fact, there were other poems from the diaspora that reached Soviet readers before the 1990s, as work by, for example, Bunin and Tsvetaeva gradually filtered through a less draconian post-Stalin censorship system together with work by poets who remained in the Soviet Union, like Akhmatova and Osip Mandelstam.

In his introduction to 'My zhili togda na planete drugoi...' the editor Evgenii Vitkovskii announces his intention to rescue 'émigré poets' from the pejorative attitudes that were formerly associated with this category of writer in the Soviet Union. His point of view is one of repatriation and assimilation: the literary emigration is viewed as a tradition that existed in parallel to other contemporary marginalized branches of literature inside the Soviet Union, the poetry of the labour camps and internal exile, as well as works which were confined to the desk drawer. All of these, he argues, were banished by the same force: the Soviet state.[72] Vitkovskii sees only a limited influence of the cultures of the host countries on the work of diaspora poets, and regrets that contacts with other literatures were so rare. His stated agenda is to 'show émigré poetry as it is', which, in his view, is to reveal its strong relationship, whether through form or content, to contemporary modernism.[73] This aspiration brings to mind Ilya Kukulin's preferred approach to reconstructing the canon of twentieth-century poetry: émigré poetry, together with underground poetry, in his view, should serve as the basis for this revised canon.[74] The literary-historical role that was assigned to diaspora poetry, as it arrived in Russia and was appropriated as part of a national canon, was that of the 'missing link' between early twentieth-century modernism and contemporary modernist writing. The 'repatriation' of modernist tradition conveniently marginalized any part that 'permitted' Soviet poetic culture might have played in the genesis of contemporary modernism.

It is instructive to consider, finally, a somewhat different anthology of Russian diaspora poetry. The year 2017 saw the publication in Germany of a massive four-volume anthology, *Sto let russkoi zarubezhnoi poezii* (A hundred years of Russian poetry abroad). The foreword to Volume 1 stresses the anthology's coverage of poetry from all the sites of Russian emigration and the range of poets included (many of whom did not feature in *Iakor'*, *Estafeta*, *Na Zapade*, *Muza Diaspory* and *Vne Rossii*).[75] Vladimir Batshev's forewords to the four volumes, taken together, reject the idea that there is one Russian poetry that forms a united whole irrespective of where it is written. Batshev's own experience most probably helped to shape his attitude towards the 'rhetoric of a unified literary canon'. He was one of the organizers of the unofficial SMOG group of poets in the 1960s, and was arrested in 1966 and sent into exile; after his return from exile Batshev was once more involved in the literary underground, joining the diaspora only in 1995 when he left Russia for Germany. In his foreword to the final volume he writes disparagingly of contemporary poets who left Russia after 1991 but are focused on publishing their work in Russia. In his view, they can barely be described as poets of Russia Abroad. He comments that some,

> driven by an insatiable desire to be published, have rushed to approach the journals and publishers run by the pogrom organizers back home …, shedding crocodile tears about their so-called 'lost homeland', which they (of course!) 'have never forgotten in a foreign land'. But they prefer to live outside the borders of their 'wonderful motherland', running to the Russian consulate for miserly handouts and taking part in suspect gatherings of their 'fellow countrymen'.[76]

This anthology does not subscribe to the rhetoric of return, but asserts a separate identity for Russian poetry written outside Russia. Batshev is clearly committed to diasporic practices of boundary maintenance and to a nuanced understanding of the meaning of home for a diaspora community marking its centenary.

## Conclusion

In conclusion, the evidence offered by the various anthologies that have been discussed in this chapter shows that while some effort has been made from the 1990s onwards to suggest that the place of diaspora poetry lies within the Russian national canon, and much work has been done by editors such as Vitkovskii to bring this material into the accessible canon for Russian readers, there remains a fundamental ambivalence in the relationship between this body of work and its putative Russian 'home'. The boundary between Self and Other is difficult to determine because diaspora poetry came from the same roots as poetry written in the Soviet Union, but developed in very different conditions, subject to the specific pressures – and opportunities – of emigration. The canon of Russian twentieth-century poetry presents difficulties because so much material that might claim a place within it has been out of wide circulation, whether in Russia or abroad, remaining for many years beyond the reach of the multiple layers of agents such as editors, booksellers, reviewers, scholars and readers whose decisions contribute to the process of canon formation and revision. While Soviet writers and critics during the Cold War era may have enjoyed privileged access to émigré and *tamizdat* writing, their discoveries could not be shared with a wider public and could play no significant role in shaping the poetic canon for anyone outside their immediate circles.

This chapter has explored the contrast between the earlier diaspora anthologies which were published mostly with the diaspora readership in mind, and the post-Soviet anthologies which were dominated by the idea of 'returning' this work as if to a place of ultimate national origin. The anthologies created in diaspora announced the survival of Russian poetry outside Russia, and offered a space in which a sense of community that was not defined by national boundaries might find expression. They asserted the existence of a community united by language, by a shared cultural heritage, by the experience of making a new life abroad, by the acceptance of diversity. The later anthologies compiled for post-Soviet Russian readers put nation back in the frame as the overriding element, foregrounding unity imagined as linguistic, cultural and national (both as imagined community and as political/historical community). Andrei Permiakov has his doubts as to the feasibility of creating an all-encompassing picture of Russian poetry 'as a phenomenon that is uninterrupted in space and time'. Because efforts to gather everything together have begun only recently, he argues, 'our numerous anthologies are like stars in a very fragmented space, and are incapable of forming a structured constellation'.[77] Given the specific conditions in which Russian diaspora poetry and Russian poetry written inside the Soviet Union emerged and developed, we should at least entertain the possibility that these stars may belong to the same universe, but in solar systems that are still perhaps light years apart.

## Acknowledgement

I would like to express my gratitude to Pamela Davidson and Kevin Platt for their insightful and very helpful comments on an earlier draft of this chapter.

## Notes

1   Rubins 2015, 9.
2   Brubaker 2005, 6.
3   Brah 1996, 192.
4   Brah 1996, 182.
5   Brah 1996, 193.
6   Golding 1995, 3–40.
7   Dostoevsky 2010, 17–19.
8   Slobin 2013, 23.
9   Fowler 1979; Golding 1995, 7.
10  Iassen, Andreev and Terapiano 1948, 5. Translations from Russian to English, unless otherwise indicated, are by the author.
11  Kuz'min 2001, 53.
12  Slobin 2013, 24.
13  See, for example, Eliasberg and Eliasberg 1920; Sviatopolk-Mirsky 1924.
14  Slobin 2013, 22.
15  Ivask 1953, 7.
16  Winko 2002.
17  Guillory 1994.
18  Bloom 1995, 522.
19  Kermode 2004, 36; Lauter 1991, 58.
20  The term 'imagined community' is from Anderson 2006, 6.
21  Slobin 2013, 16.
22  Slobin 2013, 27–8.
23  Shraer 2014, footnote 253.
24  Raeff 1990, 74.
25  Karpovich 1957, 53–8; Saunders 2013, 118.

26  Adamovich and Kantor 2005, 253.
27  Adamovich and Kantor 2005, 5. Translations are the authors, unless indicated otherwise.
28  Adamovich and Kantor 2005, 264.
29  Adamovich and Kantor 2005, 287.
30  Adamovich and Kantor 2005, 7.
31  Kostiukov 2007.
32  Iassen, Andreev and Terapiano 1948, 5.
33  Iassen, Andreev and Terapiano 1948, 6.
34  Ivask 1953, 5.
35  Ivask 1953, 7.
36  Terapiano 1960, 5.
37  Slobin 2013, 20.
38  Tjalsma 1978, v.
39  Adamovich and Kantor 2005, 7.
40  Iassen, Andreev and Terapiano 1948, 5.
41  Ivask 1953, 8.
42  Ivask 1953, 6.
43  Adamovich and Kantor 2005, 6.
44  Ivask 1953, 6.
45  Terapiano 1960, 15.
46  Terapiano 1960, 20.
47  Raisa Blokh, 'Prinesla sluchainaia molva', in Adamovich and Kantor 2005, 165.
48  Ivan Bunin, 'Poteriannyi rai', in Ivask 1953, 21.
49  Dmitri Merezhkovskii, 'Inogda byvaet tak skuchno', in Ivask 1953, 56.
50  Irina Knorring, 'Ia uzhe ne tak moloda, chtoby ekhat' v Rossiiu', in Ivask 1953, 149.
51  Lidiia Chervinskaia, 'Kogda-to byli my – i bedniaki', in Ivask 1953, 253.
52  Boym 2001, 49, 41.
53  Konstantin Bal'mont, 'Ia pomniu, mne chetyre bylo goda', in Ivask 1953, 18; Vladislav Khodasevich, 'Ne mater'iu, no tul'skoiu krest'iankoi', in Ivask 1953, 72–3.
54  Don Aminado, 'Uezdnaia siren'', in Ivask 1953, 16.
55  Galina Kuznetsova, 'Takoe nebo byvaet nad snegom', in Ivask 1953, 161.
56  Sofiia Pregel', 'Stalo v ulitsakh dymno i shumno', in Ivask 1953, 220.
57  Dovid Knut, 'Kishinevskie pokhorony', in Tjalsma 1978, 108–10; Marina Tsvetaeva, 'Stikhi k Pushkinu', in Tjalsma 1978, 40–4. Khodasevich alludes to Gavriil Derzhavin in 'Ne iambom li chetyrekhstopnym' in Tjalsma 1978, 16–17; Georgy Ivanov to Mikhail Lermontov in 'Melodiia stanovitsia tsvetkom', in Tjalsma 1978, 56; Irina Odoevtseva to Nikolai Gumilev in 'Ballada o Gumileve', in Tjalsma 1978, 66–9; Lidiia Chervinskaia to Alexander Blok in 'Khochetsia Blokovskoi, shchedroi napevnosti', in Tjalsma 1978, 107.
58  Nikolai Morshen, 'Ia svoboden, kak brodiaga', in Tjalsma 1978, 1551. Morshen's collage is made up of the following, in order: Aleksei Khomiakov, 'Vysoko peredo mnoiu'; Alexei Tolstoi, 'Kolokol'chiki moi'; Lermontov, 'Rodina'; L. N. Modzalevsky, 'S dobrym utrom!'; Derzhavin, 'Solovei vo sne'; Blok, 'Pushkinskomu domu'; Afanasii Fet, 'Shepot. Robkoe dykhan'e'; Fedor Tiutchev, 'Poshli, gospod', svoiu otradu', Pushkin, 'Prorok' and 'Besy'.
59  Slobin 2013, 221.
60  Kreid 1995, 20–1.
61  Oushakine 2009, 4.
62  Starostina 2015, 82.
63  Slobin 2013, 210.
64  Slobin 2013, 217, 219.
65  See Hodgson 2012.
66  The Bunin poems referred to are 'Izgnanie' and 'Iz knigi proroka Isaii', in Kostrov and Krasnikov 1999, 51–2.
67  The poems by Klenovskii referred to are 'Boldinskaia osen'', 'Pirog s gribami stynet na stole', 'O, tol'ko by pripomnit' golos tvoi', 'Stikhi o Peterburge', in Kostrov and Krasnikov 1999, 183–4.
68  Demidova 2000.
69  According to Permiakov 2018.
70  The poem itself is not included in the anthology. It can be found in Evtushenko 1995, 266.
71  I am grateful to Kevin Platt for bringing this particular point to my attention.
72  Vitkovskii 1995, 1:6–7.

73  Vitkovskii 1995, 1:16, 33.
74  Kukulin 2001, 438.
75  Vladimir Batshev, 'O poezii pervoi volny emigratsii', in Kiprischi 2017, 1:14.
76  Batshev, 'O poezii emigratsii 21 veka', in Kiprischi 2017, 4:10.
77  Permiakov 2018.

# Bibliography

Adamovich, G. V. and M. L. Kantor, compilers. *Iakor': antologiia russkoi zarubezhnoi poezii.* St Petersburg: Aleteiia, 2005. (Reprint of 1936 original.)

Anderson, Benedict. *Imagined Communities: Reflections on the origin and spread of nationalism.* Revised edition. London: Verso, 2006.

Bloom, Harold. *The Western Canon: The books and school of the ages.* London: Macmillan, 1995.

Boym, Svetlana. *The Future of Nostalgia.* New York: Basic Books, 2001.

Brah, Avtar. *Cartographies of Diaspora: Contesting identities.* London and New York: Routledge, 1996.

Brubaker, Rogers. 'The "diaspora" diaspora', *Ethnic and Racial Studies* 28(1) (January 2005): 1–19.

Demidova, Ol'ga. '"Emigrantskie docheri" i literaturnyi kanon russkogo zarubezh'ia'. In *Pol. Gender. Kul'tura*, vol. 2, edited by Elizabet Shore and Karolin Khaider, 205–19. Moscow: Izdatel'skii tsentr Rossiiskogo gosudarstvennogo gumanitarnogo universiteta, 2000. http://www.a-z.ru/women_cd1/html/pol_gender_cultura_m2000_d.htm (accessed 5 September 2020).

Dostoevsky, F. M. 'On Russian distinctiveness and universality'. In *The Russia Reader: History, culture, politics*, edited by Adele Barker and Bruce Grant, 16–19. Durham, NC, and London: Duke University Press, 2010.

Eliasberg, Aleksandr and David Eliasberg, compilers. *Russkii Parnas.* Leipzig: Insel Verlag, 1920.

Evtushenko, Evgenii, compiler. *Strofy veka: antologiia russkoi poezii.* Moscow: Polifakt, 1995.

Fowler, Alastair. 'Genre and the literary canon', *New Literary History* 11(1) (1979): 97–119.

Golding, Alan. *From Outlaw to Classic: Canons in American poetry.* Madison: University of Wisconsin Press, 1995.

Guillory, John. *Cultural Capital: The problem of literary canon formation.* Chicago and London: University of Chicago Press, 1994.

Hodgson, Katharine. 'Two post-Soviet anthologies of the 1990s and the Russian 20th-century poetry canon', *Slavonic and East European Review* 90(4) (2012): 642–70.

Iassen, Irina, Vadim Andreev and Iurii Terapiano, eds. *Estafeta: sbornik stikhov russkikh zarubezhnykh poetov.* Paris and New York: Dom knigi, 1948.

Ivask, Iurii, compiler. *Na Zapade: antologiia russkoi zarubezhnoi poezii.* New York: Izdatel'stvo imeni Chekhova, 1953.

Karpovich, Michael. 'The Chekhov Publishing House', *Russian Review* 16(1) (January 1957): 53–8.

Kermode, Frank. *Pleasure and Change: The aesthetics of canon.* Oxford: Oxford University Press, 2004.

Kiprischi, Gershom, ed. *Sto let russkoi zarubezhnoi poezii.* 4 vols. Frankfurt am Main: Literaturnyi evropeets, 2017.

Kostiukov, Leonid. 'Iakor': antologiia zarubezhnoi poezii', *Znamia* 2 (2007). https://magazines.gorky.media/znamia/2007/2/yakor-antologiya-russkoj-zarubezhnoj-poezii-1936-sostavlenie-g-v-adamovich-m-l-kantor-pod-red-o-korosteleva-l-magarotto-a-ustinova.html (accessed 5 September 2020).

Kostrov, Vladimir and Genadii Krasnikov, compilers. *Russkaia poeziia, XX vek: antologiia.* Moscow: Olma-Press, 1999.

Kreid, Vadim, compiler. *Vernut'sia v Rossiiu – stikhami: 200 poetov emigratsii.* Moscow: Respublika, 1995.

Kukulin, Il'ia. 'Proryv k nevozmozhnoi sviazi (pokolenie 90-kh v russkoi poezii: vozniknovenie novykh kanonov)', *Novoe literaturnoe obozrenie* 50 (2001): 435–58.

Kuz'min, Dmitry. 'V zerkale antologii', *Arion* 2 (2001): 48–61.

Lauter, Paul. *Canons and Contexts.* New York and Oxford: Oxford University Press, 1991.

Oushakine, Serguei. *The Patriotism of Despair: Nation, war, and loss in Russia.* Ithaca, NY, and London: Cornell University Press, 2009.

Permiakov, Andrei, 'Vremia antologii, ili Mechta ob ideale', *Arion*, 1 (2018): 73–87.

Raeff, Marc. *Russia Abroad: A cultural history of the Russian emigration, 1919–1934.* New York: Oxford University Press, 1990.

Rubins, Maria. *Russian Montparnasse: Transnational writing in interwar Paris.* Basingstoke: Palgrave Macmillan, 2015.

Saunders, Frances Stonor. *The Cultural Cold War: The CIA and the world of arts and letters.* New York: New Press, 2013.

Shraer, Maksim D. *Bunin i Nabokov: istoriia sopernichestva.* Moscow: Al'pina non-fikshn, 2014. E-book.

Slobin, Greta. *Russians Abroad: Literary and cultural politics of diaspora (1919–1939).* Boston, MA: Academic Studies Press, 2013.

Starostina, Natalia. 'The construction of a new émigré self in 20th-century Russian Paris in short stories by Nadezhda Teffi', *Canadian Review of Comparative Literature* 42(1) (March 2015): 81–93.

Sviatopolk-Mirsky, D. P., compiler. *Russkaia lirika: malen'kaia antologiia ot Lomonosova do Pasternaka.* Paris: La Presse Franco-Russe, 1924.

Terapiano, Iurii, ed. *Muza Diaspory: izbrannye stikhi zarubezhnykh poetov, 1920–1960.* Frankfurt am Main: Posev, 1960.

Tjalsma, H. W., ed. *Vne Rossii: antologiia emigrantskoi poezii 1917–1975.* Munich: Wilhelm Fink Verlag, 1978.

Vitkovskii, Evgenii, ed. *'My zhili togda na planete drugoi...': antologiia poezii russkogo zarubezh'ia.* 4 vols. Moscow: Molodaia gvardiia, 1995.

Winko, Simone. 'Literatur-Kanon als "invisible hand"-Phänomen'. In *Literarische Kanonbildung,* special issue of *Text + Kritik*, edited by Hermann Korte (2002): 9–24.

# 7
# Is there room for diaspora literature in the internet age?
Mark Lipovetsky

According to Rogers Brubaker, the term 'diaspora' comprises, even in its broadest definition, such criteria as 1) dispersion: 'any kind of dispersion in space, provided that the dispersion crosses state borders'; 2) homeland orientation: 'the orientation to a real or imagined "homeland" as an authoritative source of value, identity and loyalty'; and 3) boundary maintenance: 'the preservation of a distinctive identity vis-à-vis a host society (or societies).'[1] These criteria appear to be applicable not only to Russian-speaking diaspora in the traditional sense of the word, but also to the self-proclaimed liberal intelligentsia of contemporary, 'post-Crimean' Russia – i.e., those representatives of the self-appointed 'creative class' who don't share a governing nationalist sentiment and are appalled by the jingoist spectacle of Russia's supposed greatness dominating media and political spheres.

Given how highly this intelligentsia values the opportunity to travel and live outside Russia for significant periods of time (study, grants, fellowships, frequent vacations), thus becoming semi-professional globe-trotters, the applicability of Brubaker's first criterion of spatial displace-ment might not seem so much like a stretch. As for the other two criteria, homeland orientation and boundary maintenance, they describe more than adequately the self-identification of the contemporary Russian liberal, for whom concerns about the state of the homeland are inseparable from a sense of alienation from the 'host population'. Their position is not only comparable but, in fact, symmetrical to the diasporic alienation of Russian-speaking Americans, Germans or Brits from their environment and its values and dominant discourses.[2]

Furthermore, the development of internet-based social networks tangibly increases communication and, resultantly, strengthens the similarity between the two diasporas – in Russia and outside it – whose intellectual and even emotional life appears to be synchronized by Facebook: its hot topics for discussion, shared readings and screenings, frequent exchanges of opinions, and online friendships that either serve as extensions of long-running offline relationships or, on the contrary, generate new associations offline.

Considering these circumstances, one may assume that a side-by-side analysis of the literary output of these two tightly interwoven communities would blur any distinction between the diasporic and homeland literatures. Parallels between the 'external' and 'internal' diasporas in this case reflect a cognate existential condition, while their differences register only in the exterior setting – professional life, daily routine, additional media background, etc. – which may or may not affect the intellectual and emotional experience and identity of the writer. If this supposition is correct, then the concept of diaspora should be radically reassessed for the internet age, in which geographical distances and corresponding allegiances appear to be less important than discursive divides and cultural (or ideological) citizenships.

In my chapter, I am testing this hypothesis by analysing comparable texts about the Siege of Leningrad written by émigré authors and homeland writers from the liberal milieu. The selection of this theme is far from accidental. In the 1960s–1980s, the difference between literature about the Siege published in the Soviet Union and that published abroad was clear as concerned such aspects of the Leningrad ordeal as cannibalism, privileges for party and NKVD officials in contrast to the starvation of ordinary people, continuing political oppressions, and so on. In Soviet literature these motifs were either completely absent – for example from Aleksandr Chakovsky's celebrated novel *Blokada* (1969) – or minimized by censorship, as in the documentary *Blokadnaia kniga* (1977–81) by Daniil Granin and Ales' Adamovich.[3] Conversely, in émigré literature such as Anatolii Darov's novel *Blokada* (1964) the same facets of the Siege were represented fully. Furthermore, they were not neglected in the homeland texts that remained in 'desk drawers' until perestroika, such as Lydia Ginzburg's *Zapiski blokadnogo cheloveka* (1984).

Since perestroika, thematic differences between 'domestic' and émigré writings about wartime Leningrad have become irrelevant in the wake of multiple journalistic and scholarly publications about the historical realities of the Siege.[4] However, it is universally acknowledged that in the post-Soviet period, and especially in the 2000s and 2010s, victory in the Great Patriotic War (i.e., World War II minus the Soviet alliance with Germany) has become the cornerstone of post-Soviet identity making and has acquired increasingly nationalist overtones.[5] They have accelerated the transformation of the Great Patriotic War into the foundational post-Soviet sacred, harvesting multiple mythological narratives: the victorious greatness of the Soviet empire, Russia's endless suffering as the flipside of its messianic role, Europe's and America's 'indebtedness' to Russia because of its unprecedented suffering, etc.

The Leningrad Siege, in many respects, constitutes the heart of this new sacred discourse. Many may recollect a political campaign in the finest traditions of Soviet *prorabotka*, only here with capitalist overtones, against the cable channel *Dozhd'*, triggered by its 'blasphemous' poll from January 2014 (i.e., before the annexation of Crimea), which included a question about the potential upshot of surrendering Leningrad to the Germans: 'Should Leningrad have been given up in order to save hundreds of thousands of lives?' The public campaign of indignation following the poll included an audit of the station conducted by the Prosecutor's office, demands to the State and the St Petersburg Duma to shut the channel down, multiple sponsors withdrawing their investments, and thousands of ordinary citizens expressing anger and disgust towards so-called shameless journalists.[6]

At the same time, after the dissemination of Lydia Ginzburg's previously unpublished works, along with several other memoirs (by Olga Freidenberg, Liubov' Shaporina, Sofia Ostrovskaya, to name a few) and literary works (Gennady Gor's poetry),[7] the Leningrad Siege, which seemed to be completely museified, inspired a new generation of scholars and writers both in Russia and abroad to seek to release it from these Soviet and post-Soviet political interpretations. New works about the Blockade have highlighted specific discourses of Soviet traumatic writing,[8] survival skills as a form of political resistance,[9] and even the grotesque concentration of Soviet existential experience.[10] The Siege experience has re-emerged in the 2000s and 2010s as a nexus of competing identity constructions. Being the epitome of heroism, self-sacrifice and exalted suffering in the official mythology, Leningrad also offers itself as an ideal 'crisis' heterotopia (per Michel Foucault): a de-realized space perfectly matching 'a new diasporic, hybrid subjectivity' with its gravitation towards 'in-between spaces'.[11] All these factors explain the emergence of literary texts about the Siege in the homeland and diasporic literatures alike.

In this chapter I discuss three groups of texts, comparable in their poetics: two poems, by Vitaly Pukhanov and Sergei Zav'ialov; two plays, by Iurii Klavdiev and Polina Barskova; and two modernist/postmodernist novels, by Andrei Turgenev (aka Viacheslav Kuritsyn) and Igor

Vishnevetsky. Pukhanov lives in Moscow, Kuritsyn and Klavdiev both live in St Petersburg, and all belong to the liberal community, while Zav'ialov and Barskova live outside of Russia. As for Vishnevetsky, he lived in the US for more than 10 years, returned to Russia in 2008, and in 2010 won a prestigious NOS (Novaia slovesnost' / New literature) prize for his novel *Leningrad* (2010); he wrote that book, however, while living in Pittsburg, Pennsylvania, where he now resides permanently.

Certainly, given the biographical circumstances of these writers, it becomes almost impossible to clearly delineate homeland from diasporic texts: when exactly does a text become a diasporic text? The anonymous reviewer of this chapter asked this question and added a series of derivative ones: 'How long must an author have lived outside Russia to become a diasporic writer – days, months, years? Can the affiliation or non-affiliation to diaspora be measured in time or is it maybe a question of new experiences, engagement with the host culture, etc.?' I have no answers to the first two questions – and this, I guess, is indicative of the fuzziness of the category of 'diaspora' itself. Indeed, diasporic writing would be associated with new experiences and engagement with the host culture, but these experiences can be effectively obtained through internet-based communication, while the real-life experiences of émigrés can be marked by isolation from the host culture.

Therefore, I would suggest looking at my experiment in comparison of texts about the Siege of Leningrad written in the 2000s and 2010s as an attempt to define *typologically different approaches* to the same historical event, or to the representation of traumatic history in general – one group of these approaches I will more or less tentatively define as 'diasporic', and another as 'homeland', with a full understanding of the instability of these terms and their applications.

## Poems

Vitaly Pukhanov (born 1966), a Moscow-based poet, author of several books of poetry, and the executive secretary of the state-sponsored literary prize Debut (2003–18), published in February 2009 the poem 'V Leningrade na rassvete' ('In Leningrad at dawn') on the website LiveJournal. The piece triggered a heated internet discussion.[12] Some readers of the poem were sincerely shocked and plainly disgusted by the tangible conflict between its rhythm and its subject matter. Naturally, the use of the trochaic tetrameter produces a scandalous effect in conjunction with the theme of the Leningrad Siege, since in Russian tradition this metre, as Ilya Kukulin demonstrated,[13] is primarily associated with children's verses (from Pushkin's fairy tales to Kornei Chukovsky's 'Moidodyr' and Sergei Mikhalkov's 'Diadia Stepa'). Alexander Zholkovsky, in his analysis of Zabolotsky's 'Merknut znaki zodiaka', another poem that uses this metre, discusses its connection with the writings of OBERIU (a group of absurdist poets in Leningrad of the late 1920s) and their playful and surreal phantasmagorias.[14]

'V Leningrade na rassvete' reads as follows:

*Александру Секацкому*

В Ленинграде, на рассвете,
На Марата, в сорок третьем
Кто-то съел тарелку щей
И нарушил ход вещей.

Приезжают два наряда
Милицейских: есть не надо,
Вы нарушили режим,
Мы здесь мяса не едим!

Здесь глухая оборона.
Мы считаем дни войны.
Нам ни кошка, ни ворона
Больше в пищу не годны:

Страшный голод-людопад
Защищает Ленинград!
Насыпает город-прах
Во врагов смертельный страх.

У врага из поля зренья
Исчезает Ленинград.
Зимний где? Где Летний сад?
Здесь другое измеренье:

Наяву и во плоти
Тут живому не пройти.
Только так мы победим,
Потому мы не едим.

Время выйдет, и гранит
Плоть живую заменит.
Но запомнит враг любой,
Что мы сделали с собой.

Февраль 2009

> *to Alexander Sekatsky*

In Leningrad, at dawn,
On Marata, in '43,
Someone ate a bowl of cabbage soup
And violated the way of things.

There come along two police crews:
You don't need to eat,
You've disobeyed the regime,
We don't eat meat here!

A deep defence is here.
We count the days of the war.
For us neither a cat nor a crow
Is fit to eat any more:

A fearsome hunger-people-fall
Protects Leningrad!
Fear of death pours city-ashes
On the enemies.

Leningrad disappears
From the field of the enemy's vision.
Where's the Winter Palace? Where's the Summer Garden?
Here's a different dimension:

In reality and in the flesh
There is no passing for the living here.
Just so we will win,
For that we do not eat.

Time will prevail, and granite
Will replace living flesh.
But any enemy will remember
What we have done to ourselves.

February 2009

In the subsequent discussion in the Moscow-based journal *Novoe literaturnoe obozrenie* (*New literary observer*), three critics – Kukulin, Stanislav L'vovsky and Irina Kaspe – thoroughly analysed the poem's form and content. Kukulin interprets this poem as a dramaturgic and unresolved conflict of at least two discourses, one reminiscent of OBERIU and another of Anna Akhmatova's 'Requiem' ('Эта женщина больна…' / 'This woman is sick …'). According to Kukulin, 'V Leningrade' shows how the perspective of the dead is appropriated by the authorities, who devalue their tragedy by turning it into a grotesque fairy tale and in doing so block historical memory. Stanislav L'vovsky draws attention to the poem's dedication to the conservative Petersburg philosopher Alexander Sekatsky and argues that Pukhanov is attacking the neo-imperialist, 'Hyperborean' ideology epitomized by Sekatsky, according to which the intentional and exalted sacrifice of physical needs and life altogether for the sake of the symbolic superiority of spirit constitutes the main lesson and legacy of Soviet culture.[15]

I could add to this that Pukhanov's poem offers a travesty of the very process of *symbolization*, fundamental to the Soviet memorial policy. As Irina Kaspe writes, the Leningrad Siege was not merely sacralized in late Soviet and post-Soviet culture, but sacralized as the predominant visceral manifestation of death – or more specifically hell, symbolically antipodal to the invisible heavenly city of either the communist future or the capitalist present, depending on the reader's inclinations.[16] The poem depicts this transference of the real, albeit dying, city into a transcendental dimension:

У врага из поля зренья
Исчезает Ленинград.
Зимний где? Где Летний сад?
Здесь другое измеренье:

Наяву и во плоти
Тут живому не пройти.

Leningrad disappears
From the field of the enemy's vision.
Where's the Winter Palace? Where's the Summer Garden?
Here's a different dimension:

In reality and in the flesh
There is no passing for the living here.

This transformation seems intentional and 'strategic': the city, removed from the sphere of life, becomes invincible and undefeatable, which indeed reproduces both Soviet and post-Soviet symbolic rhetoric behind the mythology of the Great Patriotic War. This very process of symbolization appears identical to historical commemoration. However, a relocation into the dimension of historical memory suggests the replacement of the 'living flesh' with stone or other non-organic substances: 'Время выйдет, и гранит / Плоть живую заменит' (Time will prevail, and granite / Will replace living flesh). Thus, both symbolization and commemoration suggest, and even require for triumph, an intentional torture by hunger and the eventual murder of Leningrad's still-living inhabitants. All in all, Pukhanov's poem situates the Siege exclusively in the discursive sphere and rather allegorically materializes effects that provide a discursive reshaping of the Siege's reality. The latter is replaced by the warring discursive interpretations of the Siege experience, interpretations characteristic of the present-day dominant discursive regime.

A similar process of the evacuation of the Siege experience into a purely discursive dimension plays a constitutive role in Sergey Zav'ialov's long poem (поэма / poema) 'Rozhdestvenskii post' (Christmas fast, 2010).[17] Zav'ialov (born 1958), a classical philologist by academic training, started publishing in the samizdat magazines of the 1980s, was a member of Club-81, and during the post-Soviet period has published six books of poetry and a number of important essays. In 2004 he emigrated to Finland, and since 2011 he has been living in Switzerland. Zav'ialov is confident that 'there is no discourse which would be adequate to the material of [historical] catastrophe and there is no narrator who would be able to narrate this catastrophe'.[18] In accordance with this thesis, he constructs his poem as a montage of *equally inadequate* discourses about the Siege. Each of the poem's seven parts is titled by a calendar date, from 29 November 1941 to 7 January 1942. Each includes a weather report, a quotation from the monastery order with its dietary recommendations for the Christmas fast, actual Leningrad food rations for the given moment of the Siege, fragments from a mundane conversation, a highly poetic, if ironic, stanza, and a quotation from the daily military report regarding the situation on the front. Each part ends with a prayer.

Naturally, every segment in these seven 'entries' implies a certain interpretation of the Siege, from the Christian testing of spirit to the contemporaneous military operations. Although none of these excerpts is fully representative of the described catastrophe, taken together they produce a polyphonic, if somewhat mechanical, effect. And herein lies the principal difference between 'Rozhdestvenskii post' and Pukhanov's poem. If 'V Leningrade na rassvete' reveals the murderous power of the discourse that *disperses and petrifies* what was yet alive, Zav'ialov apparently believes that each of the vistas in his montage *revives* a certain aspect of the catastrophic past and in this respect *conveys* the tragedy, albeit partially. In Pukhanov's poem the transposition of historical past into the realm of the discourse is a destructive gesture, while in Zav'ialov's the same operation is a part of culture's hard work towards the understanding of catastrophic experiences.

Pukhanov's poem, however, exemplifies a discursive *battle*, whereas those discourses that elevate and glorify the Blockade as a triumph of will and resilience are subversively downplayed as 'children's tales', *skazki* that do not deserve to be trusted and should be perceived as pure fiction. Although the discursive fabric of both poems is highly heterogeneous (Ilya Kukulin shows that even the metre in Pukhanov's poem fluctuates along with its rhyme structures), in Zav'ialov's poem the collation of disagreeing discourses does not suggest an internal conflict but rather a chorus of mutually complementary inadequacies. Furthermore, these poems are oriented differently in time: while the 'domestic' text treats the Siege as a *contemporary* discursive problem, the diasporic text strives to restore the multidimensional scope of its historical state. To use Bakhtin's famous dichotomy, the homeland text is novelistic, since it opens onto the 'unfinished present', while the diasporic text is epic: it works with the Siege as a completed and completely locked-up experience, which needs to be somehow unlocked. Hence, we are presented with different discursive keys to the same historical problem.

## Plays

Iurii Klavdiev's drama *Razvaliny* (*The Razvalins / Ruins*, 2010)[19] and Polina Barskova's 'document / fairy tale' *Zhivye kartiny* (Living pictures / Tableau vivants, 2014)[20] present more contrasts than concords. Klavdiev (born 1974) belongs to the circle of the New Drama playwrights. He is also known as a co-author of screenplays for such important films of the new century as *Kremen'* (Firestone, dir. Aleksei Mizgirev, 2007), *Vse umrut, a ia ostanus'* (All will die, but I will live, dir. Valeriia Gai-Germanika, 2008), and the TV series *Shkola* (The School, dir. Valeriia Gai-Germanika, 2010). Born in Tolyatti, he has lived in St Petersburg since the mid-2000s. *Razvaliny*, a play about cannibalism during the Siege, was staged by several Russian theatres (Moscow Playwright and Director Centre, St Petersburg Étude-Theatre, Samara's Drama theatre).

Barskova (born 1976), an émigré from Petersburg, is a famous poet and the author of many books of lyrics. She has also obtained a PhD in Slavic Studies from UC Berkeley and published a monograph, *Besieged Leningrad: Aesthetic responses to urban disaster*, while working as a professor at Hampshire College. Her first book of non-poetry, *Zhivye kartiny*, which includes her non-fictional prose beside the eponymous play, was awarded the Andrei Bely Prize. The play itself was produced at the Moscow Theatre of Nations.

Both plays depict the same period: the most horrible winter in the Siege's history, from December 1941 to February 1942. Both deal with the question of the intelligentsia's moral and cultural norms vis-à-vis the bleak reality of the dying city, and both employ the model of mentor–mentee relationships. In Klavdiev's play, the mentor role is embodied in the former peasant Maria Razvalina, who has escaped from her village, devastated by collectivization, only to find herself under the heel of the Leningrad Blockade, unemployed and unregistered, with three little children and no food ration cards. Her mentee is a stereotypically impractical professor Iraklii Niverin, who lives in the apartment next door. Niverin gratefully accepts Razvalina's help until the moment when he realizes that she and her teenage children cut and eat the meat from human corpses. He refuses to join them in their ways and later, weakened and isolated, is shot down by a Soviet sniper who mistakes him for a German agent. Conversely, Niverin's daughter, Anechka, accepts Razvalina's brutal truth and joins her gang of children-cannibals.

The critic Pavel Rudnev believes that Niverin's death logically follows from an act of transgression: his looting of a scarf from a corpse, which symbolizes the betrayal of his moral principles (hence his last name, a derivative of the Russian phrase 'I don't believe').[21] Maria Razvalina's moral principles are shaped by the horrors she went through during the collectivization: she is focused on the survival of her family, and the author eagerly justifies her actions with the need to save her children from starvation. Thus Klavdiev, not very subtly, first transforms a stoical professor into a caricature of intelligentsia and then elevates a cannibalistic peasant to the stature of the beacon of faith (despite her practical cynicism, she constantly utters prayers). Tellingly, if Razvalina has a tragic story of collectivization behind her, Niverin is completely deprived of any prehistory, as if the Soviet intelligentsia existed in a sealed paradise, safely protected from all the shocks of Soviet society.

In Barskova's play, the entire action takes place in the cold and dark rooms of the Hermitage Museum. Its protagonists are a 37-year-old art scholar, Totia (Antonina Izergina), and a 25-year-old artist, Moisei (Vakser). Their loving and tragicomic dialogues, interrupted sometimes by the appearance of the Hermitage attendant Anna Pavlovna, manage in spite of an apparent lack of action to express the entire repertoire of intellectual and cultural resistance to the physical destruction of Leningrad, from loving tenderness to flights of imagination, memory, creativity and humour. Initially Totia teaches Moisei, filling him with life energy, but by the play's end they switch roles, and it is Moisei who, despite his weakness, continues to paint his invisible pictures, while Totia loses patience and yells at him in despair. Similarly to Niverin in Klavdiev's play, Moisei dies in the end; but unlike in *Razvaliny*, his death is in no way surrounded by an aura of defeat. It is no coincidence that in one of the final scenes, Barskova's protagonists inadvertently re-enact the composition of Rembrandt's *Return of the prodigal son*, which, in the palette of the play's motifs, connotes the highest manifestation of life and the antithesis of universal death.

Barskova's play contradicts Klavdiev's by its firm allegiance to the values of the intelligentsia, ridiculed and trampled in *Razvaliny*. Klavdiev justifies cannibalism as a necessary means of survival, and in this he involuntarily follows Varlam Shalamov's maxim: 'Голодному человеку можно простить многое, очень многое' (A hungry person can be forgiven for much, for very much).[22] However, he does not forgive the unwillingness of a stubborn *intelligent* to give up his disgust towards cannibalism: he mocks Niverin's humanism, which would permit his daughter's death from starvation rather than the consumption of human flesh.

Barskova's play bears a notable subtitle: *document–fairy tale*. Although based on documentary materials, *Zhivye kartiny* displays mundane marvels of the spirit. Survival here is derived from vital forces associated with intellect, talent, humour, memory, imagination, love and, only after the exhaustion of all these, anger and aggression. Indeed, this looks like a fairy tale, but it is substantiated by historical documents that confirm the Siege's mass cannibalism.

On the surface, Klavdiev's play preaches a greater breadth of moral criteria. In actuality, it enhances and 'essentializes' the binary opposition between the intelligentsia and 'the people'. Barskova's play, indeed, isolates her intelligentsia characters from the 'greater world', including 'the people', but not from the Siege's destructive effects. The weakness of her play is precisely the opposite of Klavdiev's biased representation of conflicting sides: Barskova's characters are surrounded by the hostile and invisible forces of death and history, but between themselves they are united by their love and intellectual energy. There is no space for any real conflict between Totia and Moisei, which suggests that *Zhivye kartiny* is truly a tableau vivant, a pantomime of kinds, but hardly a drama.

In a certain way, the distinction between *Razvaliny* and *Zhivye kartiny* is similar to the one we detected between Pukhanov's and Zav'ialov's poems. While the 'domestic' author uses the Blockade as a rhetorical instrument in the present-day discursive wars, the diasporic writer seeks to transform historical catastrophe into the isolated space (the Hermitage indeed!) on which people sunbathe and feed each other the most cherished fruits – from love to art, irony, wit, and so on. Klavdiev's humanism implies the humiliation of the *intelligent* and approves the equation of the notorious 'people's truth' with cannibalism, while Barskova's version of Siege-tested humanity, in full agreement with the intelligentsia's axiology, places Rembrandt at the top of the pyramid of nutrition. Furthermore, one may argue that for Klavdiev the Siege is simply a metaphor for his generation's experience in the 1990s, with its brutally cynical means of survival and the attendant disdain for helpless (or treasonous) perestroika-infatuated intelligentsia. On the contrary, for Barskova the documentary character of the material she uses is critical, as it secures the distance between 'us' and 'them'. However, this distance is not epic as in Zav'ialov. Rather, it is more akin to the condition of isolation in time and space that is a prerequisite for utopia, since Barskova's goal is to create an ideal utopian community out of her categorically tragic material.

## Novels

Andrei Turgenev's novel *Spat' i verit'* (*To sleep and to believe*, 2008)[23] and Igor Vishnevetsky's *Leningrad* (2010),[24] despite obvious differences between them, are comparable in that both strive to transform the well-absorbed factuality of the Siege into a (post)modernist fantasy. Many critics were inclined to label *Spat' i verit'* a postmodernist novel – mainly because its actual author, Viacheslav Kuritsyn, is known as a promoter and practitioner of postmodernism when not employing the Turgenev alias. Vishnevetsky's models, on the other hand, are more openly associated with high modernism: besides depicting the very process of transfiguration of the Siege's horror into ecstatic poetry and music, a large part of *Leningrad* is written in rhythmical prose or verse (summoning the shade of Andrei Bely). However, Vishnevetsky stresses that even in the poetic portions of his novel he is citing and paraphrasing documentary material, while Kuritsyn demonstratively combines historic details with counter-historical fiction.

Despite this, the resonance between these two novels is at times uncanny. For example, Vishnevetsky mentions that the mouth of the Neva since 1941 was guarded by the battleship *Marat* and the cruiser *Kirov* (119); Kuritsyn reconstitutes these historical details into the fictional figure of Marat Kirov, head of the Leningrad party organization, the city's darling and Stalin's rival.[25] In each novel there appears an NKVD officer: the one in Kuritsyn's plots, on his own initiative, a failed assassination of Marat Kirov and pointlessly dispatches reports in bottles to Hitler concerning different projects to deal with Leningrad after its appropriation by the German army; in Vishnevetsky's, the NKVD officer is in fact a German emissary who arrives in Leningrad intending to secretly form an alternative government out of the surviving intelligentsia. Both in *Spat' i verit'* and *Leningrad*, the protagonist translates the Leningrad tragedy into the language of high romantic *musical* genres – Wagnerian opera in Kuritsyn's novel and dithyrambic oratory in Vishnevetsky's. In both novels, the lead female character is sacrificed, almost ritualistically, yet at the same time most mundanely. In *Spat' i verit'*, Leningrad is saved by the restoration of Tamerlane's remains to his tomb, which in actuality was excavated just before the war began, while in *Leningrad* the city is protected by the magic of Russian etymology and the icon of Our Lady of Kazan, hidden in the icy basement of Kazan Cathedral.

Most importantly, both novels, while not veiling the horrors of the Siege, depict it as a moment of liberation. For both protagonists – the NKVD colonel Maxim sent to Leningrad from Moscow in Kuritsyn's novel, and Gleb Alfa, the musicologist and composer in Vishnevetsky's – the Siege offers a bizarre but at the same time exciting dismissal from social, political and even existential restraints and boundaries. Maxim's freedom is the freedom of a morose trickster (no wonder he uses the codename 'Joker' in his letters to Hitler), one who deliberately fuses in himself opposite and incompatible characteristics: he faithfully serves the NKVD, arrests and submits innocent people to torture, yet despises his bosses and the entirety of the Leningrad population, and rescues outcasts and fugitives whom he later employs for the would-be assassination of Marat Kirov. Realizing that he is cornered after that mission's failure, Maxim shoots his beloved, Varya, in order to save her from the NKVD tortures, and plans to join the Germans in the novel's finale. The horrors of the Siege generate in the novel a sense of *normality* attached to the utter and universal dehumanization, and Maxim epitomizes this process by re-enacting superhuman demonism, in many ways shielded by his NKVD stature and privileges, which he detests and enjoys at the same time. This anti-hero can best be characterized, in fact, by a sentiment from Vishnevetsky's novel: 'мы как люди наступающего послечеловеческого будущего, как люди после крушения человека...' (we are like people from the post-human future ahead, like people after the fall of man ...) (137).

Maxim's love for the young and innocent Varya is intended to manifest his lasting and tender human feelings, but it is drawn in such a formulaic way, composed entirely of popular romantic clichés, that it becomes parodic: 'Глянул и онемел. Лицо идеальным овалом, из-под стильной шапочки черная челка, ресницы длиннющие, как антенны, вспушенные, нос с тонкой горбинкой... и глаза – чистой воды изумруды. Все это он углядел в скупом струении синего маскировочного света. Девушкино лицо как бы само освещалось внутренним тихим светом' (He looked and went numb. A perfectly oval face, a black fringe emerging from a stylish cap, huge eyelashes like antennae sticking out, a nose with a gentle crook ... and the eyes, pure emerald water. All this he saw in the miserly glow of the blue camouflage light. The girl's faced seemed to illuminate itself with some soft light within) (194–5). For Gleb Alfa, on the contrary, the Siege becomes an inspiration not only for his illicit love for Vera Beklemisheva, but also for a surge of creativity – bordering on orgiastic erotic excitement, triggered by daily images of death and destruction. The oratory that he creates is also ecstatic in its tonality, celebrating the freedom of the return to prehistory: '*миг, становящийся мифом*' ('a moment, becoming myth') (61).

Another *Leningrad* character, the philologist Fedor Chetvertinsky, arrives at a similar revelation through his linguistic analysis. Chetvertinsky also conceptualizes the Siege – in a fashion similar to that of the Silver Age modernists – as the global sacrificial ritual needed to lay the cornerstone of the new world and the new heaven: 'Пусть происходящее, мысленно продолжал Четвертинский, приведёт к высвобождению – ударом метафорического копья – солнца света, солнца правды. А моё, ваше, общее наше тело даже в гибели, в сокрушении – оттого и не страшных – ляжет в основание нового мира' (Let what's happening, Chertvetinsky went on in his head, lead to the release – with a prod from the metaphorical spear – of the sun of light, the sun of truth. And my, your, our collective body even in death, in being crushed – and this is why it isn't scary – will lay the foundation of the new world) (54). However, this poetic theory substantiates itself on the most horrible evidence: the death of the pregnant Vera, killed by cannibals, news of which demolishes Gleb when he belatedly hears it. The author illustrates the connection between Vera's fate and the Siege-based myth-making with one striking detail: an acquaintance recognizes Vera's severed head near the Tavrida Garden, situating her cannibalization in the context of Russia's attempts to connect to European antiquity: '... на ослепительном, сверкающем снегу недалеко от Таврического сада ей привиделась свежеотрезанная, необычайно хорошенькая голова молодой женщины, почему-то напомнившей чертами Веру Беклемишеву, с такой же, как у Веры, короткой стрижкой. Рядом – окровавленное бельё и тёплые чулки. Тело, очевидно, "пустили в дело"' (... on the blinding, sparkling snow not far from the Tavrida Garden appeared before her the freshly severed, unusually pretty head of a young woman, somehow reminiscent of the features of Vera Beklemisheva, with the same short haircut that Vera had. Nearby there were bloody underwear and winter stockings. The body, obviously, had been "utilized".) (113–14).

Kuritsyn's and Vishnevetsky's works generally follow the same pattern of differences we identified between homeland and diasporic poetry and dramaturgy. Kuritsyn, similarly to Pukhanov and Klavdiev, blatantly projects the Siege experience onto the present. Incidentally, this is underscored by his demonstrative linguistic anachronisms in the characters' speech: '... мужик номер раз, без параши. Уважуха до потолка!' (... man number one, no shit. Respect to the sky!) (53), 'толпа в экстазе колбасится' (the crowd is raving in ecstasy) (157), 'он сегодня подробности не пробил' (he didn't crunch the particulars today) (269), 'вы же, говорят, сверхгипер' (they say you're a super-hyper) (322), 'Нужен дополнительный мониторинг! – Так мониторьте, черти полосатые!' (We need additional monitoring! – So, monitor the striped bastards!) (340), as well as consistent 'internet' spelling of the word 'яд' (poison) as 'йад' (35). All these anachronistic verbal signal flares suggest a reading of the Siege as a historical metaphor for the 1990s, which places the survivors of the collapse in a post-human condition, epitomized by the murderous trickster. Meanwhile, Vishnevetsky, echoing Zav'ialov and Barskova, tries in his text to extract stylistic essences from the lost and crushed discourses of the last modernists, preserved in their private historical documents (letters, memoirs) which his novel reworks. The result is paradoxical: experimental in its form, *Leningrad* thematizes the concept of distancing familiar from other diasporic works.

In Vishnevetsky's novel, a discursive distance manifests neither epic completeness and the closeness of the past (as in Zav'ialov), nor its utopian isolation (as in Barskova), but instead the return to a mythic non-time – or rather, to the non-time of myth-making, wherein death and ultimate freedom are conflated. In sync with these characterizations, Kuritsyn presents the Blockade as a war of all against all (similarly to Klavdiev) and thus as the normalization of utter inhumanity, while Vishnevetsky, conversely, tries to elevate the Siege experience, without idealizing it, to the level of a high Symbolist tragedy.

## Conclusion

To conclude, contemporary diasporic texts about the Siege demonstrate the following recurring qualities, which are notably absent in 'homeland' works on the same subject and in the same genre:

- distancing of the Siege experience from the present moment, as opposed to its almost declarative 'modernization' in the homeland texts;
- high dependence on historical documents as a replenishment of the surreal non-reality of the Siege experience, versus the homeland works' divergence from such documents;
- minimization of internal conflicts within the representation of the Siege, as distinguished from their accentuation in homeland texts, which also explains the more static character of diasporic narratives;
- a more idealizing, decisively non- or even counter-cynical approach to the Siege and its experiences, as opposed to the radical deconstruction and sometimes cynical mockery of outdated humanistic principles allegedly devalued by the Siege (as seen in the works of Klavdiev and Kuritsyn);
- an oxymoronic combination of an elevating vector in the artistic style (the form) with the brutality of Siege conditions (the content) compensates for the weakened conflict in diasporic pieces and distinguishes them from the more homogeneous homeland texts.

How could one explain these differences between the diasporic and homeland discourses of the Leningrad Siege? Can this difference tell us anything about diasporic writing in general?

Along with other narratives of the War, the Siege is constantly present on the information horizon for everyone living in Russia.

Therefore, a homeland liberal author feels the need to deconstruct and de-realize Siege narratives in order to connect them – as a multilayered cluster of metaphors – with his or her own historical experience and memory, that is, with the recent past and the present. On the contrary, for diasporic authors the Siege is an example of the unreal non-time, which they strive to fill with a sense of reality through their attention to documentary evidence. Yet these attempts only intensify the sense of non-reality, mainly on account of the surreal nature of the Siege experience.

Following Foucault's hint, one may define the Siege as a 'crisis heterotopia'. Its effect fully embodies the heterotopia's mirroring function:

> [B]etween utopias and these quite other sites, these heterotopias, there might be a sort of mixed, joint experience, which would be the mirror. The mirror is, after all, a utopia, since it is a placeless place. In the mirror, I see myself there where I am not, in an unreal, virtual space that opens up behind the surface; I am over there, there where I am not, a sort of shadow that gives my own visibility to myself, that enables me to see myself there where I am absent: such is the utopia of the mirror. But it is also a heterotopia in so far as the mirror does exist in reality, where it exerts a sort of counteraction on the position that I occupy. ... The mirror functions as a heterotopia in this respect: it makes this place that I occupy at the moment when I look at myself in the glass at once absolutely real, connected with all the space that surrounds it, and absolutely unreal.[26]

The conflation of reality and non-reality presented in this characterization of the heterotopia explains why the unreal non-time of the Siege may resonate with the construction of the diasporic subjectivity. In Maver's words, 'the problem, of course, lies in the question [of] how to identify [Us vs. the Others], since binary constructions clearly no longer work today. Identify oneself with what? With "Home" which holds a mythic place of desire in the diasporic imagination and subjectivity and is, paradoxically, a place of no return? Even if it is actually possible to visit the actual geographical territory which is seen as the place of "origin", the lived experience of the locality of Home is very different from that of an imaginary or imagined homeland.'[27] For residents of the former Leningrad (and not only for them), the Siege serves as a rich metaphor of the imagined 'Home', which is not only the place of no return, but also a dimension outside of the flow of time, one that offers an explosion of creative energy but demands your life instead.[28] It is the place where creativity and destruction fuse inseparably. The Siege, in other words, emerges as the new diasporic myth of the Home. Distancing from it is necessary for its functioning – and for the writer/reader's survival.

All this suggests a positive answer to the question that forms the title of this chapter. Yes, there is room for diasporic writing in the age of the internet and Facebook. Apparently, diasporic sensitivity reaches deeper levels than simple belonging or non-belonging to the informational and cultural context of the homeland. The trauma of separation generates specific but always new and unexpected modalities of writing that preserve and explore the unbreakable distance from the home. This distance one may perceive tragically or otherwise, but it inevitably serves as a source of creativity and aesthetic estrangement.

Having said that, I wish to emphasize that the same sensibility can be expressed from within the homeland experience (see for example, Maria Stepanova's *Pamiati pamiati* (2017)) – the biographic circumstances only enhance this potentiality, but the displacement that this sensibility registers is broader and deeper than the displacement associated with emigration. It is the displacement in time and cultural context to a greater extent than just in geography.

## Notes

1   Brubaker 2005, 5–6.
2   Recently, a famous Russian critic and the editor of an allegedly liberal literary magazine published on Facebook a diatribe against Russian émigrés who cannot stop talking about Russia, which they left decades ago: '"Listen," I stop her. "Russia is deep in the past perfect tense for you. You will never go back to it or let your children go there, right?" "Yes, it would be a jungle," was the answer. "So then why do you think not about Angela Merkel or German issues, but only about ours, to which you have virtually no connection?"' (https://www.facebook.com/permalink.php?story_fbid=1774507359249256&id=100000700270259, 27 December 2017; accessed 6 September 2020). As an experienced polemicist, the editor fails to notice that his rhetoric symmetrically reproduces a traditional nationalist rebuttal to liberal critics of Russia: If you hate all things Russian so much, why are you living here, why wouldn't you move elsewhere?
3   See Blium 2004.
4   See, for example, such collections of documents as Demidov 1995; Volkovskii 2004; Murav'eva 2014.
5   See, for example, Gudkov 2005.
6   'Prokuratura' 2014; 'Skandal'nyi opros' 2014.
7   See such publications as Ginzburg 2011; Freidenberg 1987; Shaporina 2011, 247–436; Ostrovskaia 2013, 247–393; Gor 2012; Barskova 2016.
8   See Sandomirskaia 2013.
9   See Yarov 2012, 2014.
10  See Barskova 2017.
11  Maver 2009, x.

12   See http://fayzov.livejournal.com/909897.html (accessed 6 September 2020).
13   Kukulin 2009.
14   Zholkovsky 2010.
15   See L'vovskii 2009.
16   See Kaspe 2018, esp. 100–2.
17   Published in *Novoe literaturnoe obozrenie* 102 (2010), https://magazines.gorky.media/nlo/2010/2/rozhdestvenskij-post.html (accessed 16 October 2020).
18   Zavialov 2015, 41.
19   Klavdiev 2010.
20   Barskova 2014, 133–73.
21   Rudnev 2018, 367.
22   Shalamov 1992, 1:72.
23   Hereafter, I quote from this novel using the following edition: Turgenev 2008, indicating a page number in brackets after a quotation.
24   *Leningrad* first appeared in *Novyi mir* 8 (2010). I will be quoting it using Vishnevetsky 2012. Hereafter, page numbers are indicated in brackets after a quotation.
25   The name of this fictional character intentionally resonates with a real-life Sergei Kirov (1886–1934), the head of the Leningrad Party organization from 1926 until his death in 1934. On 1 December 1934, Kirov was shot and killed by one Leonid Nikolayev at his offices in the Smolny Institute for unknown reasons. Kirov's death served as a pretext for the beginning of the Great Terror. Multiple mysteries surrounding Kirov's assassination suggest that it had been engineered by Stalin who could see in Kirov a rival for power. Khrushchev supported this theory in his Secret Speech at the 20th Party Congress (1956).
26   Foucault 1986, 24.
27   Maver 2009, x.
28   On the artistic and heuristic potential of diasporic extraterritoriality see Kevin Platt's article in this volume.

# Bibliography

Barskova, Polina. 'Zhivye kartiny (document-skazka)'. In Polina Barskova, *Zhivye kartiny*, 133–73. St Petersburg: Limbus Press, 2014.
Barskova, Polina, ed. *Written in the Dark: Five poets in the Siege of Leningrad*. New York: Ugly Duckling Presse, 2016.
Barskova, Polina. *Besieged Leningrad: Aesthetic responses to urban disaster*. DeKalb: Northern Illinois University Press, 2017.
Blium, Arlen. 'Blokadnaia tema v tsenzurnoi blokade: Po arkhivnym dokumentam Glavlita SSSR', *Neva* 1 (2004): 238–45.
Brubaker, Rogers. 'The "diaspora" diaspora', *Ethnic and Racial Studies* 28(1) (January 2005): 1–19.
Demidov, Viktor, ed. *Blokada rassekrechennaia*. St Petersburg: Boianych, 1995.
Foucault, Michel. 'Of other places'. Translated by Jay Miskowiec. *Diacritics* 16(1) (Spring 1986): 22–7.
Freidenberg, Olga M. 'Osada cheloveka', edited by K. Nevel'skii, *Minuvshee: istoricheskii al'manakh* 3 (1987): 7–44.
Ginzburg, Lydia. *Prokhodiashchie kharaktery: Proza voennykh let. Zapiski blokadnogo cheloveka*. Edited and compiled by Emily Van Buskirk and Andrei Zorin. Moscow: Novoe izd-vo, 2011.
Gor, Gennadii. *Krasnaia kaplia v snegu: Stikhotvoreniia 1942–1944 godov*. Edited and compiled by Andrei Mudzhaba. Moscow: Gileia, 2012.
Gudkov, Lev. 'Die Fesseln des Sieges: Rußlands Identität aus der Erinnerung an den Krieg', *Osteuropa* 55(4) (April 2005): 56–72 ('The fetters of victory: How the war provides Russia with its identity', *Eurozine*, 3 May 2005. https://www.eurozine.com/the-fetters-of-victory/ (accessed 16 October 2020).)
Kaspe, Irina. 'Mesto smerti: o znachenii Leningradskoi blokady v pozdnesovetskoi kul'ture', *Russian Sociological Review* 17(1) (2018): 59–105.

Klavidiev, Iurii. *Razvaliny*, 2010 (unpublished).

Kukulin, Ilya. 'Stroficheskaia dramaturgiia: katarsis otkladyvaetsia', *Novoe literaturnoe obozrenie* 96 (2009). https://magazines.gorky.media/nlo/2009/2/stroficheskaya-dramaturgiya-katarsis-otkladyvaetsya.html (accessed 16 October 2020).

L'vovskii, Stanislav. '"Vidit gory i lesa": Istoriia pro odno stikhotvorenie Vitaliia Pukhanova', *Novoe literaturnoe obozrenie* 96 (2009). https://magazines.gorky.media/nlo/2009/2/vidit-gory-i-lesa-istoriya-pro-odno-stihotvorenie-vitaliya-puhanova.html (accessed 16 October 2020).

Maver, Igor. 'Introduction: Positioning diasporic literary cultures'. In *Diasporic Subjectivity and Cultural Brokering in Contemporary Post-Colonial Literatures*, edited by Igor Maver, ix–xiv. Lanham, MD: Lexington Books, 2009.

Murav'eva, I. A., ed. *Leningradtsy. Blokadnye dnevniki iz fondov Gosudarstvennogo memorial'nogo muzeia oborony i blokady Leningrada*. St Petersburg: Lenizdat, 2014.

Ostrovskaia, S. K. *Dnevnik*. Edited by Polina Barskova and Tatiana Pozdniakova. Moscow: NLO, 2013.

'Prokuratura nachala proverku "Dozhdia" posle oprosa o blokade Leningrada', *RIA News*, 30 January 2014. https://ria.ru/20140130/992152684.html (accessed 7 September 2020).

Rudnev, Pavel. *Drama pamiati: Ocherki istorii rossiiskoi dramaturgii. 1950–2010-e*. Moscow: NLO, 2018.

Sandomirskaia, Irina. *Blokada v slove: Ocherki kriticheskoi teorii i biopolitiki iazyka*. Moscow: NLO, 2013.

Shalamov, Varlam. *Kolymskie rasskazy*. 2 vols. Moscow: Russkaia kniga, 1992.

Shaporina, Liubov'. *Dnevnik. Volume 1: 1898–1945*. Edited by V. F. Petrova and V. N. Sazhin. Moscow: NLO, 2011.

'Skandal'nyi opros na "Dozhde"', NTV.ru, 28 November 2014. https://www.ntv.ru/theme/42664/ (accessed 16 October 2020).

Turgenev, Andrei. *Spat' i verit': Blokadnyi roman*. Moscow: Eksmo, 2008.

Vishnevetsky, Igor'. *Leningrad*. Moscow: Vremia, 2012.

Volkovskii, N. L., ed. *Blokada Leningrada v dokumentakh rassekrechennykh arkhivov*, Moscow: AST, and St Petersburg: Poligon, 2004.

Yarov, S. V. *Blokadnaya etika*. Moscow: Tsentrpoligraf, 2012.

Yarov, S. V. *Povsednevnaia zhizn' blokadnogo Leningrada*. Moscow: Molodaia gvardiia, 2014.

Zavialov, Sergei. *Sovetskie kantaty (2012–2015)*. St Petersburg: Translit and Svobmarksizdat, 2015.

Zholkovskii, A. K. 'Zagadki "Znakov Zodiaka"', *Zvezda* 10 (2010). http://magazines.russ.ru/zvezda/2010/10/zh13.html (accessed 7 September 2020).

# 8

# The benefits of distance: extraterritoriality as cultural capital in the literary marketplace

Kevin M. F. Platt

> The literary universe obeys Berkeley's famous *esse est percipi* – to be is to be perceived – [writers] gradually perfect a set of strategies linked to their positions, their written language, their location in literary space, to the distance or proximity they want to establish with the prestige-bestowing centre. ... [T]he majority of compromise solutions achieved within this structure are based on an 'art of distance', a way of situating oneself, aesthetically, neither too near nor too far; and ... the most subordinated of writers manoeuvre with extraordinary sophistication to give themselves the best chance of being perceived, of existing in literary terms.
>
> Pascale Casanova, 'Literature as a world', 2005[1]

## Global Russian cultures and extraterritorial authors

Since the opening and collapse of the USSR at the start of the last decade of the twentieth century, the Russian literary world has become more fragmented and dispersed than at any time in the past, as millions of Russians and Russian speakers have fanned out across the globe or been stranded in what sociologists call beached diasporas in former Soviet states like Latvia or Ukraine, where they have busily set about writing poems, stories and novels in and against the cultural scenes of the new polities in which they now find themselves.[2] As I and others have argued elsewhere, to treat this panoply of dispersed communities and scenes as a singular 'Russian world', presuming a root commonality that relates to an essentializing conception of territorially bound 'Russianness', is to concede too much to nationalistic frames of interpretation.[3] Where are the proper boundaries of a singular 'Russian homeland' and who can decide what cultural formations properly inhabit it? We should not blindly grant the singular 'Russian world' ontological self-evidence in an era in which official Russian political and social institutions emphatically reject some members of the cultural establishment of the Russian Federation as 'fifth columnists', while at the same time insisting on the Russian state's prerogative to 'defend the rights of Russians everywhere', to the point of armed intervention in neighbouring countries. To the contrary, we should recognize that Russian cultures and Russian literatures are multiple, everywhere at home, always distinctive, across the reaches of the globe, inside and outside of the political formation that is by chance of fate and history named the 'Russian Federation'. Moreover, many of these variegated and dispersed Russian cultures are engaged in worlding projects of their own – projecting competing conceptions of a Russian world and its cultural meanings. As Katharine Hodgson's contribution to this volume suggests, despite flashes of optimism in the 1990s that a singular Russian literary canon might be reconstructed following the Cold War out of the shards of disparate Soviet and émigré traditions, it is now more and more clear that the past century has been one of ever-increasing variety and differentiation of globally dispersed cultural landscapes. In short, never before have there been so many 'Russian cultures' and 'Russian worlds', so amply populated, so scattered across global geography, as there are today.

Yet paradoxically, we must also recognize that since the end of the twentieth century global Russian literary formations have also become more closely adjacent and more systematically integrated than ever before. During the Cold War, surveilled and policed borders structured the largely separate realities of what were then called Soviet and émigré literature, as well as the mechanisms for their limited contacts (*tamizdat*, cultural diplomacy, smuggling, ideologically driven Soviet book exports, etc.), not only limiting the physical movement of printed matter and bodies but also diminishing the mutual comprehensibility and integration of opposed systems of literary value. Now, close to three decades on since the fall of the USSR, those secure borders have faded to a distant memory, as they have been effaced by the frenetic exchange of the globalized market, disseminating books by container vessel and aeroplane across the world's expanses, as well as by other attendant effects of cultural globalization and virtualization, enabling authors to communicate with readers and publishing institutions through electronic networks or to engage in extended global book tours. As Mark

Lipovetsky observes in his contribution to this volume, the result is literary works that criss-cross the globe, written in one place and performed in another, linked together by common concerns – the history and myth of the Leningrad Blockade, in his case – derived from a shared context of global electronic media.

This paradox of continually increasing fragmentation and integration of global Russian cultures raises fundamental definitional questions for the study of literature, geography, identity and belonging. Whereas Hodgson and Lipovetsky approach these questions by means of assessments of publication formats and canonization, in the former case, and concrete literary works and overarching themes, in the latter, my contribution will consider authorship and interlinked markets in cultural and economic capital. Consider, as an initial example, the highly successful author Irina Murav'eva, who has resided for decades near Boston, Massachusetts in the United States, yet who writes in Russian for an audience located primarily in the Russian Federation and has rarely been translated into English: is she a Russian writer, an American writer, or a global writer?[4] Clearly, she and other authors like her might be all or none of these things, depending on precise definitions of the terms in question and on the self-fashioning of individual authors and their communities. For authors such as Murav'eva, I propose the term 'extra-territorial' – one that captures their complex geographical positionality, writing for audiences located in territories distant from those of their residence, and chiefly in the Russian Federation, but also – with stress on the 'extra' – the manner in which their identity and activity as authors in a multiply worlded Russian cultural reality may ultimately obviate or confound considerations of territorial fixity *tout court*. One might name, in addition to Murav'eva, such extraterritorial russophone authors as: the poet Polina Barskova of the United States (whose play about the Blockade is treated in Lipovetsky's contribution); the poets Gali-Dana Singer and Leonid Schwab of Israel; the novelist Mikhail Shishkin of Switzerland; the poets and multimedia artists Sergei Timofejev, Arturs Punte and Semyon Khanin of the Orbita group in Riga, Latvia; the poet and novelist Alexandra Petrova of Italy, and many others whose biographies are as varied as the countries in which they now reside and who have matured as authors outside of 'Russian territory', yet whose audiences are found within it.

The category of 'extraterritorial authors' may also arguably include such figures as: the postmodern prose author Vladimir Sorokin, who resides much of the time near Berlin, Germany; the popular fiction author Boris Akunin (Grigori Chkhartishvili), who moves continually between

France, Spain, the UK and Russia; Mikhail Idov, a serial migrant whose biography has taken him from Soviet Riga, to the USA in the 1990s, to Moscow in the early 2000s, then to Berlin, and most recently to Los Angeles;[5] or the poet and publisher Dmitrii Kuz'min, who has migrated from Moscow to Latvia – members of a growing class of established Russian authors who, largely for political reasons, have established residence outside of Russia, yet continue to participate actively in its literary realities.

Yet we must also observe that this latter subset of extraterritorial writers is highly variegated in terms of geographical self-fashioning: whereas the wildly successful, cosmopolitan Akunin lives abroad because he can afford to do so and prefers to keep his distance from the Kremlin, but has not (as yet) 'onboarded' his new social environment(s) as an element of his highly public image, Kuz'min is participating in concerted fashion in the literary life of Latvia, has learned Latvian, and increasingly broadcasts his geographical position as an element of his authorial persona. One might point, in this regard, to his founding of the Literature Without Borders (Литература без границ) project, comprising a press, a residency and a festival series based in Ozolnnieki, Latvia. This is an alternate Russian literary worlding project, if ever there was one. The Literature Without Borders website explains:

> The necessary conditions for the existence of contemporary literature include freedom for creative exploration and inclusion in a single space of dialogue without borders between people and cultures. Our project helps authors to find a path to one another and to readers by means of collective work on translations and multi-lingual books. We devote special attention to Russian literature, which must survive the current political catastrophe and set a course for a post-totalitarian future.[6]

Or one might cite Kuz'min's 2018 poem, 'Удобно ненавидеть Россию…' (It's easy to hate Russia …):

> Удобно ненавидеть Россию из Латвии.
> Удобно ненавидеть Россию из Америки.
> Более или менее удобно ненавидеть Россию из некоторых районов Украины,
> но из Крыма и из Донбасса не очень удобно.
> Сравнительно удобно ненавидеть Россию из Москвы.
> Гораздо неудобнее – из Перми или Омска,

где горожан развлекают моделью виселицы в натуральную
величину.
Очень неудобно ненавидеть Россию из Лабытнанги.
Голова кружится, сильная слабость,
покалывания в пальцах, онемение рук.
Сухость во рту постоянная, не получается напиться водой.[7]

It's easy to hate Russia from Latvia.
It's easy to hate Russia from America.
It's more or less easy to hate Russia from some parts of Ukraine,
But from Crimea or Donbass it's not so easy.
It's relatively easy to hate Russia from Moscow.
It's a lot less easy from Perm or Omsk,
Where they entertain locals with life-sized model gallows.
It's not easy at all to hate Russia on a hunger strike in Labytnangi
prison.
Your head spins, weakness overpowers,
your fingers tingle, touch is numb.
Your thirst is too great for water to quench.[8]

The work is dedicated to the Ukrainian film-maker Oleg Sentsov, who
was arrested in Crimea in 2014 and convicted in Russia the following
year on trumped-up charges of terrorist conspiracy. At the time of the
poem's composition, Sentsov was being held in the Labytnangi Penal
Colony in Northern Russia and was engaged in an extended hunger strike
in protest against his own imprisonment and that of other Ukrainian
nationals held in Russian prisons in connection with post-Maidan
separatist conflict. The poem's rhetorical structure, listing locations from
which it is 'easy to hate Russia', beginning with Latvia, clearly illustrates
the complexity of Kuz'min's relationship to 'metropolitan' Russian
cultural life: although the poem works to knit together a universal
opposition to 'Russia', worlding its own 'other global Russia', this other
Russia is granted unity by a shared antipathy to the Russian political
regime. To use the terms of Pascale Casanova, as cited in the epigraph,
Kuz'min is certainly 'situating [himself], aesthetically' with this poem
and with his project more generally, adopting 'strategies linked to [his]
positions, [his] written language, [his] location in literary space'. Yet
here, his situation is one of coordinated resistance to the authority of the
national literary centre – and what are we to make of the fact that Kuz'min
himself wields considerable authority in Russian experimental writing,
in and outside of the Russian Federation? Literature Without Borders is

an alternative 'prestige-bestowing centre' for a competing Russian literary world. In short, 'It's easy to hate Russia ...' dramatizes in maximal fashion the complex geographical position of the extraterritorial writer in an era of contested nationalism and globalization, when literary personae and transnational community may be built, to greater or lesser degree, on the contradictory foundations of both belonging to and alienation from the social, cultural and political realities of nationally defined polities like the Russian Federation.

Treatment of the literary activity of such figures demands an analytical matrix flexible enough to capture the fluidity of such terms as global, local and extraterritorial at various scales of study – a mode of analysis that can account for the dynamism of the multiple geographical imaginaries and economic and institutional networks in which Russian cultures and authors currently exist. The present chapter attempts to develop such a matrix via case studies of the careers of two similar, yet distinct, extraterritorial authors and of the works that propelled them to prominence in the post-Soviet era: the russophone Israeli author Dina Rubina and her runaway best-seller of 1996, *Вот идет Мессия!* (*Here comes the Messiah!*); and the russophone Uzbek poet Shamshad Abdullaev and the poetry he published in the Tashkent-based journal for which he served as poetry editor in the early 1990s, *Звезда Востока* (*The Star of the East*). The basis for selection of these two cases relates to their prominence (both have achieved extraordinary success despite, and also because of, their roles as extraterritorial authors) and to the distinctions between the two in their territorial trajectories and in the character of their literary profiles, which will become clear in what follows. The rise to prominence of both authors took place in the early to middle 1990s, and so casts into relief the imaginaries and institutions of post-Soviet global Russian cultures as they were themselves taking shape.

My ultimate aim is to describe and differentiate between con-temporary variations of global Russian authorial identities and the dynamics of global Russian literary institutions. This is an object of study akin to that of Pascale Casanova, with her conception of the World Republic of Letters, yet rather than focusing on the interrelationships between diverse national literatures in a world literary system as she does, I seek to grapple with the internal complexities of a single, ostensibly 'national' literature when it has itself gone global and multiple, when multiple literary worlds have lifted up from geography into competition and interaction.[9] What institutions and readerships drive the success of authors like Rubina and Abdullaev? How are their cases exemplary of the coming into being of the present dispersed yet integrated global Russian literary scene? What special literary capital accrues to extraterritorial authors – which is to say, how may we describe the interrelationships of authorial reputation and literary value with territorial dispersion and audience fragmentation? In short, what are the benefits and challenges of writing and reading at a distance for audiences and for authors like Rubina, Abdullaev, the additional figures listed above, and the many others like them. Ultimately, as I will show, the study of such figures throws light on the growing instability of the structures of global literary life on which Casanova's analysis is based in the present era.

## Dina Rubina and the (im)possibility of extraterritoriality

Rubina's debut novel *Here comes the Messiah!* occupies a special place not only in her own oeuvre but in post-Soviet global russophone writing in general. This was not only Rubina's first big hit after migration from the Soviet Union to Israel as part of the enormous Aliyah of more than a million people who made the same choice as she in the late 1980s and early 1990s, but also in many ways her first really big hit in any sense, and, perhaps more importantly for the purposes of the current investigation, one of the first literary works to emerge from the context of post-Soviet immigration to become a true blockbuster in the Russian Federation, with hundreds of thousands of copies in print. Its publication and republication have literally created Rubina as a successful post-Soviet author, and arguably have done more to create the institution of the extraterritorial russophone writer for broad swathes of Russian readers than any other single work. In short, *Here comes the Messiah!* put extraterritorial writing on the Russian literary map.

Rubina was born and raised in Soviet Tashkent. Her Soviet literary career was not without notable successes: she emerged as a teenaged author with well-received stories in the journal *Юность* (*Youth*) that gained her entry into the Union of Soviet Writers at the age of 24. This led to a decade and a half of productive publication of additional stories and *povesti* (novellas) as a regularly contributing author in that journal, punctuated by several collected volumes of her stories published in Tashkent, as well as theatrical and film adaptations of her work, and ultimately a move to Moscow in the middle 1980s. Her Soviet literary career culminated in a collection published by the powerful central publishing house Советский писатель (Soviet writer) in 1990, the year of her departure for Israel.[10]

However, Rubina really made it big in Russia only several years after leaving it. In an interview, she recalls being turned down for publication in the last years of the Soviet era by the more prestigious all-union 'thick journals': the powerful and pedigreed journal Знамя (*The banner*), in particular, rejected her novellas 'Двойная фамилия' ('Dual surname') and 'На верхней Масловке' ('On upper Maslovka Street') as too 'belletristic', meaning, presumably, too 'middlebrow' and lacking in higher artistic ambition.[11] Yet just a few years after emigration she began to be published in these same most prestigious Russian journals. In particular, in 1993 she placed the novella 'Во вратах твоих' ('At thy gates'), treating with some anguish the experience of Russian Jewish emigration to Israel, in perhaps the most prestigious Russian thick journal, Новый мир (*New world*). *Here comes the Messiah!*, which is the first full-length novel of Rubina's career, appeared in late 1996 in another high-profile journal, Дружба народов (*Friendship of peoples*). Clearly, extraterritorial positionality and literary self-fashioning as an émigré author treating the theme of emigration, at a time when such subject matter was highly topical in Russian society, began to work almost immediately to gain traction for Rubina in prestigious Russian institutions, allowing her career within Russia to continue to progress, despite her relocation to the shores of the Mediterranean.

Yet the 1996 publication of *Here comes the Messiah!* in *Friendship of peoples* was not the first appearance of this work in print. Earlier that same year, the novel had already been published in Tel Aviv by the émigré press IvRus. (This edition was greeted with a literary prize awarded by the Union of Russian Writers of Israel.[12]) More importantly, the journal publication was not – by far – to be its last. Almost immediately after the journal publication, it was brought out in Moscow by the publishing house Остожье (Ostozh'e). In 1999, the novel was republished by Подкова (Horseshoe) in St Petersburg, then again in two editions in 2000, by St Petersburg's Ретро (Retro) press and by У-Фактория (U-Faktoriia) in Ekaterinburg, both of which were followed by multiple reprintings in the next four years. In 2004, Rubina signed an exclusive contract with Эксмо (Eksmo publishing company), Russia's largest publishing conglomerate, which has since that time reissued the novel in multiple stand-alone editions, collections and collected works, leading up to the most recent republication in 2020.

The story of the astounding success of this novel, which laid the cornerstone of Rubina's literary career, is revealed not only in this impressive history of editions, but also in their scales. I don't have information about the print run of the first publication of the novel in

Tel Aviv, but one may assume that it was minor: Rubina recalls in an interview that the print run of her very first book publication in Israel, her 1994 collection of stories *Один интеллигент уселся на дороге* (*An intelligentsia fellow sat down on the road*), was fewer than a thousand.[13] The first publication of *Here comes the Messiah!* in Moscow with Ostozh'e was, similarly, in an edition of one thousand. By way of contrast one may consider the print run of her 1990 collection with Soviet writer, which, at thirty thousand, one may suggest, was a reflection less of Rubina's authorial visibility at that moment than of the Soviet tendency to large print runs, cheap books and mass distribution regardless of demand. In any case, by the late 1990s, *Here comes the Messiah!* had equalled and surpassed that number, in an indisputable response to actual market conditions. Its re-editions in the late 1990s were in the tens of thousands. In the 2000s and 2010s, the novel was reissued in multiple printings of one hundred thousand copies and, at the time of writing, sales show little sign of slowing down. It is safe to say that this work became must-read literature for a very broad readership, and has retained this status for two decades.

One may contrast this resounding triumph in Russia with the fate of the novel in transnational literary life. In this regard, *Here comes the Messiah!* has achieved only the measured success that is signalled by translations into English (in 2000), German (2001) and Polish (2006) – stand-alone editions with small print runs intended for libraries and minor markets of Russian literature enthusiasts and students. And yet, we should also recognize another global literary market – that of Russian readers in cultural enclaves across the world. It is difficult to gauge the penetration of *Here comes the Messiah!* in these contexts in any precise way. At least since the start of the new millennium, global Russian-language populations have been linked by active distribution networks to powerful central publishers such as Eksmo, to say nothing of the increasingly robust global market for electronic distribution and internet piracy of Russian books. My hypothesis, bolstered by personal observation, is that *Here comes the Messiah!* is as avidly read by Russian speakers across the reaches of the globe as it is in the Russian Federation. As one may conclude from a glance at Rubina's extraordinarily active schedule of peregrinations for reading engagements to America, Canada, Ukraine, the Baltic States, Russia, Central Asia and, of course, Israel (as is visible in the events list on her official Facebook page), she herself identifies a significant readership in these many 'other Russian cultures' of the world. Undoubtedly, the global penetration of the novel is supported by its subject matter – Jewish post-Soviet emigration – which appeals to former Soviet Jews wherever they might be. Yet this cannot explain its success completely, and certainly not in the Russian Federation, which by some counts now is home to only 150,000 Jews – many multiples fewer than the nearly one million copies that have been printed.[14]

In short, *Here comes the Messiah!* has been the engine of a kind of literary success within Russia that Rubina never knew in her Soviet days, and of a global visibility – at least among Russian readers – that is reserved for very few contemporary authors. So how did this novel, written by an author who had never been exceedingly prominent when she lived in the USSR, now removed to the marginal status of Russian-speaking emigrant in Israel, achieve this astounding success? Two additional facts about the work's publication history can serve as a starting point towards an answer to this question, if only by way of heightening the mystery. First of all, we may note that the initial publication of the novel, in Israel, was actually under a different title, *Вот идет Машиах!*, employing the Hebrew word for Messiah 'mashiach' (which persists only in the text itself in all later editions) as opposed to the Russian *Вот идет Мессия!* to which Rubina switched for publication in *Friendship of Peoples* and subsequently. Secondly, and strikingly, despite this indication that the novel was initially imagined to occupy a translingual space between Russian and Hebrew, and despite the modest wave of translations of the work into other languages, it has never been translated into Hebrew.[15] In fact, Rubina has published only one collection of work in Hebrew – a partial translation of her 1990 Soviet writer collection, which appeared in 1993 in a small print run.[16] Since that time, she and the Hebrew book market appear to have largely given up on one another. Yet at the time of the writing of *Here comes the Messiah!*, it seems, Rubina imagined her work and her future career as potentials, poised between these languages and cultural spaces. In other words, at the time of its writing, Rubina imagined her future as that of an Israeli writer of Russian origin. Instead, she became one of the first of a new category of authorship: an extraterritorial Russian writer.

Let us turn now to the content of the novel, which offers a great deal of additional evidence concerning Rubina's positionality with regard to audiences, markets, societies and cultural scenes in the early 1990s. *Here comes the Messiah!* is a meditation on the Russian émigré experience in Israel, focused in an autobiographical key on figures who represent refractions of Rubina's own experience and, in particular, her conceptions regarding the possibility of continued professional literary activity in Israeli emigration. The work begins with musings on the fate of Russian literature. During a radio interview, Ziama, the editor of a literary supplement to a Russian weekly newspaper, is asked 'whether, in her view, the continued development of Russian literature in the circumstances of the Middle East is possible' ('Возможно ли, по ее мнению, дальнейшее развитие русской литературы в условиях Ближнего Востока')?[17] Her answer shows her ambivalence: 'Yes, to her mind … a unique cultural situation … thanks to the mass repatriation, a concentration of creative forces has taken shape in our country … impetus towards a future flowering …' ('да, она считает, что… уникальная культурная ситуация… благодаря массовой репатриации, в нашем государстве образовалась концентрация творческих сил… влияние на дальнейший расцвет…', 6). Yet she is thinking to herself: 'What flowering?! A flowering of what?! Just grant a peaceful death already …' ('Какой расцвет?! Расцвет – чего?! Дайте спокойно умереть…', 6).

However, Ziama is not, apparently, entirely certain that Russian literature is dead in the Israeli waters, and as her thinking unfolds her calculations turn from purely literary matters to economics. At the conclusion of the interview, which, she notes, is being recorded for broadcast in Russia (which means that 'no one will ever hear it' ('никто не услышит')), the radio host presses her about her plans for the future. In response, she announces 'proudly, and even triumphantly' ('гордо, и даже торжественно'), that 'in future we intend to pay authors a small but solid honorarium' ('мы и впредь намерены выплачивать авторам небольшой, но твердый гонорар', 6). When the host objects that an honorarium is 'not the main thing in literary creativity, but merely an insignificant side-product' ('не главное в творчестве, а лишь незначительное производное') she agrees, but holds her ground: 'Yes, insignificant, unfortunately. … On the other hand, my graphic designer Vitya and I are drawing a normal salary for the fifth year now. Would you disagree that that's a triumph over the chaos of emigration?' ('к сожалению, незначительное, … Зато мы с моим коллегой, графиком Витей, вот уже пятый год получаем приличное жалованье. Разве это – не победа над хаосом эмиграции?', 7).

Like Ziama, Rubina worked in her first years of emigration as the editor of a literary supplement (*Пятница* (*Friday*), issued by the newspaper *Наша страна* (*Our country*)), and, like Ziama's, Rubina's principal education was in music – although, before emigration, Ziama was a musicologist, not a writer. Yet Ziama is not the only semi-autobiographical figure in the novel. The other main character is the 'well-known writer N.' ('известная писательница N.'). As this character muses, in a transparent reflection of Rubina's own experience in these years,

В России ее – грех жаловаться – продолжали печатать в солидных журналах. Но там ведь нынче как: чем серьезней журнал, тем он меньше платит. В прошлом году напечатали повесть и даже гонорар выплатили, симпатяги, – тринадцать долларов. Милые вы мои, – она прослезилась, так была тронута. Заграница тоже ... нам поможет. Так как известно: переводная литература на Западе не раскупается. И несчастный тираж в тысячу экземпляров расходится по университетам, где его жуют старательные слависты, которые еще никогда ничего в русской литературе не понимали. (229–30)

In Russia – it would be a sin to complain – they continued to publish her in respectable journals. But nowadays the situation there was like this: the more serious the journal, the less it paid. Last year one of her novellas got published and they even paid an honorarium, the darlings – thirteen dollars. Sweethearts! She teared up, she was so touched. But foreign lands can also ... come to the rescue. As is well known, no one buys translated literature in the West. A sad little print run of a thousand copies gets sent out to the universities, where it gets chewed over by earnest Slavicists who have never understood a thing about Russian literature.

N., in other words, works according to her profession, but makes ends meet with great difficulty. No one needs her writing – at least not enough to pay for it.

Without offering a comprehensive close reading of the novel, we may summarize it as the story of two versions of immigration – allegorizing two fates for Russian writing in Israel – between which both the plot and the autobiographical potential of the work are in suspension.[18] Ziama's path in emigration has been oriented on assimilation and adaptation. She lives in a West Bank settlement, speaks Hebrew with her neighbours and observes Jewish dietary restrictions, and her husband is a doctor who works according to his profession. The writer N., who is married to an artist (like Rubina herself), lives in a Russian enclave, struggles financially, and is alienated from Israeli social life. The lives of the two women come into contact in entirely minor and unrecognized ways in the course of the novel, the fashionably postmodern meta-literary plot of which involves the writer N.'s desire to compose her own novel about a character who is recognizable as none other than Ziama (and note, too, that her husband, having once seen Ziama's dog when the two families happened to spend a holiday at the same kibbutz, paints the animal into many of his works). At the conclusion of the novel, as the result of a completely arbitrary chain of events, both women are separately celebrating the conclusion of Yom Kippur with their families, by chance in one and the same restaurant, where the writer N.'s hapless soldier-son accidentally shoots and kills Ziama in an effort to save her from an equally hapless Palestinian would-be terrorist. The writer N. is a witness: 'And the writer N., practically mesmerized, gazed at this woman, killed by Shmulik, lying three steps away from her: the heroine of her novel – of the novel that she would now have neither life nor strength to finish writing' ('А писательница N. почти завороженно глядела на лежащую в трех шагах от нее, убитую Шмуликом, героиню своего романа. Того романа, дописать который у нее уже не достанет ни жизни, ни сил', 315).

In short, the novel appears to present an allegory concerning its own impossibility: assimilation (Ziama) and Russian literature (the writer N.) are not only incompatible, but engaged in mortal combat. Assimilation is akin to death (the death of the literary to which Ziama jokingly refers in the first pages), while stubborn persistence in the service of Russian literature is isolating and economically unfeasible, and faces a vacuum of subject matter, apart from the topic of its own mortality. Of course, this account of the novel's contents only serves to emphasize the paradox of its eventual fate, for its main premise was to express pessimism about the kind of success – economic and literary – that Rubina and her work in fact went on to achieve.

In sum, both the publication history of the novel and its autobiographical content attest to the fact that, when Rubina wrote it, she had very little conception that it would go on to find readers. This is unsurprising, given the state of the Russian literary world at the time. The publishing industry in Russia had collapsed. Channels of interrelationship between extraterritorial authors and authors in the Russian Federation were only just taking shape. As Rubina records in recollections of her early years of emigration, the economic mechanisms of such exchange were entirely incoherent in these years. Not only were Russian honoraria laughably small, as her character the writer N. notes, but the honoraria that were at times paid by Israeli publishers were large enough to provide significant aid to Muscovites, whose works were published in Israel from time to time with Rubina's help.[19] Like the characters of her novel, Rubina appears to have been feeling her way through the limited and not fully lucid possibilities of professional literary life in her new circumstances. Was this novel going to be read only by Russians in Israel? Would its future consist of being translated into Hebrew, as Rubina would come to claim a place as an Israeli writer? The possibility that her readership would turn out to be composed primarily of Russians in the Russian Federation was clearly nothing like a certainty, and perhaps not even the central possibility on Rubina's horizon as she wrote her novel.

We may thus rephrase our question concerning this novel in even stronger form: how did a book about the impossibility of being a Russian writer in Israel launch the career of this Russian-Israeli writer in Russia? Not by means of critical success, at least at the time of its first publication, when it was largely panned, despite its laudatory presentation as an example of Jewish-Russian writing by Lev Anninsky, the editor of *Friendship of peoples*.[20] T. Kravchenko, in the *Литературнаягазета* (*Literary gazette*), described it as an entertaining, but overly intentionally constructed 'mosaic' that, nevertheless, failed to cohere into a whole.[21] Alla Marchenko, writing in *New world*, offered similar complaints concerning the jumbled plot of the novel, yet also recognized that it was a highly readable potboiler, a page-turner that would be pleasing to the 'unsophisticated reader' ('простодушный читатель').[22] In this dismissive remark, which recalls those of the editor of *The banner* from the late 1980s, Marchenko may have unwittingly put her finger on an important factor in Rubina's success. Rubina, like other Russian writers at the time, was charting new modes of interrelationship between critical recognition and authorship in the post-Soviet era. Obsolete forms of literary elitism, formerly perpetuated by the gatekeepers of the Soviet literary-critical establishment, confronted the reality of the market mechanism, and discovered their own irrelevance in the face of readers (and profit-minded publishers), who want to read what they want to read, whether or not it meets critical standards. Rubina's work is not highbrow literature. Neither is it pulp fiction. Rather, it is 'good' literature for the middlebrow reader, who appreciates a touch of craft, perhaps even a bit of postmodern play, but also simply wants to listen to a good yarn.

Yet we should also take Rubina's extraterritorial position into account here. No critic, including Annensky, Marchenko and Kravchenko, fails to note that the novel's topic is the Russian Jewish emigration to Israel (one may note that, since the late 1980s, as she was coming to her decision to leave the USSR, Rubina's works had consistently focused on Jewish topics and characters). At the time of the writing and publication of *Here comes the Messiah!*, Rubina and her critics apparently assumed that few Russian readers would be interested in such a subject. They were wrong. The novel is invested in an ethnographic description of Israeli social life, built environment and landscapes, as well as in a 'light' magical-realist mixture of Jewish and scriptural mythological elements. Further, as other commentators have noted, Rubina pays close attention to the varieties of accented and non-standard Russian one might meet in Tel Aviv or Jerusalem: for instance, the narrator notes that a former lover of Ziama's deceased grandfather mispronounces hard and soft consonants ('это ария из другой оперы (она говорила "аръя" и "опэры")').[23] In short, the novel offers a form of travel literature for readers in the Russian Federation – a journey through the exotic, diasporic spaces of Israel.

Yet for all that, the success of *Here comes the Messiah!* undoubtedly also related to its game with negativity concerning emigration and the very possibility of its own existence. Is it an accident that reading publics in Russia responded so positively to a novel that successfully grafts an ethnographic journey through Israel's 'mosaic' of 'eastern' peculiarities onto a demonstration that Russian Jews, Jews though they be, will always remain a part of Russia? The pathos of this work, and of Rubina's other early writing on related topics like the novella *At Thy Gates*, derives from her often anguished recognition of the Russian-Israeli division of affective loyalties between two homelands. This is a particular, intensified form of the typical immigrant experience of social alienation and nostalgia, magnified by the insistent Zionist conceptualization of Aliyah not as immigration but rather as homecoming, a condition that has been described as one of 'dual diaspora'.[24] Rubina's novel shows how Russian Jews, in Israel as everywhere else, continue with their recognizable, stereotypical customs – with their drinking parties, their intelligentsia cult of literature, and their impractical tendency towards grand gestures – all those elements of identity that Rubina's novel describes as dooming the project of Russian-Israeli culture, but which, perhaps unexpectedly even for the author herself, ultimately cemented a place for this novel in Russian literature proper.

In his influential essay 'Conjectures on world literature', Franco Moretti distinguishes between two basic cognitive metaphors in literary studies: the tree, which describes the diachronic development of literature in national traditions, and the wave, which describes the diffusion of diverse literary forms across territory. In the conclusion of his essay, he remarks, 'This, then, is the division of labour between national and world literature: national literature, for people who see trees; world literature, for people who see waves.'[25] Yet Rubina's novel is both national and world literature, and a description of her place in the geography demands mixed metaphors. The expansion of Russian literature represented by this novel is the encounter of a Russian writer with the novel circumstances of Israel and the productive shift in the literary fabric achieved by means of the integration of some elements of Israeli reality in a recognizable Russian literary form. In her we see the tree of culturally and politically disparate national terrains joined together by the wave of Russian emigrants, as well as the wave of market forces that moves their books across global geography. In sum, we are encountering a form of the paradox with which this chapter begins – the current combination of unprecedented fragmentation and unprecedented integration of global Russian cultural space. For Rubina, the demonstration of the realities of fragmentation led to the profitable discovery of integration. Here, the global and the national, tree and wave, converge.

## Shamshad Abdullaev and the global avant-garde of the East

Shamshad Abdullaev is an ethnic Uzbek from the city of Fergana, who debuted as a Russian-language author in the last years of the Soviet Union and went on to achieve considerable success in the Russian Federation and, indeed, in the global arena of experimental poetry.[26] Yet beyond the fact that both he and Rubina began their careers in Soviet Uzbekistan and have found their primary readerships in Russia while living outside of it, his case contrasts with hers in nearly every respect. Whereas Rubina is a true emigrant from the USSR, Abdullaev is part of the beached diaspora of Russian speakers left behind in a newly independent state by the receding tide of the Soviet collapse, and a particular case in comparison with other, similarly positioned authors, in that his attachment to the Russian cultural scene is derived not from national identity but entirely from linguistic and literary affinities.[27] Most importantly for the purposes of the present analysis (and as we shall see below), the factors contributing to Abdullaev's prominence as an experimental poet are distinct from those driving Rubina's success with the mass-educated audience.

The launch of Abdullaev's career was linked closely to the story of the Tashkent Russian-language journal ЗвездаВостока (Star of the East), which in the last years of the Soviet Union achieved broad popularity with readers both in the centres and across the expanses of the USSR through its publications of translations of classics of Western mass literature such as Robert Heinlein, Agatha Christie and Dashiell Hammett, as well as republications of previously officially suppressed Russian modernist literature.[28] In some sense, the publication strategy of the journal in these years was an efflorescence of the geographical positioning of Tashkent as a cosmopolitan centre in the late Soviet period, when it served as the site of Soviet outreach to the developing world, as evidenced in institutions such as the Tashkent International Film Festival of Countries of Asia, Africa and Latin America, and the Association of Writers of Countries of Africa and Asia, the Soviet base of which was also located in Tashkent. In this light, Rossen Djagalov has described Soviet Tashkent as a postcolonial 'contact zone', as defined by Mary Louise Pratt, in that it was the scene both of Russian intermingling with the colonized cultures of Central Asia, and of Soviet cultural interchange with the decolonizing world.[29] Yet the journal's prominence in the late 1980s and early 1990s also reflected a broader phenomenon – that of the peripheral publication that claimed a place at the forefront of Soviet liberalizing tendencies by virtue of its geographical remove from the authority and oversight of the centre. It has been compared, in this sense, to the Latvian journals *Rodnik* and *Daugava*, which were among the first outlets for the publication of Moscow conceptualist poetry, among other things, during the late 1980s.

In April 1991, *Star of the East* gained a new chief editor, Sabit Madaliev, who in June appointed Abdullaev as the journal's poetry editor. Under their leadership, the journal developed a more radical vision of its outward-facing programme, especially with regard to poetry. While it continued to publish translations of Western mass prose genres (Stephen King's *The Shining*, for instance), it now added emphatically more intellectually ambitious works, such as translations of the classics of global modernist literature, critical writing and contemporary experimental prose: D. H. Lawrence, Adunis, T. S. Eliot, Sylvia Plath, Maurice Blanchot, Ezra Pound, Federico García Lorca, Czesław Miłosz, Michael Palmer, Robert Creeley, etc. These cosmopolitan voices were joined on the journal's pages by those of formerly underground and newly emerging Russian experimental authors such as Arkady Dragomoshchenko and Sergej Timofejev, as well as translations from the Koran and other mystical literature and writings on Eastern religions. Central Asian writing was represented by Abdullaev's own poetry and essays, as well as by the work of other members of his Fergana School – the grouping of experimental russophone poets of Uzbekistan, including Khamdam

Zakirov, Ol'ga Grebennikova, Daniil Kislov and Khamid Ismailov, of which Abdullaev was the leading figure.

This was a novel configuration of Central Asian cultural life, embracing the inheritance of Russian language from the imperial and Soviet past, yet oriented on a newly constructed prehistory of global modernist and avant-garde contexts, interwoven with Central Asian cultural traditions from the deep past of Islamic culture. Notably, Russian literary traditions per se do not enter overtly into the equation. As Abdullaev explained in a 2004 interview, 'Unfortunately, I find Russian literature rather uninteresting. It remains, as in the past, for all its greatness, archaic, fixated on moral reflections and structural tendencies of the nineteenth century.'[30] This visionary project of Madaliev, Abdullaev and their colleagues intended to bring together the Russian literary language, Central Asian collective identities and pasts, and cosmopolitan global culture, over the head of Russian literature, the official culture of the Soviet era, and the geography of the former Soviet lands that stood between it and the centres of world culture as these writers understood it.[31] In short, this was yet another alternative worlding of Russian culture for the post-Soviet era, in some ways a precursor to Dmitrii Kuz'min's Literature Without Borders project, described in the introduction to this chapter (and we may note that Kuz'min is one of Abdullaev's publishers). We may recognize the quixotic nature of this cultural project: although much of this aspirational novel global literary pantheon was constructed on the basis of the Russian translations that Abdullaev and his collaborators commissioned or produced and published in Star of the East, they were also dependent on a prehistory of Russian and Soviet conceptions of world literature, both official and unofficial, and an existing tradition of translations into Russian: one cannot simply 'bootstrap' out of one's own cultural milieu overnight. The group's ambition to leave behind Russian literature, with its canons and hierarchies, while remaining nevertheless in the Russian language, presents yet another version of the paradox of the rising fragmentation and integration of post-Soviet global Russian cultures with which this chapter begins.

The proclamation of the existence of the Fergana School and Abdullaev's own first publications in Star of the East appear in the second issue of the journal under Madaliev's editorship, in May 1991. In an unsigned introductory essay, Abdullaev explains:

The Fergana School is a group of authors writing in Russian and united by a commonality of atmosphere, aesthetic passions and sense of locality. They are distinguished by a tendency towards meditative, ontological (existential) poetry. They are primarily oriented on the achievements of Anglo-American imagists and Italian Hermeticists and freely make use of cinematic allusions (from Méliès to Ermanno Olmi), striving to maintain transparency and wholeness of sensation, the multifaceted nature of a concrete world. Their motto is taken from the words of Paul Klee: not to reflect the world, but to make it visible.[32]

From this same issue, we may consider a single poem as an illustration of Abdullaev's poetry – the master prism through which the publishing programme of the journal was refracted – his 'End of the week: A walk with a friend' ('Конец недели: прогулка с другом'):

И вышли на бугристую площадь – такую широкую,
что заметней проделанный путь, но обшарпанный сгиб
забора с едко-зеленым, мшистым покровом
и грязный ветродуй, из тупика
нагнавший нас, как всегда, со спины,
заглушили эпический декор, словно Париж,
увиденный впервые глазами Руссо
в жирной, кудахтающей серости.
Спрессованный ползучей пылью и побегами косматых кустов
дешёвый простор – именно здесь.
Замедляем шаг, зараженные тишиной. И всюду
дышит Оно. Что-то.
Лёгкая длительность, солнце пылает, жуки
смещаются тяжело, как хмурые пилигримы, по стерне
и – всякий раз внезапно – обнажают бледные,
бледно-розовые крылышки, срываясь в полет.
Думаешь, мы спасемся, вот так
постоянно держась на весу, как 'они'. Я сыт
по горло этой притворной обыденностью летнего пространства.
Мы лежим, раскинув руки, на протоптанном поле – два крестика
с птичьей высоты; я щупаю молодую тростинку,
цепляя ногтем ускользающую ломкость; а ты
читаешь, как умирал (умирает) Рембо:
слова, подсказанные болью, – 'аллах карим',
но ангел уже на подхвате (в каждый
воскресный день).[33]

So we came out on the pockmarked square – so broad
the path traversed is clear, but the rough curve
of the clay-walled street with its sour-green moss cover
and the dirty windblast that overtakes us
from the blind alley, as always, from behind,
have silenced the epic scrim, like Paris,
seen by Rousseau for the first time
in its greasy, squawking greyness.
This is the spot – a cheap expanse
Compressed by crawling dust and shoots of brush.
We slow our step, stricken by tranquillity. And
everywhere It breathes. Something.
A light duration, the sun beats down, beetles
shift heavy, like grim pilgrims over the furrow
and – suddenly each time – bare their pale,
pale-pink wings, breaking into flight.
You think we'll be saved, just like that,
always floating in the air, like 'them'. I'm fed
up with the everyday pretence of this summer landscape.
We lie arms outstretched on the trampled field – two little crosses
in a bird's-eye view; I reach for a young reed,
catching its fragility with my nail; and you
read about how Rimbaud died (keeps dying):
words prompted by pain, – 'Allah Karim',
but the angel is already at hand (on every
day of rest).[34]

Abdullaev's poem is a report on a walk through a cityscape that is recognizably Central Asian, but that renders it equivalent to Rousseau's Paris and lands in its conclusion on a meditation on Arthur Rimbaud's repetition of the Arabic invocation of a merciful God, 'Allah Karim', as he lay dying in Marseille, attempting to return to his beloved Abyssinia. Abdullaev's roving poetic attention dwells intensely on the materiality and the sensorial potentials of time and place, yet it is often difficult to pin down the precise era and location in question because, as in this case, his works continuously toggle between experience of the poet's near-at-hand physical location and a superordinate plane of culturally transmitted elsewheres, often inflected with the themes of interplay between European cultural centres and Orientalized peripheries, matching the partial self-Orientalization that suffuses the poem itself.

The project of this poem, which matched that of the poetic group and of the journal it controlled, was utopian – a leap out of a Soviet periphery into the most cosmopolitan dimensions of avant-garde poetics, staged in a mass-circulation journal addressing readers with no context for reading the multiple traditions in 'difficult' writing that Abdullaev was recombining in his own. In the early 1990s this vision stood in opposition to more potent countervailing tendencies in Uzbekistan. Although I do not have numerical data at my disposal, one may speculate with a high degree of certainty that with the breakdown of the all-Soviet distribution networks that allowed the journal to address readerships outside of Uzbekistan, not to mention the rapid post-Soviet decline of the thick journals from the enormous prominence, status and circulation figures they commanded during the last Soviet years, the actual readership of *Star of the East* was rapidly diminishing and becoming more localized in Central Asia during the early post-Soviet years. And that local population was itself becoming less russophone, as a result of the quickly unfolding mass migration of repatriating Russians from Central Asia. Meanwhile, Uzbek state and elite institutions were more and more fixated on nation building and the development of Uzbek-language culture. In 1995, the editorial board of *Star of the East* became the target of a smear campaign led by the conservative membership of the Uzbek Union of Writers. Madaliev and Abdullaev were forced to resign their positions. Subsequently, most of the Fergana School authors emigrated or simply gave up writing. Since that time, Abdullaev has continued, largely in isolation, his utopian russophone Central Asian cosmopolitan project.[35]

Yet if the audiences and institutions of independent Uzbekistan had no use for Abdullaev, certain readerships in the Russian Federation absolutely did. From the early 1990s onward, Abdullaev has been published in the most prestigious Russian journals, such as *The banner*, *Friendship of peoples*, and the *New literary observer* (*Новое литературное обозрение*), while his books have since that time been published by presses at the cutting edge of Russian literary life, from the leading experimental St Petersburg press of the early 1990s associated with the *Митинжурнал* (*Mitin journal*) to the leading press for innovative poetry of today, Издательский дом 'НовоеЛитературноеобозрение' (New literary observer Publishing house) and Argo-Risk, the publishing house associated with Kuzmin's influential journal of experimental poetry *Воздух* (*Atmosphere*).[36] In 1994 Abdullaev was recognized with the Andrei Bely Prize, Russia's oldest non-state literary distinction (the only such prize to be granted between 1991 and 1997). And his visibility has, ultimately, granted him global significance, resulting in invitations to international festivals, translations into English and other languages, a DAAD, a Joseph Brodsky Fellowship in 2015, and other honours and recognitions.

In short, Abdullaev's global cosmopolitan Central Asian project resonated with audiences in the Russian Federation. Yet in distinction from Rubina's case, Abdullaev's audiences are those of the Russian cultural elite, who control the institutional heights of Russian literature, if not its broadest circulations. He was one of the first not only provincial, but even utterly peripheral poets to be consistently included in literary life in Russia's twin capitals in the post-Soviet era. Like Rubina's, Abdullaev's attractions for the metropolitan audience are linked directly to that peripheral position and the manner in which he leveraged it into a sense of openness to a new construction of globality, as Arkady Dragomoshchenko put it in his trademark boundary-pushing rhetoric, during the Andrei Bely Prize award ceremony in 1994:

> Having the honour of offering accolades to a wonderful poet, essayist, prose author, and editor of the journal *Star of the East*, we are offering accolades to the region, to the world, that this poet has created. … I have been most amazed at how he can weave together the finest threads of various cultures into a particular pattern, understanding that he is present in a conversation with great European culture from the shores of Algeria, and at the possibility of a response from Europe by whatever roundabout paths it returns there, at how mighty these invisible linkages can be. I think that precisely this second part, the co-articulation, the creation of these linkages, of these separate cultures (of course they are separate, or they wouldn't be other) is the most important task of the poet.[37]

For institutional gatekeepers of Russian elite poetic culture such as Dragomoshchenko, Abdullaev's outward-facing literary project, linking russophone writing with world culture and largely eliding Russian literary traditions in their own right, resonated with their own strivings in the early post-Soviet years for literary innovation and reconnection with global avant-garde traditions. Abdullaev and his colleagues transformed the furthest peripheries of Soviet geography into a staging area from which to gather together 'threads' from even further afield, 'weaving them' into a new pattern of radical departures and novel literary forms for Russian writing. In the attraction of metropolitan literary innovators like Dragomoshchenko to Abdullaev's peripheral experiments, we may comprehend the complex structure of Russian cultural geography, in which the absolute centre and the distant periphery both constitute apt loci for the most future-oriented activity, each eschewing the 'provincial' and the 'traditional', associated with the 'heartland' of the cultural landscape.[38] Unfortunately, however, as Abdullaev and his colleagues learned, this conception of Tashkent and Fergana as peripheral Russian cultural geography was in no way compatible with the tenor of dominant Central Asian cultural projects of the post-Soviet era, which was oriented rather on articulation of the newly independent states as centres of national cultures in their own right.

## The unanticipated rise and structuring principles of extraterritorial Russian writing

Early in the post-Soviet era, Rubina and Abdullaev discovered new niches in global Russian literary geography, but not those that they anticipated. Both were correct in their assumptions that movement beyond the borders of Russian territory (or in Abdullaev's case the movement of borders across his home territory) would make possible new forms of writing – physical departures that led to novel literary departures. Each, in their own way, discovered to their surprise that the primary audience for this territorially and culturally displaced writing was not to be found in their new location, but in the one they left behind. Each uncovered the paradoxical logics of Russian cultures in an era of globalization, more interlinked and more fragmented than ever previously.

We may think in a theoretically robust manner about Rubina, Abdullaev and the interrelationship of national and global categories of literary production by turning once again to Casanova's writings on world literature. In that theorist's account, the global scene of literary exchange is organized into an unequal hierarchy of national literatures. Some, by virtue of history and contingency, occupy the prestige-granting centre of the global literary universe (Paris being the absolute centre of the literary world for the French researcher), and others located on the peripheries, competing for the literary capital that is gained from recognition in such centres. According to Casanova, the nation is the only operative frame for participation in the global system: 'the writer stands in a particular relation to world literary space by virtue of the place occupied in it by the national space into which he has been born.' Yet a given writer may adopt various attitudes towards this necessary national frame: 'He may reject his national heritage, forsaking his homeland for a country that is more richly endowed in literary resources than his own, as Beckett and Michaux did; he may acknowledge his patrimony while trying at the same time to transform it and, in this way, to give it greater autonomy, like Joyce ...; or he may affirm the difference and importance of a national literature, like Kafka.'[39]

To some extent the national space relates in synecdochic manner to global space, including within it its own subsystem of centre and peripheries: 'the internal configuration of each national space precisely mirrors the structure of the international literary world as a whole.' Furthermore, the dynamic relationship between global and national literary prestige generates subsidiary distinctions in literary profile and practice within literary space. Casanova distinguishes between '"national" writers (who embody a national or popular definition of literature) and "international" writers (who uphold an autonomous conception of literature)'. The former are read by the mass of their compatriots, the latter are read by the elites of their own nation, but also by those of other nations.[40]

Yet what are we to make of Rubina within this set of categorical distinctions? Unlike Joyce, Beckett, Gertrude Stein and Hemingway, international authors who left their home territories in order to break free from the confines of the national tradition as exiles, Rubina was part of a mass emigration that joined a new polity, yet also came to constitute an island outpost of their former nation, at a distance from the homeland. In distinction from Casanova's iconoclastic international authors, valued by an international circle of elite readers, Rubina is a middlebrow author who is read by her own compatriots and by Russian readers everywhere precisely because she combines universal standards of 'good writing' with the fresh materials of Israeli cultural and geographical difference. She is not the sort of author one chats about in effete St Petersburg literary salons.

Abdullaev, however, is just such a writer. In some ways, he does correspond to Casanova's category of international authors, such as Beckett, who reject their own national literature in an avant-garde search for a radical new path to innovation. Yet as a russophone Uzbek author who lives in the city of his birth, it can hardly be said that he has forsaken his own literature 'for a country that is more richly endowed in literary resources than his own'. And if Abdullaev takes Russian literature forward by means of exploration of new geographies, they are the geographies of the cosmopolitan globe as a whole, made uniquely available by his apparent suspension in a land without a firm position in the elitist, Eurocentric system of literary value to which he gravitates.[41] In short, this is a radical gesture of rejection of the past of Russian literature, emphasized by the peripheral, even centrifugal motion of life in Central Asia that, paradoxically, became emblematic of avant-garde explorations in the centre, and at the heights, of Russian literature at its moment of perhaps greatest momentum towards precisely such a cosmopolitan avant-gardism following the Soviet collapse.

To Rubina and Abdullaev we may add the many authors mentioned in the introduction of this chapter: Murav'eva, Singer, Schwab, Timofejev, Punte, Khanin, Petrova, Barskova, Shishkin and others. Together, they exemplify new wrinkles or folds in the articulation of world literary space that are not fully accounted for in Casanova's scheme of international versus national authors, a new category that has been brought into being by the global dispersion and fragmentation of ostensibly national literary territories. They are national and international at the same time. To quote my epigraph from Casanova once again, all writers 'gradually perfect a set of strategies linked to their positions, their written language, their location in literary space, to the distance or proximity they want to establish with the prestige-bestowing centre'. Some global Russian authors continue to exemplify the category of exilic, international and autonomous literature; one might think here of Petrova or Barskova. Yet Rubina and Abdullaev, by chance and contingency it seems, found their way to the precise articulation of distance and proximity that appeals to specific markets within Russia, allowing them to pioneer more paradoxically concatenated categories of 'global yet national, Russian yet Jewish' (Rubina) or 'avant-garde yet peripheral' (Abdullaev) that are the unique result of mass emigration and global dispersion, combined with global interconnectedness – this mix of cultural and demographic processes characteristic of cultural geography in the twenty-first century. Perhaps more importantly, they each exemplify the importance of self-fashioning with relation to one or many alternative Russian literary worlds. This is a new coin of literary capital, made possible by the new markets and modes of circulation of our era.

What are the historical conditions and future prospects of these phenomena? In the first decade of the century, one might have speculated that the rise of such authors, as the historical efflorescence of a particular moment in history – of the actual fragmentation and dispersion of what was previously the unified cultural and social whole of the USSR – was a generational effect that would dwindle in future decades in parallel with the numbers of 'global former Soviet authors'. Yet with the politically motivated emigration of authors such as Kuz'min, or the less definitive departure from Russian territory of figures such as Akunin, Sorokin and Idov, the category of extraterritorial Russian authors appears capable of 'restocking' for at least several more decades. Beyond this, one may anticipate, the infrastructure and reality of global social and cultural life will itself be transformed in ways that are difficult to predict, resulting in novel additional niches in the global cultural ecology. Will national frames of reference experience a resurgence in importance as the era of intensified globalization of the 1990s–2010s comes to an end and locations like Russia return to a more autarkic model? Will the rise of increasingly successful forms of machine translation and the globalization of communications media continue to erode borders between languages and societies? As the description above of the cases of Rubina and Abdullaev demonstrates, as geopolitical and technological transformations render the structuring categories of literary geography increasingly variegated and mobile, the study of literary meaning and prestige must account for ever more complex interrelationships of fragmentation and integration among diverse literary contexts, readerships, markets and worlds.

Ultimately, even if the category of the 'national' makes a comeback in the decades to come, and even if that of the extraterritorial Russian author, as exemplified in the above, fades, there will be no way back to the organization of global literary life described by Casanova, an organization that relates to the heyday of the national as ideology and as organizing principle for global political life (even within the supposedly internationalist USSR). As a result of the increasing rise of human mobility, multilingual polities, electronic communications and the erosion of the nation (quite apart from its continuing acceptance by many and its cynical amplification by political elites), the structuring principles of national territories and literatures in hierarchical interaction will increasingly be effaced, reduced to the condition of one cultural imaginary among many others in global literary life. As in the above analyses, an adequate description of literary institutions and the vagaries of particular authors and works will increasingly demand attention to their positioning and self-fashioning in relation to diverse global or regional cultural projects and frames, in one or many languages, all of which rise up above the physical landscape as competing worldings of human culture.

# Notes

1 Casanova 2005, 89.
2 On 'beached' and 'accidental' diasporas, see Laitin 1998 and Brubaker 2000.
3 This is among the fundamental claims of Platt 2019. Within that volume, see in particular: Rubins 2019, Kukulin 2019 and Gorham 2019.
4 Murav'eva, whose publications in Russian are numerous and prominent, has a low profile in English. Aside from inclusion in a number of anthologies, she has only two book-length publications in English, neither with extensive print runs: Muravyova 1999 and 2013.
5 On Idov, see Wanner 2019.
6 Literatura bez granits 2016. All translations in this chapter are the author's, unless otherwise noted.
7 Kuz'min 2018.
8 Kuz'min 2019.
9 Casanova 2004.
10 For biographical information about Rubina in this and subsequent paragraphs, I rely on Adamovitch 2004.
11 Rubina 2012.
12 Additionally, Rubina's collection of stories *Один интеллигент уселся на дороге* (An intelligentsia fellow sat down on the road), published in Jerusalem in 1994, was recognized with the Arie Dulchin prize, granted by the Federation of Writers' Associations of Israel, with national state support (the prize was cancelled in 1996). Later, she won the 2007 Russian Booker for *На солнечной стороне улицы* (*On the sunny side of the street*).
13 Rubina 2012.
14 The accurate counting of Jews in Russia is a fraught matter, considering histories of intermarriage and assimilation, the complexities of self-identification on censuses, and the religious and political parameters of Jewish identities. Mark Tolts distinguishes between a 'core' population of self-identified Jews, estimated to be 183,000 in 2015, and an 'enlarged' group with some professed Jewish ancestry, estimated at 380,000 that same year. See Tolts 2018, esp. p. 217.
15 This is, of course, a reflection not only of Rubina's primary orientation towards and success with Russian readers, but also of deep divisions between the Russian and Hebrew enclaves in contemporary Israeli cultural life. See Moshkin 2018. A probable additional factor contributing to the reluctance to translate the novel into Hebrew relates to its approach to Israeli domestic politics and the Palestinian-Israeli conflict, which, as will be seen below, is at odds with the generally liberal and progressive tenor of the Hebrew cultural mainstream. The author's thanks go to Alex Moshkin for pointing to this possible factor.
16 Rubina 1993.
17 Rubina 1999, 5–6. Subsequent references to this edition are given in parentheses in the text.
18 I am indebted in my reading of this novel to Moshkin 2018.
19 Rubina 2012.
20 One may note that this publishing venue signals, in some sense, Rubina's position as a 'not quite Russian' author: the journal's initial mission upon its creation in 1939 was the publication of literature created by all of the peoples of the Soviet Union; in the post-Soviet era it transitioned to publishing 'new publications of works of writers and poets of Russia and of the countries of the near and distant abroad'. See Druzhba narodov 2013.
21 Kravchenko 1996.
22 Marchenko 1997.
23 Zeberek 2011; Ronell 2008.
24 Krutikov 2003; Moshkin 2019; Rubins 2019.
25 Moretti 2013, 61.
26 His first significant publication was a selection of poetry in a multi-authored volume: Krasil'nikov 1987. It was to be his only collection of poetry in book form to be published in Uzbekistan.
27 Of course, the significance of authorship driven by linguistic and cultural versus ethnic and national identification with Russian literature depends, in its variation across discrete cases, on the specificities of the interrelationships of the cultural traditions in question. In some sense, Abdullaev's continued participation in Russian cultural life is no different from

Rubina's – they are both representatives of 'non-Russian nationalities of the USSR' who write in Russian. Yet the status of Jews in Russian culture and society, in comparison with that of a titular nationality of a Soviet republic, is thoroughly distinct. Abdullaev is more like, in this respect, a poet such as the russophone Latvian poet Artur Punte, although one may note in the latter case that his mother was Russian, as is his first language.

28 On the history of the journal, in the context of a discussion of the Fergana School of poets of which Abdullaev is the leading figure, see Korchagin 2017.

29 Djagalov 2020, 17–19 and passim; Pratt 1991. For a cultural history of Russian cultural life in Central Asia, see Kosmarskaya and Kosmarski 2019.

30 Abdullaev 2004.

31 The Fergana school has been treated in Kukulin 2002 and Korchagin 2017.

32 Abdullaev 1991a. Attribution of the essay to Abdullaev is made possible by stylistic considerations, as well as by his partial recycling of it in a later, retrospective account of the project of *Star of the East* and of the Fergana School in the early 1990s (Abdullaev 1998). The structural position of the essay in the journal suggests that Abdullaev was already serving as the unannounced poetry editor of the journal for this issue.

33 Abdullaev 1991b.

34 Abdullaev 2018.

35 For an account of the editorial shake-up, see Korchagin 2017.

36 See Abdullaev 1992, 1997, 2013 and 2017.

37 'Premiia Andreia Belogo' 1994.

38 This configuration of the cultural landscape is not a novel post-Soviet phenomenon, but has important prehistories in Soviet constructions of the periphery as a site for experimental and avant-garde culture. In this regard, see for instance Maxim Waldstein's (2008) account of the Soviet school of cultural semiotics that coalesced in the 1960s and 1970s in Tartu, Estonia, around the figure of Yury Lotman. It also has parallels in other post-Soviet peripheral locations. As Ilya Kukulin (2002) has noted, the Fergana School is comparable in its poetics to the Riga-based poetic collective Orbita. In another essay (Platt 2013), I have described the poetics of the Orbita group in terms comparable to those I employ here with regard to Abdullaev and his colleagues.

39 Casanova 2004, 41.

40 Casanova 2004, 108.

41 Abdullaev himself has applied the term 'Eurocentric' to himself, noting as well the complexity of his relationship to Central Asia: 'It is precisely thanks to them, my ancestors, that a certain *Eastern-ness* is accumulated in me – at concealed, instinctive-unconscious levels of my nature, continuously experiencing abyssal fracturing, although the vector of my intentional conceptions is now inalterably oriented towards the Eurocentric world and there's nothing to be done about it' (Abdullaev 2004).

# Bibliography

Abdullaev, Shamshad (unattributed). Introduction to 'Poeziia' ('poetry') section. *Zvezda vostoka* 5 (1991a): 3.

Abdullaev, Shamshad. 'Konets nedeli: progulka s drugom', *Zvezda vostoka* 5 (1991b): 7.

Abdullaev, Shamshad. *Promezhutok*. St Petersburg: Mitin zhurnal, 1992.

Abdullaev, Shamshad. *Medlennoe leto*. St Petersburg: Mitin zhurnal, 1997.

Abdullaev, Shamshad. 'Poeziia i Fergana', *Znamia* 1 (1998): 209–10.

Abdullaev, Shamshad. 'Razgovornyi zhanr zhiznetvorchestva. Shamshad Abdullaev: konvul'sii peska na grebne rasstoianii'. Interview by Denis Ioffe. *Topos*, 4 April 2004. http://www.topos. ru/article/2215 (accessed 8 September 2020).

Abdullaev, Shamshad. *Priblizhenie okrain: stikhi, esse*. Moscow: Novoe literaturnoe obozrenie, 2013.

Abdullaev, Shamshad. *Pered mestnost'iu*. Moscow: Argo-Risk, 2017.

Abdullaev, Shamshad. 'End of the week: A walk with a friend'. Translated by Susanne Frank, James McGavran, Kevin M. F. Platt, Ariel Resnikoff, Val Vinokur and Michael Wachtel. In Shamshad Abdullaev, 'Zoom-shots: Four poems', translated by Kevin M. F. Platt et al., 470–1. *Common Knowledge* 24(3) (2018): 464–73.

Adamovitch, Marina. 'Dina Il'inichna Rubina (19 September 1953–)'. In *Russian Writers since 1980*, edited by Marina Balina and Mark Naumovich Lipovetsky (Dictionary of Literary Biography 285), 248–53. Farmington Hills, MI: Gale, 2004.

Brubaker, Rogers. 'Accidental diasporas and external "homelands" in Central and Eastern Europe: Past and present'. Political Science Series, no. 71, Institute for Advanced Studies, Vienna (2000). https://irihs.ihs.ac.at/id/eprint/1299/ (accessed 8 September 2020).

Casanova, Pascale. *The World Republic of Letters*, translated by M. B. DeBevoise. Cambridge, MA: Harvard University Press, 2004.

Casanova, Pascale. 'Literature as a world', *New Left Review* 31 (2005): 71–90.

Djagalov, Rossen. *From Internationalism to Postcolonialism: Literature and cinema between the Second and the Third Worlds*. Montreal, Canada: McGill-Queen's University Press, 2020.

Druzhba narodov. 'Zhurnal'nyi klub DN/Druzhba narodov', 2013. http://xn--80aabggdk2dkbof7a.com/magazines/druzhba-narodov (accessed 8 September 2020).

Gorham, Michael S. 'When soft power hardens: The formation and fracturing of Putin's "Russian World"'. In *Global Russian Cultures*, edited by Kevin M. F. Platt, 185–206, 2019.

Korchagin, Kirill. '"Kogda my zamenim svoi mir…": Ferganskaia poeticheskaia shkola v poiskakh postcolonial'nogo sub"ekta', *Novoe literaturnoe obozrenie* 144 (2017): 448–70.

Kosmarskaya, Natalya and Artyom Kosmarski. '"Russian culture" in Central Asia as a transethnic phenomenon'. In *Global Russian Cultures*, edited by Kevin M. F. Platt, 69–93, 2019.

Krasil'nikov, Nikolai, ed. *Vstrecha: Stikhi molodykh poetov*. Tashkent: Izd-vo TsK LKSM Uzbekistana 'Esh gvardiia', 1987.

Kravchenko, T. 'Dve zhenshchiny i vse ostal'nye', *Literaturnaia gazeta* 4(5630), 27 November 1996, 4.

Krutikov, Mikhail. 'Constructing Jewish identity in contemporary Russian fiction'. In *Jewish Life after the USSR*, edited by Zvi Gitelman with Musya Glants and Marshall I. Goldman, 252–74. Bloomington: Indiana University Press, 2003.

Kukulin, Il'ia. 'Fotografiia vnutrennostei kofeinoi chashki', *Novoe literaturnoe obozrenie* 54 (2002): 262–82.

Kukulin, Ilya [Il'ia]. 'Russia as whole and as fragments'. In *Global Russian Cultures*, edited by Kevin M. F. Platt, 151–82, 2019.

Kuz'min, Dmitrii. 'Udobno nenavidet' Rossiiu…'. Dreamwidth (blog site), 12 August 2018. https://dkuzmin.dreamwidth.org/593395.html (accessed 8 September 2020).

Kuz'min, Dmitrii. 'It is easy to hate …'. Translated by Michael Wachtel, Charles Bernstein, Leonid Schwab, Katherine O'Connor and James McGavran. *Matter*, 19 August 2019. https://mattermonthly.com/2019/08/19/it-is-easy-to-hate/ (accessed 8 September 2020).

Laitin, David. *Identity in Formation: The Russian-speaking populations in the near abroad*. Ithaca, NY: Cornell University Press, 1998.

Literatura bez granits. 'O proekte', 2016. http://www.literaturewithoutborders.lv/ru (accessed 8 September 2020).

Marchenko, Alla. '…s prekrasnym vidom na Ershalaim', *Novyi mir* 3 (1997): 217.

Moretti, Franco. 'Conjectures on world literature'. In Franco Moretti, *Distant Reading*, 43–62. London: Verso, 2013.

Moshkin, Alex. 'Forty years in the wilderness: Russian-Israeli literature, film, and painting, 1978–2018'. PhD dissertation, University of Pennsylvania, 2018.

Moshkin, Alex. 'History, diaspora, and geography: The case of Russian-Israeli cinema, 1991–2016'. In *Global Russian Cultures*, edited by Kevin M. F. Platt, 113–34, 2019.

Muravyova, Irina. *The Nomadic Soul: A story of modern-day Anna Karenina*, translated by John Dewey. Moscow and Chicago, IL: GLAS, 1999.

Muravyova, Irina. *Day of the Angel*. Translated by John Dewey. London: Thames River Press, 2013.

Platt, Kevin M. F. 'Eccentric orbit: Mapping Russian culture in the near abroad'. In *Empire De/Centered: New spatial histories of Russia and the Soviet Union*, edited by Sanna Turoma and Maxim Waldstein, 271–96. Aldershot and Burlington, VT: Ashgate, 2013.

Platt, Kevin M. F., ed. *Global Russian Cultures*. Madison: University of Wisconsin Press, 2019.

Pratt, Mary Louise. 'Arts of the contact zone', *Profession* (1991): 33–40.

'Premiia Andreia Belogo za 1993 god (stenogramma tseremonii vrucheniia)', *Mitin zhurnal* 51 (Spring 1994): 277–86. Republished at Vavilon.ru, 1998. http://www.vavilon.ru/metatext/mj51/bely.html (accessed 8 September 2020).

Ronell, Anna P. 'Some thoughts on Russian-language Israeli fiction: Introducing Dina Rubina', *Prooftexts* 28(2) (2008): 197–231.

Rubinah, Dinah (Rubina, Dina). *Shem mishpahah kaful: novelot.* Translated by Imanuel Bihovski. Tel Aviv: ha-Kibuts ha-meuhad: Agudat ha-sofrim ha-`Ivrim, 1993.

Rubina, Dina. *Odin intelligent uselsia na doroge.* Jerusalem: Verba, 1994.

Rubina, Dina. *Vot idet Messiia!* Moscow: Podkova, 1999.

Rubina, Dina. *Na solnechnoi storone ulitsy.* Moscow: Eksmo, 2006.

Rubina, Dina. 'Moia kar'era nachalas' s trex slov'. Interview by Varvara Bogdanova. 7dnei.ru, 19 April 2012. 7days.ru/stars/privatelife/dina-rubina-moya-karera-nachalas-s-trekh-slov. htm (accessed 8 September 2020).

Rubins, Maria. 'A century of Russian culture(s) "abroad": The unfolding of literary geography'. In *Global Russian Cultures*, edited by Kevin M. F. Platt, 21–47, 2019.

Tolts, Mark. 'Post-Soviet Jewish demographic dynamics: An analysis of recent data'. In *Jewish Population and Identity: Concept and reality: In honor of Sidney Goldstein*, edited by Sergio DellaPergola and Uzi Rebhun, 213–29. Cham: Springer, 2018.

Waldstein, Maxim. *The Soviet Empire of Signs: A history of the Tartu School of Semiotics.* Saarbrücken: VDM Verlag, 2008.

Wanner, Adrian. 'The most global Russian of all: Michael Idov's cosmopolitan oeuvre'. In *Global Russian Cultures*, edited by Kevin M. F. Platt, 230–49, 2019.

Zeberek, Teresa. 'Homeland as exile and exile as homeland in the works of Dina Rubina'. In *Poles & Jews: History–culture–education*, edited by Mariusz Misztal and Piotr Trojanski, 148–57. Cracow: Wydawnictwo naukowe Uniwersytetu pedagogizcnego, 2011.

# Beyond diaspora? Brief remarks in lieu of an afterword

Galin Tihanov

This seminal volume illuminates diasporic writing from different perspectives; crucially, it also engages, at times critically, with the very notion of diaspora that has been sustaining these perspectives. Here I wish to offer some brief reflections on the status of diaspora studies, what it can and cannot do, and where it fits in the current, and perhaps also the future, landscape of the humanities.

It is among the strengths of this volume that it begins to question, often implicitly, the suitability of a diasporic approach to literature and culture today. The real problem here is that diaspora, as a methodological perspective, defines itself through the nation: the diaspora might seem distant in its own preoccupations, or close, displaying varying degrees of commitment to the national agenda, but it is in the end always the nation that posits the diaspora as its extension. This dependency could be best conveyed by saying – in a somewhat pointed fashion – that diaspora studies is the last remaining refuge of methodological nationalism, modelling as it does its object of research with constant reference to a nation whose presence is both mediated and inescapable. Despite mounting scepticism towards globalization, there continues to be a strong underlying sense of global interconnectedness sustained by the (often alienating) experiences of virtual reality, simultaneity and incessant information flow which the rebirth of various nationalisms fails to disrupt. Globalization, in this deeper meaning beyond the surface manifestations of economic exchange, is proving a resilient reality that has the power to bind and isolate in the same breath. Seen in this light, diaspora becomes a problematic concept also in the sense that it deposits in the fabric of a globally interconnected yet dispersed and atomized world a somewhat dated notion of tribal solidarity and cohesion constructed from the remnants of loyalty and attachment to the nation.

In other words, diaspora often serves to resurrect the idea of an imagined *community*, grounded in certain expectations of homogeneity and yet operating at the heart of a world organized around the principles of *society* that guarantee anonymity, equidistance from communitarian agendas and, above all, liberal individualism (current illiberal pressures notwithstanding). Diaspora, in brief, can potentially function as an archaic formation that keeps alive a sense of tribalism amidst a globalized economy of (non-)belonging that features culturally hybrid agents (the norm, in recent decades, and not just in the West, following unabating mass labour migration and waves of refugees). This constant referral back to the nation (in social anthropology, the term 'long-distance nationalism', introduced by Benedict Anderson, is sometimes used as an appellation that captures the underlying modus vivendi of diaspora[1]) is what makes diaspora a problematic term – and observation platform – today. Shu-mei Shih, critiquing the way in which the term diaspora is always conjuring the spirit of the nation and the nation state, on which it depends, has proposed that 'diaspora has an end date',[2] resisting the narrative of cross-generational, open-ended sustainability of cultural patterns inherited from the ancestral land. In turning 'against diaspora', as the title of her important essay on global sinophone culture would have it, Shih refuses to embrace notions of imposed ethnic, linguistic and cultural homogeneity.

As one contemplates an epistemological move beyond diaspora, one should retain the considerable heuristic potential of the essays in this excellent collection which raises awareness of the asymmetry between nation state and Empire, and in so doing seeks to demarcate the applicability of diaspora to the Russian case. For most of its history, Russia has functioned as an empire rather than as a pure nation state. Research on Russian culture thus assists us in asking important questions. How does diaspora relate to Empire, keeping in mind the latter's tendency to transcend ethnic and linguistic homogeneity in ways that erode the very foundations of diasporic cultures? Once a polis recalibrates following the disintegration of Empire, does this polis transition to a formation that shares the features of a nation state, or does it remain dominated by the characteristics of what one could call post-Empire, an intricate form of political and cultural organization that is no longer a full empire, just as it is not a nation state in the habitual understanding of the term? Diaspora here, certainly in the Russian case (but also in the case of the Central European states that emerged following the collapse of other empires after World War I: multilingual, ethnically mixed, often with large diasporas present on the territory of their immediate neighbours, in other words states that were, at their birth, less than Empire and more than a mere nation state), serves as a helpful litmus test of how one delineates these formations; the lessons to be learnt in the process would have validity, now and in the future, that extends far beyond Russian studies. Conversely, Russian studies stands to learn from the work on diaspora and diasporic cultures that has been going on for a long time in postcolonial studies (a pertinent question here is how diasporas that originate in the disintegration of the Soviet Union but are not predominantly russophone relate to Russian literature and culture).

Some of the contributions to this collection also return to the question of exile and exilic culture. Exile as concept always comes laden with existential baggage: it stands for trepidation, anxiety, cultural energy that is often directed backwards, to the past, and, ultimately, a deeply personal sense of loss and gain in the same breath. Just like diaspora, exile operates differently under Empire. Ovid's *Ex Ponto*, one of the prototypical texts of imperial exile, bemoans the fact that the poet is thrust onto the edge of Empire – still within its borders, yet overwhelmed by a sense of exclusion. In his solitude in the fold of Empire, Ovid draws up a list of other exiles, sourced from history and from literature, and this is the company he keeps most faithfully. But there is, at least historically, also a most significant demarcation line between exilic and diasporic writing: the propensity of the former to accommodate narratives about individual experiences, and the proclivity of the latter to transform these narratives into accounts of collective destiny.

To maximize the intellectual benefits of reading the chapters included in this important collection, we have to come to terms with the fact that both the notion of exile and, as I have argued, that of diaspora may be gradually ageing. Modernity has ruthlessly pegged these two notions to the ideological horizon of the nation state, severely narrowing the repertoire of meanings and experiences they could convey; from the perspective of a *longue durée* that would consider the vast body of writing before the arrival of national cultures, this repertoire is bound to have been – and could prospectively still be – richer and much more varied. What is more, exile as a prism for the analysis of current cultural phenomena sits somewhat uncomfortably in the present intellectual context, not least because of the lingering shadow traditional humanism, by now under unrelenting interrogation, casts over it. The exilic narratives of suffering and creativity, of authenticity and its relinquishing, which I have written about elsewhere,[3] are enfleshments of a humanist outlook that presumes certain core values, including, but not confined to, human dignity and singularity; and it is precisely these core values that are no longer self-evident or available in an uncontested fashion.

I wish to conclude by praising the sustained attention this volume gives to the cardinal question of language. Phenomena such as self-translation, translingual experiences, comings and goings between languages are very much at the centre of this collection of chapters. Exilic and diasporic writing have the capacity to estrange language from its identity as a *national language*; they thus lay the foundations of world literature, which would be absolutely unthinkable without destabilizing the sacrosanct (but in fact historically produced and thus limited) Western model of identity between a single national language and its corresponding national literature. In a sense, the main protagonist of exilic writing is language itself; we cannot really comprehend the history of world literature unless we understand what happens to language as it travels across political, cultural and linguistic borders. The two principal scenarios are well known: either embracing a new language (Nabokov is one salient example that stands for many others), or continuing to deploy the language of one's pre-exilic environment. There is, however, a powerful third way. Witold Gombrowicz, the Polish émigré writer who has a place in the extended canon of Western modernism, elected to do something different. His relatively short novel, *Trans-Atlantyk*, published in Paris in 1953, is written in a language that deliberately reactivates the resources of Polish Baroque and Romanticism, adding to the mix a *skaz*-like handling of language. The result is a language that emphatically liberates and estranges both Gombrowicz and his readers from the Polish that was written and spoken in Poland in the early 1950s, i.e. from Polish as the language of the nation (*the national language*). This purposely odd language, not recognizable as the national language shared by Gombrowicz's contemporaries, but still identifiable as an iteration of Polish, is the compass his readers must use in order to be led 'out of their Polishness', as Gombrowicz puts it in his *Diary*.

Exilic writing is thus inextricably bound up with, and participating in, the making of world literature – by disaggregating language and nation, and by emplotting mobility, multiplicity and foreignness.

## Notes

1   See Anderson's 1992 working paper 'Long-distance nationalism'; for a more sustained articulation, see Glick Schiller and Furon, *Georges Woke Up Laughing,* 2001.
2   Shih, 'Against diaspora', 37; the first version of this essay, reworked for the 2013 volume cited here, appeared in 2007.
3   Tihanov, 'Narratives of exile', 2015, 141–59.

# Bibliography

Anderson, Benedict. 'Long-distance nationalism: World capitalism and the rise of identity politics', Center for German and European Studies, University of California, 1992.

Glick Schiller, Nina and Georges Eugene Furon. *Georges Woke Up Laughing: Long-distance nationalism and the search for home*. Durham, NC: Duke University Press, 2001.

Shih, Shu-mei. 'Against diaspora: The Sinophone as places of cultural production'. In *Sinophone Studies: A critical reader*, edited by Shu-mei Shih, Chien-hsin Tsai and Brian Bernards, 25–42. New York: Columbia University Press, 2013.

Tihanov, Galin. 'Narratives of exile: Cosmopolitanism beyond the liberal imagination'. In *Whose Cosmopolitanism? Critical perspectives, relationalities and discontents*, edited by Nina Glick Schiller and Andrew Irving, 141–59. New York and Oxford: Berghahn, 2015.

# Conclusion

## Maria Rubins

Examining Russian diasporic literature as a complex but integral phenomenon evolving for over a century in multiple contexts opens up additional perspectives on the current reframing of culture as multifocal, hybrid and contingent. Located in the contact zone between national and global networks, diaspora unsettles ideas of an essentialist Russian identity. Asserting alternative definitions of Russianness, extraterritorial authors contest their alleged marginality vis-à-vis the homeland. At the same time, through their participation in transnational literary systems they facilitate the making of World Literature.

The purpose of our collective discussion was not to come to a consensus on all aspects of extraterritorial identities as they are expressed in and through literary narratives, but to start the process of rethinking the place and function of diaspora in global Russian literature. As the various interpretations of 'diaspora' evoked in this volume demonstrate, this concept remains fluid and subject to constant interrogation and redefinition. While the continuing relevance of diaspora as a methodological lens for the study of hybrid transnational cultural production needs to be tested in future studies, should we rush to move 'beyond diaspora', as Galin Tihanov appears to suggest in his contribution to this volume? For Tihanov it is a problematic concept because, in his words, diaspora defines itself through the nation, re-surrecting the idea of a homogeneous imagined community and keeping alive a sense of tribalism 'amidst a globalized economy of (non-)belonging that features culturally hybrid agents'. He draws on the work of Shu-mei Shih, who proclaimed 'an end date for diaspora' in the context of her polemic against 'Chinese diaspora' a category that she considers 'mis-conceived' and 'universalizing', founded on a notion of unified ethnicity, culture, language and place of origin.[1] While the current debates among sinologists appear far removed from our present concerns, a comparison between the ways of construing 'Chineseness' and 'Russianness' may be instructive.

Shu-mei Shih views 'Chinese' largely as a Han-centric designation, exclusive of some 56 other ethnic groups (Uyghur, Tibetan, Mongolian, etc.) whose place in the Chinese diaspora is largely determined by the degree of their Sinicization. She argues that the reduction of Chineseness to Han ethnicity in places outside China is the inverse of the hegemonic claims to Chineseness made by the Han majority inside the country. Shih speaks up against the narrative of 'Chinese diaspora' that reproduces the mainland's practices of cultural homogeneity and insufficiently reflects place-based experiences of sinophones found in various locations around the globe.

How far can this specific case of discursive uses and misuses of *Chinese* diaspora affect our understanding of the *Russian* diaspora? If we look back at diverse meanings of Russian diaspora as a social formation, we will also find occasional attempts, particularly in the years following the initial post-revolutionary dispersion, to create a mini-replica of the homeland and to cement émigré identity through a set of definitive markers promoted by diasporic institutions. In practical terms, what have come to be known as Russian diasporas have been defined primarily by their russophone nature. Even if ethnic Russians predominated within such networks, they incorporated other ethnicities of the former Russian and Soviet empires with a shared historical, cultural and linguistic background. But as I mentioned in my introductory chapter, this function of diaspora has become progressively more irrelevant in the contemporary world. So in this sense we have already moved 'beyond diaspora'.

Significantly, Shih specifies that in her discussion of the inadequacies of 'Chinese diaspora' she does not refer to the literary domain. Rather, she deals with it as a geopolitical, ideological and social construct. Unlike Shih, we are here primarily concerned with literature. Does extra-territorial writing in Russian automatically reproduce the hegemonies of the mainland, assume a homogeneous Russian ethnicity, or refer back to the Russian nation? Does it resurrect a 'sense of tribalism'? Many of the case studies presented in this volume develop quite different scenarios. 'Diaspora' emerges as a typological category, a displacement not so much in geography as in cultural context, a severing of networks and communicative circuits. This severing may be triggered by a dislocation in space but it also can happen without any spatial movement at all, as in the case of internal exile or when political entities modify state borders and create new polities (as happened, for example, in Riga after the Revolution or in the Near Abroad after the collapse of the Soviet Union). Diaspora is also discussed as a discursive 'space', an imagined distance, a virtual community, and a new maze of cultural networks that come to replace the old ones. Most of our contributions show how diasporic narratives that emerge from this repositioning disrupt nation-bound homogeneous narratives, and highlight instances of cultural hybridity, fluidity and multiplicity. In the large corpus of theoretical literature to which we refer throughout this volume, diaspora as a paradigm is discussed in a way that privileges migration, mobility, border crossing and new patterns of circulation. For many scholars looking at diverse cultural contexts, 'diasporic' connotes anti-nationalist and culturally pluralistic aesthetic practices.[2]

Not only is our central concept of 'diaspora' periodically called into question, but even its definition as 'Russian' can be contested. Adrian Wanner draws attention to its inadequacy as a marker of the complex diasporic identity and proposes to replace it with 'russophone':

> Which criteria allow us to decide who belongs to a putative diasporic community and who doesn't? Russia is a country that hovers uneasily between a nation state and an empire. For that reason, ethnicity and religion have been less than satisfactory yardsticks in delineating the contours of the Russian diaspora. Instead, language is usually seen as the determining factor. In that view, what we call the 'Russian' diaspora is really a russophone diaspora.

Replacing Russian with russophone is no easy solution, however, because not all that falls within a broader definition of Russian diasporic writing is indeed russophone. Further complicating any clear-cut definitions is the work of 'cultural hybrids', native speakers of Russian who may or may not be ethnically Russian, and who turn their insider knowledge of Russianness into a 'cultural commodity' while mostly writing in adopted tongues.[3]

This volume does not purport to cover the entire ground, nor to point out all possible nuances. Here, we have been mostly testing the paradigm of East–West exile (from Russia to the West). It would be interesting to ponder an alternative paradigm of West–East exile, where geographically (and perhaps culturally) Russia would be seen as 'the West'. It should not be forgotten that in the wake of the Revolution numerous routes led in an easterly direction. Did Russians, as self-fashioned carriers of European cultural values, feel superior to the surrounding Asian populations? Did local cultures inspire their curiosity, respect and admiration? Were they exoticized or ignored? Did émigrés experience the same sense of intellectual and emotional connection to Asia that many felt towards Europe? Nicholas Roerich's enthusiastic exploration of Eastern spirituality in his painting, writing, expeditions and direct encounters with a broad range of notable Asian personalities, from Tibetan lamas to politicians, stands out as a powerful but arguably unique example. We know that Russian literati of interwar Harbin and Shanghai pined for Paris as the 'cultural capital' of Russia Abroad and desired to be published in Europe-based émigré journals, and so at least indirectly to maintain their link to presumed 'civilizational origins'. The legacy of Roerich, his family and his close associates notwithstanding, the Asian Russian diasporas did not produce bilingual and bicultural 'hybrids' whose writing would realize a symbiosis of Russia and the East. Valery Pereleshin is a rare case of an émigré poet who was genuinely interested in the Chinese cultural tradition, translated from Chinese (including the ancient classical poem *Li Sao*), and integrated Chinese literary models, as he understood them, into his original poetry. But with all the uncertainty about Pereleshin's fluency in Chinese, his acquired 'Chineseness' was a far cry from the 'Europeanness' of the likes of Viacheslav Ivanov. And other émigrés in Asia were much more culturally insulated from the surrounding environment. What does this tell us about Russian cultural universals, namely the presumed East/West dichotomy in Russian identity, to this day symbolized by the double-headed eagle in the Russian state emblem? Has any Russian writer contemplated Asia as 'the birthplace of our thought', as Alexander Herzen did in reference to Europe in his letters from France and Italy? In the same breath, Herzen expressed a typically arrogant and superficial view of the 'East', viewed from his faraway Western location:

> In the East, for example, only faces and generations change; the true living is a hundredth repetition of the same theme with minor variations brought about by contingencies: harvest, famine, cattle mortality, the character of the shah or his satraps. This life produces no experience, *keine Erlebnisse*; the everyday life of Asian peoples may be amusing but their history is tedious. We have made a grand step forward away from Asia: we had an opportunity to understand our situation and to reject it.[4]

Has Russian culture indeed reoriented itself completely towards Europe, as Herzen and other Westernizers believed more than 150 years ago? Has it stamped out all Asian cultural aspects and, as contemporary liberal discourse would have it, preserved an 'Asiatic' legacy only as part of the political tradition of authoritarianism? And what is the place of Asia in today's Russia's self-definition, after all the 'disappointments' with Europe over the last century? Perhaps a closer look at various forms of contact between the Russian diaspora and Asian cultures would shed new light on the evolution of West versus East in Russia's dual cultural profile.

Another original facet of the diasporic model is represented by the Russian-Israeli cultural formation, discussed in part in Kevin Platt's chapter. While it does not enjoy the status of an official language in Israel like Hebrew or Arabic, Russian serves as a code of communication for almost one-fifth of the Israeli population (about 1.5 million people). In the 1970s and the 1990s, two waves of *aliyah* (literally 'ascent', as migration of Jews into Israel is defined in the Zionist narrative of return to the ancestral land) brought to the country about 250,000 and one million Russian speakers respectively. This community has not only changed the social and demographic profile of the country and had an impact on politics and voting practices, but also transformed its cultural dynamics. Unlike the earlier waves of *aliyah*, these newcomers resisted the politics of Hebraization promoted by the official establishment from the founding of the state: using Hebrew in the social and professional spheres, ex-Soviets by and large reserved Russian for private communication and artistic expression. As a result, a unique russophone literature has been produced in Israel by such writers as Dina Rubina, Svetlana Shenbrunn, Ruf Zernova, David Markish, Alexander Goldstein, Yulia Viner and Nekod Zinger, and poets Igor Guberman, Mikhail Gendelev, Elena Akselrod, Gali-Dana Zinger, Alexander Barash, and many others. In contrast to the high visibility of Russian-born scientists, musicians, actors and politicians, russophone authors remain 'silent voices' in the Israeli cultural landscape because of a lack of integration into the local cultural networks. Their works circulate primarily in the metropolitan and global Russian markets, and their translations into European languages are far more common than translations into Hebrew.

This literary corpus transcends the parameters of global Russian culture and needs to be investigated as a hybrid transnational phenomenon made up of an amalgamation of diverse elements, including Jewishness, the Russian cultural canon, the Soviet experience (with Jewish particularities, such as the history of grass-roots and institutional anti-Semitism and the Holocaust), responses to Zionism and post-Zionist revision, and the present Middle Eastern location with all its political, ethnic and religious tensions. The recent history of this literature includes strong articulations of autonomous identity, which challenge any straight-forward affiliation with metropolitan Russian culture or traditional Russian diasporas. In some of his essays, Goldstein imagined Russian Israel as a Middle Eastern province of the Russian cultural empire, where the relations between the two are based on complementarity (and therefore mutual enrichment). Together with Barash, he developed the concept of the Mediterranean Note – a Levantine brand of literature shaped by its geocultural situation and characterized by a paradoxical combination of hedonism and the imminence of death. Both projects privilege different aspects of Russian-Israeli hybridity – self-definition through, and by contrast to, the metropole in the first instance, and connection to a specific geo-mythological space in the second. Some studies have pointed to the emergence of a new, Ashkenazi nationalism as an essential feature of Russian-Jewish-Israeli patterns of self-identification.[5]

Within the Middle Eastern context, the West/East dichotomy, so central to the Russian cultural discourse, acquires additional variations and a sense of urgency. This discourse has been dislocated into the debate about the Western and Eastern elements that make up Israel's profile. Russian Jews who, upon their relocation, tried hard but unsuccessfully to shed the collective sobriquet *rusim* ('Russians' in Hebrew), as Israelis casually call them, subsequently redefined their Russianness as a genetic connection to European culture. From this perspective, in a number of narratives Israel has been construed as an Eastern backwater. The literary critic and essayist Maya Kaganskaya phrases it with striking directness in the book she published in Hebrew, *God's Twilight* (2004):

> I hate the East. Everyone has a conception of his own death, his hell. … So for me, … my hell and death, turned against me, is the East, the Muslim world. … The Mizrahim are a very archaic people, and in all archaic tribes, the central events are birth, marriages, and deaths … Culture starts beyond nature – literature, metaphysics, philosophy, music. … When Israel becomes more and more part of the East, it is the end of the world for me, the end of our dream. Israeli culture is starting to be pulled in that direction …. I do not believe in a culture without hierarchies. I will never accept that Mizrahi music and Mozart are one and the same thing.[6]

A poem by Elena Akselrod expresses the rather common bewilderment ex-Soviets experienced when faced with the unexpectedly 'Eastern' look of Israel:

Мой круг не замкнулся, и я проскочила—куда?
Европа не рядом, а рядом шатер бедуина.[7]

I didn't come full circle. And I ended up – where?
Europe is not nearby, near me is a Bedouin tent.

Many pages of Goldstein's collection of essays *Aspekty dukhovnogo braka* (Aspects of spiritual union) are dedicated to a close contemplation of various Oriental elements in Israel, going so far as to discuss peculiar scents exuded by Arab men or the residents of Jewish ultra-Orthodox districts.[8] The transition from the ex-Soviet Union to the historic homeland is pictured by the author as an unrelenting march away from the 'light' of European culture. This inexorable descent into darkness is only accelerated by the influx into Israel of Asian *Gastarbeiter*: 'Восток пеленает нас, точно саван. Тают последние европейские огоньки ашкеназской души. Так неужели должны мы ускорить кончину и, приняв филиппинцев, малайцев, тайцев, китайцев, раньше срока упасть в азиатскую ночь?'[9] (The Orient is enfolding us in a shroud. The last sparks of Europe in the Ashkenazi soul are fading. So should we precipitate our demise and, absorbing the Filipinos, Malaysians, Thai and Chinese, fall into the Asian night before it is time?). Unused to the Russian cavalier disregard for political correctness, the Israeli intellectual establishment was quick to condemn these voices from a postcolonialist perspective. For Adia Mendelson-Maoz, 'Once in Israel, members of the intelligentsia were amazed to discern the Mizrahi and Arab foundations of Israeli culture, and developed a patronizing, colonialist approach to them.'[10] Rafi Tsirkin-Sadan identifies plenty of Orientalist stereotypes in the ex-Soviets' narratives and explains them as residues of the Soviet imperial consciousness, with its pejorative attitudes to people from non-European Soviet republics.[11] These entanglements of loyalties, ideologies and aesthetics will no doubt constitute a focus of future studies of this vibrant culture.

Finally, writers in the ex-Soviet states actively change the world's vision of Russian literature, adding additional levels of complexity and ambivalence. In our volume, Kevin Platt laid out some important methodological approaches to russophone literature of the Near Abroad in the framework of his discussion of Shamshad Abdullaev. Let us briefly consider perhaps the most internationally renowned author from this category, Svetlana Aleksievich, the 2015 Nobel laureate in literature. A russophone writer of mixed Byelorussian and Ukrainian origins, a citizen of Belarus who lived for 12 years in emigration in Western Europe and who openly advocates 'European values', she is a perfect example of diasporic hybridity. Even her speech, characterized by non-literary pronunciation and elements of substandard grammar, underscores her position off the metropolitan centre. Does the fact of her writing in Russian, with a conscious and clearly articulated objective of creating 'the history of the Russian-Soviet soul',[12] of recording Soviet civilization (by examining the sensibilities of a private individual) make her a 'Russian writer' referring back to the 'nation'? And which 'nation' would that be? The aggressive reaction in Russian media towards Aleksievich's Nobel Prize and her relentless critique of the state of the politics, mentality and culture that have emerged from the ruins of the Soviet empire indicate anxiety in the metropole over the fluid status of such diasporic cultural figures. The source of this anxiety, it seems, is precisely the ambivalence of Aleksievich's position, her simultaneous proximity and distance from Russia. To readers inside Russia she is at once 'one of ours' and a foreigner, insider and outsider, one who dares to parade historical traumas in front of the whole world and to delve into topics shrouded in formal and informal taboos. It is unsurprising that Russian 'patriots' feel doubly betrayed! Characteristically, Aleksievich herself does not clearly differentiate between her various identities. When she refers to 'our' country, she implies in equal measure Russia, Belarus, Ukraine and the post-Soviet space at large. To the pointed question from Stanislav Belkovsky as to whether she stands in the position of a 'Russian writer' – a creature, according to the interviewer, with an idiosyncratic ontological status ('the pillar and affirmation of truth, the source of morality and its guardian'[13]) – she simply cited her triple heritage: Ukrainian mother, Byelorussian father and Russian culture. This third component (Russian culture) for Aleksievich is certainly not circumscribed by the borders of the Russian Federation. The same could be said of Goldstein, a Russian-Israeli writer and journalist, an Ashkenazi Jew who lived most of his life in Baku, and of many other diasporian writers around the world. These figures demonstrate how much creative innovation happens beyond traditional centres of power.

In *The Location of Culture*, Homi Bhabha argues that peripheral areas have the potential to destabilize and renew stagnating 'centres'.[14] Such a process has informed the evolution of contemporary Russian culture, giving rise to a non-hierarchical, multifocal model. Today, Russian literature is the shared legacy of many diverse agents in different parts of the world. It acquires various articulations, just as the literary Russian language appears in many different diasporic redactions, at times far removed from the prescriptive metropolitan grammar. Starting this discussion about Russian diasporic literature, we have sought to capture this multiplicity of perspectives, accents, origins and identities. Future research will no doubt illuminate numerous other diasporic configurations.

## Notes

1 Shih 2013, 30.
2 Levy and Schachter 2017.
3 On the category of writers who have emerged in the transnational cultural field yet retained a viable link with Russian culture, see Wanner 2011, as well as my own research on francophone writers of Russian origin, including Irène Némirovsky and Andreï Makine (Rubins 2004, 2008, 2015). The list of such authors has been getting progressively longer in the last decades, just as the range of adopted tongues has been getting broader, including English (Gary Shteyngart, Lara Vapnyar, David Bezmozgis and Olga Zilberbourg), German (Wladimir Kaminer), Hebrew (Boris Zaidman, Alex Epstein, Alona Kimhi and Sivan Beskin), and scores of others.
4 Gertsen 1905, 12. Translations are the author's unless specified otherwise.
5 Weisband 2018, 257.
6 Translation in Mendelson-Maoz 2014, 174.
7 Shklovskaia 2001, 15.
8 Cf. 'Iaffo, zhilishche i fotografiia', in Goldstein 2001, 7–11.
9 'Nashestvie', in Goldstein 2001, 26.
10 Mendelson-Maoz 2014, 165.
11 Tsirkin-Sadan 2014.
12 'V poiskax vechnogo cheloveka.' http://alexievich.info/ (accessed 18 September 2020).
13 'Belkovsky's interview with Svetlana Alexievich', TV Rain, 9 June 2017. https://www.youtube.com/watch?v=5Tu7TgJF9FY (accessed 18 September 2020).
14 Bhabha 1994.

## Bibliography

Bhabha, Homi. *The Location of Culture*. London: Routledge, 1994.
Gertsen, A. I. 'Pis'ma iz Frantsii i Italii. Pis'mo pervoe'. In *Sochineniia A.I. Gertsena i perepiska s N.A. Zakhar'inoi v semi tomakh*, vol. 5. St Petersburg: Tipografiia Iu.N. Erlikha, 1905.
Goldstein, Alexander. *Aspekty dukhovnogo braka*. Moscow: NLO, 2001.
Levy, Lital and Allison Schachter. 'A non-universal global: On Jewish writing and World Literature', *Prooftexts* 36(1) (2017): 1–26.
Mendelson-Maoz, Adia. *Multiculturalism in Israel: Literary perspectives*. West Lafayette, IN: Purdue University Press, 2014.
Rubins, Maria. 'Russko-frantsuzskaia proza Andreia Makina', *Novoe literaturnoe obozrenie* 66 (2004): 208–29.
Rubins, Maria. 'Irène Némirovsky: Strategii integratsii', *New Review* 253 (2008): 228–58.
Rubins, Maria. *Russian Montparnasse: Transnational writing in interwar Paris*. Basingstoke: Palgrave Macmillan, 2015.
Shih, Shu-mei. 'Against diaspora: The Sinophone as places of cultural production'. In *Sinophone Studies: A critical reader*, ed. Shu-mei Shih, Chien-hsin Tsai and Brian Bernards, 25–42. New York: Columbia University Press, 2013.
Shklovskaia, Margarita, ed. *Orientatsiia na mestnosti: Russko-izrail'skaia literatura 90-kh godov*. Jerusalem: Biblioteka-aliia, 2001.

Tsirkin-Sadan, Rafi. 'Between marginal and transnational: Post-Soviet immigration in Hebrew literature', *East European Jewish Affairs* 44 (2–3) (2014): 253–68.

Wanner, Adrian. *Out of Russia: Fictions of a new translingual diaspora*. Evanston, IL: Northwestern University Press, 2011.

Weisband, Edward. 'Alexander Goldstein's "Tethys or Mediterranean Mail": A Russian-Israeli Levantine literary idea reconsidered', *Ab Imperio* 4 (2018): 253–80.

# Index

Chukovsky, Kornei 198
Chulkova, Nadezhda 97
civilizational advance 19, 41, 59–60, 256
Clifford, James 12
Cohen, Robin 11
Cold War 189, 215
Communism 8, 30
community, sense of 189
Conrad, Joseph 124
cosmopolitanism 173, 230–1, 234–8
Creeley, Robert 230
cultural capital 27–8, 51, 55, 172, 252
cultural geography 238–9
cultural nationalism 57
Curtius, Ernst 93–4

Dante Alighieri 13, 38, 96
Darov, Anatolii 195
Darwin, Charles (and Darwinian theory) 139–41, 153, 156
*Daugava* (journal) 230
Davidson, Pamela vii 22–3, 55, 120; *author of Chapter 3*
Dawkins, Richard 149, 156–7
Decembrists 42–5, 48, 55
Demidova, Ol'ga 186–7
diaspora
    concept of 10–11, 91, 112, 138, 176, 195, 197, 244–6, 249–51
    *external* and *internal* 194–5
*diaspora space* (Brah) 11
diaspora studies 166, 244
diasporic communities 10–13, 29–30, 99
    dispersed and fragmented nature of 172
    distinct literary culture of 166–7
diasporic experience 50, 55
diasporic journeys 165–6
diasporic writing 7–13, 25–6, 165, 184–90, 197, 205, 208–11, 244–9, 256–7
Dienes, Laszlo 9
displaced persons 170
dissidents 54
Djagalov, Rossen 230
Dobzhansky, Theodosius 25, 137–8, 141–4, 147–50, 153–9
Dom knigi (publisher and bookshop) 173
Donne, John 123–4
Dor, Daniel 139–40
Dostoevsky, F. 67, 93, 141, 168–9
double agents 21
*Dozhd'* (cable channel) 196
Dragomoshchenko, Arkadii 230, 235–6
'dual diaspora' 228
Du Bos, Charles 90, 93
Donne, John 123

Efron, Sergei 21
electronic distribution of books 222
Elijah the prophet 83–5
Eliot, T. S. 230
elites 20, 53–5, 235, 239
elitism, literary 227
émigrés and émigré writing 6–9, 59, 78–9, 82–3, 94–9, 152, 168, 176, 178, 184–8, 195, 215, 221, 223, 250, 252

'mission' of 79, 94
    outside the main diaspora 170
emotions, exploration of 179
English language 28, 129, 183
Enlightenment thought 37, 43, 47–8, 52, 57, 59
Epstein, Alex 257
Epstein, Mikhail 24–5, 128–31, 151
Esenin, Sergei 65, 71–3, 80
*Estafeta* (poetry anthology) 170, 173–81
Etkind, Efim 119
Eurasianism 21
Eurocentrism 237
Europe, Russian disillusionment with and rejection of 16–19, 253
European culture and values 16–20, 256
Europeanization 48–9
evocriticism 25
evolutionary biology 138–41, 146, 158
exile 14–15, 20–1, 37, 52–4, 98, 177, 246, 250–1
    ambivalence about 37–8, 51–4
    de-romanticization of 59
    enforced 114
    and exceptionalism 38, 59–60
    experience of 38–9, 55, 60
    *internal* and *external* 21, 55–8, 187, 250
    narrative of creativity 59
    narrative of suffering 59
    negotiation of 13, 15, 21, 54, 59
    *performance* of 7, 18, 37–9, 52–60, 99
existentialism 17
expulsion from Russia 69, 114, 185
extraterritorial russophone authors 216–23, 226–7, 236–9, 249–50

Facebook 195, 211
'Father's butterflies' 137, 142–9, 158
Fergana School 230–1, 234, 236
Feuerbach, L. A. 57
Fink, Wilhelm 174
First World War 16–18, 59
Florensky, Pavel 70
foreignization 5, 117, 123
Forster, Leonard 113
Foucault, Michel 196, 210
Fowler, Alastair 169
Frank, Semen 19

García Lorca, Federico 230
Gazdanov, Gaïto 9, 17
Gendelev, Mikhail 4, 253
'genetic drift' 142, 151, 157
George, Stefan 113
Germany 53, 113
Gilroy, Paul 12, 15, 55
Ginzburg, Lydia 195–6
Gippius, Zinaida 67, 95–6
Glad, John 124
global literary life 220, 239
global Russian culture 5, 27, 121, 152, 215–16
globalization 28, 59, 99, 131, 152, 215–16, 219–23, 231, 236–9, 244–5, 249, 253
Goethe, J.W. von 73, 115
Gogol, Nikolay 52, 88